OLD SPANISH TRAIL
NORTH BRANCH
and its travelers

Cover Photo:

Wagon ruts shown here are worn into the fish canyon tuff. They are located between Monte Vista and Del Norte, Colorado south of US Highway 160, southwest of Coyote Hill. These ruts are lasting evidence or scars worn in the fragile desert earth as well as this stone. They mark a trail left by the migration of Mammoth, Bison Antiquuis, early Spanish Travelers and traders. Though it is known that thousands of pack animals on the Old Spanish Trail did not leave this evidence. It is known that the wheeled vehicles traveling these trails shown to later travelers by those who followed the game animals. And have left this evidence of our ancestors, journey which is well preserved in the soft stone. The weather exposed furrows are more than 12" deep in some areas.

OLD SPANISH TRAIL
NORTH BRANCH
and its travelers

Ron Kessler

SUNSTONE
PRESS

SANTA FE
New Mexico

Sunstone books may be purchased for educational, business, or sales promotional use. For information please write: Special Markets Department, Sunstone Press, P.O. Box 2321, Santa Fe, New Mexico 87504-2321.

FIRST EDITION

10 9 8 7 6 5 4 3 2 1

Library of Congress Cataloging in Publication Data:
Kessler, Ronald, 1943-
    Old Spanish Trail North Branch and its travelers / by Ron Kessler.
        p. cm.
    ISBN: 0-86534-270-9 (soft)
    1. Old Spanish Trail—History.   2. Pioneers—Southwest, New—Biography.
3. Southwest, New—Biography.   4. Frontier and pioneer life—Southwest, New.
I. Title.
F786.K43   1998
979—dc21   97-50404
                                                      CIP

Published by   SUNSTONE PRESS
                  Post Office Box 2321
                  Santa Fe, NM 87504-2321 / USA
                  (505) 988-4418 / *orders only* (800) 243-5644
                  FAX (505) 988-1025

CONTENTS

ILLUSTRATIONS

All photos in this book were taken by Ron Kessler unless otherwise noted.

ACKNOWLEDGMENTS

Many people have contributed in one form or another to the organization of this book. My special thanks to all of them:

My parents, Ernest and Lola *Brown* Kessler, for their patience in enduring and answering my endless questions after visiting the foothills near our home. Grandparents, Pete and Amy *Phillips* Kessler, long deceased, also shared countless stories in response to my eternal quest for answers about "the old trail and the rock art that I had discovered".

Albert "Pop" Getz, deceased, was one of the first to shed light on the fact that this trail was an old wagon road. Ruth Marie Colville was the person who introduced me to the book by Leroy and Ann Hafen, *Old Spanish Trail*. It opened up a whole new world for me.

My continued gratitude goes to the libraries in Monte Vista, Alamosa and the others who generously share their books. Diane Machado and Diane Koshak at Adams State College Library and Becky Gossard at Monte Vista Carnegie Library have been of tremendous help.

A big debt of gratitude is owed to each of the travelers who took the time to create their diaries along with their special thoughts. Without their notes this book would not have been possible. I sincerely hope that those who read this book enjoy the diaries as much as I have. And may Jacob Fowler's diary be an encouragement to all of us who struggle to write!

Thanks to Yvonne Halburian for her fabulous maps and to Jack Nelson for his help in identifying the route on the maps from Green River to Gunnison.

A special thanks to Frances McCullough, Carol Ann Wetherill Getz, Jack Nelson and Sam & Yvonne Halburian for patiently reading my manuscript and offering suggestions. I believe they have helped make this a better book.

INTRODUCTION

The Old Spanish Trail has long intrigued me. The fact that it is conveniently located in "my back yard" has surely added much to its allure. My endeavors to discover as much as possible about this ancient trail have put me in contact with kindred souls who exuberantly share their knowledge, resources and fascination for the Old Spanish Trail. They, like myself, are all hopelessly hooked.

I first discovered evidence of what Leroy Hafen called the West Fork of the North Branch of the Old Spanish Trail in the late 1950s. It was while riding colts for local ranches that I began to discover evidence of what appeared to be an old wagon road. There my struggle began. I was in high school, but not able for many years to put a name on the wagon ruts and other evidence that I had discovered. After each ride to the foothills west of Monte Vista, Colorado, I would spend countless hours questioning people who I thought might have the answers.

Since I was still living at home, my first contact was my parents, Ernest and Lola Kessler. My father had ridden horseback in much of the same country. He and his father had often traveled to Dry Creek, southwest of Monte Vista, to cut firewood. From Dad I learned that my grandfather, Pete Kessler, had came to the San Luis Valley as a young man and had trapped wild horses in the area where I was finding these wagon ruts. But they had no knowledge of the history of this trail.

Albert Getz was one of the first to shed light on the fact that this was an old wagon road. He graciously returned with me to the location of the wagon ruts and Año 1858 rock which was a marker locating the trail crossing on Raton Creek. Also, on one of my many trips to the Rio Grande County Museum, I discovered a map which Ruth Marie Colville had copied from Leroy and Ann Hafen's book "Old Spanish Trail." This map and book were a big contribution to my search for information. The bibliography led to many more books and ultimately to the sixteen diaries which have portions related to the North Branch of the Old Spanish Trail.

Suddenly, the pieces began to fit. This wagon road, almost forgotten, had been the link between the early settlements in the San Luis Valley. But it had a much older beginning. The wagon road had originally been a game trail used by larger animals as they migrated south. As early man began to hunt these creatures for food, he too traveled this ancient trail, as is evident in the petroglyphs and pictographs found along it.

As the Spanish began to advance farther into the frontier, "Al Norte," to trade with the Ute, they also began a period of many years' use of this trail. It was not until 1844 that John C. Fremont labeled it the Spanish Trail. Leroy and Ann Hafen, like myself, had grown up near a portion of the Old Spanish Trail. Their sharing of the information they had found fueled my research. As I gathered more and more information on the Old Spanish Trail, I became acquainted with Ruth Marie Colville. It was she who encouraged me to record my findings.

Many miles of the Old Spanish Trail have been tramped or traveled by saddle horse, foot, vehicle, airplane and covered wagon in the past two-score years. Countless photographs have been taken. Finally, I have gathered enough information to make this worthwhile to share with you. This book contains portions of diaries of those adventurous people who left the security and safety of their homes to ensure a better life for their loved ones or perhaps for adventure and profit. It was my difficulty in locating these documents which has led to editing and including them in this book. And now, here's a bit of background to help make sense of the upcoming diaries and reports. After Mexico gained her independence from Spain in 1821, two commercial lines began to develop from Santa Fe, New Mexico. The Santa Fe Trail evolved and broke to the east to establish trade with the Americans in the "outside world". The Mexican people struggled to maintain a supply line within their ranks on the Old Spanish Trail to the west.

The Old Spanish Trail started out as a trade route which connected the Spanish colonies of Santa Fe and Los Angeles, California. It stretched nearly 1200 miles and ran through six western states: New Mexico, Colorado, Utah, Arizona, Nevada and California. It connected two of Spain's largest colonies and strengthened the Northern Frontier of New Spain against her enemies who were encroaching from the north and east.

The route of the Old Spanish Trail looped northwesterly from New Mexico with two branches crossing Colorado. They joined in eastern central Utah before turning southwesterly into northwestern Arizona, across southern Nevada and into southern California. This trail tied together a number of shorter and much older trade routes. The Spanish were apparently the first compelled to cross this entire area and also the first with a written language. Hence, the name *Spanish Trail*. With reference to "anyone preceding us," the term *Old Spanish Trail* came into use.

I believe that my hero, Juan Bautista de Anza, helped create the need for the Old Spanish Trail. His efforts in bringing settlers from Mexico into California to establish San Francisco helped create the need for this trail. And it is ironic that Santa Fe was home to Anza during his reign as New Mexico Governor. It is likely that no one was more familiar with both these two colonies than Anza. He and others created a record in their diaries of their northward advance.

Father Garces, who had accompanied Anza, set out in February 1776 from Yuma, Arizona to become the first white man to traverse the Mojave River segment of the Old Spanish Trail. In July of that same year, Father Dominguez and Father Escalante left Santa Fe with others, including the noted mapmaker, Don Bernardo Miera y Pacheco. Their travels took them to Abiquiu, along the Chama River, into southwestern Colorado where they turned north, then west into the Uintah Basin of Utah to the southwest. They returned through northern Arizona, east into New Mexico to Santa Fe in January 1777.

Slave traders soon followed the Escalante route to the northwest from Santa Fe through western Colorado via the South Branch of the Old Spanish Trail to the Uintah Basin. In 1805 and 1813 there is evidence of slave traders being tried for their crimes against the crown. This attests to the fact that the Old Spanish Trail was being used at that time.

In August 1826 Jedediah Smith set out from the Great Salt Lake with a party of fifteen men. He followed the Escalante trail south to the Sevier River and then to the mouth of Clear Creek, passing the town sites of Salina and Richfield. Jedediah reached the Mojave village in October 1826, thus connecting the routes of Escalante and Garces. Smith had successfully completed the first recorded journey from the Missouri River to California and opened the Old Spanish Trail, a central route to the Pacific.

Antonio Armijo left Abiquiu, New Mexico in August 1829, starting out on the traditional South Branch of the Old Spanish Trail. His party consisting of thirty-one men arrived at Santa Barbara, California three months (less six days) from the time they left Santa Fe, New Mexico. They spent the winter trading *serapes* and wool blankets from New Mexico for California horses and mules. In the spring of 1830 they returned to Santa Fe, New Mexico.

William Wolfskill is recognized as the first to traverse the entire route of the traditional Old Spanish Trail from Santa Fe to California. The Wolfskill-Yount company consisted of about twenty men. Eleven of these were Wolfskill's employees, the others were Yount and his free trappers. The party also contained a number of New Mexicans who had taken *serapes* and *fresadas* (woolen blankets) with them to trade to the Indians for beaver skins. However, on their arrival in California they traded for mules. They left Taos the last of September 1830, trapping as they traveled, and arrived in Los Angeles in February 1831.

This commerce between the Spanish colonies was to last only for about two decades. Two serapes from New Mexico would buy one horse or mule in California. There were thousands of these horses and mules that traveled from California to Santa Fe. From there they were driven to Missouri where there was a great demand for these animals. The opening of the Oregon California Trail created the need for animals to ride and to pull their wagons. The price of a team of mules in Westport, Missouri in 1820 was $20. That same team of mules was soon worth $200 dollars. Thus, a very lucrative business was developed by hard-working and enterprising frontier men.

The Old Spanish Trail runs from Santa Fe northwest to San Juan Pueblo, the first Spanish capital of New Mexico. Here the Old Spanish Trail splits into three trails. The South Branch of the Old Spanish Trail runs from San Juan Pueblo northwest along the Chama River to Abiquiu, then into southwest Colorado. Passing through Arboles, Ignacio and Mancos, Colorado, then on to Moab, Utah and finally, to Green River.

Perhaps least known of all of the Old Spanish Trail is the North Branch of the Old Spanish Trail. Its two forks passed through northern New Mexico and the San Luis Valley of Colorado. They reunited at Saguache, Colorado and crossed Cochetopa Pass to follow the Gunnison River and at last joined the South Branch near Green River, Utah. Colorado contains the largest and probably the oldest portion of the Old Spanish Trail.

The East Fork of the North Branch possibly shows the oldest use of any portion of the trail. Near the Great Sand Dunes, in the north end of the San Luis Valley (SLV), several sites have been discovered which contained bones of a large buffalo, "Bison Antiquus". This is of the same species found at the site of Folsom, New Mexico in 1926. These bones, as well as Folsom points, indicate the existence of ancient camps of buffalo hunters in the SLV 10,000 or more years ago. The teeth, tusks and bones of some extinct species of elephants such as "Wooly Mammoth" have also been found as well as Clovis Points. The similarity of the artifacts in the SLV and those at Folsom, New Mexico, indicate possible travel by early man to and from these areas. This travel brings up the possibility of very early use of the East Fork of the Old Spanish Trail.

In the San Luis Valley of Colorado there are two forks of the North Branch of the Old Spanish Trail. The Old Spanish Trail runs northwest from Santa Fe to Pojoaque then to San Juan Pueblo, which is north of Española, New Mexico. At this point the trail splits. The East Fork runs north to Taos staying east of the Rio Grande along the west side of the Sangre de Cristo Mountains. The West Fork runs north to Ojo Caliente, then on to Tres Piedras along the east side of the San Juan Mountains. U.S. Highway 160 crosses the East Fork at Blanca, Colorado and the West Fork about five miles east of Del Norte, Colorado at Martinez Hill. These two forks of the North Branch join at Saguache, Colorado to cross Cochetopa Pass.

All the streams in southern Colorado were named by the Spanish by 1650. One can look at a map of the Southwest and see that these names still exist.

The East Fork of the North Branch of the Old Spanish Trail from Taos to Fort Garland was the first mail route in the San Luis Valley. Traversing a distance of seventy-five miles, it served the communities of Costilla and San Luis in the Colorado Territory. The mail carrier would leave Taos on Wednesday at 1:00 P.M. and arrive at Fort Garland on Friday at 11:00 A.M. This route was started April 10, 1862 when an office was established at Fort Garland. It was discontinued on January 21, 1865.

The West Fork of the North Branch of the Old Spanish Trail served as the second mail route in the SLV from Conejos to Saguache which is a distance of seventy-five miles. It provided mail to the communities of La Jara, Piedra, La Loma del Norte (East Del Norte founded in 1861), La Garita, Carnero, and Saguache. The mail carrier would leave Conejos on Monday at 7:00 A.M. and arrive in Saguache the next day by 7:00 P.M. This route was established on April 1, 1869.

There are many other names for portions of the Old Spanish Trail. On one of the survey plat maps, I found the designation "Old California Road" marked on the map in the area west of Saguache. South of Saguache the maps are marked "Del Norte-Saguache Road." South of Del Norte the maps are marked "Del Norte-Conejos Road." Countless modern names have been tacked onto parts of the Old Spanish Trail in other areas.

Although the use of Old Spanish Trail lasted only for about forty years as a trade route, its use continued. The pack route became the wagon roads linking the early settlements and these wagon roads have become our modern highways.

The importance of the Old Spanish Trail has been overlooked far too long. Think about it! It was the horse and mule trade on the Old Spanish Trail that brought those animals from California to Missouri to facilitate the settling of the West! Perhaps neither the Santa Fe Trail nor the Oregon Trail would have developed as readily as they did without the aid of the Old Spanish Trail.

Many travelers used the Old Spanish Trail but left no memento of their passing. Included in this book are but a few of the records or diaries that attest to the use of this very important part of our history. Thankfully, more of these records are being found everyday.

In 1994 a portion of the West Fork of the Old Spanish Trail was endangered by a regional landfill project. Concerned citizens, BLM employees and Rio Grande County Commissioners helped prevent this from happening. As a result, the Old Spanish Trail Association (OSTA) was formed. The OSTA proposes to identify, protect and educate others about the Old Spanish Trail. To obtain more information about joining the OSTA write to Old Spanish Trail Association, P.O. Box 510, Monte Vista, CO 81144.

—Ronald E. Kessler

OLD SPANISH TRAIL NORTH BRANCH MAP

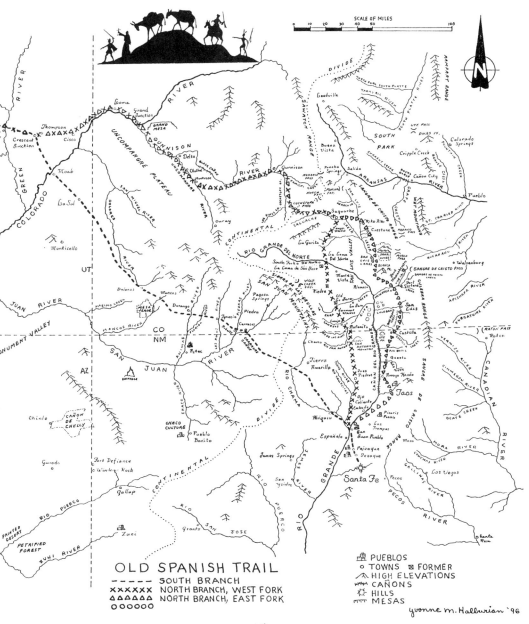

OLD SPANISH TRAIL

- – – – – SOUTH BRANCH
- XXXXXX NORTH BRANCH, WEST FORK
- ▲▲▲▲▲▲ NORTH BRANCH, EAST FORK
- 000000

⌂ PUEBLOS
o TOWNS ⊠ FORMER
⋀ HIGH ELEVATIONS
ᨑᨑ CAÑONS
✗ HILLS
▭▭▭ MESAS

yvonne m. Halburian '96

15

1

1694/DON DIEGO DE VARGAS

Don Diego José de Vargas Zapata Luján Ponce de León y Contreras was the second child born to Alonso de Vargas and María Margarita Contreras y Arráiz. He was baptized on Wednesday, November 8, 1643 in Madrid Spain, the city of his birth. María was not quite eighteen years old at the time of their marriage on January 6, 1641. Alonsa and María had three children, two boys and one girl, Lorenzo, Diego, and Antonia. Their mother died on April 17, 1649, when Diego was five years old. At eighteen Diego was taught by a tutor and later attended the University of Valladolid although he never received a degree.

Doña Beatriz Pimentel de Prado Vélez de Olazábal, twenty-two years of age and Don Diego de Vargas, twenty, signed a marriage contract on April 1, 1664 in front of a notary. They were married on May 5, 1664. Don Diego and Doña Beatriz had five children; Isabel María February 9, 1665; Juana Viviana December 2, 1666; María Antonia December 18, 1667; Francisco Alonso October 4, 1669; and Juan Manuel December 20, 1670. On July 10, 1674 Don Diego's wife died at the age of thirty-two. Shortly thereafter he met Nicolosa Rincón. Although they never married they had three children, Juan Manual, Alonso and María Teresa.

Diego became heir to his father's estate upon the death of his brother Lorenzo, who died at about seventeen or eighteen years of age. After the death of Don Alonso de Santander y Mercado, his father's agent, Don Diego became active in the family affairs. By mid-1666 the Vargas family had received word of the death of Alonso de Vargas. His will left instructions that his properties in Spain were to go to Don Diego. The properties were badly in need of repair. Don Diego borrowed money against the income of the properties to make the necessary repairs. Due to the indebtedness of the family Don Diego decided to come to New Spain to settle his father's estate there. His coming to America was to have an enormous impact in the settling of the northern frontier.

Don Diego de Vargas received an appointment as a royal courier of New Spain. He arrived in Mexico City in April 1673 delivering the dispatches to the Viceroy, whom he petitioned for an appointment. In 1674 Don Diego was appointed the Mayor of the mining district of Teutila with an annual salary of 250 pesos. In 1679 Don Diego was appointed the Mayor of Tlalpujahua. He was appointed the Governor of New Mexico in 1690. On September 14, 1692 Diego took possession of the Palace of the Governors in Santa Fé. Don Diego José de Varges Zapata Luján Ponce de León y Contreras was the thirtieth and the thirty-second Governor of what is now the State of New Mexico.[1]

Don Juan de Oñate, the founder and first Governor of New Mexico, traveled an existing Indian trail north from San Juan Pueblo to Taos Pueblo in July 1598.[2] This is a piece of the trail that would become known as the East Fork of the North Branch of the Old Spanish Trail. To my knowledge he left no detailed journal of his travel along this route.

Don Diego left Santa Fé on June 30, 1694 traveling north to Taos. From Taos he followed the North Branch of the Old Spanish Trail north to the Culebra River. Travel continued west to the Rio Grande. Unable to cross at the confluence of the Culebra and Rio Grande they turned south crossing at the site later known as the Ford Ferry Site. Then the expedition traveled west to the Rio San Antonio. His party followed the east side of the river west of San Antonio Mountain along the West Fork of the North Branch on their return trip to Santa Fe, New Mexico.

Diego's diary which was kept on the expedition is the oldest known record of travel north of the New Mexico capital of Santa Fé on what was to become known as the North Branch of the Spanish Trail. References from Diego's diary to the Rio Culebra, Rio San Antonio and other landmarks in the San Luis Valley indicate in a most familiar manner the presence of New Mexico Spanish prior to the 1680 era. Close study of this journal will reveal that his was not the first journey along this Indian Trail, as he states on Tuesday, July 6, 1694.

"The elders, experienced in this country, who were coming with the camp told me not to worry, that if I could tolerate the great distance and the detour, they would get me out with the royal army through the country so that we could succeed in bringing help to the Villa of Santa Fé with the supplies that our Lord had seen fit to give us, delivering us for that purpose from danger, which we have experienced in this location up to the present time. Thus we could be assured of his divine mercy.[3]

After serving thirty punishing years as a royal administrator in the Indies of New Spain, Vargas died of dysentery in 1704.[4]

Wednesday, June 30, 1694

On the thirtieth day of the month of June of the present date and year, about nine or ten in the morning, when they were ready in the Plaza de Armas of this

Palace of the Governors was the starting point of the Old Spanish Trail. This late 19th century photo is courtesy New Mexico State Records & Archives. Dod Collection #1467

Villa of Santa Fé, with the camp of the men-at-arms and militia readied, I, the said governor and captain general, departed from this villa. (The Santa Fé plaza today is a park which contains reminders of early day importance. This park was the staging area for expeditions traveling on the Old Spanish Trail.) In the vanguard were the soldiers of the garrison guarding the royal standard and my person and the distinguished council, and in the rear guard were the aforementioned militia. And having arrived at the Pueblo of Cuyamungué (The Old Spanish Trail is made up of ancient trails which had been used for centuries by early man.) four leagues from the villa, Sergeant Major Antonio Jorje, who was the captain of the garrison as well as of the vanguard, saw that there was near the said pueblo a group of rebel Indians who, as soon as they sighted him, took up their arms.

The captain of the garrison having gone ahead with five, discovers near the Pueblo of Cuyamungué a group of Indian fighters with whom they fight. They kill eleven.

The said governor and captain general orders a corporal to go with a dozen soldiers for reinforcement of the escort of the horses and mules and train. And he goes to sleep with his camp on the bank of the Rio del Norte one league from the said mesa.

With his corporal, to take charge of the horses and mules and field train of the camp to better safeguard it, I indicated to the corporal the place where he was to go to make night camp on the bank of the river (Campsites along the Old Spanish Trail were located near a source of water for both men and animals.) at a distance of a little more than one league. As the sun set he was at said camp. And in this place was captured an Indian woman of the rebels who informed us she was from the mesa and had come down to see her corn field. So that what has been narrated may be of record, I sign it with capitan and sergeant major and with the Adjutant Antonio de Baluerde together with my secretary of government and war, Don Diego José de Vargas Zapata de Luján Ponce de León y Contreras, Antonio Jorje, Antonio de Baluerde, before me, Alpfonso Rael de Aguilar, Secretary of Government and War.

Thursday, July 1

On the first of July of this present year of the said date, 1694, I, said governor and captain general, having been with this camp on this river bank and place of the Rio del Norte with the concern that perhaps the enemy would dare to attack at night after having heard about my arrival, from the smoke signals with which they are communicating from all sides, I set out from this place and go a distance seven leagues to the ravine of the abandoned Moraga Hacienda. (At this point Vargas took a route different from that of the later traders. Later traffic followed the trail across the mountain from Velarde to Picurís while some appear to travel more closely to the Rio Grande del Norte as far as Embudo then cross the mountains to Picurís.) Because it was a place of less risk, I was obliged to halt and to quarter the royal army here, having passed through the Pueblos of San Lázaro and San Cristobal, and recognized that these enemy rebels have most of their corn fields planted, the sight of which gives me much cause for joy and the people of the camp.

And that it may be on record, I sign it with my secretary of war, doing it together with the corporals, captain and second lieutenant of the royal standard, Don Diego José de Vargas Zapata Luján Ponce de León y Contreras, Antonio Jorje, Diego Arias de Quiros, Antonio de Baluerde, before me, Alphonso Rael de Aguilar, Secretary of Government and War.

Friday, July 2

On the second day of the month of July of the date and year about six in the afternoon, I, said governor and captain general, with said camp, set eyes upon the

Pueblo of the nation of the Picurís, having come by the said road which is very mountainous with dangerous slopes to climb and descend with care and suspicion lest the said rebel enemy will gather together to ambush. As we came in view they were making and sending up their smoke signals of warning. And having descended to a mesa which overlooked the cornfields of this pueblo, at what seemed to be a distance of half a league away, it seemed to me to be a good campsite for the royal army to pass the night on the outskirts of the pueblo near the river and valley. And to safeguard against damage by horses and mules, I then ordered the corporals and officers of war that they should halt here and quarter the royal army so that these rebels would know by this intention my good will, that the Spanish would not damage their cornfields. And for better judgment and to insure their confidence I went down to see the way to their pueblo. I found it abandoned which I much regretted for their ignorance and rebelliousness. And for my part by demonstrations in order to show them even more the desire for their peace and return to their former style, I ordered my secretary of government and war and Captain and Sergeant Major Antonio Jorje that they should leave and place in said plaza a cross. And I did not allow the soldiers to break a single wall, nor search the houses of the pueblo in case they had food supplies within, since my intent was only their submission and to pay for whatever they gave me as much as they wished. And so that it may be recorded, I sign it with the leaders and officers of war together with my secretary of government and war, Don Diego José de Vargas Zapata Luján Ponce de León y Contreras, Antonio Jorje, Diego Arias de Quiros, Antonio de Baluerde, before me, Alphonso Rael de Aguilar, Secretary of Government and War.

Saturday, July 3

On the third day of the present month of this date and year, I, said governor and captain general, passed the night in view of the said Pueblo of Picurís, although near the said camp the rebels made a fire, by means of which they could let us know that they would come in pursuit of us and that they would be in sight. It being a distance of ten leagues to the Pueblo of Taos, and the road very dangerous, eight leagues of wooded mountains and sierra of greatest danger which could slow the passage, I took into consideration the increasing numbers of this enemy who could attain part of their desire in this region, which many of the soldiers and some leaders of the illustrious town council pointed out. To all of these I responded that I had set out for supplies and that I would buy them from said villa of Taos by purchase or by bullets and the case was up to his Divine Majesty whose Divine Law I was defending.

And the royal army, going with orderly and military discipline, I arrived with it. Having gone with order and military discipline of the royal army, we arrived. And

21

I was freed from said risk, having succeeded in entering in view of the Pueblo of Taos at four in the afternoon, a distance of one short league from it on the bank and on the island of its river because it was a place outside the cornfields of this pueblo which would secure it from the harm the horses and mules could do. I ordered the royal army to set up camp.

The Taos Indian Pueblo was built about 1450 A.D. and is the largest multi-story pueblo structure still in existence. It has been continuously inhabited for over 500 years. Taos Pueblo photo c. 1940s is courtesy of New Mexico State Rcords & Archives Dod Collection #2761.

And I went to the said pueblo with a squadron of forty men and on entering into the pueblo I found it abandoned, although there were crosses recently placed at their houses and storerooms and they also had them in most of the cornfields where we passed, which made me and all the rest very happy, for it meant to me a sign and a demonstration establishing peace, and because they had retreated, it was not to fight but out of fear for their transgression. To let them know for my part and to assure them pardon, I then ordered that no one should climb up to a single house and they should put in the two plazas of the two villages two big crosses, returning to them by means of them the desire that they could have and assuring them by the crosses of the said reason, the pardon and of receiving them in peace. I also ordered that the captain and sergeant major should take a cross put it at a distance of half a league on the road to the sierra on whose side fresh tracks of said rebels and Taos natives showed that they had retreated and fortified themselves on the mountain and narrow canyon because it was safe ground for them. On previous times when they had rebelled they had taken refuge in this well chosen place and spent a long time there so it was necessary to return to reconquer them by force of arms in order to conquer and reduce them to their pueblo, as is well known, as some of the older men of the camp related. And I stayed at this camp and pueblo waiting for said captain as he went with some of the soldiers to set up and raise the cross. And in the middle of this road he found a large band of Apache Indians with their captain with whom they shook hands. And as a sign of friendship they then laid down their arms, and having seen the Captain and Sergeant Major Antonio Jorje, that they asked for me, said governor and captain general, he told them that I had stayed in the pueblo and the reason for my coming. And the Apache Indians also told him that he had come with his rancheria and that they were from the plains and had come to trade with the pueblo, as was the custom. And captain Antonio Jorje immediately sent information to me by a soldier and as a result of this I went with a squadron of up to ten men, and having gone to said place, I then found the Apaches who shook hands and gave me many embraces, and Don Juan de Yé, the Governor of the Pecos, who was accompanying me with even greater rejoicing, as their friend and acquaintance who he was.

The Apaches said they were in the Pueblo of Taos when the news came from the Tewas of the Rio Grande Valley and Picurís that I was on my way down to their pueblo. And at once the Taos left it and although the Apache told them not to, they could not detain them.

That Taos might not think badly of the Apache friendship was the reason why they had gone with them, but with a difference. The Taos had gone into the sierra and embudo, where, at other times, the Apache had remained at the entrance of the sierra where I, said governor and captain general, would see where his camp was. And the Apache captain of his own free will carried the said Holy Cross which he had, as has been said, to place at a half-way point and in sight of the sierra, saying that he could by virtue of that assurance, Francisco Pacheco, Governor of Taos, who was near the entrance, could come down.

And so, I, said governor and captain general, went with the Apache and only fifteen soldiers followed me. Nevertheless, I went up to the entrance of said sierra, less than a pistol-shot away, where the Captain of the Apaches having gone in advance, Governor Pacheco with many of the Taos was already. And I saw there the camp of the Apaches of the plains who were recognized by Don Juan de Yé of the Pecos who acted as interpreter with Governor Pacheco. And although Yé used forceful words and clear arguments for his desire to show safety the confidence with which Pacheco and his people could come down to see me, since they had already had experience from the time of my first entrada and conquest of their pueblo in the month of October of ninety-two, the arguments of the aforesaid Don Juan de Yé were not sufficient. He acted with such kindness as will be known from the tragic outcome with which they repaid his trust that they were his friends.

And although I, said governor and captain general, carried by impulse and fervent Catholic zeal, without considering the risk to my life and the small numbers of men mentioned, left said line, going near some rock cliffs where Governor Pacheco was, after his people had surrounded me on both sides to seize me, which my few men watched carefully, nevertheless they did not dare to. And I, realizing that the sun had already set and that my words were not effective, took leave of them with much affection and friendliness an indication of my desire saying to Pacheco I would await him with his people the next day in their pueblo where I would go from the river where I had left the royal army and troops so they would not damage the cornfields with the horses and mules.

The aforesaid Don Juan repeated my words and reassured them since he was such a good friend of Pacheco. Pacheco, with treacherous and pretented friendliness told Yé for his consolation and that of the Taos natives, his friends, as they were of the nation of the Pecos, and asked that they were asking Yé to spend that night with Pacheco in order to talk at leisure about that which he would say about me, said governor and captain general, and of the Spaniards, in presence of his people of the Taos nation, and they would decide, according to what he would say to them, whether or not to come and see me and also to go down to their pueblo as they said and I ordered.

And then Governor Don Juan de Yé with more joy, than if he were entering into his own house, wholeheartedly agreed to stay. And although Sergeant Juan Ruíz de Cazeres and the Sergeant Major Francisco de Anaya Almazan told him that he should watch well what he was doing, not to put himself in danger because some misfortune could befall him, he replied that he was going in safety and had confidence in Governor Pacheco, his friend.

And said sergeant came to me, said governor and captain general, to ask whether they should take from him the arquebus he was carrying, which was mine, and the mule. I said they should let Don Juan go without showing a sign of distrust. And I went with said sergeant the short distance where Don Juan de Yé was already dismounted and expressed to him the reply and warning mentioned above concerning the danger, to which he replied to me that he was secure and content. He took off the spurs and the gunpowder bags from his waist, handing them over along with his mule and cloak to said sergeant, with his arquebus and shield, telling him to take

24

care of them for him. And he took leave of me giving me an embrace and his hand, and did likewise with the others.

The Taos were watching this attentively along with their Governor Pacheco, to whom I repeated that he remain with God, and that with Don Juan de Yé I would expect him in my tent early in order to give him chocolate. And I left this place, taking leave of the Apaches, with whom, since we were their friends, I presume that what I said gave Don Juan great confidence and satisfaction to spend the night and stay with the Taos. Going with pleasure and concern about what was referred to, on the way to the pueblo, I found out that most of the royal army and troops were on their way to overtake me to aid and assist me. The Reverend Father Procurator Fray Francisco Farfan, who had come voluntarily on the said campaign, had gone to relate the danger I was in, and therefore with speed they set out. I gave them thanks and told them what had occurred. We spent the night with the protection and necessary precautions against any mishap which one could expect since we were now in the middle of so many enemies.

And so that the said entrada may be of record and what was referred to in it, I sign it with the leaders and officers of war who were there present and with the assistance of my secretary of government and war who also signed, Don Diego José de Vargas Zapata Luján Ponce de León y Contreras, Antonio Jorje, Diego Arias de Quiros, Antonio de Baluerde, before me, Alphonso Rael de Aguilar, Secretary of Government and War.

Sunday, July 4

On the fourth day of the present month of July of the date and year, now being nine o'clock in the morning, Don Juan de Yé, Governor of the Pecos, has not yet arrived. He had remained by his own free will by request of Governor Pacheco of the Pueblo of the Taos, as it is noted and affirmed in the entrada of said governor and captain general in said pueblo. And also having met and spoken with him (Pacheco) yesterday, at sunset, and being late, I was suspicious, since Juan de Yé had not come, they had treacherously killed him or held him prisoner to punish him more.

In reference to this, I ordered one hundred men from the garrison with their arms and horses dispatched as well as leaving the remaining people guarding the horses and mules. And having mounted, by virtue of this order I, said governor and captain general, mounted as well as the reverend Fathers, chaplains of the army and the members of the illustrious town council, and forming a squadron of two files of said people, I repeated with them the said entrada to the village of Taos giving orders to all in general. In loud voices they cried out, "Praise be the Most Holy Sacrament."

And it was seen in the village that no people had come down. And going on with the squadron to the stopping place and camp of yesterday, said day, in view of the sierra and embudo all the people were found to have gone inside, they were only discovered because some Indians who were keeping watch with the sentinels in the places where they were hidden and fortified among the thickets and rock cliffs of the mountain range shouted.

I questioned them by means of Matias Luján, who was acting as interpreter for their Governor, Francisco Pacheco. They responded that they had entered with the people within said mountains. I asked where Don Juan de Yé, Governor of the Pecos, was. They said that night he had gone with four young men to the mountains. Sometimes they said he had gone to his pueblo, and other times said that he had gone to bring his people to fight against us in his behalf, for which they had all the people prepared, with the Apaches from the Red River. The Spanish-speaking Indians were saying all this, that they had placed for that purpose.

And among all there was one outstanding Indian of the Tewas who those of said camp recognized that, like Sergeant Juan Ruíz, because he understood the language, he was the one on the mesa, where they are, of San Ildefonso, who spoke and answered for all the people. In a loud and angry voice, I told him that he was not a Taos Indian to reply and speak for them, that he should go with the Tewa and Tano liars, that I already knew him and that he and all the others had rebelled or stirred up all the people of the other nations. And with these and many other reasons he shut up as if mute. And continuing to insist about Don Juan de Yé, they repeated the same thing. Insisting they should call the said Governor Pacheco. Sometimes they replied that they had already sent for him, other times that he could not come down, that he was far away with said people.

And already being late, in order not to lose the day, having seen from the clock it was eleven o'clock, that I was going down to their pueblo, I told them that I would await them without doing any harm until one o'clock. And if the said Juan de Yé and Governor Pacheco were not there at said hour I would take the corn.

And having descended to the pueblo with the men and having been there a good while I checked the clock and since it was past one, and since the sentinels that I ordered to be placed on the high houses did not see anyone coming down nor detect the presence of the rebels, I ordered the men-at-arms to enter openly into the houses. And they had removed from them what they contained having left only old corn and some pottery jars. Nevertheless, I ordered a squad of fifteen men to go back with their leader to the camp where the royal army was, that one of them should promptly bring me a prybar, and that the rest should have the muleteers prepare the sacking to load on the mules of the pack trains. And then they would come as soon as possible, as they were ordered, which order was performed. And it being about three in the afternoon, they had already with said prybar broken and torn open the lower rooms and new corn was discovered. Thus malice and treacherous heart with which these rebels operated were known for they placed the crosses only with cunning and trickery, to see if through them they could again withdraw to give themselves time to take their food supplies to the mountains where they were secure.

And the muleteers aided by the militia busied themselves until the church service late in the afternoon loading the cobs of corn, when I left with the men of the escort, returning to spend the night at the outpost.

And so that which is referred to that day may be of record, I noted it as an action that I sign with the leaders and officers of war together with my secretary of government and war, Don Diego José de Vargas Zapata Luján Ponce de León y Contreras, Antonio Jorje, Diego Arias de Quiros, Antonio de Baluerde, before me, Alphonso Rael de Aguilar, Secretary of Government and War.

Monday, July 5

On the fifth day of the month of July of said date and year, none of the rebel Taos having appeared, except for on all sides of the mountainous countryside, in order to communicate with each other, making many smoke signals, in particular, continuing them on the route to the place where the royal army and camp were located in order to manage to take out the supplies, carting off the ears of corn from said pueblo to protect it better and after the grain was shelled, to sack it in the camp. I ordered that Captain and Sergeant Major Antonio Jorje, currently holding that rank in the garrison, should go immediately with the officers along with the muleteers and carts. And as its escort he should take up to 30 soldiers, and from the new corn the best that he might find, he should load the pack train, coming with it to said royal camp. He did so and many people of the camp who had animals also did this. So that the action may be of record, I noted it as a proceeding and signed it with my secretary of government and war, Don Diego José de Vargas Zapata Luján Ponce de León y Contreras, before me, Alphonso Rael de Aguilar, Secretary of Government and War.

Said governor and captain goes out at 10 o'clock at night to reconnoiter the countryside and said pueblo. By means of a large cloud of smoke coming out of the mountainous countryside he knows there is a council of the said enemy there.

On said fifth day of the present month of July of the date and year, it must have been 10:00 o'clock at night when, by means of the moon so much smoke was seen coming out of the ravine of the sierra that comes from the road of the Picurís it almost covered the countryside—in this regard and because it could be a warning that the rebel enemy Taos could attack the royal camp with the confidence of having help from said rebel people, it occurred to me that I should go out to reconnoiter the countryside and thus I then mounted, as did the military leaders and officials of war. And with my secretary we traveled throughout all the country.

We went to the Pueblo of Taos and from it up to the foothills of the mountains. There was no enemy to be found nor sound of them. Returning to said royal camp, I ordered that everyone should be ready with their arms and saddled horses, for the rest of the night, having a squad of ten men alternate as a night patrol around the royal camp. And so that it may be of record, I noted it as an action that I signed with my secretary of government and war, Don Diego José de Vargas Zapata Luján Ponce de León y Contreras, before me, Alphonso Rael de Aguilar, Secretary of Government and War.

Tuesday, July 6

On the sixth day of the present month of July of the date and year, I, said governor and captain general, seeing that the grains of corn were shaken out in their transportation for the two previous days to this camp is of record; in order to finish and load the pack train, considering that more than half was lost, not only because of shelling it but because of the green corn, I ordered that getting and transporting it be repeated in the same manner, as was ordered yesterday, the fifth day of the present month. The aforementioned captain, having brought it to the royal camp, I ordered that it should be distributed among all of the men, as they were interested, because it was for their sustenance and that of their families, they should diligently shell it. Once that was done, the muleteers should sack it and should be careful with the adjustment of their packtrains and the number of mules each one loads, so that when everything was finished and outfitted, I may determine the order of their leaving this campsite.

And so that this action may be of record, I noted it as a proceeding which I signed with my secretary of government and war, Don Diego José de Vargas Zapata Luján Ponce de León y Contreras, before me, Alphonso Rael de Aguilar, Secretary of Government and War.

The smoke signals of the said rebels increase on all quarters; as they are opponents they warn each other where they are and that they have the camp surrounded.

On the sixth day of the present month of July of the date the smoke signals greatly increased throughout the mountainous country which surrounds the Valley and Pueblo of the Taos, so that it was known that all the rebel nations were there together; and to show the location where each one was located; as well as by the outcry, since they thought that they safely would have the victory in destroying us, as a result of their increased number; for their reason, having realized that the said road and exit were of the nature that is of record and referred to in the entrada of the day into this valley and Pueblo, to deduce that it was impossible with the heavily-loaded pack train, and more, those which the soldiers and citizens have outfitted without the well-known risk of being attended to; and fearing total ruin, a plan was formed, although it would be a detour, going where the enemy would be fooled, for they thought that the royal army would only go through this road.

The elders, experienced in this country, who were coming with the camp told me not to worry, that if I could tolerate the great distance and the detour, they would get me out with the royal army through the country so that we could succeed in bringing help to the Villa of Santa Fé with the supplies that our Lord had seen fit to give us, delivering us for that purpose from danger, which we have experienced in this location up to the present time. Thus we could be assured of his divine mercy.

And I answered them that I was ready for everything willingly and very happy with his Divine Will and that thus I would leave the success to his will and to them to guide me through where they were saying, and that I was only seeking the safety of the camp and not the shortness of the road. In that regard it was determined that the way out would have to be to the land of the Utes whose nation is very friendly toward the Spaniards. The Utes felt sorry for the loss and departure of the Spaniards when the revolt of the said kingdom took place. From knowing the Spaniards are again settled in it will follow the congruence of their interests, by means of the increased exchange of local goods which enter and that they trade in. By turning to leave through the mouth of the Chama River the buffalo will also be found which may help to feed the men who will be able to support themselves, with the toasted corn, since fortune obliges them to wander such a long way. These reasons were so that, I, said governor and captain general, resolved to delay returning to Santa Fé secure and even more so, when the enemy could invade or overrun it, since I was in their land. It was up to me to protect the people. Thus, so that my said departure would not be detected, and to hide the return from them so that in case some should notice it, and those who were farther away might not notice it, I ordered that at ten at night the men should begin to load or get ready said royal army. And so that it could be done by the hour of six in the evening, I ordered that the horses be brought near for the guards to change horses and that the horses at night should all be outfitted, and the saddle horses, saddled and the pack horses, having men armed and each one prepared in their campsites for the said hour of ten to begin to load.

And the leaders and officials of war being present said that it was resolved and was what should be done. And they did what was ordered and commanded of them. And so that it may be of record, they signed it with me, said governor and captain general and my secretary of government and war, Don Diego José de Vargas Zapata Luján Ponce de León y Contreras, Antonio Jorje, Diego Arias de Quiros, Antonio de Baluerde, before me, Alphonso Rael de Aguilar, Secretary of Government and War.

On said day at night, sixth of the present month of July of the date and year, judging it to be the hour indicated by me, the governor and captain general, in the aforementioned command, so that with the efficiency and precision which is required for the brevity and preparation of the camp, since the loading of the supplies is so difficult, I, then mounted with the leaders and officials of war, and, at the same time as I, they assisted in giving encouragement for the rapid preparations.

The camp, being ready at about one o'clock in the night of the seventh, Wednesday of the present July of the date and year, I, governor and captain of said camp, in order to take the direction and route of the Utes, (The decision was made to travel north to the land of the Ute. It was here that Vargas continued traveling north of Taos on the East Fork of the North Branch of the Old Spanish Trail.) took Matias Luján as guide and also the Rexidor and Captain Lázaro de Mizquía for the said entrada, since it was he who proposed it and made the decision at the conference referred to.

Wednesday, July 7

The camp, prepared, being ready to march from this place at about one at night of the seventh, Wednesday, of the present month of July of said date and year, I said governor and captain general, took the direct road and route of the Utes; taking with me Matias Luján as interpreter, and the Rexidor and Captain Lázaro de Mizquía, also for said entrada, the one who proposed it and made the decision the conference referred to yesterday. Having gone barely half a league, when the rebel enemy, Taos, passing near the road of the mountains inhabited by them, they made a small fire, which is the accustomed warning indicating that they are following the camp. In order to protect the camp, I arranged for the campaign Captain, Juan de Olguín to take the vanguard with forty soldiers and for the train of the camp and the transport of supplies to go then.

And in the main body was the squadron of the battle and infantry, the squad of the royal standard, with my person; along with the garrison for the flying squadron, militia company. In the rear guard the campaign Captain, Eusébio de Vargas, was coming with his squad of thirty soldiers of horse guard, and mules who were carrying that he was leading, in his charge.

Also, next to me the military leaders came with Sergeant Juan Ruíz de Cazeres, and in that order, the march continued. And having gone two leagues up to the river, which they call Arroyo Hondo, we entered.

We passed on the road of hills and mountainous countryside, which had some security because there were, on the hills of the land, clearing of large trees, and making some avenues to give rest to the camp.

And when it was ten in the morning, after having gone from five to six leagues, some smoke was seen in the sierra, which was high, facing the valley leaving it on the right hand. After a little while and distance, fresh tracks were seen, showing that a large troop of Indians had come down, which caused Captain Juan de Olguín to inform me and to keep back the royal army, and then to order that the soldiers whose horses were tired be changed.

Continuing the march into a deep and wooded ravine, the enemy appeared in ambush. And our Lord permitted that with care and following the tracks the enemy was fought by the said captain, Olguín, and his squadron leaving as he could, withdrawing through the brambles and ravines, which escape was managed because the ruggedness of the terrain was in his favor. Five were killed and some were badly hurt and one was very badly wounded. Because of the repeated shots the soldiers fired, many must have been badly wounded.

Having captured two alive, one badly wounded, by means of intelligent people, knowledgeable in that language, Taos, and among them, Sergeant Juan Ruíz de Cazeres, I asked them various questions. They said that they were from Taos and that every night their Governor Pacheco had placed thirty Indians as spies, and that last night, as soon as we began to load, they saw it and came following me. And because of that they lit the signal fire referred to. And having the report from the rest, from Governor Pacheco about leaving on that road he ordered that eighty young Indians should leave immediately with their war captains to give me the said ambush and to kill me. All the people of the rebel Tanos, Tewa and Picurís were on the road of the sierra through where I descended. Don Juan de Yé was still alive, but they had tied him up. After these statements were made, I asked the Reverend Missionary Father, one of the chaplains of the army, Fray Juan de Alpuente, that he should prepare them to be shot and I gave the order to Sergeant Major Antonio Jorje, Captain of the garrison, that he should select and appoint from the soldiers who were present so that they should shoot them dead. After such was done, I continued the march to the Red River, (The Red River continued to be a popular stopping place on the East Fork. See later chapters.) and choosing the most appropriate place to set up the royal camp, I ordered them to quarter themselves on it, the march having more than ten long leagues.

Since the sun had already set when all the royal army and camp arrived, and so that this and what is referred to may be of record, I sign it with the military leaders and my secretary of government and war, Don Diego José de Vargas Zapata Luján Ponce de León y Contreras, Antonio Jorje, Diego Arias de Quiros, Antonio de Baluerde, before me, Alphonso Rael de Aguilar, Secretary of Government and War.

Thursday, July 8

On the eighth day of the present month of July of the date and year, I, the said governor and captain general called the guides of this journey. They informed me that in the mountains that border the Red River live the Apaches that are called the "Acho" and the nations of the Utes, whom we are going to look for, do not allow them in their land, for which reason they live in this place as though cornered in. The interpreters said this is also as far as the rebel Taos who have many spies and sentinels watching, come in to hunt for the bovine cattle, the buffalo, whose dung was seen in various places and descents from this mountain range to the said river. And in order that the Utes whom we seek may know of our arrival in this Kingdom of New Mexico and the Villa of Santa Fé, I ordered that many large smoke signals be made.

I set out marching with our camp to the Rio de la Culebra, (It would appear that this stream was already known by this name and possibly some of these Spanish people had been here before.) the distance being nine long leagues, all land of extensive valleys and many streams with groves of trees. It is seen the buffalo graze here because of the dung that was found.

And having arrived at the Rio de la Culebra, I ordered a halt to spend the night with the camp on its bank at six in the evening. So that the march may be of record, I signed with the said military leaders and my secretary of government and war, Don Diego José de Vargas Zapata Luján Ponce de León y Contreras, Antonio Jorje, Diego Arias de Quiros, Antonio de Baluerde, before me, Alphonso Rael de Aguilar, Secretary of Government and War.

Friday, July 9

On the ninth day of the present month of July of the said date and year, having gone about four long leagues to the left, I came upon the Rio del Norte flowing by; sending some swift swimmers in to discover its ford. It was found that there was none, that the river was very high. It makes us very sad to see that rafts will be necessary to cross it.

The whole royal army having arrived, I, the governor and captain general, called a halt to unload because it was almost midday. And I ordered that some soldiers go with an Indian, who came in the service of the Maestro de Campo and Alcalde Ordinario, Lorenzo Madríd, who said he knew the way because he was a Tewa of the Pueblo of San Juan, whose natives set out by the mouth of the Chama River which was the departure place that they had used; and it saved much distance. This route the experienced ones did not know since they said it went to the gap far in the interior of the land of the said Utes. They had to plan that, being found or when they found us, they would take us out. It was Divine Providence that on this occasion this Indian of so much intelligence should be sure of this road. And so from this place it was he who went as guide.

And going on to the business of looking for a ford of this river, at a little less than two leagues, it was found. It had a flow of two branches and a meadow and a

This crossing is known as the Ford Ferry Site. The two small hills at the left in the photo, one on each side of the river, mark the location where Don Diego de Vargas crossed the Rio Grande in 1694.

little island of beautiful pasture. And at the descent of a little mountain range the river, which was very wide, was forded. By means of its two branches the flow of its current was broken and, although deep, it could be crossed. The muleteers in two trips carried over the cargo by putting a half-load on the back of each mule. Having crossed and reconnoitered it, it was crossed over. And I spent the night at the meadow and little island with the joy of having secured and seen this ford which was the worry that generally repressed the spirit of all. So that this march may be of record, I signed with said military leaders and secretary of government and war, Don Diego José de Vargas Zapata Luján Ponce de León y Contreras, Antonio Jorje, Diego Arias de Quiros, Antonio de Baluerde, before me, Alphonso Rael de Aguilar, Secretary of Government and War.

Saturday, July 10

On the tenth day of the present month of July of this said date and year, I, the said governor and captain general, crossed the aforesaid discovered and reconnoitered ford of the Rio del Norte, with the squad of the royal banner. It was much work for the militia to build brush bundles that were necessary on the embankment and bank to ensure its descent both on the entrance as well as the way out of this river for there would be no other chance to cross it for it was boxed in with walls. So by this endeavor and repair it was conquered and an easy and possible crossing was made.

So that it may be of record, we proceeded a distance of four leagues to the Rio de San Antonio, thus named for the hill located opposite it; and in its meadow, because it was a land of good pasture, I called a halt to pass the night with the royal army, having arrived with the joy of having no misfortune, at about three in the afternoon, I signed so that this march may be of record with the military leaders and my secretary of government and war, Don Diego José de Vargas Zapata Luján Ponce de León y Contreras, Antonio Jorje, Diego Arias de Quiros, Antonio de Baluerde, before me, Alphonso Rael de Aguilar, Secretary of Government and War.

The said camp being quartered some who had stationed themselves on said hill to see what the country was like informed me that many of them had noted a large quantity of buffalo. And they killed some and they told what is related here.

And then immediately, short after having made camp and quarters some of those with a desire to eat meat were moved to go up on this hill and mountain range of San Antonio. They sighted and descried at a distance of two leagues by their guess that there was on a spacious meadow a big bunch of wild cattle. Their desire to eat meat as well as to see this herd of buffalo alive led more than eighty persons to mount and go to this meadow where they found more than five hundred head of buffalo. They did not make the best of the opportunity for they barely killed with the lance fourteen or fifteen cattle and some other very large deer almost the size of those they call elk. And with this meat the men were helped in part for all they had been eating was toasted corn. So that it may be of record, I signed with my secretary of government and war, Don Diego José de Vargas Zapata Luján Ponce de León y Contreras, before me, Alphonso Rael de Aguilar, Secretary of Government and War.

Sunday, July 11

On the eleventh day of the present month of July of the date and year, having recognized the need of the camp and to give some rest to the horses and mules because of the load and long journeys they had made and to give the people the relief they can get by going today to see if any stray buffalo took refuge in the nooks and groves of the river whose course moves snake-like I gave permission to go on this hunt. And therefore along with me, the said governor and captain general, nearly a hundred men, mounted on their horses, with the servants some had with them, equipped with their animals to load the cattle they might kill. And in order that I might do likewise for those in general who were not equipped for this, I ordered the muleteers to make ready about twenty mules to go with them. And by two in the afternoon of this day, only seven or eight cattle and a few deer could be obtained because of the stampede and flight that happened yesterday.

So this business, and that we continued the smoke signals for the Utes to make them go out to search for those who were making them and who were the people to be found in their country may be of record, I signed with him, my secretary of government and war, Don Diego José de Vargas Zapata Luján Ponce de León y Contreras, before me, Alphonso Rael de Aguilar, Secretary of Government and War.

Monday, July 12

On the twelfth day of the present month of July of the date and year the Ute Nation attacked, the above mentioned nation which had been sought by smoke signals previously made to attract them so that they might recognize the Spaniards and me, the said governor and captain general, that they might know of our return to settle the Villa of Santa Fé and its Kingdom of New Mexico. I, said governor and captain general, had notified Sergeant Juan Ruíz de Cazares yesterday evening and ordered that at the rise of the morning star the horse and mule herd should be gathered and brought in so that the royal army might make an early start and have time to get ready. And by virtue of this order being executed by the Captain and Guard Eusébio de Vargas, it was a great advantage during the event and surprise attack which the aforesaid Ute Nation unexpectedly made. They, having reconnoitered our campfires with their spies on the said night, believed us to be the Indians of this Kingdom, and our enemies, the rebels mentioned in these proceedings the Tewa, Tano, Taos, Picurís, Jemez and Keres with all of whom the Utes are now at war and were before the rebellion. And because of this and the slaughter the Pueblo had treacherously inflicted on the Utes, Spanish friends and the killing of their friars, they have waged war on them with great vigor, saying that until the Spaniards should return again they would come to their very Pueblos to make war until all were destroyed, for the Pueblo have not only killed the Spaniards, their brothers and friends but also caused them to leave the Kingdom.

And so at the time that the Pueblo rebels came in to hunt buffalo they had used the scheme and ruse to come mounted with suits of armor and leather jackets and hats made of hide like those the Spaniards wear, carrying also the firearms they had taken and even their bugle. And in this guise and scheme they entered this land and present place. And at the times that the Utes had strength of people they have

35

fought and they have killed many and had made the rest run away.

They related and told all these things to excuse the attack and furious on-slaught they made on the camp, aiming their closed volley of arrows and war clubs at it from all sides. There is no doubt that their finding most of our force awake and up, with the horse herd at hand ready for each man to get his ready for the trip, was the reason and essential circumstance which prevented these Utes from killing many of the people, for it was not even the break of dawn when their furious clamor fell, as had been said, on all the royal camp. The horse herd and mules being nearby with their guard they could not drive them off. And since we had come looking for them and did not believe they could be another kind of enemy, we tried on our own part not to start hostilities, but only to defend ourselves and hold off the attack, talking to them and telling to them we were Spaniards and their friends.

Not believing for the reason given above, they charged with more force, judg-ing we were afraid. And even when we did not fire they were still convinced that we were the rebellious Indians, their enemies. And thus our consideration put us in obvious danger, giving them more confidence and courage to come in among the shelters of our royal army and troops. When all the Spaniards were armed and many of them mounted, some volleys of shots were finally fired at them because six of our own men had fallen wounded and it was now necessary to fire in our defense. And so with this moderate discharge eight of them were killed. Realizing the strength with which resistance had been made, they decided to clear out of the camp, taking to flight, during which many were wounded because of the obstacle of crossing the river to which they had taken.

And finding themselves safe on the other side they came to their senses, and daylight now being clear, they waved a buckskin in sign of peace, yelling in their language "*anche*," "*pauiche*," which means "brother," "friend." And those of our camp, natives of the land, recognized them to be Utes not only in their words but also in the appearance of their faces, shields and dress. And so our natives answered them with gestures because they understood them for they too communicate with them. Because there was no interpreter it was necessary to resort to gestures and panto-mime and they made great show of joy as soon as they were sure that we were Span-iards. Then without showing regret about the above recorded damage that was done to them, joyful, peaceful, complaisant they came to us with as much confidence as if war had not been made.

And I received and treated them kindly giving them corn that they asked of me and valuables such as trinkets for hats and a wool poncho, knives and ribbons and such. And the rest of my men of the royal army did the same, giving them some of the dried meat and meat and corn that they had. And I also gave to the captain of war who was prominent among them, a horse in recompense and payment for the death of another brother of the captain of war, the one who came in the lead and was one of the first to receive a shot, nearing the camp of the royal ensign. My said notary of government and war, who was with it, shot him.

All generally in the said camp acted with great courage fulfilling their obligations as did the captains of the campaign, Eusébio de Vargas and Juan Olguín, and the captain of the garrison and of the militia. To all I gave thanks in the name of His Majesty and we thanked the Divine Mother amazed at the outcome in achieving our aim after the war and fight. One of the Indians, content to be friends with us, helped to heal our wounded. And we could have killed them all and captured their women and children whom they had brought with them. We refrained from doing it, always believing that they were Utes. Their number was seen to be about three hundred in all. When about to return to their rancheria they told us as they took their leave that they had much trade goods and clothing of the country, buckskin, urging us to go there. We replied by signs showing them the loads of provisions we were going to take to the villa and that by our tracks they could go there to see us.

So that the said success may be of record, I signed with the said military leaders jointly with my secretary of government and war, Don Diego José de Vargas Zapata Luján Ponce de León y Contreras, Antonio Jorje, Diego Arias de Quiros, Antonio de Baluerde, before me, Alphonso Rael de Aguilar, Secretary of Government and War.

Tuesday, July 13

On the thirteenth day of the month of the date and year, I, said governor and captain general, went six or seven leagues stopping in a narrows on whose right is a mountain they also call San Antonio, (North of San Antoine Mountain the river turns from traveling to the northeast to east. Just after it changes direction is where the ford is located.) because the San Antonio descends in a gorge on the left. And the said Indian guide saying the stopping place where we go to sleep was similar country, not having water for our horses and mules, except for a very small spring that could give just enough for our people. In this regard, I commanded then that the royal army should make a halt and pass the word to make mid-day càmp and allow time for the horses and mules to drink slowly.

Having stayed until three in the afternoon and experienced a great storm and tempest, I set out from this place, arriving at the appointed place of the Indian at the coming of dark. And there was water in the little spring (The little spring is located west of present day Tres Piedras and was a stopping place used by many travelers.) for our people as the Indian said previously. I ordered the same form and order as the one of the day before, being even more certain of the evil intentions of a

San Antonio Mountain marked the east side of the West Fork of the North Branch of the Old Spanish Trail for centuries before being discovered by the Spanish.

surprise attack that it is feared the said Ute may repeat. And taking precautions against this, I ordered the captain and sergeant to bring in the horses when the morning star rises, for this reason and for having slept without water. And so that it may be of record, this march was twelve or thirteen leagues, most of it land very rough and rocky. I signed with my secretary of government and war, Don Diego José de Vargas Zapata Luján Ponce de León y Contreras, before me, Alphonso Rael de Aguilar, Secretary of Government and War.

Wednesday, July 14

On the fourteenth day of the present month of July of the date and year, the said royal army being readied early in the morning, the same Indian guide having said that today's journey would be to the Rio del Ojo del Aqua Caliente (Ojo Caliente was a popular resort visited by the Indians and later by the Spanish. For a number of years it was to become the northern-most outpost on the Spanish Frontier.) about nine or ten long leagues away. Having traveled until four in the afternoon, I arrived at it, taking the vanguard with me. The camp was there altogether at a little after five. And having reconnoitered the place where lodging would be, it was found the bank and the valley of this said river was not wide enough, but it was necessary after having traveled this day's journey to quarter the troops there for the night keeping all the precautions of proceeding nights and even greater ones this night, because we were boxed in between two mountains which was advantageous to the enemy, since this place is ten leagues from the rebellious Tewa. So that this march may be of record, I signed it with my secretary of government and war, Don Diego José de Vargas Zapata de Luján Ponce de León y Contreras, before me, Alphonso Rael de Aguilar, Secretary of Government and War.

Thursday, July 15

On the fifteenth day of the present month of July of the said date and year, having also taken the morning, because of the journey of ten or eleven leagues, and because of the difficulty of having to pass the mouth of the Chama River and likewise the Rio del Norte, in view of the Pueblo of the rebel Tewa up in arms against the Kingdom of New Mexico, whose distance our Indian guide said would be about ten leagues, but better going than the day before; and so at a little after three in the afternoon, I said governor and captain general, was there, bringing the vanguard, having traveled and set out for the said mouth of the Chama River. (The South Branch of the Spanish trail was to take this fork of the Rio Grande to the southwest.) Where begins the brow of the mesa they call San Juan, because the said pueblo is three leagues away, some of the rebel native Tewa were spotted on it. And the moment they saw me and said troops they raised their smoke signals of warning, and the lookouts that they had placed on the other mountains answered them immediately. This was the reason for making a halt in the grove of trees of the said Chama River, in order to give time and to assure that the royal army which was straggling along might pass by. And the horses and mules being gathered were gotten out of the valley and trees of the said river which runs one long league along the said road. I returned to continue with said march and reached the ford of the pass of Rio del Norte, (Just south of Black Mesa was a ford on the Rio Grande which was used for many years by the Indians and later Spanish. See documents to follow.) designated by the Indian, in view of the Pueblo of San Juan, (It is here at San Juan Pueblo that Juan of the Oñate established the first capital of New Mexico in 1598. The Old Spanish Trail divided here into three trails. The East Fork of the North Branch went to Taos. The West Fork Of the North Branch followed the Rio Ojo Caliente north to the Ojo Caliente Spring. The South Branch followed the Rio Chama northwest to Abiquiu.) recognized by the breaking of the said river into two branches. Although the second one was deep I crossed it without any misfortune.

Because the distance of the Villa of Santa Fé was ten leagues, in order to shorten tomorrow's journey, I went to half the distance, staying in the middle of three leagues that would put us at the mesa inhabited by the uprisen rebels of the Pueblo of San Ildefonso. (Don Diego of the Vargas had made a circle to the north and returned to that portion of the Spanish Trail which he had traveled earlier.) Arriving at this place and bank of the Rio del Norte at six in the evening with the royal army, we gave thanks to His Divine Majesty for the happy outcome and for getting out by a route so different and so lengthy with the result related in this report.

And in order that the present march may be record, and that the arrangements and precautions of preceding nights were observed, because we are in view of the rebels, I added a squadron to take night watch, so that in case the enemy should try to spring a surprise attack by the river they would be heard and it would be possible to resist them with success in destroying them. This order I gave to the said military leaders and so that it may be record, I signed it with my secretary of government and war, Don Diego José de Vargas Zapata de Luján Ponce de León y Contreras, before me, Alphonso Rael de Aguilar, Secretary of Government and War.

Friday, July 16

On the sixteenth morning of the present month of July of the said date and year, the said force, having in accordance with my order, made ready to enter the Villa of Santa Fé at a good hour, because of my worry I, said governor and captain general, wished to know if they had any misfortune during my long absence. In order that the said army might proceed by the direct route because of the supplies they carried, I gave orders, after having separated and assigned forty soldiers, including the two captains, of the garrison and of the militia, military officers including my secretary of government and war. I gave orders, as has been said, to the maestro de campo to proceed with the said royal army by the direct road which comes out to the Pueblo of Jacona, in order to enter the Villa of Santa Fé by the direct route. I would have passed them in the meantime if I had not scouted and seen some smoke signals made other times by the rebels on the mesa of the Pueblo of San Ildefonso. And therefore, the said maestro de campo immediately set out with the said royal army and I, said governor and captain general, proceeded to reconnoiter the mesa, which was not only occupied as I left it, but also the rebellious tribes of Tanos, Tewas, Picurís, Taos and Jemez were gathered together there. And when I arrived at the point that falls to the Rio del Norte, there were many people on the lower mesilla, who, seeing how few I had, thought I had come, like other times, to attack them. And although some shots were fired at them, they were not as timid as in previous times when I had come to reconnoiter. As a result I noted and realized the presence of new people and fearing that they might lay some ambush when they saw me divided from said army and troops, taking precaution lest a misfortune befall me or said troops, I ordered my men to close ranks and retreat, telling them that I had only come to reconnoiter and see if this mesa was occupied. And so that the camp might not miss the road I had separated from them, in order not to have any misfortune in this campaign by lingering to kill four to six Indians; that at the right time I would come with their graces to make war on the rebels so their desire might be accomplished. And I told Sergeant Juan Ruíz to start out and take a shortcut to join said royal army and troops, that I would follow him with my men. And he did so, leaving by the way which cuts along the cliff which is very difficult, dangerous and lengthy. I came down from it until I came in sight of and near the said Pueblo of Jacona where I joined said army and troops when they were going by. I traveled under its protection, because many of the said rebels had come down and followed me along the road by the cliff to yell at me, and show themselves among the sharp ridges where I had come down.

And so, having descended to the Pueblo of Tesuque, I was also detained there for more than two hours, waiting for the whole army to pass, in order to give it time to go through part of the three rough, wooded leagues with many gullies from there to said villa. After the horse herd having arrived and I changed horses, as did the others, I set out, leaving many soldiers of said squadron on the road to outfit and escort said troops that I had left behind, in the charge of the captain of the soldiers of the garrison.

And it was about two o'clock in the afternoon when I entered the villa, where I was received with happiness for my successful arrival and for the supplies of food for they did not have any.

And it was Divine Providence that impelled me to go to the said Pueblo of Taos for supplies. My lieutenant reported to me, as the rest, that it was very quiet here in the villa, without a single rebel Indian even coming to reconnoiter as they had done on other occasions. The one in charge has sent different soldiers every day to see whether they had found tracks, which were not seen during my absence.

And it was between three and four in the afternoon when all the said army and troops were within the villa, all being well with them and the villa.

And so that this entrada and campaign made in seventeen days, including coming and going, staying and returning, having traveled from one hundred to one hundred twenty leagues, may be of record, I signed this along with my military leaders and secretary of government and war, Don Diego José de Vargas Zapata Luján Ponce de León y Contreras, Antonio Jorje, Diego Arias de Quiros, Antonio de Baluerde, before me, Alphonso Rael de Aguilar, Secretary of Government and War.

March 20, __13 G. D. Cordova & Cross
Was this an earlier explorer? What century (16, 17, 18) was this? This carving in the face of a cliff is located up the same canyon in which the 1744 date is located. This route was used by travelers to reach the Pagosa Springs area from the San Luis Valley.

2

1705/ROQUE MADRID

Roque Mardid was born in New Mexico about 1644 to Francisco and Sebastiana Ruíz de Cáceres Madrid II. He had one brother, Lorenzo, who also played an important part in the reconquest of New Mexico.[1]

Roque married Juana *López Pacheco de Arvid*. Roque and Juana Madrid had four children: Pedro born in 1673, Matías born in 1675, José born in 1678 and Josefa, no date of birth noted.[2] His hacienda was located south of Santa Fe about six miles near the Arroyo de San Marcos.[3] Juana *de Arvid* Madrid died in 1713 and Roque married Josefa Durán. Roque and Josefa *Durán* Madrid had three children by some reports: Antonia, Julián and Miguel Angel.[4]

Roque Madrid had achieved the rank of Captain by 1686 and was promoted a year later to the rank of Sargent Mayor of all troops in New Mexico. Roque took a leading part in the reconquest of New Mexico as part of the Vargas Expeditions of 1692 and 1693, as well as the Pueblo uprising in 1696.[5]

Roque Madrid led his 1705 Navajo expedition north from Santa Fe on the Old Spanish Trail to San Juan Pueblo where he reviewed his troops. From San Juan Pueblo they continued north on the East Fork of the North Branch of the Old Spanish Trail. Leaving the Rio del Norte, they traveled northeast to Picurís Pueblo. From there they turned west to Cieneguilla (Pilar) where they crossed the Rio Grande below the Rio Grande Gorge. After crossing the Rio Grande, they traveled northwest to the West Fork of the North Branch of the Old Spanish Trail. They traveled north on the Trail to Piedra del Carnero (Tres Piedras) and continued north to the Rio de Los Pinos where they left the Trail.

Roque Madrid served as an officer in the Royal Army of New Mexico under many New Mexico Governors: Otermín, Jironza, Posada, Vargas, Cubero, Páez, Cuervo, Chacón, Mogollón, Martínez, and Valverde. Although the exact date is not known, Roque Madrid died about 1723.[6]

July 31, 1705

In this village of San Juan de los Caballeros on the 31st of July 1705, (Juan de Oñate arrived at the Tewa Pueblo of Oke Oweenge and renamed it San Juan de los Caballeros in July of 1598. The name has been shortened to San Juan Pueblo.)[7] I, the Company Commander, Roque de la Madrid, chief military officer, by order of the Governor and Captain General, don Francisco Cuervo y Valdés, knight of the Order of Santiago and treasurer and factor of the Royal Treasury office of the city of Guadalajara, declare war by blood and fire on our enemies, the Apache Navajo nation. (The Na-dene (Athabaskan) had crossed the Bering Straight from Asia to North America. Later they were pushed south by the Shoshone. The names Apache and Navajo are the names given to these people by the early Spanish.)[8]

And for fulfillment of the orders that I was given it was my duty to inspect the arms of the Spanish and Indians alike. This was carried out on the same day, month, and year. Lieutenant General don Juan de Ulibarrí was present, and after the inspection was passed much to my satisfaction, he handed the company over to me. Taking the Rio del Norte (This is the present-day Rio Grande or Rio Grande del Norte which begins in the San Juan Mountains southwest of Creede, Colorado, crosses New Mexico and Texas, dumping into the Gulf of Mexico. The East Fork of the North Branch of the Old Spanish Trail follows the east side of the Rio Grande.) route, I encamped on its pleasant banks, near the funnel.

August 1, 1705

On the first day of August of that year I left the banks of that river bound for the village of Picurís. Along the way sixteen Indians from the village of Tesuque joined my company and I made camp a quarter of a league from that village, having marched that day a little more than five leagues.

August 2, 1705

On the second day of that month and year I departed, marching with my company, taking the difficult high ground of a steep, rocky terrain. And arriving at a spring called La Cieneguilla, (La Cieneguilla was an older name for present-day Pilar, New Mexico. At Pilar Roque Madrid left the East Fork and crossed the gorge to the West Fork of the North Branch of the Old Spanish Trail.) I was fortunate to have waiting for me the Reverend Father Chaplain named to be chaplain of my company by the Father Vice Guardian, Father Friar Francisco Jiménez, who has charge of the mission of the village of San Gerónimo de Taos. (San Gerónimo de Taos is suggested by Harrington as being the name of the Taos Pueblo.)[9] I gave orders for my company to march there. I went to see the Reverend Father, and enlisted there the Indians of the Taos nation, forty in number. There I inspected their arms, since they had not been included in the inspection in the Plaza de Armas, and was pleased to find them sufficient.

Following the route of my company I led them along the canyon and banks of the Rio del Norte, fording it with increasing difficulty and obvious risk of our lives, which it pleased God to preserve from danger, and when the entire company had crossed I settled them on a narrow beach with much brush and little grass, since there was no better place available. I marched six leagues that day. (They crossed at the south end of the Rio Grande Gorge which extends from Pilar, New Mexico north into the San Luis Valley in southern Colorado.)

August 3, 1705

On the third day of that month and year my company departed, marching with increasing difficulty up the gorge toward the north. It became necessary for the entire mounted squadron to dismount and lead the horses, due to the thick brush and the steepness of the terrain, holding always to the direction toward the camp called Piedra de Carnero, ten leagues from the river gorge, and there I encamped my company. (Traveling northwest from Pilar could put troops in Comanche (La Cañada de los Comanches) Cañon which is the route of the old wagon road from Ojo Caliente to Tres Piedras. This route follows the west boundary of Taos County.)

August 4, 1705

The the fourth day of that month and year we departed from the campsite of Piedra del Carnero, (Piedra del Carnero is an early day name for Tres Piedras, New Mexico. The Indians referred to this location as the mountain sheep rocks.)[10] marching toward the west along a pleasant ravine with good grazing until we arrived at the middle of the mountain range a place I named Tierra Florida for the diversity of flowers, that because of its lack of steep and rugged terrain, the presence of many small streams, fed by rain showers and heavy dew. I halted my company on the banks of a shallow river whose current flows south to a colorful terrain and extended valley where that night we experienced a frost. This day I traveled six leagues.

August 5, 1705

On the fifth day of that month and year we departed the camp of the Sierra Florida and its river, following always the same route toward the west, and I stopped at an extensive alluvial fan that forms the skirt of the mountain where there was much good grazing. This day I made a short march, since the Indians who were acquainted with the country told me that beyond this camp, that I named Nuestra Señora de Covadongo, there was no water except at a great distance. I marched this day three leagues. I encamped my company on that same river of the Florida Mountains.

That same day I sent the war chiefs of the Tewa and Picurís nations, who were accustomed to those steep climbs and wild country, to find the pass through which, Spanish Arms had entered some thirty years earlier.

The above-mentioned chiefs returned from their excursion on the sixth of that same month. And as soon as they returned to this camp and my presence they started telling me how impossible and ill advised the penetration was saying that if we proceeded we would likely lose all the horses and at best would thank God that we could ride out on the same horse we rode in on, due to the density of the forest, the fallen timber, the cliffs and precipices, saying that since they had told me the truth I should not complain when I saw it with my own eyes.

August 7, 1705

On the seventh day of that month and year, in spite of the news the war chiefs brought me, I decided to follow the sierra with its windfalls and rock slides by a way never traveled before that time by any Spaniard, or by any other nation, first taking the precaution of doubling the escort of the horses, so that with everyone helping we would be able to drive them without any losses. I took the point as guide, invoking Our Lady of Conquest to open the way for us to emerge from that difficulty.

And after a short march the forest was so dence it shut out the light of day, but it pleased God that after a quarter of a league I broke out into country easier to travel and with good grazing and beautiful partridges big as Castilian hens. (Dendragapus obscurus, commonly known as Blue or Dusty Grouse, inhabit the pine forests of western North America and often weight up to 3-1/2 pounds.)[11] And in about four leagues as we traveled toward the north I came out into a small valley, with good grazing, marches and springs, which I called the Valley of Santiago. By way of two ravines that are very close together containing two shallow creeks that run toward the east. They are very boggy, and it required much work to cross them. Today, I encamped my company after having traveled six leagues, and as soon as they were encamped I sent the war chief of all the nations to see if they could discover a path or way for me to continue on my route. From this Valley of Santiago one can see the Sierra de las Grullas (Mountains of the Cranes) and hear the singing of the cranes.

(It would appear that Roque Madrid was responsible for the name "Sierra de Las Grullas". This name was used in 1779 by Juan Bautista de Anza (see chapter three.) and also appears on the Alexander de Humboldt map of 1804. Roque comments about hearing the singing of the Cranes. Although this is in the flyway used by the Sandhill and Whooping Cranes, they normally migrate North in March and South in October. A few cranes stay in the San Luis Valley all summer.)

The Big Bird or Crane petroglyph is located in the San Juan Mountains (Sierra de Las Grullas). The petroglyph is located in a rock shelter. The ceiling has been smoke blackened and the petroglyph was produced by scratching through the darkened surface.

August 8, 1705

On the eight of said month and year, the allies came and expressed greater objection to the penetration, but I paid no attention to them, having determined to carry it to its conclusion, and so I ordered that the horses be rounded up, and I went ahead, always traveling along the front of the Sierra de las Grullas (San Juan Mountains) through the middle of a forest so dense, with the trees so close together that the horses got stuck. They could go neither backward nor forward. So I ordered that campaign captain, Juan Roque Gutierrez take charge of extricating the horses, an order he carried out with some misgivings, dismounting in many places to assist his companions. Together they accomplished the task by dint of much work, falling and rolling. This being the reason that Alejo Gutierrez and Juan de Zamora broke their muskets and not that they had abused them. So I gave two pistols to each of them who had broken their weapons.

In this forest there are many creeks with different currents. I reached the summit of the very high peak of Las Grullas and I reached its river. (Roque Madrid's "Rio de Las Grullas" is probably the present-day Rio de los Pinos which crosses a little valley southwest of present-day Antonito, Colorado near Ortiz, Colorado. This is Juan Bautista de Anza's "Rio Conejos" and it was in this little valley that Anza met his Ute and Apache allies. See chapter three. Roque Madrid left the Old Spanish Trail here and proceeded west. He and Juan Bautista de Anza had traveled nearly the same route from the Rio de Los Nutrias (Tusas River) to the Rio de Los Pinos.) There I happened to roll down the mountain together with the horse I was riding. Only by a miracle from Our Lady of Conquest was I able to escape with my life.

This River of the Cranes flows from west to east, dividing two very high rocky cliffs. Its waters are cool and fresh with many trout. I crossed over to the other side to a ravine where it pleased God that the going should be somewhat better. Having already traveled more than six difficult mountain leagues, I came to a splendid beach at the banks of that rivers edge. There I camped with my company and then dispatched spies to reconnoiter to see whether they could see fires or other traces of the enemies. At the same time giving orders that no fires should be lighted, lest the enemies should see the smoke or the light from the fires at night. I placed the sentries and lookouts on the alert to which Captain Juan Roque Gutiérrez attended with all vigilance.

1744 Date is located about 1.52 miles west of the route which Juan Bautista de Anza was to travel in 1779. The trail divided and along the route where the date is located was a route used by the Ute's to travel from the San Luis Valley to the Pagosa Springs area. Was it French or Spanish?!

3

1779/JUAN BAUTISTA de ANZA

Don Juan Bautista de Anza, the second, was born in the town of (Cordéguachi) Fronteras, Sonora, Mexico, probably in the year of 1736. Records show that he was baptized by Padre Carlos de Roxas on July 7, 1736 at the small church in Cuquiarachi about eight miles west of Fronteras.[1] His education and early childhood before the age of sixteen is unknown. Whether he was educated by the Jesuits or a military school, two legends, it is certain that his godfather and first

The Church in Cuquiarichi, Sonora, Mexico.

cousin Pedro Felipe de Anza had a hand in his education. His handsome handwriting shows both a desire to learn and the dedication of caring teachers. Since Basque, which he learned as a first language, lacks a written component, young Anza was taught to read and write, as well as speak, Spanish.

Juan Bautista de Anza the first had come to North America in 1712 arriving in Culiacan, Sinaloa at the age of nineteen. He was born in Hernani, Guipuzcoa, Spain on June 29, 1693 to Antonio and Lucia Sasoeta Anza. Perhaps it was the lure of adventure which brought him to New Spain since Hernani was a crossroad of the traffic headed for the Indias. As was typical of many who traveled to New Spain on the North American Continent, he probably grew up hearing the stories of adventure told by travelers returning from far distant lands.

Anza senior soon became involved in mining as he was one of three Basques who owned mining properties at Aguaje in 1718. Of the ten stores in Aguaje, one belonged to Anza. His mining interests expanded to the newly discovered silver mines at Tetuachi, Sonora. His interests not only included mining and a store but soon included several ranches. Anza senior was appointed inspector of the mines in Sonora. He moved to the presidio of Janos where he was appointed second lieutenant. He and María Rosa Bezerra Nieto, the daughter of his comanding officer, were married in April 1722. In 1726 Anza senior was appointed commandante of the presidio of Fronteras located on a rocky promontory overlooking the valley of the Rio Fronteras. Fronteras was located far out onto the northern frontier with danger from many enemies on all sides. Anza soon gained the reputation as an Apache Indian fighter as his troops pursued the Apache who raided the settlement. It was on one of these punitive expeditions on May 9, 1740, that Anza senior's troops were ambushed by the Apache. As the fury of battle subsided the troops found their leader dead at the hands of the Apache. No longer able to occupy the commander's quarters at Fronteras, the young widow moved the family to Basochuca where they lived for several years. The Anza family then moved to the Divisadero Ranch on the Rio Santa Cruz in the San Luis Valley of the Pimería Alta where they made their permanent residence.

At the age of sixteen, in 1752, Juan Bautista de Anza the second was following family tradition when he volunteered for military service. His grandfather had served for thirty years on the Northern Frontier of New Spain. Anza's father served both as Captain at Fronteras and as temporary Governor of Sonora. Young Anza served as a cadete under his "cuñado" (Brother-in-law), Captain Gabriel de Vildósola, who was appointed captain of the Royal Presidio of Fronteras in 1754. By the year 1755 the young Anza had achieved the rank of lieutenant.

In 1758 Anza campaigned against the Apaches at the Gila River. In 1760, after the death of its first commander, Captain Anza became the Commander of the Presidio of Tubac. In 1766 he again campaigned against Apaches, and during 1768-1771 he played a brilliant part in Elizondo's conquest of Sonora. Anza was wounded twice in fighting the Seri Indians and twice in battles with the Apache Indians. This fighting with the Indians of Mexico and his victories gained him a reputation as one of the best Indian fighters on the frontier.

On June 1, 1761 Juan Bautista de Anza petitioned Bernardo de Urrea, the Governor of Sonora, for permission to marry Ana María Perez Serrano. The Governor granted permission and dispatched the marriage license from his residence in San Migual de Horcasitas on June 8th.

Juan Bautista de Anza and Ana María Perez Serrano were married in front of the main alter of "La Iglesia Nuestra Señora de la Asunción" in Arizpe, Sonora, Mexico on June 24, 1761. The ceremony was performed by Padre Carlos de Roxas who had also baptized the groom twenty-five years earlier. (It is ironic that Anza was to later be buried only a few feet from where he and María were married.)

On January 8, 1774 Anza set out at the head of thirty-four men to explore a route to San Francisco, California. In November of that year he was promoted to the rank of Lieutenant Colonel. On September 29, 1775 Anza led forth from Sonora an expedition of two hundred and forty people to establish San Francisco. He arrived on March 10, 1776, with three hundred people, a proud accomplishment. One woman had died along the way, but three babies were born on the trip. This journey was so difficult that it cost the lives of nearly a hundred head of livestock along the way. Anza's journey to and from California covered more than two thousand miles. To go to Mexico City to report his work to the Viceroy and return to his post involved a horseback trek of an additional three thousand miles for a total of five thousand miles on horseback in a little over two years.

On May 19, 1777 Anza was appointed the Governor and Military Commander of New Mexico, by King Charles III of Spain. Anza remained in Sonora for one year as Military Commandant where he took charge of fighting the Apache. On August 8, 1778 Anza was given the oath of office as Governor of New Mexico by Teodoro de Croix, Commandant General of the Provincias Internas. Anza didn't reach Santa Fé until late in 1778. He took census of the province and visited all of the pueblos. He then reorganized the settlers into towns or plazas (See the statment made by Pike in chapter four regarding these fortifications in 1807) containing at least twenty families. Each small plaza contained two bastions to give the guns better range. Taos was fortified with four bastions as were all of the larger plazas so that they could be more easily defended. He then ordered the Miera y Pacheco map prepared and made his plans to campaign against the Comanches who had been continually raiding the Spanish settlements.

Governor Anza traveled north through the San Luis Valley at night along the

West Fork of the North Branch of the Old Spanish Trail, which would indicate a well worn trail. He returned to Santa Fé along the East Fork of the North Branch after defeating the Jupe Comanche Chief Cuerno Verde near Rye, Colorado.

Anza's diary which he kept on the Comanche Campaign contains a great deal of information that is of importance to the study of what later became known as the Old Spanish Trail. His comment "three civilians who have explored it" on the 23rd of August tell us that his was not the first group to travel the area. Then again on the 27th of August the comment "it being very rarely crossed" indicates that the trail was one used by the Spanish frequently, though the route to the north through Poncha Pass was seldom used. This leads me to believe that the Spanish were familiar with the trail that had been used by the Indians for a very long time. The Utes and other Indians had traveled to the Spanish settlements first to trade with the Spanish, but also to raid the settlements to steal horses, one of the items most prized by the Indian.

The church of our lady of the Assumption Arizpe, Sonora, Mexico.

After successfully dealing with the Indian problems of New Mexico, Anza furnished labor and materials to establish a pueblo on the Arkansas River. The pueblo was built for the Jupe Comanches who had become friendly with the Spanish. Governor Anza left New Mexico in November and arrived in Sonora in the spring of 1788. There he became Provisional Commander of the armed forces of that province and captain of the Presidio of Tucson.

On December 19, 1788 Governor Anza died in Arispe, Sonora, and was buried in the church of Nuestra Señora de la Asunción. In 1963 the church needed a new floor. At that time, Anza's remains were dug up and reburied in a marble sarcophagus. A celebration was held in honor of Anza's many accomplishments and a plaque was placed upon his tomb for all who would visit to see. The church also received a tile floor instead of the oak floor originally planned.[2] Since this project was completed, the burial record for Juan Bautista de Anza has been found. It states that he was buried in the Chapel of Loreto, which is located off the west side of the main church floor. Unless Anza's body had been moved, the body found near the center of the main floor of the church is not that of Anza.

Sunday, August 15, 1779

At three o'clock in the afternoon the march was begun, route to the north on which six leagues were covered on the Camino Real. Halt was made to pass the night in the vicinity of the Pueblo of Pujuaque. (The Pueblo of Pojuaque today is spelled Pojoaque. It was abandoned from 1912 to 1932 because of disease epidemics. Today it has no clearly defined village center. The original name of Pojoaque Pueblo is Po suwae geh, which means "Water Drinking Place" in the Tewa language.)

Monday, August 16

At half-past six in the morning we continued our march on the road, route north, one-quarter to the northwest. On this six leagues were traveled, in the wood of San Juan de los Caballeros. (San Juan de los Caballeros was the location of the first capital of New Mexico. Juan de Oñate arrived at this Pueblo in July 1598.)[3] Camped.

This place I designated for the assembling of the combatants mentioned above. Accordingly, I reviewed all on the afternoon of this day. In this review I found the troops provided with three horses to each soldier with arms, munitions of war,

San Juan Pueblo is the location where Juan de Oñate arrived on July 11, 1598. Called Ohke by the Pueblo Indians, it was renamed San Juan de los Caballeros by Oñate. San Juan Pueblo c. 1881, Museum of New Mexico photograph #99997.

and food supplies more than enough for forty days. This was not the case with the settlers and Indians. Because of their well-known poverty and wretchedness, the best equipped presented themselves with two riding beasts, the most of them almost useless; their guns were the same, very few of them having three changes of powder; in everything else the proportion was similar. In view of this, I supplied the most needy, each with a good horse from the two hundred that I have extra in the herd at the presidio and all of them with firearms with ten ball cartridge belts.

I immediately provided for the best arrangement of the people making up the expedition, by forming the whole into three divisions, which can be of advantage to it in any event. I gave each one its respective commander whom I appointed. The divisions understood their position which I also indicated for any affray and for the entire march. The first was the vanguard under my command; the second, the rear guard under the first lieutenant; and the third, under command of the second lieutenant, the center between the two aforesaid and the reserve corps.

At the end of the afternoon I sent two scouts in advance to reconnoiter the point of entrance and departure of the enemy with orders that if they should find no indication or other development not to return until the 20th.

It will not be out of place to note here that I am directing the present expedition along a route and through regions different from those which have been followed previously. (Three other New Mexico Governors had tried to punish the Comanche. They had traveled east over the Sangre de Cristo Mountains either east of Taos or at Pecos.)[4] Thus I shall not suffer what has always happened so often, that is to be discovered long before reaching the country in which the enemy lives, as they inform me this is very common and is the reason for the failure of most of the campaigns, and so that I may be able to gain the border or boundary of the country indicated for the best success of the undertaking.

Tuesday, August 17

At a little after six we proceeded along the same road, the Rio del Norte crossed, route to the north-northwest. On this seven leagues were made as far as the deserted pueblo of Ojo Caliente, (Ojo Caliente, New Mexico was abandoned when Anza arrived in 1779, but Zebulon M. Pike found five-hundred people there in 1807.) where camp was pitched for the night, having reached the end of the Camino Real that we have been following.

The above mentioned pueblo is one of those abandoned on account of the hostilities of the enemy, as well as one proposed for the establishment of a presidio. For this reason I devoted myself today surveying it. I found it lacking all the conditions and advantages required for such an establishment. Those who have left it can only make this *(selection)* possible. Altogether they are twenty-five or thirty families scattered over more than four leagues, their houses unfortified. For this reason it is not strange that there were such attacks, as this disorder brought upon them the loss of their poor fields to which in substance the possessions of the inhabitants were reduced.

Wednesday, August 18

At seven o'clock we set out again on our way with the route to the north through terrain considerably broken. Through this eight leagues were made up to the Rio de las Nutrias (The name of the river has been changed from Rio de las Nutrias to Rio Tusas. It appears as Rio de los Nutrias on the Miera y Pacheco map of 1779 and the Alexander Humboldt map of 1804.) where the journey ended.

Thursday, August 19

A little before seven we pushed on toward the north. On this we traveled seven leagues through a country similar to that of the preceding day as far as the Rio de San Antonio (Rio San Antonio is a name which has been used for this river for a long time. See chapter one.) where we stopped to pass the night.

Friday, August 20

On this day frost and cold as though it were the months appropriate to this weather. At half-past six we resumed our march toward the north through broken terrain which lasted as far as the Rio de los Conejos. (Rio de los Conejos is the name which appears on the Miera y Pacheco map of 1779, but on modern day maps this river is called the Rio de los Pino.) To this seven leagues were made with which the day's journey ended.

Today the scouts mentioned on the 16th returned to me. They had found no other sign of the enemy than the trail in this very place of the last ones who encroached on our territory.

At the end of the afternoon two hundred men of the Ute and Apache nation also joined me with four of their principal captains. (The two-hundred Utes and Apaches joined Anza near the New Mexico/Colorado state lines of today.) Of the first were those who ever since my assumption of this government have asked me, and have reiterated incessantly with prayers that they be admitted into my company in confirmation of our friendship, provided I should go on a campaign against the Comanches. I agreed to grant this to them, as much to take advantage of this increase of people as to try in this way to civilize them so that they may at least be more useful to us against the enemy itself than they have been formerly.

With this intent I indicated that they must be at my orders as to what of spoils belonged to them in case of encounters and defeats of the enemy. This, with the exception of personal captures, they would have to agree to divide equally with all my men. To these proposals they consented, promising to observe them.

Saturday, August 21

At six we again returned to our route to the north-northeast through bad country with many ravines, among which after two leagues, the Rio del Pino (It would appear that the name Rio del Pino as it is listed in Anza's diary is today's Conejos River.) was crossed. To these three more leagues were added until Las Jaras (Las Jaras has been changed to La Jara.) was reached where the day's journey ended.

Sunday, August 22

It was necessary to make the next march at night so that the enemy might not descry the dust of our troops and horseherd from the sierra, not very distant, which we are keeping on our right. (The distance from the San Juan Mountains to the Sangre de Cristo Mountains is about fifty miles but the atmosphere is very clear and you would have been able to see the dust from even a small herd of horses.) For that reason the march of this day was reserved for the night.

At sunset the journey was taken up with route to the north and after a league was made in that direction, the Rio de las Timbres (The name Rio de las Timbres has changed to the Alamosa River.) was crossed; beyond that another six leagues were made in the same direction, upon which the Rio de San Lorenzo (Rio de San Lorenzo and Piedra Creek were early day names used for present-day Rock Creek.) was reached at two in the morning.

Monday, August 23

At nightfall we again held our course towards the north in which direction we traveled four leagues through fairly good country. At the end of this march we inclined toward the north-northwest for two more leagues upon which the march ended at the Rio del Norte where the ford was named El Paso de San Bartolomé. (El Paso de San Bartolome as it was called by the Spanish has been a fording place on the Rio Grande del Norte for many hundreds of years. In 1861 it became the location of La Loma del Norte or east Del Norte.)

This river, as it is known, empties into the Mar del Norte and the Bay of Espíritu Santo. (Bay of Espritu Santo is the Gulf of Mexico.) It has its own source fifteen leagues more or less from this place in the Sierra de la Grulla, (Sierra de la Grulla, which means Mountains of the Cranes, is the early day Spanish name used for what today we call the San Juan Mountains.) which is that on the skirts of which we have traveled since the 17th, it being the one to the west and closest on this route to the principal Villa of this government under my charge.

The Ute nation which is accompanying me, who reside at the said source, and three civilians who have explored it, tell me that the river above proceeds from a great swamp, this having been formed, in addition to its springs, by the continuous melting of snow from some volcanos which are very close.

The same persons also assure me that after fifteen leagues on the breadth of the sierra, one sees seven rivers in a very short distance. These united form in the same way one of considerable size which flows to the west. For this reason and others which I omit, I judge this river to be that which they call the Rio Colorado, which merging with the Gila empties into the Gulf of California. There from the nations who lived on it and whom I have communicated in my travels along it I have quite detailed information of the Ute nation. From this I infer that the two are not far distant from each other.

The same settlers mentioned, who explored the seven rivers refered to, by order of Governor Don Tomás Velez, affirm that on all of them, which are very fertile, they observed that in ancient times they were well populated with Indians, this being demonstrated by the large size of the formal pueblos of three stories and other remains. Among these was (evidence) that the settlers themselves had practiced the art of taking out silver, as their ore dumps and other remains of their use were found.

They assured me, moreover, they delivered these fragments to the aforesaid governor, who, according to other reports, sent them to the city of Mexico.

Tuesday, August 24

As soon as it was night we picked up our route in the same northern direction, by which, and through good land, eight leagues were made. After this we descended four to the north-northwest (northeast), upon which we arrived at the break of day following at a pleasant pond named San Luis. (From the area of present-day Saguache, Colorado to that of the confluence of the Rio de La Culebra and the Rio Grande is very marshy and on some maps is recorded as being a lake.)

From the beginning of the march we suffered from bitter cold. When as we ended the journey we promised ourselves relief with fires which we were about to kindle, we discovered many fires to the east of us, and believing them of the enemy, we gave up what we had intended. Later these fires were found to be from a camp of long standing, (The distance from the area where Anza and his men crossed Saguache Creek to Rattlesnake Hill is about one hour's travel by horseback. Just to the east side of this hill is a dry spring called Hunt Spring. This has been the location of many camps throughout history. It was used by Gunnison in 1853 and in

Hunt Spring is dry now but it was "an Indian camp of long standing" per Governor Juan Bautista de Anza in 1779. The spring is located at the lower right of Ratttlesnake Hill which is in the foreground.

1939 it became the home of the CCC camp. Artifacts have been picked up at this location for many years.) but the mistake was not learned until eight o'clock in the morning.

At this place on the 18th of July of the present year, a large number of Comanches attacked a greater force of Utes who were camped there with their families. Although the former succeeded in the darkness of the night in capturing all the Ute horses, the latter recovered them, with the added advantage of killing twelve of the robbers, among them a captain. Their bodies with other evidence proved the fact; besides the very victors themselves pointed it out to us.

Wednesday, August 25

At nightfall we began our march, route to the north for one league, at the end of which we inclined for another two the north. After three more were made to the northwest, we reached an arroyo which was named Santa Xines. (Santa Xines is near the present-day town of Villa Grove.)

Thursday, August 26

At four o'clock in the afternoon we continued our route to the northeast. Along its four leagues were marched at the end of which we halted to pass the night

El Aguage de los Yutas or Ute Spring can be seen just north of the top of Poncha Pass and to the south side of Highway 285.

and wait the following day in order to cross the bad land which follows. This place was named El Aguage de los Yutas.

Since the swamp of the San Luis was left, up to the above-named water-hole, the sierras that we have had to the right and left of us (between which runs the Rio del Norte) have drawn much closer together. Those there conjoined run thus to the northwest, their end being unknown.

Anza's return trip on the East Fork of the North Branch of the Old Spanish Trail followed his successful campaign against the Jupe Comanche chief, Cuerno Verde and his people. Not one of Anza's men perished.

Saturday, September 4

A little before seven we continued our route along the same direction, and from the first we began to recross the sierra that we had on our right in going. It was extremely fatiguing from its constant alterations of ascents and descents and to this was added a violent wind and fog. At five in the afternoon we came down to its foot, after eight leagues of travel to the place of the Ciénega. (This ciénega or march is located east of Mountain Home Reservoir on Trinchera Creek. This camp site was used by many people throughout history, including George Frederick Ruxton in 1847.)

Sangre de Cristo Pass is the low saddle in the center of this ridge of mountains.

Sunday, September 5

At half-past seven we again set out on our march on the said route through good country, during which we progressed ten leagues in the whole day. At the end of this, we arrived at the Rio de la Culebra (The camp on the Rio Culebra was another used by many people including Fowler, Ruxton, and Richerdson. In 1851 the town of San Luis, Colorado was built near here.) and the day's journey was ended.

Because on reaching this place we found seven horses killed by the enemies whom we had met on the third, and other signs of treatment of wounds, I had it examined with great care. This resulted in the discovery of a grave in which were the same number of bodies which proved to us that they perished in the attack which we suppose they made on the pueblo of Taos, whence it appears the trail comes.

On this same day, before twelve o'clock, that part of the Ute nation which had remained, left for their country enriched and satisfied, and without farewells, for their barbarity and desire again to see their country did not admit this civility. (The remainder of the Utes left the expedition. They were in their home country.)

Monday, September 6

At seven o'clock we continued our route with destination for the pueblo of Taos to obtain information of what had happened there. We traveled to the south and after making ten leagues during the entire day, the journey came to an end at the Rio del Datil. (The Rio Datil name appears on the Alexander Humboldt map of 1804.)

Tuesday, September 7

A little before seven we proceeded and after concluding three leagues, forded the Rio Colorado. Up to this we had had good country. From here we began to skirt the sierra which we had on our left. Along this route and with its many difficulties another five leagues were marched until we arrived at four o'clock in the afternoon at the pueblo of Taos, which is the most northern one of all those of this kingdom.

Before reaching the pueblo, its alcalde, with whom I had communicated in advance my coming in order not to cause him surprise, came out to meet me. He informed me that having been notified by our Apache friends six days before they attacked the pueblo under his command, which occurred on the 31st of the last month, that many enemies were coming, he prepared to receive them. He even advised the interior of the kingdom to do the same, in case the attack should turn in another direction. In consequence of this, he placed scouts on the usual roads of the barbarians. In this way it was possible on the night of the 30th for the scouts to signal him with fires that the enemy was marching on the pueblo which he then put under arms. They found it so on the day mentioned.

The first attack of the enemy, made at twilight, (The Jupe Comanche attacked Taos just after daylight on the same day that Anza's troops attacked the Comanche village near Fountain, Colorado at about noon.) he assured me was vigorous, but as soon as they recognized the new state of defense which the place has because it is one of those I had made into a square with triangular fortification on the corners, their surprise was so great that he was able to fire on them sallying forth from the wall, *(tactics)* which from *(within)* they could not attempt, nor attack the enemy. With this foray he succeeded in killing three, wounding many and frightening off all whom he judged to number two hundred and fifty. They then took the prudent part of retiring to much greater distance, to examine the town in this way. There they remained until nine in the morning when their retreat began, preceded by a great havoc which they wrought in the cornfields.

The only loss this pueblo sustained was that of a young man who, although he was inside at the time of the attack, went out unknown to the alcalde to see if he could save a horse which he saw in a cornfield, judging it to be his own. He found that it belonged to the enemy who killed him.

The enemy's loss, from what the alcalde states from what is related on the 6th, amounts to ten deaths in this attack alone, a disaster which in the many attacks that they have made has never been experienced. This is attributed to the fact that as all its inhabitants were not needed as before to defend the seven corners and as many other salient or exposed parts it had. They employed themselves in attacking the assailants, being able to sally out for the purpose for more than seventy varas from the new wall.

Wednesday, September 8

At half-past seven we continued our march along the Camino Real to Santa Fe, which in general runs toward the south. After ten leagues were made on it we arrived at the pueblo of Embudo.

Thursday, September 9

At half-past seven we again set out over the above mentioned route and direction. On this nine leagues were traveled. The march ended at the Pueblo of Pujuaque.

Friday, September 10, 1779

At seven o'clock we continued our way by the aforesaid direction and course, and then after six leagues arrived at the Villa of Santa Fe. There I received information communicated by the Ute nation from those who, as recorded, left us on the 2nd at the Rio de Napestle, that they had the good fortune to surprise seven

Comanches in their houses with their families, the latter being nine, women and children, who perished at their hands with the men, with the exception of one child who surrendered alive to them. At the same time they seized forty saddle horses the barbarians had, with the rest of the articles of their use and service.

With this loss, those which have been referred to, which the Comanches suffered on the 31st, 2nd, and 3rd, with that which is stated at the pueblo of Taos amount to fifty-eight men and sixty-three women and children, making a total of one hundred and thirty-one persons. With this information, and the statement that the sum of leagues amounted to two hundred and five covered on this expedition, ends the diary which it relates.

—*Juan Bautista de Anza*
September 10, 1779

4

1807/ZEBULON MONTGOMERY PIKE

Zebulon Montgomery Pike was the second son of Zebulon and Isabelle *Brown* Pike of Lamington, New Jersey. He was born January 5, 1779.[1] This was the same year that Juan Bautista de Anza punished the Jupe Comanche for raiding the Spanish settlements (chapter three) in northern New Mexico. This punitive action by the Spanish Governor was what made it possible for Pike to travel safely in New Spain.

Zebulon had two brothers, James Brown and George Washington, and one sister, Maria Herriot, who lived to maturity.[2]

Pike enlisted in the United States Army in 1794 at the age of fifteen. Zebulon Montgomery was first attached to his father's company. On March 3, 1799 Pike was given the rank of Second Lieutenant and in November of the same year was promoted to First Lieutenant.[3]

One of Lieutenant Pike's duties was to purchase supplies for the troops at the frontier forts. He made frequent trips up and down the Ohio River. A regular stop was at his Uncle Captain James Brown's plantation near Sugar Grove, Kentucky. This is where he became acquainted with cousin, Clarissa (Clara) Brown. When Captain Brown refused to grant permission for the two to get married, they eloped and were married in 1801 at Cincinnati. Zebulon Montgomery and Clara *Brown* Pike had five children of whom Clarissa, a daughter, was the only surviver.[4]

Lieutenant Pike was assigned to exploring the head waters of the Mississippi River. He arrived in Saint Louis with his family and about a dozen soldiers. Here he recruited additional solders from Fort Bellefontaine and purchased enough supplies for four months.

Pike and twenty soldiers sailed up the Mississippi River for the first few days with the aid of the large square sail of their keelboats. As the river became smaller they began using canoes and carrying them around water falls as they proceeded up river. Near present-day Little Falls, Minnesota, Pike built a stockade to house about half of his men through the winter. Here they also built canoes to continue up river. Pike and eleven men proceeded up river, led by a guide. After the river froze over,

Pike built sleds to transport his supplies. Pike and his party reached Lake Leech on February 1, 1806, thinking that this was the source of the Mississippi River. Thus, having completed his mission, Pike and his men traded and visited with the Indians before beginning their return journey on February 18, 1806. They were now equipped with snowshoes and dogsleds to transport their supplies.

By March 1, the expedition reached the Mississippi River and continued down river. Pike reached the stockade and found Seargent Kennerman had used up most of the supplies stored for the return trip and was both drinking and selling the supply of whiskey. After reducing Seargent Kennerman to the rank of Private, Pike continued down river, reaching Saint Louis on April 30, 1806 after nine months of exploring.[5]

Lieutenant Pike returned to Saint Louis certain that his achievements would earn him a promotion and much needed rest. General Wilkinson had other plans. Pike was now assigned to explore the head waters of the Arkansas and Red Rivers in the newly acquired Louisianna Purchase. The weeks following his return were busy ones as Pike organized his notes of the Mississippi Exploration and purchased supplies for the journey west. His promotion didn't come until August 12 after he and his men had departed for the west. Pike's expedition was made up of twenty-two men: Captain Zebulon M. Pike, leader and journalist; Lieutenant James B. Wilkinson; Sergeants: Joseph Ballenger and William E. Meek; Corporal Jeremiah R. Jackson; Privates: John Boley, Samuel Bradley, John Brown, Jacob Carter, Thomas Dougherty, William Gorden, Solomon Huddleston, Henry Kennerman, Hugh Menaugh, Theodore Miller, John Mountjoy, Alexander Roy, Patrick Smith, John Sparks, Freegift Stoute and John Wilson; civilians: (Dr. John Hamilton Robinson,) Surgeon and A.F. Baronet Vasquez, interpreter. Henry Kennerman deserted on July 19, 1806. Lieutenant James B. Wilkinson, Sergeant Joseph Ballenger and Privates: John Boley, Samuel Bradley, Solomon Huddleston and John Wilson accompanied Wilkinson to descend and explore the Arkansas River from near Great Bend, Kansas. This left Pike with sixteen men.[7]

The expedition started west from St Louis, Missouri on Tuesday, July 15, 1806. Pike followed the Arkansas River to the site of present-day Pueblo, Colorado, having entered the state on November 11. After exploring the upper Arkansas River and South Park, they entered the San Luis Valley on January 28, 1807. Pike's diary and maps are not detailed enough to determine whether he entered the San Luis Valley through Medano or Mosca Pass. The author hopes to present facts from other diaries that will lead us to believe that it was Mosca Pass through which Pike traveled.

After entering the San Luis Valley, Pike and a few of his men traveled down the Rio Grande to the Conejos River. Ascending the Conejos River a short distance,

Pike began to build a crude shelter and store a supply of meat.

Dr. Robinson left the party to find the Spanish Capitol of Santa Fe. After a few days travel Ute Indians found and escorted him to Santa Fe. On finding that Americans were in Spanish Territory, Governor Juaquin del Real Alencaster sent troops north along the West Fork of the North Branch of the Spanish Trail to locate these intruders and bring them to Santa Fe. Half of the Spanish Troops escorted Pike and part of his men to Santa Fe, while the rest remained to gather up the rest of Pikes destitute expedition.

Pike tried to maintain possession of his notes, maps, and journal, but after searching all of Pike's men, the Spanish confiscated all documents. These notes were later located by H. E. Bolton in the archives of Chihuahua, Mexico and were returned to the United States Government. The notes that made Pike famous were reconstructed by him from memory after returning to Washington. This was Pike's attempt to put his expedition in better stature after the much troubled expedition. His notes were edited by Elliott Coues and published in three volumes as *The Expeditions of Zebulon Montgomery Pike* in 1895 by Frances P. Harper.

Pike's statements are not fully credible. Anyone who has spent the winter in the San Luis Valley knows that one cannot construct a stockade, of the magnitude described later in his notes, in the frozen ground, particularly with no tools and with men who were suffering from frostbite. This is also attested to by the vain attempts of historians to locate the site, much less a structure.

The reference by Pike to Spanish roads indicates that the Spanish were traveling this area frequently. The Miera y Pacheco map used by Juan Bautista de Anza gives the names of all of the streams, mountains, and rivers. Most of the names still exist today. Anza's diary chapter three makes one aware that certain civilians were very familiar with the area in 1779, indicating that they had traveled it before.

Ignacio Sotelo traveled north out of Santa Fe, New Mexico through Espanola, Ojo Caliente and Tres Piedras to the San Luis Valley of Colorado on the West Fork of the North Branch of the Old Spanish Trail. He returned with Pike and his men by the same route. If Ignacio Sotelo had not rescued Pike and his men, they would have surely perished.

The route of travel into the San Luis Valley was well-known by the Spanish and frequently traveled. These facts will be shown by later chapter.

Captain Zebulon Montgomery Pike was first taken to Santa Fe, New Mexico and questioned by Governor Juaquin del Real Alencaster. Later he was transported south along the Camino Real by soldiers accompanying a caravan returning to Chihuahua, Mexico. After being detained for several months and questioned by the Viceroy in Mexico, Pike was returned through Texas and Louisianna to Natchitoches where he was met by his wife and daughter. After reaching Saint

Louis, Captain Pike took a couple of months rest and time to organize his maps and papers. Pike, his wife and daughter, boarded a sailing ship in New Orleans and set out on September 19, 1907 for New York. After enjoying a few weeks in New York the Pikes' continued to Washington by stage coach. While in Washington, Pike finished his final report of his explorations and obtained President Jefferson's blessing to have his journals published. The next two years were spent preparing his journals for publication.

On May 3, 1808 Pike was promoted to Major in the Sixth Infantry where he was in command of a small detachment at Fort Bellefontaine from late summer until December. Pike was then transferred to Fort McHenry, Baltimore, Maryland. In 1911, Pike's Journals were republished by a London Publisher and translated to French, German and Dutch. Not only was this a tribute to Pike's writing but it showed an interest in the southwestern United States. This interest still exists today.

At the outbreak of the War of 1812, General Pike was sent to Canada where his troops attacked present-day Toronto, Canada. They defeated troops under General R. H. Sheaffe. After the fighting was over, an enemy powder magazine exploded, scattering rocks and debris hundreds of yards. A piece of rock tore a large hole in General Pikes back, killing him on April 27, 1813 at the age of thirty-four.

Tuesday, January 27, 1807

We marched, determined to cross the mountains, (Pike had left the area of present-day Cañon City, Colorado and was traveling south through the Wet Mountain Valley. Upon reaching a point east of the Sangre de Cristo Mountains, Pike was determined to cross them to the west.) leaving Menaugh encamped with our deposit. After a bad day's march through snows, in some places three feet deep, we struck on a brook which led west. This I followed down, and shortly came to a small stream, running west, (The author believes that this evidence indicates that Pike crossed Mosca Pass. Therefore, the stream that he was descending was Mosca Creek.) which we hailed with fervency as the waters of Red River. Saw some sign of elk. Distance 14 miles.

Wednesday, January 28

Followed down the ravine and discovered after some time that there had been a road cut out; (His journal does not provide enough detailed evidence to indicate which pass he used. We must rely on facts in other documents in the hope of achieving any amount of certainty regarding which pass he used. See chapters three, eight & nine.) on many trees were various hieroglyphics painted. After marching some miles, we discovered through the lengthy vista, at a distance, another chain of mountains; (Across the San Luis Valley to the west, Pike could see the San Juan Mountains. They were known to the early day Spanish as the Sierra de las Grullas or the Mountains of the Cranes, see chapter two & three.) and nearer by, at the foot of the White mountains which we were then descending, sandy hills. (The sand hills that Pike found to the west of the Sangre de Cristo Mountains are the Great Sand Dunes.) We marched on the outlet of the mountains, left the sandy desert to our right, and kept down between it and the mountain. When we encamped, I ascended one of the largest hills of sand, and with my glass could discover a large river, (Rio Grande del Norte) flowing nearly N. by W. and S. by E., through the plain. (The plain referred to by Pike is the San Luis Valley which is about 100 miles long, north to south and about sixty-five miles wide at the widest point, east to west.) This river came out of the third chain of mountains, about N. 75° W.; the prairie between the two mountains bore nearly N. and S. I returned to camp with the news of my discovery. The sand-hills extended up and down the foot of the White mountains about 15 miles, and appeared to be about five miles in width. Their appearance was exactly that of the sea in a storm, except as to color, not the least sign of vegetation existing thereon. Distance 15 miles.

Thursday, January 29

Finding the distance too great to attempt crossing immediately to the river, in a direct line, we marched obliquely to a copse of woods, which made down a considerable distance from the mountains. Saw sign of horses. Distance 17 miles.

Friday, January 30

We marched hard, and arrived in the evening on the bank of the Rio del Norte, then supposed to be Red River. Distance 24 miles.

Saturday, January 31

As there was no timber here we determined on descending until we found timber, in order to make transports to descend the river with, (The Rio Grande del Norte is frozen over in the winter months. Therefore, Pike and his expedition could not have floated down it.) where we might establish a position that four or five might defend against the insolence, cupidity, and barbarity of the savages, while the others returned to assist the poor fellows who had been left behind at different points. We descended 18 miles, when we met a large west branch, (The largest stream entering the Rio Grande from the west is the Rio Conejos.) emptying into the main stream, about five miles up which branch we took our station. Killed one deer. Distance 18 miles.

Sunday, February 1
Laid out the place for our works, and went out hunting.

Monday, February 2
The doctor and myself went out to hunt, and with great difficulty, by night, at the distance of seven or eight miles from camp, killed one deer, which we carried in.

Tuesday, February 3
Spent in reading, etc.

Wednesday, February 4
Went out hunting, but could not kill anything.
One of my men killed a deer.

Thursday, February 5
The doctor and myself went out to hunt. After chasing some deer for several hours, without success, we ascended a high hill which lay south of our camp, whence we had a view of all the prairies and rivers to the north of us. It was at the same time one of the most sublime and beautiful inland prospects ever presented to the eyes of man. The prairie, lying nearly north and south, was probably 60 miles by 45. The main river, bursting out of the western mountains, meeting from the northeast a large branch (The stream which follows along the west side of the Sangre de Cristo Mountains is San Luis Creek.) which divides the chain of mountain, proceeds down the prairie, making many large and beautiful islands, one of which I judge contains 100,000 acres of land, all meadow ground, covered with innumerable herds of deer. About six miles from the mountains which cross the prairie at the south end, (The hills which cross the south end of the San Luis Valley are called the San Luis Hills.) a branch of 12 steps wide pays its tribute to the main stream from the west course. (The next stream north of the Rio Conejos is the combined water of Alamosa and La Jara Creeks.) Due W. 120. N. 75°. W. 6°. Four miles below is a stream (Trinchera Creek) of the same size, which enters on the east and up which was a large road; its

View of Mount Blanca from the top of Sierro Del Ojito.

View from the top of Sierro Del Ojito looking toward Greenie Mountain. Zebulon Pike and Dr. Robinson climbed this hill.

general course is N. 65° E. From the entrance of this was about three miles, down to the junction of the west fork, (Rio Conejos) which waters the foot of the hill on the north, while the main river wound along its meanders on the east. In short, this view combined the sublime and the beautiful. The great and lofty mountains, covered with eternal snows, seemed to surround the luxuriant vale, crowned with perennial flowers, like a terrestrial paradise shut out from the view of man.

Friday, February 6

The doctor, having some pecuniary demands in the province of New Mexico, conceived this to be the most eligible point for him to go in, and return previous to all my party having joined me from the Arkansaw, and that I was prepared to descend to Nachitoches. He therefore this day made his preparations for marching to-morrow. I went out hunting, and killed at three miles' distance a deer which, with great difficulty, I brought in whole. We continued to go on with the works of our stockade or breast-work, which was situated on the north bank of the west branch, about five miles from its junction with the main river, and was on a strong plan.

The stockade was situated in a small prairie on the west fork (Conejos River) of the Rio (Rio Grande del Norte) del Norte. The south flank joined the edge of the river, which at that place was not fordable; the east and west curtains were flanked by bastions in the northeast and northwest angles, which likewise flanked the curtain of the north side of the work. The stockade from the center of the angle of the bastions was 36 feet square. Heavy cottonwood logs, about two feet in diameter, were laid up all round about six feet, after which lighter ones, until we made it 12 feet in height; there logs were joined together by a lap of about two feet at each end. We then dug a small ditch on the inside all round, making it perpendicular on the internal side and sloping next the work. In this ditch we planted small stakes, about six inches in diameter, sharpened at the upper end to a nice point, and slanted them over the top of the work, giving them about 2 1/2 feet projection. We then secured them above and below in that position, which formed a small pointed frise, which must have been removed before the works could have been scaled. Lastly, we had dug a ditch round the whole, four feet wide, and let the water in all round. (The description given here fits a stockade which Pike and twenty able-bodied, well equipped men had taken two weeks to complete on the Mississippi. Also, what purpose would his trench serve around the stockade? When, if it filled with water, it would have frozen the first night!) The earth taken out, being thrown against the work, formed an excellent rampart against small-arms, three or four feet high.

Our mode of getting in was to crawl over the ditch on a plank, and into a small hole sunk below the level of the work near the river for that purpose. Our port-holes were pierced about eight feet from the ground, and a platform was

This is a recreation of the structure which Pike claimed to have built at this site on the Conejos River.

This photo of a shelter similar to that Pike built on the Arkansas River and is probably similar to what was actually built on the Conejos River.

prepared to shoot from. Thus fortified, I should not have had the least hesitation of putting the 100 Spanish horse at defiance until the first or second night, and then to have made our escape under cover of the darkness; or made a sally and dispersed them, when resting under a full confidence of our being panic-struck by their numbers and force.

Saturday, February 7

The doctor marched alone for Santa Fe; and as it was uncertain whether this gentleman would ever join me again, I at that time committed to paper the following testimonial of respect for his good qualities, which I do not, at this time, feel any disposition to efface. He has had the benefit of a liberal education, without having spent his time, as too many of our gentlemen do in colleges, in skimming on the surfaces of sciences, without ever endeavoring to make themselves masters of the solid foundations. Robinson studied and reasoned; with these qualifications he possessed a liberality of mind too great ever to reject an hypothesis because it was not agreeable to the dogmas of the schools; or adopt it because it had all the eclat of novelty. His soul could conceive great actions, and his hand was ready to achieve them; in short, it may truly be said that nothing was above his genius, nor anything so minute that he conceived it entirely unworthy of consideration. As a gentleman and companion in dangers, difficulties, and hardships, I in particular, and the expedition generally, owe much to his exertions.

The demands which Dr. Robinson had on persons in New Mexico, although legitimate, were in some degree spurious *in his hands*. The circumstances were as follows: In the year 1804, William Morrison, Esq., an enterprising merchant of Kaskaskias, sent a man by the name of Babtiste La Lande, a Creole of the country, up the Missouri and La Platte, directing him if possible to push into Santa Fe. He sent in Indians, and the Spaniards came out with horses and carried him and his goods into the province. Finding that he sold the goods high, had land offered him, and the women kind, he concluded to expatriate himself and convert the property of Morrison to his own benefit. When I was about to sail, Morrison, conceiving that it was possible that I might meet some Spanish factors on the Red River, intrusted me with the claim, in order, if they were acquainted with La Lande, I might negotiate the thing with some of them. When on the frontiers, the idea suggested itself to us of making this claim a pretext for Robinson to visit Santa Fe. We therefore gave it the proper appearance, and he marched for that place. (The author believes that Pike knew exactly where he was on the Rio Grande, not the Red River. It also seems that Dr. Robinson knew where to travel to find Santa Fe. He had only to follow the well-worn road that Pike described in his February 5th notes.) Our views were to gain a knowledge of the country, the prospect of trade, force, etc.; while, at the same time, our treaties with Spain guaranteed to him, as a citizen of the United States, the right of seeking the recovery of all just debts or demands before the legal and authorized tribunals of the country, as a franchised inhabitant of the same, as specified in the 22d article of said treaty.

In the evening I dispeched Corporal Jackson with four men, to recross the mountains, in order to bring in the baggage left with the frozen lads, and to see if they were yet able to come on. This detachment left me with four men only, two of whom had their feet frozen; they were employed in finishing the stockade, and myself to support them by the chase.

Sunday, February 8
Refreshing my memory as to the French grammar, and overseeing the works.

Monday, February 9 Hunting, etc.

Tuesday, February 10 Read and labored at our works.

Wednesday, February 11 Hunting. Killed three deer.

Thursday, February 12 Studying.

Friday, February 13 Hunting. Killed two deer.

Saturday, February 14
Crossed the river (Conejos) and examined the numerous springs which issued from the foot of the hill, (South of Pike's camp is Sierro Del Ojito and to the west of this hill are the springs that he went to investigate. These springs today are known as McIntire Springs. They were named after Colorado's former governor, Albert W. McIntire, who at one time made his home near the location.) opposite our camp. These were so strongly impregnated with mineral qualities, as not only to keep clear of ice previous to their joining the main branch, but to keep open the west fork until its junction with the main river and for a few miles afterward, while all the other branches in the neighborhood were bound in the adamantine chains of winter.

Sunday, February 15 Reading, etc. Works going on.

Monday, February 16
I took one man and went out hunting; about six miles from the post, shot and

wounded a deer.

Immediately afterward I discovered two horsemen rising the summit of a hill, about half a mile to our right. As my orders were to avoid giving alarm or offence to the Spanish government of New Mexico, I endeavored to avoid them at first; but when we attempted to retreat, they pursued us at full charge, flourishing their lances; and when we advanced, they would retire as fast as their horses could carry them. Seeing this, we got in a small ravine, in hopes to decoy them near enough to oblige them to come to a parley; which happened agreeably to our desires, as they came on, hunting us with great caution. We suffered them to get within 40 yards—where we had allured them; but they were about running off again, when I ordered the soldier to lay down his arms and walk toward them, at the same time standing ready with my rifle to kill either who should lift an arm in an hostile manner. I then hollowed to them that we were "Americans," *(Americanos)* and "friends," *(Amigos)* which were almost the only two words I knew in the Spanish language; when, with great signs of fear, they came up, and proved to be a Spanish dragoon and a civilized Indian, armed after their manner, of which we see a description in the Essai Militaire. We were jealous of our arms on both sides, and acted with great precaution.

They informed me that this was the fourth day since they had left Santa Fe; that Robinson had arrived there, and been recieved with great kindness by the governor. As I knew them to be spies, I thought proper to inform them merely that I was about to descend the river to Nachitoches. We sat on the ground a long time, till, finding they were determined not to leave us, we rose and bade them adieu. But they demanded where our camp was; and, finding they were not about to leave us, I thought it most proper to take them with me, thinking we were on Red River, and of course in the territory claimed by the United States.

We took the road to my fort, and as they were on horseback, they traveled rather faster than myself; they were halted by the sentinel, and immediately retreated much surprised. When I came up, I took them in, and then explained to them, as well as possible, my intention of descending the river to Nachitoches; but at the same time told them that if Governor Allencaster would send out an officer with an interpreter who spoke French or English, I would do myself the pleasure to give his Excellency every reasonable satisfaction as to my intentions in coming on his frontiers. They informed me that on the second day they would be in Santa Fe, but were careful never to suggest an idea of my being on the Rio (Grande) del Norte. As they concluded, I did not think as I spoke. They were very anxious to ascertain our numbers, etc.; seeing only five men here, they could not believe we came without horses. To this I did not think proper to give them any satisfaction, giving them to understand we were in many parties, etc.

Tuesday, February 17

In the morning, our two Spanish visitors departed, after I had made them some trifling presents, with which they seemed highly delighted. After their departure, we commenced working at our little stockade, as I thought it probable the governor might dispute my right to descend the Red River, and send out Indians, or some light party, to attack us; I therefore determined to be as much prepared to receive them as possible.

This evening the corporal and three of the men arrived, who had been sent back to the camp of the frozen lads. They informed me that two men would arrive the next day, one of whom was Menaugh, who had been left alone on the 27th of January; but that the other two, Dougherty and Sparks, were unable to come in. They said that they had hailed them with tears of joy, and were in despair when they again left them, with the chance of never seeing them more. They sent on to me some of the bones taken out of their feet, and conjured me, by all that was sacred, not to leave them to perish far from the civilized world. Ah! little did they know my heart, if they could suspect me of conduct so ungenerous. No! before they should be left, I would for months have carried the end of a litter, in order to secure them the happiness of once more seeing their native homes, and being received in the bosom of a grateful country. Thus those poor lads are to be invalids for life, made infirm at the commencement of manhood and in the prime of their course, doomed to pass the remainder of their days in misery and want. For what is the pension? Not sufficient to buy a man his victuals. What man would even lose the smallest of his joints for such a trifling pittance?

Wednesday, February 18

The other two boys arrived. In the evening I ordered the sergeant and one man to prepare to march to-morrow for the Arkansaw, where we had left our interpreter, horses, etc., to conduct them on, and on his return to bring the two lads who were still in the mountains.

Thursday, February 19

Sergeant William E. Meek marched with one man, whose name was Theodore Miller, and I took three other men to accompany him some distance, in order to point out to him a pass in the mountain which I conceived more eligible for horses than the one by which we came. I must here remark the effect of habit, discipline, and example, in two soldiers soliciting a command of more than 180 miles, over two great ridges of mountains covered with snow, inhabited by bands of unknown savages, in the interest of a nation with which we were not on the best understanding. To perform this journey, each had about ten pounds of venison. Only let me ask, what would our soldiers generally think, on being ordered on such a tour, thus equipped? Yet those men volunteered it with others, and were chosen; for which they thought themselves highly honored. We accompanied them about six miles, and pointed out the pass alluded to, in a particular manner. But the corporal afterward reported that the new one which I obliged him to take was impassable, he having been three days in snows nearly middle deep.

We then separated and, having killed a deer, sent one of the men back to the fort with it. With the other two, I kept on my exploring trip down the river on the east side, at some leagues from its banks, intending to return up it. At nine o'clock at night we encamped on a small creek which emptied into the river from a nearly due east course.

Friday, February 20

We marched down the river for a few hours; but, seeing no fresh sign of persons, or any other object to attract our attention, took up our route for the fort. Discovered the sign of horses and men on the shore. We arrived after night and found all well.

Saturday, February 21

As I was suspicious that possibly some party of Indians might be harboring round, I gave particular orders to my men, if they discovered any people, to endeaver to retreat undiscovered; but if not, never to run, and not to suffer themselves to be disarmed or taken prisoners, but conduct whatever party discovered them, if they could not escape, to the fort.

Sunday, February 22

As I began to think it was time we received a visit from the Spaniards or their emissaries, I established a lookout guard on the top of a hill all day, and at night a sentinel in a bastion on the land side. Studying, reading, and working at our ditch to bring the river round the works.

Monday, February 23

Reading, writing, etc.; the men at their usual work.

Tuesday, February 24

Took one man with me and went out on the Spanish road hunting; killed one deer and wounded several others. As we were a great distance from the fort, we encamped near the road all night. Saw several signs of horses.

Wednesday, February 25

Killed two more deer, when we marched for our post. Took all three of the deer with us, and arrived about nine o'clock at night, as much fatigued as ever I was in my life. Our arrival dissipated the anxiety of the men, who began to be apprehensive we were taken or killed by some of the savages.

Thursday, February 26

In the morning was apprized of the approach of strangers by the report of a gun from my lookout guard. Immediately afterward two Frenchmen arrived. My sentinel halted them, and ordered them to be admitted, after some questions. They informed me that his Excellency, Governor Allencaster, had heard it was the intention of the Utah Indians to attack me; had detached an officer with 50 dragoons to come out and protect me; and that they would be here in two days. To this I made no reply: but shortly after the party came in sight, to the number, as I afterward learned, of 50 dragoons and 50 mounted militia of the province, armed in the same manner with lances, escopates, and pistols. My sentinel halted them at the distance of about 50 yards. I had the works manned. I thought it most proper to send out the two Frenchmen to inform the commanding officer that it was my request he should leave his party in the small copse of woods where he was halted, and that I would meet him myself in the prairie in which our work was situated. This I did, with my sword on me only. I was then introduced to Don Ignatio Saltelo and Don Bartholemew Fernandez, two lieutenants, the former the commandant of the party. I gave them an invitation to enter the works, but requested the troops might remain where they were. This was complied with. When they came round and discovered that to enter they were obligated to crawl on their bellies over a small draw-bridge, they appeared astonished, but entered without further hesitation.

We first breakfasted on deer, meal, goose, and some biscuit which the civilized Indians who came out as a spy had brought me. After breakfast the commanding officer addressed me as follows:

"Sir, the governor of New Mexico, being informed you had missed your route, ordered me to offer you, in his name, mules, horses, money, or whatever you might stand in need of to conduct you to the head of the Red River; as from Santa Fe to where it is sometimes navigable is eight days' journey, and we have guides and the routes of the traders to conduct us."

"What" said I, interrupting him, "is not this the Red River?"

"No, Sir! The Rio del Norte."

I immediatly ordered my flag to be taken down and rolled up, feeling how sensibly I had commited myself in entering their territory, and conscious that they must have positive orders to take me in.

He now added that he "had provided 100 mules and horses to take in my party and baggage, and how anxious his Excellency was to see me at Santa Fe." I stated to him the absence of my sergeant, the situation of the balance of the party, and that my orders would not justify my entering into the Spanish territory. He urged still further, until I began to feel myself a little heated in the argument; and told him, in a peremptory style, that I would not go until the arrival of my sergeant with the balance of the party. He replied, "that there was not the least restraint to be used; that it was only necessary his Excellency should receive an explanation of my business on his frontier; that I could go now, or on the arrival of my party; that, if none went in at present, he should be obliged to send in for provisions; but that, if I would now march, he would leave an Indian interpreter and an escort of dragoons to conduct the sergeant into Santa Fe." His mildness induced me to tell him that I would march, but must leave two men to meet the sergeant and party, to instruct him as to coming in, as he never would come without a fight, if not ordered.

I was induced to consent to this measure by the conviction that the officer had positive orders to bring me in; and as I had no orders to commit hostilities, and indeed had committed myself, although innocently, by violating their territory, I conceived it would appear better to show a will to come to an explanation than to be in any way constrained; yet my situation was so eligible, and I could so easily have put them at defiance, that it was with great reluctance I suffered all our labor to be lost without once trying the efficacy of it. My compliance seemed to spread general joy through their party, as soon as it was communicated; but it appeared to be different with my men, who wished to have "a little dust," as they expressed themselves, and were likewise fearful of treachery.

My determination being once taken, I gave permission for the Spanish lieutenant's men to come to the outside of the works, and some of mine to go out and see them. The hospitality and goodness of the Creoles and Metifs began to manifest itself by their producing their provision and giving it to my men, covering them with their blankets, etc. After writing orders to my sergeant, and leaving them with my corporal and one private, who were to remain, we sallied forth, mounted our horses, and went up the river about 12 miles, to a place where the Spanish officers had made a camp deposit, whence we sent down mules for our baggage, etc.

Friday, Feburary 27

In the morning I discovered that the Spanish lieutenant (don Ignatio Sotelo) was writing letters addressed to the governor and others; on which I demanded if he was not going on with me to Santa Fe. He appeared confused and said, No; that his orders were so positive as to the safe conduct and protection of my men, that he dare not go and leave any behind; that his companion (don Bartolomé Fernandez) would accompany me to Santa Fe with 50 men, while he with the others would wait for the sergeant (Meek) and his party. I replied that he had deceived me, and had not acted with candor; but that it was now too late for me to remedy the evil.

We marched about eleven o'clock, ascending the Rio del Norte (Pike is mistaken here. They ascended the Rio Conejos, not the Rio del Norte.) five miles more, S 60° W., when we went round through a chain of hills and bore off to the south. We proceeded nine miles further, when we crossed the main branch of that stream, which was now bearing nearly west toward main chain of the third chain of mountains. We encamped on the opposite side. Intensely cold; obliged to stop frequently and make fires. Snow deep. Distance 15 miles.

Saturday, February 28

We marched late. One of the Frenchmen informed me that the expedition which had been at the Pawnees had descended the Red river 233 leagues, and from thence crossed to the Pawnees expressly in search of my party. This was afterward confirmed by the gentleman who commanded the troops. He then expressed great regret at my misfortunes, as he termed them, in being taken, and offered his services in secreting papers, etc. I took him at his word, and for my amusement thought I would try him; so I gave him a leaf or two of my journal, copied, which mentioned the time of my sailing from Belle Fontaine, and our force. This I charged him to guard very carefully and give to me after the investigation of my papers at Santa Fe. This day we saw a herd of wild horses. The Spaniards pursued them and caught two colts, one of which the Indians killed and ate; the other was let go. We pursued our journey over some hills, where the snow was very deep, and encamped at last on the top of a pretty high hill, among some pines. We left the river, which in general ran about six, eight, and 10 miles to the left or east of us. Saw great sign of elk. Distance 36 miles.

Sunday, March 1

We marched early. Although we rode very hard we only got to the village of L'eau Chaud, or Warm Spring, (The village of L'eau Chaud or Warm Spring is the present-day Ojo Caliente.) some time in the afternoon. The distance was about 45 miles. The difference of climate was astonishing; after we left the hills and deep snows, we found ourselves on plains where there was no snow, and where vegetation was sprouting.

The village of Warm Springs, or Aqua Caliente in their language, is situated on the eastern branch of a creek of that name, and at a distance presents to the eye a square inclosure of mud walls, the houses forming the walls. They are flat on top, or with extremely little ascent on one side, where there are spouts to carry off the water of the melting snow and rain when it falls; which, we were informed, had been but once in two years previous to our entering the country. Inside of the inclosure were the different streets of houses of the same fashion, all of one story; the doors were narrow, the windows small, and in one or two houses there were talc lights. This village had a mill near it, situated on the little creek, which made very good flour. The population consisted of civilized Indians, but much mixed blood.

Here we had a dance which is called the fandango; but there was one which was copied from the Mexicans, is now danced in the first societies of New Spain, and has even been introduced at the court of Madrid.

This village may contain 500 souls. The greatest natural curiosity is the warm springs, which are two in number, about 10 yards apart, each affording sufficient water for a mill-seat. They appeared to be impregnated with copper, and were more than 33° above blood heat. From this village the Tetaus (Comanche) drove off 2,000 horses at one time, when at war with the Spaniards.

Monday, March 2

We marched late, and passed several little mud-walled villages and settlements, all of which had round mud towers of the ancient shape and construction, to defend the inhabitants from the intrusions of the savages. I was this day shown the ruins of several old villages which had been taken and destroyed by the Tetaus (Comanche). We were frequently stopped by the women, who invited us into their houses to eat; and in every place where we halted a moment there was a contest who should be our hosts. My poor lads who had been frozen were conducted home by old men, who would cause their daughters to dress their feet, provide their victuals and drink, and at night give them the best bed in the house. In short, all their conduct brought to my recollection the hospitality of the ancient patriarchs, and caused me to sigh with regret at the corruption of that noble principle by the polish of modern ages.

We descended the creek of Agua Caliente about 12 miles, where it joined the river of Conejos (This was not the Conejos but the Rio Chama.) from the west. This river was about 30 yards wide, and was settled for 12 miles above its junction with the Agua Caliente, as the latter was in its whole course from the village of that name. From where they form a junction it was about 15 miles to the Rio del Norte, on the eastern branch of which was situated the village of St. John's, (This was San Juan Pueblo, the first capital of New Mexico, where Juan de Oñate arrived in July 1598.)[8] which was the residence of the president priest of the province, who had resided in it 40 years.

The house-tops of the village of St. John's were crowded, as well as the streets, when we entered, and at the door of the public quarters we were met by the president priest. When my companion, who commanded the escort, received him in a street and embraced him, all the poor creatures who stood round strove to kiss the ring or hand of the holy father; for myself, I saluted him in the usual style. My men were conducted into the quarters, and I went to the house of the priest, where we were treated with politeness. He offered us coffee, chocolate, or whatever we thought proper, and desired me to consider myself at home in his house.

As I was going, some time after, to the quarters of my men, I was addressed at the door by a man in broken English: "My friend, I am very sorry to see you here; we are all prisoners in this country and can never return; I have been a prisoner for nearly three years, and cannot get out." I replied: "that as for his being a prisoner, it must be for some crime; that with respect to myself I felt no apprehension; and requested him to speak French, as I could hardly understand his English." He began to demand of me so many different questions on the mode of my getting into the country, my intention, etc., that by the time I arrived in the room of my men, I was perfectly satisfied of his having been ordered by some person to endeavor to obtain some confession or acknowledgment of sinister design in my having appeared on the frontiers, and some confidential communications which might implicate me. As he had been rather insolent in his inquiries, I ordered my men to shut and fasten the door. I then told him that I believed him to be an emissary sent on purpose by the governor, or some person, to endeavor to betray me; that all men of that description were scoundrels, and never should escape punishment, whilst I possessed the power to chastise them—immediately ordering my men to seize him, and cautioning him, at the same time, that, if he cried out, or made the least resistance, I would be obliged to make use of the saber which I had in my hand. On this he was so much alarmed, that he begged me for God's sake not to injure him; he also said that he had been ordered by the government to meet me, and endeavor to trace out what and who I was, and what were my designs, by endeavoring to produce a confidence in him, by his exclaiming against the Spaniards and complaining of the tyranny which they had exercised toward him. After this confession, I ordered my men to release him, and told him that I looked upon him as too contemptible for further notice; but that he might tell the governor, the next time he employed emissaries, to choose those of more abilities and sense; and that I questioned if his Excellency would find the sifting of us an easy task.

This man's name was Baptiste Lalande; he had come from the Illinois to the Pawnees, to trade with goods furnished him by William Morrison, a gentleman of the Illinois, and thence to New Mexico with the goods which he had procured, and established himself; he was the same man on whom Robinson had a claim. He returned into the priest's house with me, and, instead of making any complaint, he in reply to their inquiries of who I was, etc., informed them that when he left Louisiana I was governor of the Illinois. This I presume he took for granted from my having commanded for some time the post of Kaskaskias, the first military post the United States had established in that country since the peace; however, the report served to add to the respect with which my companion and host treated me.

I had at this place the first good meal, wine, etc., which with the heat of the house, and perhaps rather an immoderate use of the refreshments allowed me, produced an attack of something like cholera morbus, which alarmed me considerably, and made me determine to be more abstemious in future.

This father was a great naturalist, or rather florist; he had large collections of flowers, plants, etc., and several works on his favorite studies, the margins and bottoms of which were filled with his notes in the Castilian language. As I neither had a natural turn for botany sufficient to induce me to puzzle my head much with the Latin, nor understood Castilian, I enjoyed but little of the lectures which he continued to give me for nearly two hours on those subjects; but, by the exercise of a small degree of patience, I entirely acquired the esteem of this worthy father, he calling me his son, and lamenting extremely that my faith had not made me one of the holy Catholic church.

The father, being informed that I had some astronomical instruments with me, expressed a desire to see them. All that I had here was my sextant and a large glass which magnified considerably, calculated for the day or night; the remainder of my instruments being with my sergeant and party. On his examining the sextant, and my showing him the effect of it in the reflection of the sun, he, as well as hundreds who surrounded us, appeared more surprised at the effect of the instrument than any nation of savages I was ever among. Here an idea struck me as extraordinary—how a man who appeared to be a perfect master of the ancient languages, a botanist, mineralogist, and chemist, should be so ignorant of the powers of reflection and the first principles of mathematics. But my friend explained that enigma, by informing me of the care the Spanish government took to prevent any branch of science from being made a pursuit, which would have a tendency to extend the view of the subjects of the provinces to the geography of their country, or any other subject which would bring to view a comparison of their local advantages and situations with other countries.

St. John's was inclosed with a mud wall, and probably contained 1,000 souls; its population consisted principally of civilized Indians, as indeed does that of all the villages of New Mexico, the whites not forming One-twentieth part of the inhabitants.

Tuesday, March 3

We marched after breakfast, B. Lalande accompaning us, and in about six miles came to a village, (Santa Cruz Pueblo) where I suppose there were more than 2,000 souls. Here we halted at the house of a priest, who, understanding that I would not kiss his hand, would not present it to me. The conduct and behavior of a young priest who came in was such as in our country would have been amply sufficient forever to have banished him from the clerical association—strutting about with a dirk in his boot, a cane in his hand, whispering to one girl, chucking another under the chin, going out with a third, etc.

From this village to another small village, (Pojoaque Pueblo) of 500 inhabitants, is seven miles. At each of those villages is a small stream, sufficient for the purpose of watering their fields. At the father's house we took coffee. From this village it was 17 miles to another, (Tesuque Pueblo) of 400 civilized Indians. Here we changed horses and prepared for entering the capital, (Santa Fé became the capital of New Mexico in 1608 and Governor Peralta took over as governor in 1610. See Rocky Mountain News Wednesday, June 29, 1994.) which we came in sight of in the evening. It is situated along the banks of a small creek, (Santa Fé Creek) which comes down from the mountains, and runs west to the Rio del Norte. The length of the capital on the creek may be estimated at one mile; it is but three streets in width.

Its appearance from a distance struck my mind with the same effect as a fleet of the flat-bottomed boats which are seen in the spring and fall seasons, descending the Ohio river. There are two churches, the magnificence of whose steeples form a striking contrast to the miserable appearance of the houses. On the north side of the town is the square of the soldiers' houses, equal to 120 or 140 on each flank. The public square is in the center of the town; on the north side of it is situated the palace, as they term it, or government house, with the quarters for guards, etc. The other side of the square is occupied by the clergy and public officers. In general the houses have a shed before the front, some of which have a flooring of brick; the consequence is that the streets are very narrow, say in general 25 feet. The supposed population is 4,500 souls. On our entering the town the crowd was great, and followed us to the government house. When we dismounted we were ushered in through various rooms, the floors of which were covered with skins of buffalo, bear, or some other animal.

—Z. M. Pike
Captain, 1st United States Battalion Infantry
Washington City
January, 1808

5

1822/JACOB FOWLER

Jacob Fowler was born in 1765 in New York and moved to the state of Kentucky at an early age. He married Ester Sanders, a widow from Newport, Kentucky who was of French descent. Jacob and Ester Fowler had three children: two sons, Edward and Benjamin, and one daughter Abigail. Jacob Fowler became a surveyor. He was accompanied by his wife on a number of his surveying expeditions, but not the one to Colorado.

The Fowlers lived in a large double brick house in the midst of trees, shrubbery, flowers and bluegrass on a two-thousand-acre estate. It is the site of the present-day city of Covington, Kenton County, Kentuckey. Mrs. Fowler took care of the business affairs of the farm in the absence of her husband. The farm grew grapes for wine, and apples for cider as well as other crops.

Jacob and Robert Fowler, with a total party of twenty-four men, left Fort Smith, Arkansas on September 6, 1821. They followed the Arkansas River to the mouth of the Verdigris River. There they acquired more trade goods from the trading house of Hugh Glenn, a well-known Indian trader. From this point on, Colonel Hugh Glenn was in command of the expedition. It would appear that he provided the largest part of the trade goods, since he was in command of the expedition.

The expedition left the trading house, as it was called, with thirty head of horses and mules, seventeen of which carried traps and goods for the Indian trade, and each man was mounted on horseback. At this point, five of the original party returned home. It would appear that there was a disagreement as to the details of the expedition.

The party now was made up of Colonel Hugh Glenn, in command; Major Jacob Fowler, the journalist, second in command; Robert Fowler, brother of Jacob Fowler; Baptiste Roy, interpreter; Baptiste Peno; George Douglas; Nathaniel Pryor, ex-Sergeant of the Lewis and Clark Expedition; Bono; Barbo; Lewis Dawson, injured by a grizzly bear at the mouth of the Purgatory, November 13, 1821 and died November 16; Taylor; Richard Walters; Eli Ward; Jesse Van Biber; Slover; Simpson;

Dudley Maxwell; Findley; Baptiste Moran; and Paul, a slave belonging to Jacob Fowler.

The expedition ascended the Arkansas River to the site of the present-day city of Pueblo, Colorado where they were met by a group of sixty Spanish soldiers. On January 2, 1822 Colonel Glenn and four men left for Santa Fe with the sixty Spanish solders.

January 3, 1822 Jacob Fowler built two pens for their horses. Each pen was four logs high. On January 4 they started to build a house. By January 16, 1822 they had moved their camp to the north side of the river where they built another corral for their horses. They moved to the American side of the river just in case the Spanish on their return proved to be unfriendly. On January 18 they built a three-room house. They trapped and hunted for about a month.

On the 28th of January, Peno, a French-Indian interpreter and some Spanish soldiers returned to conduct them to the Spanish settlement. Colonel Glenn had recieved permission to trade, hunt and trap in the Spanish Province. The expedition traveled to the southwest following the Spanish Road known as the Taos Trail.

Jacob and Robert Fowler crossed Sangre de Cristo Pass on their travel on the Taos Trail. They arrived in Taos on February 8, 1822 where they met Colonel Glenn. The people of Taos were very poor. There was no bread to be had since the grasshoppers had destroyed the last two years' crops. Meat was also scarce. The Taos people offered twenty-five cents a pound for the meat that the Fowler party had packed to Taos for their own use.

The men split into three parties to trap. Each party contained four men.

On February 12, 1822 Jacob and Robert Fowler, Taylor Walters and Paul set out with eight horses to trap in the San Luis Valley of Colorado. They trapped on several of the streams and the river traveling across and up and down the valley several times. The last day that the party trapped was on the 25th of May. They had caught only thirty-seven beaver between the four men of the Fowler party.

Jacob Fowler was fifty-seven years of age when he trapped and explored in the San Luis Valley. He kept a journal of each days happenings during the expedition. After Fowler's death in Covington, Kentuckey in 1850, the journal was passed from one descendant to another. It was eventually given to Colonel R.T.Durrett of Louisville, Kentucky who contacted Elliott Coues in hopes of having it published. Elliott Coues edited the diary and the book, *The Journal of Jacob Fowler*. It was published in 1898 by Frances P. Harper.

Leon Macy from Del Norte, Colorado trapped some beaver that were giving the author trouble by plugging the irrigation tubes or culverts. This was on the author's ranch about three miles east of Del Norte in the 1980s. In one-half mile of river, Leon caught thirty beaver the first year and twenty the second. This would lead one to believe that when the Fowler's were trapping beaver in the San Luis Valley in 1822 it was nearly trapped out! This, as well as the comments in the diary, indicate that there was a great deal of traffic in the San Luis Valley in the 1800s. Note: The spelling in the following diary is verbatim.

Tuesday, January 29, 1822
Tusday 29th Jany 1822

Sent the Horses out Early the Hands to Packing up the goods So as to Set out in the morning for the Spanish Settlement (The northernmost Spanish settlement on the Taos Trail/Trappers Road was San Fernando de Taos.) agreable to advice from Conl glann We now under Stand that the mackeson provence Has de Clared Independence of the mother Cuntry and is desirous of a traid With the people of the united States (The Spanish Provinces in North America declared their independence from Spain in 1821, just the year before Jacob Fowler and his party visited New Mexico.) Conl glann also advises me that He Has obtained premition to Hunt to trap and traid In the Spanish provences—

Wednesday, January 30
Wensday 30th Jany 1822

We moved about ten oclock and Steered a little South of the 3rd mountain (If one is standing at the south side of Pueblo, Colorado, where Jacob Fowler stood when he made this statement, he or she will see the Spanish Peaks and Greenhorn Mountains. These appear to be the most prominent. Hence this must account for the statement "Steered a little South of the 3rd mountain".) over a level plain about ten miles to a Crick (Rio San Carlos or St. Charles River.) a bout 30 feet Wide and Runs north East and Heads in the mountains the Bottoms in this Crick is from three to four Hunderd yards Wide and Well Covered With Cotten Wood and Boxelder the Bluffs about one Hunderd feet High frunted With [*stone*] of a grayis Coller and to appeerence Weell adapted for Building (It is interesting that Jacob Fowler perceived that this stone was "well suited to building". There is a stone quarry located at this site.)—the Hunters killed two Buffelow Bulls—

So 25 West 10 Miles

Spanish Peaks

Greenhorn Mountain named after the Jupe Comanche Chief Cuerno Verde.

Thursday, January 31
Wensday (error) 31st Jany 1822

Set out about 10 oclock and at about two miles truck the Spanish Road (This is the same road which Zebulon Pike saw as he descended Mosca Pass, see chapter four, as he crossed the Sangre de Cristos on January 28, 1807. It was built in 1787 by Manuel Segura as he took implements and seeds with the two-wheeled Spanish carrettas from Taos to San Carlos de los Jupes. Governor Juan Bautista de Anza sent Segura to the confluence of the Arkansas and St. Charles Rivers to build a farming community for the Jupe Comanche.)[1] on our left Hand—which leads to touse (The road that Pike found led from San Carlos de los Jupes to Taos, New Mexico. This road was an east fork of what became known as the Taos Trail/Trappers Road.) Which We followed and at five miles fell on a branch of the Crick on Which We lay last night—the meet about one mile below our Camp—We kept up this Crick and out at the Head of it and over a low Ridge to another Branch of the Same Crick Which Puts in below the forkes of the other—We Went up this Crick about one mile and Camped near the Mountain (The trail followed the St. Charles River to the Greenhorn Mountains, then turned south following the east side.) makeing about 10 miles in all and a little West of South—the Hunters killed three deer and four Buffelow one of Which Was two Poor for use and two left out all night the Hunters being alone and not able to bring in the meet and it Was lost—deer is plenty Heare but Wild We Will Stay Heare to morrow for the Purpose of killing meet to load the Spare Horses—

So 25 West 10 miles

Friday, February 1
thorsday (error) 1st Feby 1822

Hunters out Early—killed one Cow Buffelow With In four Hunderd yards of Camp—but So Poor the meat Was not Worth Saveing—three Bulls killed this day and three Hors loads of meat Braught to Camp—two deer braught into Camp—it is now Sunddown and three Hunters out yet—this morning Was Clouday and the Snow fell about 2 Inches deep—about 10 oclock at night the Hunters Came In Haveing killed three Buffelow and loaded their Horses to Camp one of them Slover—got His feet a lletle frost Bitten—Conclude to Hunt to morrow as our Horses Can Carry more meet

Saturday, February 2
Friday (error) 2nd Feby 1822

up Early to Start the Hunters out—but I now discover the men are all feerfull of meeting With the Indeans as We are near the War Road and Have maid So much

Sign In the Snow that the Will track us up and Steel our Horses Whill We are So much Scattered as not to be able to defend our Selves—and to be left Heare Without Horses—at So great a distance from Home—there is no knolede of What destress We might Come to—

I then Con Cluded to load up and move on the Road Which We did and on loading up the Horses We find seven Hors loads of meet We moved on about six miles along the futt of the mountains to Crick Wheare We Camped for Wood and Watter—the Hunters killed two Bulls this day but two Poor for use—the Snow is Heare about three Inches deep on the leavel Pirarie but on the north Side of the Hills the old Snow is more than one futt deep and up the mountains it is Still deeper—

S° 25 West 6 miles

Sunday, February 3
Satterday (error) 3rd Feby 1822

Set out Early about South along the foot of the mountains for about ten miles to a Crick (Jacob Fowler crossed the Huerfano River near Badito. From Badito the Taos Trail/Trappers Road left the wagon road. (See chapters three, eight & nine) and followed South Oak Creek to the southwest.) about five miles to Whar there the Remains of a Spanish fort (In 1819 Governor Facundo Melgares had a fort built to protect the Spanish Province from the encroachment of the Americans.) to apperence ocepied about one year back—Hear We Camped for the night Which Was Cold and Windey—So that the two men kept out as gard With the Horses—Was like to frees—as We Have kept two men garding the Horses all night Ever Since We left our House on the River and Intend keeping them up till We Rech the Spanish Settlement We this day maid fifteen miles—

Monday, February 4
Sunday (error) 4th Feby 1822

the Wind High and Very Cold We set out Early up the valley a little West of South for about two miles thence up the Point of a mountain and along a Ridge leave High Peeks on both Sides till We took up a High Hill and threw a Pine groave Whar the Snow is three feet deep—and at about five miles from Camp We Came to the top or Backbon of the mountain Which devides the Watters of the arkensaw from the Delnort (The backbone or ridge that Fowler crossed is Sangre de Cristo Pass. This is the same pass that Anza, Ruxton, Heap/Beale, Gunnison and Richardson crossed. See chapters three, six, eight, nine & fifteen) Heare the Wind Was So Cold We Scarce dare look Round South 5 miles to the top of the mountain

This photos taken from 35,000 feet is an over-view of Taos Trail which crossed through Sangre de Cristo Pass.

We then Steered more West down the mountain to a branch of the delnort—and down that about South for nearly ten miles (Sangre de Cristo Creek descends from the pass of the same name. Today you cross La Veta Pass into the San Luis Valley and travel down this creek. Watch to the north of the guard rail, just after crossing La Veta Pass to the west and you can still see evidence of Gunnison's wagon road.) to Wheare the mountains are much lower Whear Capted for the We Hear find no timber but Piny and Roal Some old logs off the mountain for fier Wood—Dick Walters is mising and on Inquirey He Had lost His Blankes Comeing down the mountain and tyed His Hors to a tree and gon back to find them and that His Hors broke loos and overtook the Reer party at about four miles from Whare He tied Him the Hors Was Hear Caut and tied again it is now Sundown and no Word of Dick We are afraid He is frosen We maid fifteen miles this day—Walters got to Camp Some time In the night

S° 45 West 10 miles

INTO SAN LUIS VALLEY

Tuesday, February 5

Monday (error) 5th Feby 1822

Set out Early down the Crick nearly South at five miles the Crick on our Right Hand Came to Crick (The Taos Trail/Trappers Road leaves Sangre de Cristo Creek several miles east of present-day Fort Garland. The trail crosses Trinchera Creek just east of Mountain Home Reservoir. The author is surprised that Fowler did not camp on Trinchera Creek. This was a popular camp site.(See chapters three & six.) From Trinchera Creek to his next camp site is about thirty miles.) Running West With Some Cottenwood and Willows We Crossed this Crick Into an oppen plain (This is part of the San Luis Valley, but is separated by the Basaltic Hills which run from San Luis to Smith Reservoir south of Blanca, Colorado.) of great Exstent We Have now left the mountains behind us and on our left Hand tho there are Some to be Seen at a great distance on our Right and In frunt—our Cors is now South and Crossing a Small Crick at three miles and at twelve miles farther Camped on a Crick (This is the Rio Culebra where Anza and Ruxton camped. See chapters three & six. From here the East Fork of the North Branch of Old Spanish Trail goes north about eight miles before turning to the northwest to pass the west side of Mount Blanca.) 40 feet Wide full of Running Watter Some Cotten Wood trees and Willows We this day maid twenty one miles—South 21 miles

Wednesday, February 6

tusday (error) 6th Feby 1822

Set out the Sun about one Hour High nearly South along the mountains leave them on our left and pasing Some Small mounds (The East Fork of the North Branch/Jacals Road passed east of San Pedro Mesa and west of the Sangre de Cristos.) on the Right Which Stand alone in the Pirarie at fifteen miles Crosed a Small Crick (Costilla Creek) Runing West from the mountains a Cross the plain and In the Evening Crossed two more Small Streems Runing as before and at night Camped on a Small Crick at the lower Eand of this large vally (San Luis Valley) Heare the mountain Puts a Cross the Plain to the River Delnort about 6 miles to our Right as We Have been going down that River at about the above distance Ever Since We Came in to this plain—on this Crick there Is a Small Spanish vilege but abandoned by the Inhabetance for feer of the Indeans now at War With them We this day troted the Horses more than Half the time and maid thirty miles nor did We Stop till In the night

South 30 miles—

Thursday, February 7

Wensday (error) 7th Feby 1822

We Set at an Early Hour Crossing a Crick Well adapted for mills of Ither the Saw or the grinding and plenty of tall Pitch Pine—We Heare proceded up the Side of a High mountain and Continueing alonge the Side of it the River Runing Close under the futt of it So that the Was no other Way to pass—We Continued over Ruff grounds and deet guters for nine miles to a Small vilege on a Crick — Heare We Capped in the vileg for the night—and our gides left us as Well as the Intarpreter after Shewing us Into a Hous as He Said of Honest People—and telling on ordors that I Had no money but wold pay in Such artickels as We Had the land lord Was verry Kind I obtained Some taffe for the men as the Have not tasted any Sperits Since We left the virdegree He put all our goods in a dark Room and locked them up—and We lodged in an outer Room—the Inturpreter and guide promised us to Return to us Early—S° 30 West 9 miles

Friday, February
thorsday (error) 8th Feby 1822
We Had the Horses up Early and With Some defequeelty got out the Saddles and Bridles—and then atempted to Settle the Bill but the Spanierd Ither Cold not or Wold not under Stand me I Soposed the amt about Six dollers—and layd ten Dollers Worth of Knives and tobaco—Which He took up and put a Way I demanded the goods but to no purpose He Wold not let me Have them Still Saying that Battees told Him not to let the goods go till He Came now this Battees Was one of the men Imployed Heare and Sent by Conl glann to asist us over the mountain—and I began to ConClude that Some vilenus Skeem Was at Worke betwen Him and the landlord as He did not Return as He promised—but after about three Hours disputeing and Indevering to get the goods I Seen that nothing but force Wold do I Steped to my gun and So did Robert Fowler I told the men to do the Same—and [when] I Seen all Readey I Spoke loud Saying I Wold Have the goods and Shoing much anger—the Spanierd got in a better umer and gave up the goods— So We loaded and moved on Crossing a Crick Which Run West threw the village Steered a little South of East about twelve miles over a High Butifull plain to the village of St Flander (Ft. Flanders-San Fernando de Taos was the Spanish settlement which was located about two miles southwest of the Taos Indian Pueblo.)— In the nibor Hood of touse (Taos Pueblo is an ancient Taos Indian Pueblo. This is the Pueblo from which Don Diego de Vargas took corn. See chapter one.) about two miles from the villege We meet With Conl glann at the Crossing of a Crick Which West—on our Rivel at the village We mised one of the Hors loads of meet and on Inquiery it was found that one of the Spanierds Head taken it of to His own Hous at about three miles distance So We lost it there being no moad of Recovering it—He was one of the men Sent out to asist us over the mountains and that

93

morning With out being notised put the load on His own Hors—and falling be-
hind maid His Eskape With the meet—We Heare found the people extremly poor.
and Bread Stuff Coud not be Head amongest them as the Said the grass hopers
Head Eat up all their grain for the last two years and that the Head to Pack all their
grain about one Hunderd miles—for their own use—We found them Eaqually
Scarce of meet and Ware offered one quarter of a doller a bound for the meet We
Braght in With us—but this We Cold not spair and Haveing nothing Els to eat it
Will not last us long—and no Bread Stuff to be got Heare We must Soon leave this
Reeched place—and now in the dead of Winter and the Waters frosen tite Exsept
the River Delnort Which is Said to be oppen to Which We Intend to go as Soon as
poseble to Cetch Bever to live on as there is no other game In this part of the
Cuntry—

Saturday, February 9
Satterday 9th Feby 1822
    Remained In the villedge all day and In the Evening there Was a Colletion
men and Ladys of the Spanyerds Had a fandango in our House Wheare the appeered
to InJoy them Selves With the Prest at their to a great degree—

Sunday, February 10
Sunday 10th Feby 1822
    Remained In the village all day But Sent out two parteys of trapes to Remain
out till the first of may next—Hear it may be Remembered that a Capten and and
Sixty men of the Spanierds Came in from the arkensaw With Conl glann and little
party—and now the Same Capten and party Has Crossed the mountains again—
but before He let Home Has Interdused Conl glann and Mr. Roy to His family Consisting a Wife and two daughters both young Woman the old lady Haveing paid us
a visid In the morning appered In a few minet quite formiler and as Well aquainted
With us as If She Head knone us for several years tho She did not Stay more than
about Half an Hour—But in the after noon a boy Came With a mesege for Conl
glann mr Roy and the negro. Who after Some Ceremony acCompanyed the two
gentlemen but With Some Reluctance aledgeing that He Was not Settesfyed to go
With out His master aledgeing as the ladys appeerd more atached to Him than the
White men—that there might be Some mischeef Intended and uder those doupts
He Went as I before Stated and from the Statement of those two gentlemen I Will
Indevour to State What followed—it Is a Custom With the Spanierds When
Interdused to Imbrace With a Close Huge—this Ceremoney So Imbareshed Pall
and maid Him So Shaimed that I [if] a Small Hole Cold Have been found He Wold
Sartainly Crept Into it. but unfortnetly there Was no Such place to be found. and

the trap door threw Which the desended Into the Room being Shut down *(for the Went In at the top of the House)* there Was no Poseble Way for Him to make His Escape—now the Haveing but one Beed in the House and that So large as to be Cappeble of Holding the three Copple of poson—there Ware all to lodge to geather and the mother of the daughters being oldest Had of Corse the ferst Chois of Bows. and took pall for Hir Chap taking Hold of Him and drawing Him to the beed Side Sot Him down With Hir arms Round His Sholders. and gave Him a Kis from Sliped Hir Hand down Into His Britches—but it Wold take amuch abeler Hand than mine to discribe palls feelings at this time being naturly a little Relegous modest and Bashfull He Sot as near the wall as Was Poseble and it may be Soposed He Indevoured to Creep Into it for Such Was His atachment to the old lady that he kept His turned Constently up to the trap door—and to His great Joy Some person oppened it to Come In to the Same Room—But Pall no Sooner Saw the light than He Sprang from the old lady and Was out In an Instent—and maid to our lodgeing as fast as Poseble Wheare the other two Soon followed and told What Head Happened to Pall

Monday, February 11
monday 11th Feby 1822
Remained in the vilege all day nothin meterel took place.

Tuesday, February 12
tusday 12th Feby 1822
I Set out on traping tower With Robert Fowler—Taylor Walters and Pall With Eight Horses We Went South West about ten miles to the bank of the River (Rio Grande del Norte) Which Bank or Bluf Was So High We Cold see no Chance of getting down With the Horses for We looked some time before We Cold see the River the distance Was So great—and the River looked like a Small Spring Branch that a man might Easely Step over—and Head We not been told that the River Was In that gap (Rio Grande Gorge) We Cold not Have beleved the River Was there at all—We then Pased down a long the Bluff about two miles and found a path Way down the mountain—the Bluf or River Bank as you may Chose to Call it Which path We took but With great danger to our Horses and In about two Hours going down that mountain We got to the River Which is about one Hunderd yds Wide and is fordable With Horses—and now takeing a vew of the River I find it is at least one thousand feet below the leavel of Pirarie. and is bound With a bluf of Rocks on Each Side mostly Parpendickeler So that there Is but few plases that Ither man or Beast asend them—We are now at the mouth of the Crick (Taos Creek) Which Pases threw touse Heare is two Houses With Each one family of Spanierds and it is

95

not Poseble the Have more than Half an acer of ground to live on. and Shold a Rock Breake loos and Come down Wold destroy the Hole Settlement

S° 45 West 10 to the River

Wednesday, February 13

Wensday 13th Feby 1822

Robert Fowler and my Self Went down the River about Six miles on foot to look for Bever no Sign of any the River is So bound With Rocks that With much difequaty We maid our Way Heare We found a nother Small villege With Eight or ten Houses and a foot Bridge a Cross the River over Which We Went and Heare We found a Path up the River Hills Which full as High as Wheare We first Came to it But Heare the Rocks are So broken that a Papth Way is found up threw them after a long and tedeous Walk We a Rived at the top of the Hil and found our Selves on oppen leave Pirarie of from forty to fifty miles Wide. We are now on the West Side of the River and Went up along the Bluf about two miles and Came to a dry Crick Which put into the River but the Rocks Ware So High on Each Side that We Walked up it about one Hour before We found any Poseble Chance of Crossing it after Which We pased over the leavel Pirarie opset our Camp Wheare We found a path leading down threw the Rocks to the River and it appeers that there is no poseble Chance of going up or down these Clifts but at those paths—for as Soon as you Come to the top of these Clifts and look down you are so struck With Horror that you Will Retret In an Instant

Thursday, February 14

thorsday 14th Feby 1822

Crosed the River Early and Wound up the mountain along a path maid By the Spanierds among the Rocks till We arived at the top in the oppen World and Steereing to the north leaveing the River on our Right Hand and Camped at night opesed the villege Wheare We Head the defequeelty Withe the land lord We this day maid about fourteen miles—and found no Watter for our Horses Sent two Kittles down to the River for Watter Heare We find the mountain about the Same Hight as Wheare We Caped last night With a path up threw the Rocks maid by the People of the villege on the East side— 14 miles

Friday, February 15

Friday 15th Feby 1822

We Set out Early up the margin of the River about twelve miles to the point of a mountain Cut off by the River forming a parpendickelor Bluff of about fifteen Hunderd feet High—over this mountain We Head to Clime on the top of Which the Snow Was nee deep—tho there Was none on the Pirarie We Went four miles farther and Camped on the margen of the River Sent down two kittles for Watter and sot two bever traps—Heare the Rocks or Bluffs are a little Broken and not quite so High as Wheare We Stayed the two nights past—tho Heare they are about nine Hunderd feet High and So Steep—Exsept the Spot Wheare Sent down the kittles that a Squerel Cold not Climb them—our distance this day is Sixteen miles—16 miles

Saturday, February 16
Satterday 16th Feby 1822

found one Bever in a trap this morning Sott the two traps again and moved up the River about Six miles and Ca(m)ped on the margen of the River the Rocks not So High as last night but So Steep that We Cold not git Watter from the River and melted Snow for that Purpose Which We found among Some Rocks We found some dry Cedars for fier Wood—6 miles

Sunday, February 17
Sunday 17th Feby 1822

Very Cold Haveing Snowed a little In the fore part of the night Sent for the two Bever traps—the River Had frosen over them So that We Caught nothing—Seen two men on Hors Back at a great distance Soposed to be Indeans—the Road off as fast as their Horses Cold Carry them—We this day Seen Six Wild Horses tho two of them must Have been In Hands as their tails Ware Bobed Short—We find no game yet and our Stock of provetion Is nearly out—

Monday, February 18
monday 18th Feby 1822

We Sot out Early up the River and at about 12 miles Came to the upper Eand of the High Rocks and going down a gradual decent three or four Hunderd yds Came to a low Bottom on the River the Bank being low not more than six or Eight (*feet*) High the River butifull and a bout one Hundred yds Wide—But all frosen up tite—We Heare got Watter for the Horses—it Is Heare proper to Remark that the River as far as We Have Seen it pasing down betwen the High Rocks or mountains—dose not move In a very gentle manner as It appears much Impeded by the Rocks falling from Each Side. and is forsed forward dashing from one Rock over others In almost one Continued foam the Hole distance threw the mountains Which from What I Can larn is about seventy miles When it appeers below In an oppen Cuntry—I Have no doubt but the River from the Head of those Rocks up for about one Hundred miles Has once been a lake of about from forty to fifty miles Wide and about two Hundred feet deep—and that the running and dashing of the Watter

Has Woren a Way the Rocks So as to form the present Chanel—We this day Crosed a dry Branch. But Have Not Seen one Streem of Watter In all the distance We Have Came up on the *(west)* Side We traveled nor Cold ourHorses get one drop of Watter in all that distance but the Eat Snow When the Cold get it—We Went up the River a bout Six miles further and Camped on the East Side in a Small grove of Cotten Wood trees the Ice In *(is)* now so Strong the Horses Can Cross at pleasure—We find nothing to kill Exsept two of the Big Horned Sheep *(Ovis montana)* one of Which Robert Fowler shot but Cold not git it—

We this day maid Eighteen miles our Corse about north all the Way up the River—North 54 miles

Tuesday, February 19
tusday 19th Feby 1822

We Set out Early up along the West Side of the River and at two miles Came to High Short Hills Which Put In Cloce to the River on both Sides and Continu for about three miles Wheare We find Wide and low Bottoms—Heare We See timber a Head Wheare We Will Indevour to Camp this night—and at ten miles We Came to Slovers party In Camped about two miles up Pikes forke of the Delnort (Pike's fork of the del Norte would be the Rio Conejos.) and about three miles below His Block House Wheare He Was taken by the Spanierds—this fork Is oppen ocationed by the large Warm Spring Spoken of In Pikes Jurnal this party Has Caught Some Bever and their Is Sign of more in the River our Cors this day Was north 30 West ten miles—there is plenty of Cotten Wood trees and Willowes along this but Scarce a tree on the main River

N 30 West 10 miles

Wednesday, February 20
Wensday 20th Feby 1822

We moved up the River threw the Bottom Which is about fifty miles Wide In Cluding the second Bottom leavel and Rich and not a tree to be Seen Exsept a few along the River bank—We maid twelve miles. and Camped on the East Side among Some Willows and geathered drift Wood for our fier—the Weather Is very Cold the Snow fell last night about two Inches deep—Cors north 12 miles See nothing to kill

Thursday, February 21
thorsday 21st Feby 1822

Crosed over on the Ice and up the West Side of the River the timber and Brush Is now plenty In the low bottoms Which are from two to four miles Wide tho these are not all Covered With timber—and Hear there Is on both Sides What We Call a second bottom a little Higher than the first—the Hole now makeing a distance of from 30 to 40 miles now Since We Have Came to the timber We find much Sign of Bever—But the River Is So frosen that We Cannot ketch them We Camped on the East Side of the River and Conclude to go to the West mountains In the morning and try to kill meet to Eat as our provetions are all gon—nor Have We Seen any kind of game Since We left Slovers party N 45 West 18 miles

Friday, February 22
Friday 22nd Feby 1822

Robert Fowler and my self Set out Early on futt for the West mountains and Steered for a Small streek of Brush Wheare We Exspect to find Watter as that kind of Brush dos not grow With out We on the Way See Eight or 90 Wild Horses and In devour to git In Shot distance so as to kill one to Eat—but In that We failed for Whin We Ware at about one miles distanes the Seen us and all Run off—We Went to the mountain and Camped by the Side of a large Rock Wheare We both Wood and Watter Was plenty but nothing to Eat Pall and taylor Came up With the Horses We all Went up the mountains to Hunt But See nothing to kill—but there Was Some Sign of the Big Horned Sheep on the Sides of the mountain amongst the Short Pine Which Is plenty Heare In Some plases—the Weather Is Cold and Some flying Clouds—our Corse Was this day West 12 miles—We Heare found by going up the mountain the Snow Was so deep We Cold not travel tho there Was little or none In the valey

West 12 miles

Saturday, February 23
Satterday 23rd Feby 1822

We Conclude to go to the River and up it till We find game—Pall and my Self take the Horses and Steerd north to the River about ten miles Robert Fowler and Taylor out on the Hunt—Camped on the West Side of the River—nothing killed this day— north 10 miles West Side of the River

Sunday, February 24
Sunday 24th Feby 1822

nothing to Eat—Taylor Purposes to take Robert Fowlers Hors and Ride Hunting Which Was agread to He Went on the West Side of the River I Went my Self on the East Side up the River about ten miles to the Short Hills Seen Some Caberey but killed nothing Taylor did not Return at night—nothing to Eat but look at Each other With Hungrey faceses

Monday, February 25

monday 25th Feby 1822

this morning Taylor Came Into Camp on futt Haveing lost the Hors With Sadle Bridle Blankets nek Roap and all In the first Short Hills on the West Side of the River at Some ten or twelve miles up—and that He Said He Head Seen many deer Elk and Bares—to Which place We moved as fast as poseble and got there about 3 oclock Seen a great many deer but killed nothing—our Corse West ten miles

Tuesday, February 26

tusday 26th Feby 1822

all out and Hunt till about 10 oclock but killed nothing tho Seen Some deer— We now begin to think of killing one of our Horses—but first move to fresh Camp Wheare We Have not disturbed the game and try In the Evening again to kill Something We move about two miles to the River—as We Were now Camped on a Small Crick—and put out the Horses Robert and my Self took our guns to Hunt on futt as there Was much timber land Heare—but Taylor and Pall Began to Complain of Hunger of Which Taylor began gro black In the face and Pall Was gitting White With the Same Complaint and the both thaught the Hors Shold be killed. to Which Robert and my Self Consented and gave them liberty to kill Him as Soon as the Cold—but not Willing to see that operation Robert and my Self Went off to Hunt but We Soon Heard the gun fier that We Soposed to kill the Hors—but We kept our Corse down the River on the Ice as the Brush Was thick and dry So that If We Went on land We maid So much nois that We Could not git neer the game—but We Head not gon far before Som deer Was Seen In the Brush and Robert Went after them and killed two of them He then Went to Camp for a Hors leaveing me to take Care of the deer—but When He got to Camp He found one of the Horses about Half Skined—but another Was Soon got up and the deer Caryed to Camp Wheare We Soon Head Suntious feest and much Plesentness now appeered Round the fier tho We lamented the fate of the Poor Hors—as now Head no use for His flesh Which feel a pray to the Birds and Wolves

Wednesday, February 27

Wensday 27th Feby 1822

Sent Pall out Early to look for the Horses We Soon Heard the Report of gun and not long after Pall Came In With a deer on His back the first He Ever killed In His life—We Have meet plenty and the Weather Is now moderate Some Holes appeer a longe Shore In the Ice out at Which the bever Workes We Sot some traps this day—

Thursday, February 28

thorsday 28th Feby 1822

Caught one bever—and Hunted for the lost Hors—but Have not found Him—

Friday, March 1

Friday 1st march 1822

Taylor Caught one Bever—Hunted for the lost Hors—met With vanbeber and two of His party the had found our lost Hors—the Remained at our Camp that night the Hors Head lost all but the Bridle

Saturday, March 2

Satterday 2nd march 1822

vanbeber and His Party Set out Early up the River We Con Clude to follow them one or two days Exspecting We may find Some Elk—We Went up the twelve miles pasing at Seven miles a large pond of Watter of about 40 acers on the West Side of the River—the Bottom of Which is about one mile Wide the mountains High on Each Side—the tops of Which are a great Hight above vegatation at about ten miles We Crost a fork Puting In on the West Sid about one third as large as the River it appeers to Head to the West—Heare the River makes a turn to the north as fare as We Cold See up it—We Camped With vanbebers party the Head killed one Elk—our Cors West 12 miles—Heare the mountains Put Close to the River Which very Croked

Sunday, March 3

Sunday 3rd march 1822

I Remained at Camp Robert and Taylor Went Hunting the former killed two Elk and left the latter to butcher them While took out Horses and braught them In to Camp

Monday, March 4

monday 4th march 1822

Went up the River to look for Sign of Bever but found none

Tuesday, March 5

tuesday 5th march 1822

We moved down the River to the first High point of Rocks on the East Side at the Head of the large vally and about one mile below Where We killed the Hors— Some Snow fell last night the Weather Cold the River Is yet frosen up Close Except a few Springs in the River bank Which keeps it oppen a few feet—High Wind last night—

Wednesday, March 6
Wensday 6th march 1822

Sot Some traps—Taylor Came In late at night Reports that Some Indeans are Camped about Eight miles below us on the River

Thursday, March 7
thorsday 7th march 1822

Taylor purposes going to the Indeans Camp I gave Him Some tobaco for that purpose—He Went to the Indeans Robert my Self and Pall Road out the mountains and on our Return We See a number of Indeans at Camp Which We Cold See at Some distance from a point of one of the mountains and not noing what Indeans the Ware we vewed them about Half an Hour—the then moved off from our Camp and We Came In—Wheare We found taylor—tho the Indeans Had Stolen two Buffelow Roabs Some lead and two knives—and Ware of the utaws nation Which Roame about and live In the mountains Without Haveing any Settled Home and live alltogether on the Chase Raising no grain—Slover With His party Pased up the River this day—

Friday, March 8
Friday 8th march 1822

We Remain at the Same Camp—Caught one Bever and one aughter Ward and duglass Came to our Camp from touse and State that the Spanierds Have Sent 700 men against the nabeho Indeans—and of a battle being faught between Spanierds and the Panie Indeans East of the mountains

Saturday, March 9
Satterday 9th march 1822

Ward and Duglass Set out for vanbebers Camp—In the Evening two Spanierds Came to Camp—Hard frost last night

Sunday, March 10
Sunday 10th march 1822

Went up the River above the forkes to kill meet the two Spanierds With us—

Monday, March 11
monday 11th march 1822

We Hunted till 12 oclock for Elk but found none—We Continued up the north about Eight miles Heare the mountains Close in on both Sides So that our Pasege Was Defequal (The cañon from which the main channel of the river descends narrows at Wagon Wheel Gap.) and the River turning to the West—We maid ten miles and Camped With Slover and vanbeber Partey the Have all meet Heare together—the Have killed two Elk N° 8 miles—West 2 miles

Tuesday, March 12
tusday 12th march 1822

Robert and myself Set out Early to Hunt and Haveing been Informed that a Hot Spring (A bath house was built on this spring in the late 1800s.)[2] Had been found up the Crick Which put In to the River from the West Side a little above our Cam We Went to the Spring about one and a Half miles up the Crick—But the Smoke appeered like that of a Salt furnis—as Soon as We Came In vew of it—the Snow Was now about Six Inches deep over the valley of the Crick But the hot Watter Head kept the ground Cleane for a few Rods Round the Spring—but What appeered Straing to look at Was to see Ice Exstended about three feet from the Shore over the Watter—tho a boiling up In the middle of the Pon Which Was about three Rods a Cross and nearly Round the Spert of Watter Rose up Some distance above the leavel of the Watter In the Pon and Was about the Size of a flour Barrel—now the question Was How Can the Ice Existe on Hot Watter. I Caught hold of the Ice as I Soposed—and not only scalded With the Watter but the Burned With the Ice it being nearly as Hot as the Watter—bout on a farther Examination I found it was a mineral Substan that Had Congeled on the Watter of Which there Ware vast quantitys laying below the Spring In the Crick Which Run from it—We then Went up the mountain till the Snow got So deep We Ware obliged to Return—killed nothing—this forke of the River Heads nearly in the High mountains—the main River Heading north and from appeerence the mountains Seperates and be Comes Lower as you go up the River leaveing a large valley—and low Bottoms along the River—the two Spanierds tell us it is about one days travel to the Head of the River (Here is another indication that the Spanish had thoroughly explored the headwaters of the Rio Grande del Norte.)—the Cuntry is low a Crass to the arkensaw—about twenty miles north from Heare and Six East of this River there Is a large lake or Bodey of Watter that Has no out let that there is Some Island In it With trees on them the all So State that this lake lyes be twen the Delnort and the arkensaw and that the Cuntry is low all the Way betwen the two Rivers—

Wednesday, March 13
Wendsday 13th march 1822

We Heare left the two Spanierds With Slover as We Head Dick Walters at His Camp on Pikes fork We moved down the River a little below the main forkes and killed one Elk Wheare We Camped for the night—bothe the other partys pased us Heare and Camped about one mile below us—the Ice begins to thaw and all makeing for the Bever Sign—

Thursday, March 14

thorsday 14th march 1822

this morning two of our Horses Ware mising—about twelve oclock We found them and moved down to Hanging as We Have Called it at our old Camp—the Weather Has got Cold and the Ice Harder—We Will not be able to trap for Some time yet—We Heare find the flax In abondance the Rute Is purenal but In Every other appeerence it is like ous—

Friday, March 15

Friday 15th march 1822

Remained In Camp—the Ice begins to thaw in the day time but Hard frost at night—

Saturday, March 16

Satterday 16th march 1822

Remained in Camp all day—

Sunday, March 17

Sunday 17th march 1822

Remained in Camp all day—

Monday, March 18

monday 18th march 1822

Some difequalty With Taylor He quits us or We leave Him—and move up a Crick to the South a bout four miles to Some bever Dams—Robert Fowler Complains of the Sore throat for Some days—and is gitting Worse

South 4 miles

Tuesday, March 19

tusday 19th march 1822

Robert is Still Worse With the Sore throat—We apply a sock With ashes Round His neck—He finds Releef in about two Hours—Hard frost this morning and Cold With High Winds

Wednesday, March 20

Wensday 20th march 1822

Caught three Bever and Examin the Crick about Six miles Higher up to Wheare the mountains Close In on both Sides there Is timber and Willows all along this Crick and the bottoms about Half a mile Wid and Well adopted for Cultavation on acoumpt of Eragation—as no other lands Can be Cultivated Heare for the Want of Seasnable Rains—

S° 30 W 6 miles

Friday, March 29

thorsday (error) 29th march 1822

We Have Remained Heare Waiting for the Ice to melt out of the Crick but the Weather Continues Cold and Clouday With frequent Snow Storms the Ice is Still frosen over the bever dams So that We Caught but few—Robert Sore throat Has gon much better—We moved down to the River about 3 miles above our old Camp killed three gees—Sot Some traps—the gees is now Coming plenty and those We killed fatt Which is pleasing to us as We Have now lived a long time on Poor meet—Cloudey and begins to Snow—the Ice is nearly gon out of the River

Saturday, March 30

Satterday 30th march 1822

the Snow is about four Inches deep Caught one bever killed one Sand Hill Crain and five gees—the day is Warm—the Snow all gon out of the valleys but the mountains are all Covered moved to down to the old Camp

Sunday, March 31

Sunday 31st march 1822

Caught four Bever and killed five gees—the Weather is gitting Cold

Monday, April 1

monday 1st aprile 1822

Killed five gees—the Watter frose over the traps Caught no bever

Tuesday, April 2

tusday 2nd aprile 1822

Caught two bever—and Remained the ballence of the day In Camp

Wednesday, April 3

Wensday 3rd aprile 1822

Caught one Bever killed three gees—the Weather much Warmer We moved up the Crick to the Bever dams—find the Ice much thiner and Sot Some traps—

Thursday, April 4

thorsday 4th aprile 1822

Hard frost last night and frose up the traps Caught but one bever We now find that In this Crick the Watter Rises by Suns thaw Ing the Ioe and at night With the Hard frost so that the Rise and fall of the Watter will defeet the traping

Friday, April 5

friday 5th aprile 1822

moved Early about East threw a low In the Spurs of the mountains about ten miles and Camped a little below the Spanish Road leading to Pikes (This is the West Fork of the North Branch of the Old Spanish Trail which crossed the east end of an island in the Rio Grande east of present-day Del Norte, Colorado. It follows the east side of the San Juan from the Rio Grande to Conejos, Colorado.) gap In the mountain—We Sot Some traps—N 70 East 10 to the River

The Old Spanish Trail from 800 feet.

Saturday, April 6

Satterday 6th aprile 1822

Caught one Bever—We find the River as Well as the Crick Rises In the day with melting of the Ice for it Cannot be the Snow In the mountains the distance up to the Snow prevents the Watter from Ever Retching the vally the ground is so dry and loose that the Watter all dis appeers before it Can Rech near the futt of the mountains and Haveing Had frost at night the River falls as much as it Rises in the day—Taylor Came to our Camp to day and States that there are a great many Indeans on the River both above and below us that the Had Robed His Camp and taken all His traps but that He Had followed them and got all back but two traps

Sunday, April 7

Sunday 7th aprile 1822

Caught one Bever and moved down the River about 12 miles on the north Side We Have killed twelve gees Since We Have been on the River last—

Monday, April 8

monday 8th aprile 1822

Caught one Bever—Killed five gees moved down the River to the lower Eand of the timber—the Indeans are all gon to the West over the mountains the Ware the utaws nation—

Tuesday, April 9

tuesday 9th aprile 1822

moved down the River about ten mile—and then turned East across the valley to a crick and up it about five miles—this Crick Heds to the north as Is the Same We Came down Where We Crosse the mountains In feby last—We this day mett With venbeber and Ward—

Wednesday, April 10

Wensday 10th aprile 1822

Heare Is Some Indeans from the Spanish Settlement—We moved up the Crick about ten miles lost one bever trap—N° 10 miles

Thursday, April 11

thorsday 11th aprile 1822

Went up the Crick about three miles and found Some Sign of bever—Sot Some traps—We yesterday pased threw Some of the Richest bottom on the Crick

that I have Seen and Contains Six or Eight thousand acers
N 20 West 3 miles

Friday, April 12
friday 12th aprile 1822
Cold and Clouday the Crick frose up—We Caught nothing—We Set out threw the Pirarie down the Crick a Snow Storm Came on and Caught us In the Pirarie the Wind and Snow in our faces So that We Cold not See one another two Rods—this Storm lasted about two Hours and it Was Weel for us it Seesed for We Cold not See Which Way to go and our Setuation Was Realy unplesent—
We Camped near the mouth of the Crick (Trinchera Creek) Wheare We found Some timber—

Saturday, April 13
Satterday 13th aprile 1822
the ground is now Covered With Snow and Hard frosen—We Have not Seen one morning With out frost Since the Winter first Sot In—We Crossed the River a little above Pikes forke (Rio Conejos) and ConCluded to go back to the timber up the River for Which We Steered for three or four miles and Crossed a large Streem (La Jara Creek) of Runing Watter forty feet Wide and nearly beley deep to the Horses—We Head Crossed this Same Crick In febuy last but the Was no Watter then In it it Haveing to pass over about twenty miles of oppen leavel Pirarie it Was all frosen to Ice—at that time and Is now melted and Coming down—the Snow Has disappeered In the valey but the mountains Covered—

Sunday, April 14
Sunday, April 14th—no entry

Monday, April 15
monday 15th aprile 1822
Caught 2 beve and killed one goos We yester day Seen our Hors lost by vanbebers Party but So willd We Cold not take Him—

Tuesday, April 16
tusday 16th april 1822
Caught one Bever and moved up the River about four miles and Camped on the West Side vanbebers party pased us on the East going up all So—

Wednesday, April 17

Wensday 17th aprile 1822

Caught one bever and moved up the River about 12 miles the day Cloudey and Cold Comesed Snowing fast In the Evening and Continued till late at night—

Thursday, April 18

thorsday 18th aprile 1822

the Snow about Six Inches deep We Caught one Bever and killed four gees— the day Warm the Snow all gon before night—

Friday, April 19

Friday 19th aprile 1822

killed two gees and Caught two Bever—Remained the ballence of the day at Camp—

Saturday, April 20

Satterday 20th aprile 1822

Caught 2 Bever and killed two gees the Weather Warm the grass begins to appeer a little moved up the River a bout Seven miles Seen about twenty Elk Robert Shot one but it went off With the Rest—the mountains are Still Covered With Snow tho none In the valeys—

Sunday, April 21

Sunday 21st aprile 1822

Caught two bever killed one goos moved up the River about Six miles Seen nine Elk—

Monday, April 22

monday 22nd aprile 1822

Caught two bever killed one goos and moved up the River to the Hanging Rock and from that to the Bever dams on the Crick Wheare We left on the 6th Instent Soposeing the Ice Wold be gon out of the Crick—

Tuesday, April 23

tusday 23 aprile 1822

Caught two bever—the Weather Cold—no game Hear and the Bever Poor We Will move to the River In the morning on acoumpt of killing gees to Eat—

Wednesday, April 24

Wensday 24th aprile 1822

Caught two bever moved to the River and Crosed over to the East Side and Camped a little below the Hanging Rock killed one goos and one duck—

Thursday, April 25

thorsday 25th aprile 1822

Caught one Bever killed one goos and moved down the river about five miles—

Friday, April 26

Friday 26th april 1822

Set out down the river Intend to go to the Settlement We are giting Scarce of Powder Haveing to Shute So much at gees for Want of larger game—killed two Caberey and one Elk—maid Eight miles and Camped on the East Side of the River—

Saturday, April 27

Satterday 27th aprile 1822

killed two gees moved down the River near the lower Eand of the timber Seen many Elk the Have now left the mountains and Come Into the timber land on the River to feed on the young grass—

Sunday, April 28

Sunday 28th aprile 1822

no frost this morning and the first We Have Seen this Spring—the grass groes but Slow the trees not yet Buding the ground is as dry as dust no moisture but the Snow Since We Came to the Cuntry and the Spanierds Say that It is three years Since the Have Had Rain—we moved down the River about four miles and Crossed to the West Side of the River and Steered South at about ten miles Crosed the Willow Crick and at about fifteen miles pased a Spring (The distance doesn't fit that given by Fowler, but along the West Fork of the North Branch of the Old Spanish Trail south of La Jara Creek about three miles in the level prairie is Diamond Spring. Except for distance, the description of the spring fits that of Diamond Spring.) In the leavel Pirarie Which Contained about on Hogset of Clear Cool Watter Standing on Rise or mound of Earth a little above the leavel of the Pirarie the ground Round this Spring Was quite Soft and Wen We Ware at the Watter by Jumping on the ground you Cold See it Shake for about two Rods all Round—about five miles farther We Crosed Pikes forke at the mouth of the Warm Spring Branch

110

Spoken of by that gentleman In Jurnal We then pased threw Some low Hills a little East of South Seven miles to the River and Crossing over found the Watter up to the Saddle Sceats and one of our Pack Horses fell down with his load and Was not able to Rise So that We Had Some difequalty to Keep Him from be drounded We then pased over a low Ridge about Half a mile and Camped on a crick Wheare We found Some Woods—

Monday, April 29
monday 29th aprile 1822

Clouday With High Winds Some Snow—We moved on intending to Camp on a branch With Some timber on the East Side of the Snake Hill at twelve miles We maid the Branch but no Watter—We Went up the the Crick about Eight miles and there found it a Bold Runing Streem Hear We Camped for the night makeing in twenty miles We Seen Heare on this Crick a great many Cabery but very Wild

South 45 East 18 miles

Tuesday, April 30
tusday 30th aprile 1822

Hard frost the Ice about the 8th of an Inch on the kittle of Watter Killed a Woolf at Camp—and Set out up the Crick (Culebra Creek) to the mountains about three miles Whear We Struck the Road to touse (Jacob Fowler was back on the East Fork of the North Branch of the Old Spanish Trail which ran along the west side of the Sangre de Cristo Mountains.) Which We took and Camped at the Hords mans villege but no purson to be Seen the Have deserted that place—about Sundown Six Indeans Came to our Camp the Ware of the apacha nation now at Pace With the Spanierds—the derected us to go off Emedetly Saying that the utaws Had Stolen three Horses from our men and that Wold Steel ours if We Stayed at this place all night—We geathered up our Horses and after night moved off about three miles and lay Without fier—

Wednesday, May 1
Wensday 1st may 1822

We Went down to St flander in the nibor Hood of touse and find Conl glann Is gon to stafee (Fowler followed the Old Spanish Trail south as far as Santa Fé.) We Remained Heare two days vanbebers Party Heads Came In and the french partey Is Heare all So—We now find all the Horses that ware left Heare very Poor and the Rainge near the vilege all Eat out I then ConCluded to take all the Horses out of the Settlement to good Rainge So as to fatten them or the Will not be able to to Cross the mountains on the first of June as that Was the time We In tend to Set out I therefore derected them all to be Collected and that I Wold move them In the morning.—

We Ware Informed that Spanish army Had Returned that they Hag taken one old Indean and Some two or three old Horses that Ware So poor the Nabeho Cold not drive them up the mountains—for it appers the Went up the Steep mountain and Role down the Rocks on their Pursurs So that the Ware Compled to discontinu the pursute—

Saturday, May 4
Satterday 4th may 1822

moved up the Crick South about five miles and Camped in the forks near Some Hords men Ho kept a large lot of Cattle from We obtained Some Cows milk We took With us 16 Horses—all We Cold find

Sunday, May 5
Sunday 5th may 1822

Went up the East fork of the Crick about Eight miles—find the Bever Have been all taken out by Some trapers—the mountain is High and Steep and Croud Close to the Crick on both Sides We Returned to Camp Wheare Barbo and Simpson Had braught Eight more horses makeing in twenty four—grass is Heare very good—the Horses Will Soon get fatt—this Evening Cloudey With thonder and a little Rain the first We Have Seen on this Side of the mountain

Monday, May 6
monday 6th may 1822

Clouday and a little Rain—the Horses all Collected the are all poor but the grass is good and the Will thrive—I purchased a bull from a Spanierd for which I gave Him my great Coat and one knife—the Beef Was Perty good it Rained a little In the Evening

Tuesday, May 7
tusday 7th may 1822

Cool With flying Clouds and a little Rain Battess braught taylors mule to Camp Which He Head Reported to Have been Stolen by the Indeans Potter Came to Camp With Conl glanns Horse He Has Returned from Stafee—

Wednesday, May 8
Wensday 8th may 1822

Hard frost the Horses all presend Went down to the vilege—We Heare that the Congrass Has Convened at maxeco—and that the Indeans Have taken a great many Horses from this niborhood and killed Some Cattle

Thursday, May 9
thorsday 9th may 1822
> Hard frost In the morning and Rained a little In the Evening

Friday, May 10
friday 10th may 1822
> Cool With flying Clouds and High Wind—our Horses all present

Saturday, May 11
Satterday 11th may 1822
> Some flying Clouds and warm In the evening

Sunday, May 12
Sunday 12th may 1822
> Cloudey With flying Clouds—the trees giting green the Cotten Wood leaves Half gron the People not yet don Sowing Wheat

Monday, May 13
monday 13th may 1822
> flying Clouds and High Winds Continues Cloudey With lightning threw the night

Tuesday, May 14
tusday 14th may 1822
> Clouday and Rain threw the day

Wednesday, May 15
Wensday 15th may 1822
> the Snow from 4 to 5 Inches deep—Clers up about 10 oclock and Warm the Snow disappers in the vallys but Hangs on in the mountains

Thursday, May 16
thorsday 16th may 1822
> Some frost In the morning but Warm after Sun Rise

Friday, May 17

friday 17th may 1822

flying Clouds and High Winds—

Saturday, May 18

Satterday 18th may 1822

flying Clouds and High Wind

Sunday, May 19

Sunday 19th may 1822

Cloudey and Warm for the Season

Monday, May 20

monday 20th may 1822

High Winds and Clouds—

Tuesday, May 21

tusday 21st may 1822

Clouday and Cool in the morning—High Winds about 12 oclock and Continu till Sundown—

Wednesday, May 22

Wensday 22nd may 1822

Clouday and Winday—

Thursday, May 23

thorsday 23rd may 1822

Cloudey With thonder like for Rain—Clears off in the after noon With High Wind

Friday, May 24

friday 24th may 1822

flying Clouds and High Wind

Saturday, May 25

Satterday 25th may 1822

the Wolves maid an atackt on our Horses the Wounded one Hors and two mules We Have maid a Strong Pen Close to Camp and Still Shut up all the Horses at night While We Remain at this place—to protect them from the Wolfes—

114

Sunday, May 26

Sunday 26th may 1822

Clouday and Warm all day—

Monday, May 27

monday 27th 1822

Clouday With High Winds and thonder Several thonder gust With a little Rain in the night—

Tuesday, May 28

tusday 28th may 1822

Cool With High Winds and flying Clouds—Snow Storms In the Evening— but light—

Wednesday, May 29

Wensday 29th may 1822

Cool With flying Clouds We are now makeing Some araingements for our Jurney over the mountains Some few days back Robert Fowler killed two young White Bares and braught them to Camp

Thursday, May 30

thorsday 30th may 1822

Road down to the vilege all Hands prepairing to Set out on the first day of June for the United States—

6

1846/GEORGE FREDERICK RUXTON

George Augustus Frederick Ruxton was born in England on July 24, 1821, the third son of John and Anna Maria *Hay* Ruxton. This was also the year that William Becknell, the first American trader, successfully traded with the people of Santa Fe, New Mexico.

The Santa Fé Trail story first appeared in a little frontier newspaper in Franklin, Missouri (*the Missouri Intelligencer, April 22, 1823*). No doubt Ruxton grew up hearing these exciting stories of adventures in the far west.

Ten days before his fourteenth birthday Ruxton began his military career when he enrolled in the Royal Military Academy at Sandhurst. Bored with life at the Military Academy, Ruxton became interested in the Carlist Civil War. He made his way across the English Channel and the French countryside to arrive in Spain. Although Ruxton was first a spectator, he then obtained a commission of Cornet of Lancers in the British Auxiliary Legion. The legion was attached to the regular Spanish division commanded by General don Diego León, Viceroy of Navarre. Ruxton was soon a participant in several engagements. One of these was the Battle of the Bridge of Belascoain in which he was awarded the Cross of the First Class of the National Military Order of San Fernando. Ruxton became a knight of Spain before reaching his eighteenth birthday. It was while serving in the Spanish Army that he learned to speak Spanish, which would prove to be useful in his travels in Mexico.

Upon returning to England Ruxton was given the rank of lieutenant in the Ceylon Rifles. He never joined the Ceylon Rifles but was transferred to the 89th Foot. He served a short time in his home depot in England before being transferred to Ireland. Ruxton was then transferred to his overseas regiment. He joined his regiment at Amherstburg, Ontario, across the river from Detroit. The dull military duty ended when he sold his commission on October 6, 1843.

His travels next took Ruxton to Africa, where there was a delay of financial backing for his proposed extensive exploration. The impatient Ruxton took off to Vera Cruz, Mexico. Upon arriving in Vera Cruz he began a two thousand mile journey to the Rio Grande where he crossed into the United States. He traveled up the Rio Grande to Santa Fe, New Mexico. In December of 1846 Ruxton, on his way north from Chihuahua, Mexico, reached the settlement of Fernandez, as it was called by the Mexicans in the earlier days is the present town of Taos, in the Taos Valley, some eighty miles to the north of Santa Fe. He spent some time in Taos with an American named Stephen Lee who had been a trapper and had traded with the Indians in the mountains. Ruxton had been invited to stay with Lee for the winter. Lee was currently running a very profitable liquor business but Ruxton was anxious to experience the life of a trapper and mountain man. Hiring the guide, Mattias, Ruxton set out for Pueblo (present-day Pueblo, Colorado) with each of them having a horse and two pack mules, to spend a winter in the Rockies with the beaver-trapping mountain men.

Ruxton had traveled what today is known as the "East Fork of the North Branch of the Old Spanish Trail". At Taos the Old Spanish Trail that he followed was known by many names, one of which was the Trappers Road which ran from Taos, New Mexico to Pueblo, Colorado. On the Pueblo end of this very same trail it was known as the Taos Trail.

After having much difficulty and nearly freezing, Ruxton and Mattias arrived in Pueblo. Ruxton complained of Mattias not Knowing the trail, but Mattias had likely only traveled the trail in the summer. With the trail and terrain covered with snow, it becomes very difficult to recognize landmarks. The fact that the two were successful in making it to Pueblo attests to the fact that Mattias was somewhat familiar with the trail.

A well-educated gentleman, member of the Royal Geographical Society, mountain man, trapper, soldier, and world traveler, Ruxton returned to England long enough to write two books, the titles are: *Adventures in Mexico and the Rocky Mountains and Life in the Far West*. Ruxton came back to America where he died as the result of an injury in St. Louis, Missouri in 1848 at the age of twenty-seven. He crowded a lifetime of remarkable experience into ten years. Being a trained observer, knowing and living with the people that he wrote about, he created authentic, lively and vivid detail of the legendary mountain men that has never been equaled.

December 1847

Santa Fé, the capital of the province of *Nuevo Mejico*, contains about three thousand inhabitants, and is situated about fourteen miles from the left bank of the *Del Norte*, (The name Rio Grande del Norte, great river of the north, is often shortened to Del Norte or Rio Grande.) at the foot of a mountain forming one of the eastern chain of the Rocky Mountains. (The Sangre de Cristo Mountains extend from Poncha Pass at the north end of Colorado's San Luis Valley south into New Mexico.)

The extent of the province of New Mexico is difficult to define, as the survey of the northern sections of the republic has never been undertaken, (New Mexico was not surveyed until about 1860, after becoming part of the United States.) and a great portion of the country is still in the hands of the aborigines, who are at constant war with the Mexicans. (This continued until the Chiricahua Apache Chief Gerónimo's surrender in 1886.)[1]

It was a cold, snowy day on which I left *Santa Fé*, and the mountain, although here of inconsiderable elevation, was difficult to cross on account of the drifts. My mules, too, were for the first time introduced to snow on a large scale, and, by their careful, mincing steps and cautious movement, testified their doubts as to the security of such a road. The mountain is covered with pine and cedar, and the road (Ruxton was traveling on the Old Spanish Trail.) winds through the bed of an *arroyo*, between high banks now buried in the snow. Not a living thing was visible, but once a large grey wolf was surprised on our turning a corner of rock, and in his hurry to escape plunged into a snowdrift, where I could easily have despatched the animal with a pistol, but *Panchito* was in such a state of affright that nothing would induce him to stand still or approach the spot.

Over ridges and through mountain-gorges we passed into a small valley, where the pueblo of *Ohuaqui* afforded me shelter for the night, and a warm stable with plenty of corn for my animals, a luxury they had long been unaccustomed to.

I was here made welcome by the Indian family, who prepared my supper of *frijoles* and *atole*, (Atole is a food item much used on the Old Spanish Trail. Watch for its mention in other chapters.) the last *the* dish of New Mexico. It is made of the Indian meal, mixed with water into a thick gruel, and thus eaten—an insipid compound. Far more agreeable is the *pinole* of the *tierra afuera*, which is the meal of parched maize, mixed with sugar and spices, and of which a handful in a pint of water makes a most cooling and agreeable drink, and is the great standby of the *arrieros* and road-travellers in that starving country.

The *patrona* of the family seemed rather shy of me at first, until, in the course of conversation, she discovered that I was an Englishman. "*Gracias a Dios,*" she exclaimed, "a Christian will sleep with us to-night, and not an American!" (This is typical of the hostilities felt by many of the Mexican people even into this century, but it has lessoned in the last few years!)

I found over all New Mexico that the most bitter feeling and most determined hostility existed against the Americans, who certainly in *Santa Fé* and elsewhere have not been very anxious to conciliate the people, but by their bullying and overbearing demeanour towards them, have in a great measure been the cause of this hatred, which shortly after broke out in an organized rising of the northern part of the province, and occasioned great loss of life to both parties.

After supper the women of the family spread the floor with blankets, and every one, myself included, cigar in mouth, lay down—to the number of fifteen—in a space of less than that number of square feet; men, women, and children, all smoking and chattering. Just over my head were roosting several fowls; and one venerable cock every five minutes saluted us with a shrill crow, to the infinite satisfaction of the old Indian, who at every fresh one exclaimed, "*Ay, como canta mi gallo, tan claro!*"—how clear sings my cock, the fine fellow! "*Valgame Dios! que paxarito tan hermoso!*"—what a lovely little bird is this!

The next day, passing the miserable village of *La Cañada*, and the Indian pueblo of *San Juan*, (San Juan de los Caballeros as it was officially known, was the first Spanish capital in New Mexico. Juan de Oñate arrived here in July 1598. This is the point at which the three forks of the Spanish trail split.)[2] both situated in a wretched, sterile-looking country, we reached *El Embudo*—(This is a location also mentioned by Anza. See chapter three.) the funnel—where I put up in the house of an old Canadian trapper, who had taken to himself a Mexican wife, and was ending his days as a quiet ranchero. He appeared to have forgotten the plenty of the mountains, for his pretty daughter set before us for supper a plate containing six small pieces of fat pork, like dice, floating in a sea of grease, hot and red with *chile colorado*.

We crossed, next day, a range of mountains covered with pine and cedar: on the latter grew great quantities of mistletoe, and the contrast of its bright green and the sombre hue of the cedars was very striking. The snow was melting on the ascent, which was exposed to the sun, and made the road exceedingly slippery and tiring to the animals. On reaching the summit a fine prospect presented itself. The Rocky Mountains, stretching away on each side of me, here divided into several branches, whose isolated peaks stood out in bold relief against the clear, cold sky. Valleys and plains lay between them, through which the river wound its way in deep *cañons*. In the distance was the snowy summit of the *Sierra Nevada*, bright with the rays of the setting sun, and at my feet lay the smiling *vale* of Taos, with its numerous villages and the curiously constructed pueblos of the Indians. (It was this same Indian Pueblo at which Vargas had taken corn in 1694. See chapter one.) Snow-covered mountains surrounded it, whose ridges were flooded with light, while the valley was almost shrouded in gloom and darkness.

On descending I was obligated to dismount and lead my horse, whose feet, balled with snow, were continually slipping from under him. After sunset the cold was intense, and, wading through the snow, my mocassins became frozen, so that I was obliged to travel quickly to prevent my feet from being frost-bitten. It was quite dark when I reached the plain, and the night was so obscure that the track was perfectly hidden, and my only guide was the distant lights of the villages. Coming to a frozen brook, the mules refused to cross the ice, and I spent an hour in fruitless attempts to induce them. I could find nothing at hand with which to break the ice, and at length, half frozen, was obliged to turn back and retrace my steps to a *rancho*, which the Indian boy who was my guide said was about a mile distant. This I at length reached, though not before one of my feet was frost-bitten, and my hands so completely numbed by the excessive cold that I was unable to unpack the mules when I got in. To protect the poor animals from the cold, as there was no stable to place them in, I devoted the whole of my bedding to cover them, reserving to myself only a *serape*, which, however, by the side of a blazing wood fire, was sufficient to keep me warm. The good lady of the house sent me a huge bowl of *atole* as I was engaged in clothing the animals, which I offered to *Panchito* as soon as the messenger's back was turned, and he swallowed it, boiling hot as it was, with great gusto.

The next morning, with the assistance of some *rancheros*, I crossed the stream, and arrived at *Fernandez*, (San Fernandez de Taos was the earliest Spanish settlement in the Taos Valley. It is located about two miles southwest of the famous Taos Indian Pueblo.)[3] which is the most considerable village in the valley.

El Valle de Taos is situated about eighty miles to the northward of *Santa Fé*, on the eastern side of the *Del Norte*.

It contains several villages or *rancherias*, the largest of which are *Fernandez* and *El Rancho*. The population of the valley may be estimated at eight thousand, including the Pueblo Indians. The soil is exceedingly fertile, and produces excellent wheat and other grain. The climate being rigorous, and the summers short, fruit does not ripen to perfection, but vegetables of all kinds are good and abundant, onions in particular growing to great size and of excellent flavour. The climate is colder than at *Santa Fé*, the thermometer sometimes falling to zero in winter, and seldom rising above 75° in summer; the nights in summer being delightfully cool, but in winter piercingly cold. Although generally healthy, infectious disorders are sometimes prevalent and fatal; and periodical epidemics have on several occasions nearly decimated the inhabitants.

In all maps the valley of Taos is confounded with a city which under that name appears in them, but which does not exist, *Fernandez* being the chief town of the valley, and no such town as Taos to be found. The valley derives its name from the

Taoses, a tribe of Indians who once inhabited it, and the remains of which inhabit a pueblo under the mountain about seven miles from *Fernandez*. Humboldt mentions Taos as a city containing 8900 inhabitants. Its latitude is about 36° 30', longitude between 105° 30' and 106° west of Greenwich, but its exact position has never been accurately determined. The extent of the valley from *El Rancho* to *Arroyo Hondo* is seventeen miles, the breadth from the *Del Norte* to the mountains about the same.

Several distilleries are worked both at *Fernandez* and *El Rancho*, the latter better known to Americans as The Ranch. Most of them belong to Americans, who are generally trappers and hunters, who having married Taos women have settled here. The Taos whisky, a raw fiery spirit which they manufacture, has a ready market in the mountains amongst the trappers and hunters, and the Indian traders, who find the "fire-water" the most profitable article of trade with the aborigines, who exchange for it their buffalo robes and other peltries at a "tremendous sacrifice."

In *Fernandez* I was hospitably entertained in the house of an American named (Stephen) Lee, who had for many years traded and trapped in the mountains, but who now, having married a Mexican woman, had set up a distillery and was amassing a considerable fortune. He gave me a pressing invitation to stop the winter with him, which I was well inclined to accept, if I could have obtained good pasture for my animals; that, however, was not to be had, and I continued my journey. A few days after my departure, Lee's house was attacked by the Mexicans, at the time when they massacred Governor Bent in the same village, and himself killed, with every foreigner in the place excepting the brother of Lee, who was protected by the priest and saved by him from the savage fury of the mob.

Bent, as well as Lee, had resided many years in New Mexico, both having wives and children in the country, and were supposed to have been much esteemed by the people. The former was an old trader amongst the Indians, and the owner of Bent's Fort, or Fort William, a trading-post on the Arkansa, well known for its hospitality to travellers in the far west. From his knowledge of the country and the Mexican character, Mr. Bent had been appointed Governor of New Mexico by General Kearney, and it was during a temporary visit to his family at *Fernandez* that he was killed in their presence, and scalped and mutilated, by a mob of Pueblos and the people of Taos.

William Bent was one of those hardy sons of enterprise with whom America abounds, who, from love of dangerous adventure, forsake the quiet monotonous life of the civilized world for the excitement of a sojourn in the far west. For many years he traded with Indians on the Platte and Arkansa, winning golden opinions from the poor Indians for his honesty and fair dealing, and the greatest popularity from the hardy trappers and mountaineers for his firmness of character and personal bravery.

Notwithstanding advice I received not to attempt such a journey at this season, I determined to cross the mountains and winter on the other side, either at the head of the Arkansa or Platte, or in some of the mountain-valleys, which are the wintering places of many of the trappers and mountain-men. I therefore hired a half-breed Pueblo (Indian named Mattias) as a guide, who, by the by, was one of the most rascally-looking of rascally Mexicans, and on the first of January was once more on my way.

I left *Fernandez* late in the day, as I intended to proceed only twelve miles to *Arroyo Hondo*, and there remain for the night. After proceeding a mile or two we came to a stream about thirty feet in breadth and completely frozen. Here the mules came to a stop, and nothing would induce them to attempt to cross. Even the last resource, that of crossing myself on *Panchito*, and pretending to ride away with their favorite, entirely failed, although they ran up and down the bank bellowing with affright, smelling the ice, feeling it with their forefeet, and, throwing up their heads, would gallop to another point, and up and down, in great commotion. At length I had to take a pole, which was opportunely lying near, and break the ice away, having to remove the broken blocks entirely before they would attempt it. With all this, however, my old hunting-mule still refused; but, as I knew she would not be left behind, I proceeded on with the rest. At this she became frantic, galloped away from the river, returned, bellowed and cried, and at last, driven to desperation, she made a jump right into the air, but not near the broken place, and came down like a lump of lead on top of the ice, which, of course, smashed under her weight, and down she went into a deep hole, her head just appearing out of the water, which was "mush" with ice. In this "fix" she remained perfectly still, apparently conscious that her own exertion would be unavailing; and I therefore had to return, and, up to my middle in water, break her out of the ice, expecting every moment to see her drop, frozen to death. At last, and with great labor, I extricated her, when she at once ran up to the horse and hinnied her delight at the meeting.

By this time it was pitchy dark, and the cold had become intense; my moccasins and deerskin leggings were frozen hard and stiff, and my feet and legs in a fair way of becoming in the same state. There was no road or track, the snow everywhere covering the country, and my guide had evidently lost his way. However, I asked him in which direction he thought *Arroyo Hondo* to be, and pushed straight on for it, floundering through the snow, falling into holes and ravines, and at length was brought to a dead halt, my horse throwing himself on his haunches, and just saving his master and himself a fall down a precipice some 500 feet in depth, which formed one side of the *Arroyo Hondo*.

The lights of the *rancho* to which we were bound twinkled at the bottom, but to attempt to reach it, without knowing the road down the ravine, was like jumping from the top of the Monument. However, as I felt I was on the point of freezing to death, I became desperate and charged the precipice, intending to roll down with *Panchito*, if we could not do better; but the horse refused to move, and presently, starting to one side as I spurred him, fell headlong into a snow-drift some twenty feet in depth, where I lay under him; and, satisfied in my mind that I was "in extremis," wished myself farther from *Arroyo Hondo* and deplored my evil destiny. *Panchito*, however, managed to kick himself out; and I, half smothered and with one of my ribs disabled, soon followed his example, and again mounted. We presently came to a little adobe house, and a man, hearing our cries to each other in the dark, came out with a light. To my request for a night's lodging he replied, "*No se puede, no habia mas que un quartito*"—that there was no room, but one little chamber, but that at the *rancho* I would be well accommodated. With this hint I moved on, freezing in my saddle, and again attempted to descend, but the darkness was pitchy, and the road a wall. Whilst attempting the descent once more, a light appeared on the bank above us, and a female voice crying out, "*Vuelvase amigo, por Dios! que no se baja*"—return, friend, for God's sake! and don't attempt to go down. "*Que vengan, pobrecitos, para calentarse*"—come, poor fellows, and warm yourselves. "*Por hi se sube, por hi*"—this way this is the way up—she cried to us, holding up the light to direct our steps. "*Ay de mi, como suffren los pobres viageros!*"—alas, what poor travellers suffer!—she exclaimed, eying our frozen appearance, and clothes white with snow; and, still holding up the light, she led the way to her house, where now, lectured by his wife for his inhospitality, the man who had sent us away from his door bestirred himself to unpack the mules, which, with our numbed hands, it was impossible for us to do.

A little shed full of corn-shucks *(the leaf of the maize, of which animals are very fond)* provided a warm shelter for the shivering beasts; and having attended to their wants, and piled before them enough *hoja* for a regiment of cavalry, I entered the house, where half a dozen women were soon rubbing life into my hands and feet, which were badly frost-bitten, whilst others were busy preparing *atole* and *chile*, and making *tortillas* on the hearth.

A white stone marks this day of my journey, when, for the first time, I met with native hospitality on *Arroyo Hondo*. In this family, which consisted of about fifteen souls, six were on their beds, suffering from *sarampión*—the measles—which was at the time of my journey carrying off many victims in *Santa Fé* and Taos Valley. An old crone was busy decocting simples in a large *olla* over the fire. She asked me to taste it, giving it the name of *aceite de vivoras*—rattlesnake-oil; and as I expressed my disgust by word and deed at the intimation, which just saved my taking a gulp, the old lady was convulsed with laughter, giving me to understand that it was not really viper-oil, but was so called—*no mas*. This pot, when cooked, was set on one side, and all the patients, one after the other, crawled from their blankets and imbibed the decoction from a gourd. One of the sick was the mother of the family, who had run after us to bring us back when her husband had told her of our situation—one instance of the many which I have met of the kindness of heart of Mexican women.

The next morning we desended into the *Arroyo*, and even in daylight the track down was exceedingly dangerous, and to have attempted it in the dark would have been an act of no little temerity. On the other bank of the stream was situated a mill and distillery belonging to an American by the name of (Simeon) Turley, who had quite a thriving establishment. Sheep and goats, and innumerable hogs, ran about the corral; his barns were filled with grain of all kinds, his mill with flour, and his cellars with whisky "in galore." Everything about the place betokened prosperity. Rosy children, uniting the fair complexions of the Anglo-Saxon with the dark tint of the Mexican, gambolled before the door. The Mexicans and Indians at work in the yard were stout, well-fed fellows, looking happy and contented; as well they might, for no one in the country paid so well, and fed so well, as Turley, who bore the reputation, far and near, of being as generous and kind-hearted as he was reported to be rich. In times of scarcity no Mexican ever besought his assistance and went away empty-handed. His granaries were always open to the hungry, and his purse to the poor.

Three days after I was there they attacked his house, burned his mill, destroyed his grain and his live stock, and inhumanly butchered himself and the foreigners with him, after a gallant defence of twenty-four hours—nine men against five hundred.

I here laid in a small supply of provisions, flour and dried buffalo-meat, and got besides a good breakfast—rather a memorable occurrence. Just as I arrived, a party of Mormons, who had left Colonel Cooke's command on their way to California, and were now about to cross the mountains to join a large body of their people who were wintering on the Arkansa, intending to proceed to California in the ensuing spring, were on the point of starting. There were some twelve or fifteen of them, with four or five pack-mules carrying their provisions, themselves on foot. They started several hours before me; but I overtook them before they had crossed the mountain, straggling along, some seated on the top of the mules' packs, some sitting down every few hundred yards, and all looking tired and miserable.

Arroyo Hondo runs along the base of a ridge of mountain of moderate elevation, which divides the valley of Taos from that of *Rio Colorado*, or Red River, both running into the Del Norte. The trail from one to the other runs through and over the mountain, a distance of about twelve miles. It is covered with pine and cedar and a species of dwarf oak; and numerous small streamlets run through the cañons and gorges. Near these grows plentifully a shrub which produces a fruit called by

124

the mountaineers service-berry, of a dark blue, the size of a small grape, and of very pleasant flavour.

My animals, unused to mountain travelling, proceeded very slowly. Every little stream of frozen water was the cause of delay. The mules, on reaching the brink, always held a council of war, smelt and tried it with their forefeet, and bellowed forth their dislike of the slippery bridge. *Coronela*, my hunting-mule, since her mishap at *Fernandez*, was always the first to cross, but I had first to strew the ice with branches, or throw a blanket over it, before I could induce them to pass; and at last, tired of the delays thus occasioned, I passed with the horse, and left the mules to use their own discretion, although not unfrequently half an hour or more would elapse before they overtook me.

All this day I marched on foot through the snow, as *Panchito* made sad work of ascending and decsending the mountain, and it was several hours after sunset when I arrived at *Rio Colorado*, with one of my feet badly frozen. In the settlement, which boasted about twenty houses, on inquiry as to where I could procure a corral and *hoja* (fodder) for my animals, I was directed to the house of a French Cana-dian—an old trapper named Laforey—one of the many who are found in these re-mote settlements, with Mexican wives, passing the close of their adventurous lives in what to them is a state of ease and plenty; that is, they grow sufficient maize to support them, their faithful and well-tried rifles furnishing them with meat in abun-dance, to be had in all the mountains for the labour of hunting.

Rio Colorado (Red River) is the last and most northern settlement of Mexico. It contains perhaps fifteen families, or a population of fifty souls, including one or two Yuta Indians, by sufferance of whom the New Mexicans have settled this valley, thus ensuring to the politic savages a supply of corn or cattle without the necessity of undertaking a raid on Taos or *Santa Fé* whenever they require a remount. This was the reason given me by a Yuta for allowing the encroachment on their territory.

I was obliged to remain here two days, for my foot was so badly frozen that I was quite unable to put it to the ground. In this place I found that the Americans were in bad odour; and as I was equipped as a mountaineer, I came in for a tolerable share of abuse whenever I limped through the village or passed on the way to the shed where my animals were corraled. As my lameness prevented me from pursuing my tormentors, they became more and more daring, until at last, words not being heavy enough, pieces of adobe rattled at my ears. This, however, was a joke rather too practical to be pleasant; so the next time I limped to the stable, I carried my rifle on my shoulder, which was a hint never to be mistaken by Mexican, and hereafter I passed with impunity. However, I was obliged to watch my animals day and night, for, as soon as I fed them, either the corn was bodily stolen, or a herd of hogs was driven in to feed at my expense. The latter aggression I put a stop to by administer-

125

ing to one persevering porker a pill from my rifle, and promised the threatening crowd that I would have as little compunction in letting the same amount of daylight into them if I caught them thieving the provender; and they seemed to think me in earnest, for I missed no more corn or shucks. I saw plainly enough, however, that my remaining here, with such a perfectly lawless and ruffianly crew, was likely to lead me into some trouble if, indeed, my life was not in absolute danger. Therefore I only waited until my foot was sufficiently recovered to enable me to resume my journey across the mountains.

On the third day, the inflammation in my frost-bitten foot having in some measure subsided, I again packed my mules, and turned my back on Mexico and the Mexicans. Laforey escorted me out of the settlement to point out the trail *(for roads now had long ceased)*, he bid me good by, and recommended me to mind my hair—in other words, look out for my scalp.

I had now turned my back on the last settlement, and felt a thrill of pleasure as I looked at the wild expanse of snow which lay before me, and the towering mountains which frowned on all sides.

Our course on leaving Red River was due north, my object being to strike the Arkansa near its head-waters on the other side of the Rocky Mountains, and follow as near as possible the Yuta trail, which these Indians use in passing from the *Del Norte* to the *Bayou Salado*, on their annual buffalo-hunts to that elevated valley.

Skirting a low range of mountains, the trail passes a valley upwards of fifty miles in length, intersected by numerous streams *(called creeks by the mountain-men)*, which rise in the neighboring highlands, and fall into the *Del Norte*, near its upper waters. Our first day's journey, of about twenty-five miles, led through the uplands at the southern extremity of the valley. (This is the south end of the San Luis Valley.) These are covered with pine and cedar, and the more open plains with bushes of wild sage, which is the characteristic plant in all the elevated plains of the Rocky Mountains. On emerging from the uplands, we entered a level prairie, covered with innumerable herds of antelope. These graceful animals, in bands containing several thousands, trotted up to us, and, with pointed ears and their beautiful eyes staring with eager curiosity, accompanied us for miles, running parallel to our trail within fifty or sixty yards.

The cold in these regions is more intense than I ever remembered to have experienced, not excepting even in Lower Canada; and when a northerly wind sweeps over the bleak and barren plains, charged as it is with its icy reinforcements from the snow-clad mountains, it assails the unfortunate traveller, exposed to all its violence, with blood-freezing blasts, piercing to his very heart and bones.

Such was the state of congelation I was in on this day that even the shot-tempting antelope bounded past unscathed. My hands, with fingers of stone, refused even to hold the reins of my horse, who travelled as he pleased, sometimes slueing round his stern to the wind, which was "dead ahead." Mattias, the half-breed who was my guide, enveloped from head to foot in blanket, occasionally cast a longing glance from out its folds at the provoking venison as it galloped past, muttering at intervals, "*Jesus, Jesus, que carne*"—what meat we're losing! At length, as a band of some three thousand almost ran over us, human nature, although at freezing-point, could no longer stand it. I jumped off *Panchito*, and, kneeling down, sent a ball from my rifle right into the "thick" of the band. At the report two antelope sprang into the air, their forms being distinct against the horizon above the backs of the rest, and when the herd had passed, they were lying kicking in the dust, one shot in the neck, through which the ball had passed into the body of another. We packed a mule with the choice pieces of the meat, which was a great addition to our slender stock of dried provisions. As I was "butchering" the antelope, half a dozen wolves hung around the spot, attracted by the smell of blood; they were so tame, and hungry at the same time, that I thought they would actually have torn the meat from under my knife. Two of them loped round and round, gradually decreasing their distance, occasionally squatting on their haunches, and licking their impatient lips, in anxious expectation of a coming feast. I threw a large piece of meat toward them, when the whole gang jumped upon it, fighting and growling, and tearing each other in furious melée. I am sure I might have approached near enough to have seized one by the tail, so entirely regardless of my vicinity did they appear. They were doubtless rendered more ravenous than usual by the uncommon severity of the weather, and, from the fact of the antelope congregating in large bands, were unable to prey upon these animals, which are their favorite food. Although rarely attacking a man, yet in such seasons as the present I have no doubt that they would not hesitate to charge upon a solitary traveller in the night, particularly as in winter they congregate in troops of from ten to fifty. They are so abundant in the mountains, that the hunter takes no notice of them, and seldom throws away upon the skulking beasts a charge of powder and lead.

This night we camped on Rib Creek, the *Costilla* of the New-Mexican hunters, where there was no grass for our poor animals, and the creek was frozen to such a depth, that, after the greatest exertions in breaking a hole through the ice, which was nearly a foot thick, they were unable to reach the water. It is a singular fact that during intence cold horses and mules suffer more from want of water than in the hottest weather, and often perish in the mountains when unable to procure it for two or three days in the frozen creeks. Although they made every attempt to drink, the mules actually kneeling in their endeavors to reach the water, I was obliged to give it them, one after the other, from a small tin cup which held half a pint, and from which the thirsty animals greedily drank. This tedious process occupied me more than an hour, after which there was another hour's work in hunting for wood, and packing it on our backs into camp. Before we had a fire going it was late in the night, and almost midnight before we had found a little grass and picketed the animals; all of which duties at last being effected, we cooked our collops of antelope-meat, smoked a pipe, and rolled ourselves in our blankets before the fire. All night long the camp was surrounded by wolves, which approached within a few feet of the fire, and their eyes shone like coals as they hovered in the bushes, attracted by the savory smell of the roasting venison.

The next day we struck *La Culebra*, (The Culebra was mentioned by many of the people in these diaries: Vargas, Anza, Pike, Fowler, & Richerdson.) or Snake Creek, where we saw that the party of Mormons had encamped, and apparently halted a day, for more than ordinary pains had been taken to make their camp comfortable, several piles of twigs, of the sage-bush and rushes, remained, of which they had made beds. However, we were obliged to go farther down the creek, as there was no firewood near the point where the trail crosses it, and there we found a sheltered place with tolerable grass, near an air-hole in the ice where the animals could drink. I remarked that in the vicinity of the Mormon camp no watering-place had been made for their animals, and, as we had seen no holes broken in the ice of the creeks we had passed, I concluded that these people had allowed their animals to shift for themselves, the consequences of which negligence were soon apparent in our farther advance.

The cold was so intence that I blanketed all my animals, and even then expected that some of the mules would have perished; for it snowed heavily during the night, and the storm ended in a watery sleet, which froze as soon as it fell, and in the morning the animals were covered with a sheet of ice. We ourselves suffered extremely, turning constantly, and rolling almost into the embers of the scanty fire; and towards daybreak I really thought I should have frozen bodily. My bedding consisted of two blankets—one of them a very thin one, which was all I had between my body and the snow; and the other, first soaked with the sleet and afterward frozen stiff and hard, was more like a board than a blanket, and was in that state no protection against the cold. It is well known that the coldest period of the twenty-four hours is that immediately preceding the dawn of day. At this time one is generally awakened by the sensation of death-like chill, which penetrates into the very bones; and as the fire is by this time usually extinguished, or merely smoldering in the ashes, the duty of replenishing is a very trying process. To creep out of the blanket and face the cutting blast requires no little resolution; and, if there be more than one person in the camp, the horrible moment is put off by the first roused, in hopes that someone else will awaken and perform the duty. However, should the coughs and hems succeed in rousing all, it is ten to one but that all, with a blank look at the cheerless prospect, cover their heads with the blanket, and with a groan, cuddling into a ball, resettle themselves to sleep, leaving the most chilly victim to perform the office.

The half-frozen animals, standing over their picket-pins and collapsed with cold, seem almost drawn within themselves, and occasionally approach the fire as close as their lariats will allow, bending down their noses to the feeble warmth, the breath in steaming volumes of cloud issuing from their nostrils, whilst their bodies are thickly clad with a coat of frozen snow or sleet.

Our next camp was on *La Trinchera*, or Bowl Creek. (La Trinchera, or Bowl Creek was a popular campsite on the Taos Trail/Trappers Road. Between this and Ruxton's last camp on the Rio Culebra, the Old Spanish Trail and the Taos Trail split. The Taos Trail crossed the Sangre de Cristo Pass, while the Old Spanish Trail circled to the west of Sierra Blanca.) The country was barren and desolate, covered with sage, and with here and there a prairie with tolerable pasture. Antelope were abundant, and deer and turkeys were to be seen on the creeks. The trail passed, to the westward, a lofty peak resembling in outline that one known as James' or Pike's Peak, which is some 250 miles to the north. The former is not laid down in any of the maps, although it is a well-known landmark to the Indians.

The creeks are timbered with cotton-woods, quaking-asp, dwarf-oak, cedar, and wild cherry, all of small growth and stunted, while the uplands are covered with a dwarfish growth of pines. From Rio Colorado we had been constantly followed by a large gray wolf. Every evening, as soon as we got into camp, he made his appearance, squatting quietly down at little distance, and after we had turned in for the night helping himself to anything lying about. Our first acquaintance commenced on the prairie where I had killed the two antelope, and the excellent dinner he then made, on the remains of the two carcasses, had evidently attached him to our society. In the morning, as soon as we left the camp, he took possession, and quickly ate up the remnants of our supper and some little extras I always took care to leave for him. Shortly after he would trot after us, and, if we halted for a short time to adjust the mule-packs or water the animals, he sat down quietly until we resumed our march. But when I killed an antelope, and was in the act of butchering it, he gravely looked on, or loped round and round, licking his jaws, and in a state of evident self-gratulation. I had him twenty times a-day within reach of my rifle, but he became such an old friend that I never dreamed of molesting him.

Our day's travel was usually from twenty to thirty miles, for the days were very short, and we were obliged to be in camp an hour before sunset, in order to procure wood, and water the animals before dark. Before arriving at the creek where we purposed to camp, I rode ahead, and selected a spot where was good grass and convenient water. We then unpacked the mules and horses, and immediately watered them, after which we allowed them to feed at large until dark. In the meantime we hunted for fire-wood, having sometimes to go half a mile from camp, packing it on our shoulders to the spot we intended for our fire, the mule-packs and saddles, &c., being placed to windward of it as a protection from the cold blasts. We then cooked supper, and at dark picketed the animals round the camp, their lariats *(or skin-ropes)* being attached to pegs driven in the ground. After a smoke, we spread our blankets before the fire and turned in, rising once or twice in the night to see that all was safe, and remove the animals to fresh grass when they had cleared the circle round their pickets. Guard or watch we kept none, for after a long day's travel it was too much for two of us to take alternate sentry, thus having but half the night for sleep.

We were now approaching a part of the journey much dreaded by the Indians and New-Mexican buffalo-hunters, and which is quite another "*Jornada del Muerto,*" (journey of the dead) or dead man's journey. A creek called *Sangre* (de) *Cristo*—blood of Crist—winds through a deep cañon, which opens out at one point into a small circular basin called *El Vallecito*—the little valley.

El Vallecito, or little valley, is located on the west side of north La Veta Pass. Evidence of the old wagon road can be seen crossing this little valley from northeast to southwest.

It is quite embosomed in the mountains; and down their rugged sides, and through the deep gorges, the wind rushes with tremendous fury, filling the valley with drifted snow, and depositing it in the numerous hollows with which it is intersected. This renders the passage of the *Vallecito* exceedingly difficult and dangerous, as animals are frequently buried in the snow, which is sometimes fifteen or twenty feet deep in the hollows, and four or five on the level.

This valley is also called by the mountaineers the "Wind-trap;" a very appropriate name, as the wind seems to be caught and pent up here the year round, and, mad with the confinement, blows round and round, seeking for an escape.

Wishing to have my animals fresh for the passage of this dreaded spot, I this day made a short journey of fifteen miles, and camped in the *cañon* about three miles from the mouth of the Wind-trap. (The mouth of the Wind-trap would be at the location where the road forks at the southwest end of El Vallecito.) The *cañon* was so precipitous, that the only place I could find for our camp was on the side of the mountain, where was tolerably good gramma-grass, but a wretched place for ourselves; and we had to burrow out a level spot in the snow before we could place the packs in a position where they would not roll down the hill. The cedars were few and far between, and the snow covered everything in the shape of wood; and as in our last camp my tomahawk had been lost in the snow, I was unable to procure a log, and was fain to set fire to a cedar near which we had laid our packs. The flame, licking the stringy and dry bark, quickly ran up the tree, blazed along the branches in a roar of fire, illuminating the rugged mountain, and throwing its light upon the thread of timber skirting the creek which wound along the bottom far beneath.

All night long the wind roared through the *cañon*, and at times swept the blankets from our chilled bodies with the force of a giant. The mules and horses after dark refused to feed, and, as there was no spot near where we could picket them, the poor beasts sought shelter from the cruel blasts in the belt of dwarf oak which fringed the creek.

We passed a miserable night, perched upon the mountain-side in our lonely camp, and without a fire, for the tree was soon consumed. Our old friend the wolf, however, was still a companion, and sat all night within sight of the fire, howling piteously from cold and hunger. The next morning I allowed the animals a couple of hours after sunrise to feed and fill themselves; and then, descending from our camp, we entered at once the pass into the dreaded Vallecito. A few hundred yards from the entrance lay a frozen mule, half-buried in the snow; and a little farther on another, close to the creek where the Mormons had evidently encamped not two days before.

The *Vallecito* was covered with snow to the depth of three feet, to all appearance perfectly level, but in fact full of hollows, with fifteen or twenty feet of snow in them. With the greatest difficulty and labour we succeeded in crossing, having to dismount and beat a path through the drifts with our bodies. The pack-mules were continually falling, and were always obliged to be unpacked before they could rise. As this happened every score yards, more than half the day was consumed in traversing the valley, which cannot exceed four miles in length.

The mountain rises directly from the north end of the *Vallecito*, and is the dividing ridge between the waters of the *Del Norte* and the Arkansa or *Rio Napestle* of the Mexicans. The ascent to the summit, from the western side, is short, but very steep; and the snow was of such a depth that the mules could hardly make their way to the top. Leading my horse by the bridle, I led the way, and at length, numbed with cold, I reached the summit, where is a level plateau of about a hundred square yards. Attaining this, and exposed to the full sweep of the wind, a blast struck me, carrying with it a perfect avalanche of snow and sleet, full in my front, and knocked me as clean off my legs as I could have been floored by a twenty-four pound shot.

The view from this point was wild and dismal in the extreme. Looking back, the whole country was covered with a thick carpet of snow, but eastward it was seen in patches only here and there. Before me lay the main chain of the Rocky Mountains, Pike's Peak lifting its snowy head far above the rest; and to the southeast the Spanish Peaks (*Cumbres Españolas*) towered like twin giants over the plains. Beneath the mountain on which I stood was a narrow valley, through which ran a streamlet bordered with dwarf oak and pine, and looking like a thread of silver as it wound through the plain. Rugged peaks and ridges, snow-clad and covered with pine, and deep gorges filled with broken rocks, everywhere met the eye. To the eastward the mountains gradually smoothed away into detached spurs and broken ground, until they met the vast prairies, which stretched far as the eye could reach, and hundreds of miles beyond—a sea of seeming barrenness, vast and dismal. A hurricane of wind was blowing at the time, and clouds of dust swept along the sandy prairies, like the smoke of a million bonfires. On the mountain-top it roared and raved through the pines, filling the air with snow and broken branches, and piling it in huge drifts against the trees. The perfect solitude of this vast wildness was almost appalling. From my position on the summit of the dividing ridge I had a bird's-eye view, as it were, over the rugged and chaotic masses of the stupendous chain of the Rocky Mountains, and the vast deserts which stretched away from their eastern bases; while, on all sides of me, broken ridges, and chasms and ravines, with masses of piled-up rocks and uprooted trees, with clouds of drifting snow flying through the air, and the hurricane's roar battling through the forest at my feet, added to the wildness of the scene, which was unrelieved by the slightest vestige of animal or human life. Not a sound, either of bird or beast, was heard—indeed, the hoarse and stunning rattle of the wind would have drowned them, so loud it roared and raved through the trees.

The animals strove in vain to face the storm, and, turning their sterns to the wind, shrank into themselves, trembling with cold. *Panchito*, whom I was leading by the bridle, followed me to the edge of the plateau, but drew back, trembling, from the dismal scene which lay stretched below. With a neigh of fear he laid his cold nose against my cheek, seeming to say, "Come back, master: what can take you to such a wretched place as that, where not even a blade of grass meets the eye?"

The descent on the eastern side is steep and sudden, and through a thick forest of pines, to the valley beneath. Trail there was none to direct us, and my half-breed knew nothing of the road, having passed but once before, and many years ago, but said it went somewhere down the pines. The evening was fast closing round us, and to remain where we were was certain death to our animals, if not to ourselves: I therefore determined to push for the valley, and accordingly struck at once down the pines. (The trail led down South Oak Creek to the northeast of Sangre de Cristo Pass.)

Once amongst the trees there was nothing to do but reach the bottom as fast as possible, as it was nearly dark, and nothing was to be seen at the distance of a dozen yards, so dence was the forest. Before we had proceeded as many paces from the edge of the plateau, and almost before I knew where I was, horses, mules, &c., were rolling down the mountain all together, and were at last brought up in a snow-drift some twelve feet deep. There they all lay in a heap, the half-breed under one of the pack-mules, and his swarthy face just peering out of the snow. Before a mule would stir, every pack had to be removed; and this, with a temperature some ten degrees below zero, was trying to the fingers, as may be imagined. As it was impossible to reach the bottom from this point, we struggled once more to the top through six feet of snow and an almost perpendicular ascent. I had to beat a road for the animals, by throwing myself bodily on the snow, and pounding it down with all my weight. We were nearly frozen by this time, and my hands were perfectly useless— so much so that, when a large bird of the grouse species flew up into a pine above my head, I was unable to cock my rifle to shoot at it. The mules were plunging into the snow at every step, and their packs were hanging under their bellies, but to attempt to adjust them was out of the question. It was nearly dark too, which made our situation anything but pleasant, and the mules were quite exhausted.

At last, however, we reached the top and struck down the mountain at another point, but it was with the greatest toil and difficulty that we reached the bottom long after dark, and camped shortly after near the creek which wound through the valley, or rather in its very bed. One of the mules had slipped its pack completely under the belly, and, the girth pinching her, she started off just before reaching the creek at full gallop, kicking everything the pack contained to the four winds of heaven. This pack happened to contain all the provisions, and, as the search for them in the dark would have been useless, we this night had no supper. To shelter ourselves from the wind we camped in the bed of the creek, which was without water, but the wind howled down it as if it were a funnel, scattering our fire in every direction as soon as it was lighted, and tearing the blankets from our very bodies. The animals never moved from the spot where they had been unpacked; even if there had been grass, they were too exhausted to feed, but stood shivering in the wind, collapsed with cold, and almost dead. Such a night I never passed, and hope never to pass again. The hurricane never lulled for a single instant; all our afforts to build a fire were unavailing; and it was with no small delight that I hailed the break of day, when we immediately packed the mules and started on our journey.

The trail now led along the creek and through small broken prairies, with bluffs exhibiting a very curious formation of shale and sandstone. At one point the *cañon* opens out into a pretty open glade or park, in the middle of which is a large rock resembling a ruined castle: (Gwinn Harris Heap gives this same description as the location of a camp site on South Oak Creek!) the little prairie is covered with fine grass, and a large herd of black-tailed deer were feeding in it. A little farther on we descried the timber on the *Huerfano* or Orphan Creek, so called from a remark-

Huerfano Butte

able isolated rock of sandstone which stands in a small prairie on its left bank, and is a well-known landmark to the Indians. We camped on the *Huerfano* under some high cotton-woods, the wind blowing with unabated violence. The next morning all the animals were missing, and, following their trail, we found them on the other side of the creek, five or six miles from the camp, in a little prairie full of buffalo-grass. As it was late in the day when we returned to camp, we did not leave till next morning, when we crossed on to the *Cuernaverde* or Greenhorn Creek. (Greenhorn Creek was named after the Jupe Comanche Chief, Cuerno Verde, who was killed by Juan Bautista de Anza's troops just east of Rye, Colorado in 1779.)

On a bluff overlooking the stream I had the satisfaction of seeing two or three Indian lodges and one adobe hovel of a more aspiring order. As we crossed the creek a mountaineer on an active horse galloped up to us, his rifle over the horn of the saddle, and clad in hunting-shirt and pantaloons of deer-skin, with long fringes hanging down the arms and legs. As this was the first soul we had seen since leaving Red River, we were as delighted to meet a white man *(and him an American)* as he was to learn the news from the Mexican settlements. We found here two or three hunters, French Canadians, with their Assinaboin and Sioux squaws, who have made the Greenhorn their head-quarters; and game being abundant and the rich soil of the valley affording them a sufficiency of Indian corn, they lead a tolerably easy life, and certainly a lazy one, with no cares whatever to annoy them. This valley will, I have no doubt, become one day a thriving settlement, the soil being exceedingly rich and admirably adapted to the growth of all kinds of grain. The prairies afford abundant pasture of excellent quality, and stock might be raised upon them in any numbers.

The depreciation in the value of beaver-skins has thrown the great body of trappers out of employment, and there is a general tendency amongst the mountain-men to settle in the fruitful valleys of the Rocky Mountains. Already the plough has turned up the soil within sight of Pike's Peak, and a hardy pioneer, an Englishman, has led the way to the Great Salt Lake, where a settlement of mountaineers has even now been formed, three thousand miles from the frontier of the United States.

From the Greenhorn an easy day's travel brought us to the banks of the *San Carlos*, (The Taos Trail/Trappers Road followed the north side of San Carlos or Saint Charles River.) which, receiving the former creek, falls into the Arkansa about two hundred and fifty miles from its source. The *San Carlos* is well timbered with cottenwood, cherry, quaking-asp, box, alder, and many varieties of shrubs, and many spots in the valley are admirably adapted for cultivation, with a rich loamy soil, and so situated as to be irrigated with great facility from the creek. Irrigation is indispensable over the whole of this region, rain seldom falling in the spring and summer, which is one of the greatest drawbacks to the settlement of this country, the labour of irrigation being very great. The *San Carlos* heads in a lofty range of mountains about forty miles from its junction with the Arkansa. Near its upper waters is a circular valley enclosed by rugged highlands, through which the stream forces its way in a *cañon* whose precipitous sides overhang it to the height of three hundred feet. The face of the rock *(of a dark limestone)* is in many places perfectly vertical, and rises from the water's edge to a great elevation, *piñons* and small cedars growing out of crevices in the sides.

After leaving this creek we passed a barren rolling prairie with scanty herbage and covered with the *palmilla* or soap plant. A few antelope were the only tenants, and these so shy that I was unable to approach them. Fourteen miles from the *San Carlos* we struck the Arkansa (The wagon tracks left by Manuel Segura continued along the north side of the San Carlos to the confluence of the San Carlos and the Arkansas River. This was the location where he built San Carlos de los Jupes.)[4] at the little Indian trading fort of "Pueblo," (now Pueblo, Colorado) which is situated on the left bank, a few hundred yards above the mouth of the Fontaine-qui-bouille, or Boiling Spring River, so called from two springs of mineral water near its head-waters under Pike's Peak, about sixty miles from its mouth. Here I was hospitably entertained in the lodge of one John Hawkins, an ex-trapper and well-known mountaineer. I turned my animals loose, and allowed them to seek for themselves the best pastures, as in the vicinity of the fort the prairies were perfectly bare of grass, and it was only near the mountain that any of a good quality was to be found.

The Arkansa is here a clear, rapid river about a hundred yards in width. The bottom, which is enclosed on each side by high bluffs, is about a quarter of a mile across, and timbered with a heavy growth of cotton-wood, some of the trees being of great size. On each side vast rolling prairies stretch away for hundred of miles, gradually ascending on the side towards the mountains, and the highlands are there sparsely covered with piñon and cedar. The high banks through which the river occasionally passes are of shale and sandstone, and rise precipitously from the water. Ascending the river the country is wild and broken until it enters the mountains, when the scenery is grand and imposing; but the prairies around it are arid and sterile, producing but little vegetation, and the grass, though of good quality, is thin and scarce. The Pueblo is a small square fort of adobe with circular bastions at the corners, no part of the walls being more than eight feet high, and round the inside of the yard or corral are built some half-dozen little rooms inhabited by as many Indian traders, *coureurs des bois*, and mountain-men. (One needs to visit El Pueblo Museum. A good job of investigating the remains of this fort has been accomplished.) They live entirely upon game, and the greater part of the year without even bread, since but little maize is cultivated. As soon as their supply of meat is exhausted they start to the mountains with two or three pack-animals, and bring them back in two or three days loaded with buffalo or venison. In the immediate vicinity of the fort game is very scarce, and the buffalo have within a few years deserted the neighboring prairies, but they are always found in the mountain-valleys, particularly in one called *Bayou Salado*, (Bayou Salado is the name used by the early-day trappers and Mountain Men for present-day South Park.) which abounds in every species of game, including elk, bear, deer, bighorn or Rocky Mountain sheep, buffalo, antelope, &c.

Hunting in the mountains round the head of Fontaine-qui-bouille and *Bayou Salado*, I remained for the rest of the winter, which was unusually sever—so much so, that the hunters were not infrequently afraid to venture with their animals into the mountains.

7

1848/GEORGE D. BREWERTON

George Douglas Brewerton was born in Newport, Rhode Island, on June 3, 1827. He was the eldest son of General Henry and Caroline Louise *Knight* Brewerton. George grew up along the Atlantic seaboard and received much of his education while living at West Point. This training would prove to be valuable in the keeping of records and drawing pictures on his trip along the Old Spanish Trail to Santa Fe and then on the Santa Fe Trail from Santa Fe to Missouri.

When the Mexican War broke out, George joined the Army. On August 15, 1846, at Fort Columbus, Governor's Island, New York Harbor he was mustered into service as a second lieutenant under Captain John E. Brackett's Company C, First New York Infantry Volunteers. The regiment, under command of Colonel Stevenson, sailed for California on September 26, 1846. They arrived in San Francisco, California six months later.

After serving with several different companies of volunteers, George transferred to the regular army where he was ordered to cross the plains and join his new regiment at its station in Mississippi. Brewerton traveled south from San Francisco partway by ship, but at the town of San Pedro, he and Dr. Richard S. Den were given horses by an American rancher. They rode the remaining sixteen miles to Los Angeles. The rancher stated to Brewerton that he was "not concerned with the return of his horses but take care of my saddles." Along the road to Los Angeles Brewerton describes several ranch houses, located among stunted trees and rolling prairies, with cattle lying lazily in the shade, and children playing their favorite game of lassoing each other.

Brewerton also gave a good description of the Pueblo of Los Angeles. He says that "the white-walled city contained several hundred souls, a church, a padre, and three or four American shops; the streets were narrow, and the houses built of adobe, the roofs flat and covered with a composition of gravel mixed with a sort of mineral pitch, which the inhabitants say they find upon the sea-shore." The adobe is a brick, made of clay, and baked in the sun. Walls built of this material, from the great thickness necessary to secure strength, are warm in winter and cool in summer.

A very good description of Kit Carson was given by Brewerton, whom he apparently felt had saved his life on a number of occasions. He imagined Kit to be over six-feet tall, a modern Hercules in build with an enormous beard and a voice like the roar of a lion. The real Kit he describes as a plain, simple, unostentatious man; below medium height, with brown, curly hair, little or no beard, and a voice as soft and gentle as a *woman's*. "In fact, the hero of a hundred desperate encounters, whose life had been spent mostly in the wilderness, where the white man is almost unknown, was one of Dame Nature's gentlemen—a sort of article which she gets up occasionally, but nowhere in better style than among the backwoods of America."

Brewerton provided himself with a tin plate, a tin cup, which would hold a quart of coffee, a common fork, a large bowie-knife, and a Whitney rifle. A water container made of porous leather which held half a gallon, and suffered just enough liquid to soak through as was required to keep the outside constantly wet, so that whenever he desired cool water he had only to hang the flask in a free current of air. To make up his bedroll he purchased two Mexican blankets serving him at once for mattress, sheet, and pillowcase, while his saddle gave a rude, but never-failing pillow. The saddles were of the true Mexican pattern, wooden trees covered with leathers called macheers. Their bridles were formed of twisted hide or horse hair, were ornamented with pieces of copper, and furnished with strong Spanish bits. Their spurs were sharp and heavy enough to have driven an elephant, not to speak of a California mule, which he took to be the more unmanagable beast of the two. He had also purchased seven head of horses and mules.

George D. Brewerton left Los Angeles in early May, 1848, traveling with Kit Carson who was carrying official dispatches to Washington. Kit chose to travel the Spanish Trail on this trip to the east, following nearly the same route that he and Fremont had used in 1844. This was also the same route that had been traveled by William Pope and Isaac Slover in 1837 who were accompanied by a group of trappers in wagons as they moved their families from Santa Fe, New Mexico to Los Angeles. According to Antoine Leroux, they took the route north from Taos crossing the San Luis Valley, Cochetopa Pass and followed the Gunnison river to the Colorado River.[1]

Brewerton's first days' march was full of problems. Many of the mules had not been saddled for several months and got up all sorts of antics and were as vicious and obstinate as possible.

After traveling for eight days in the desert, Brewerton and Carson's party overtook a group of two to three hundred Mexican traders. They were driving a herd of nearly one thousand head of horses, which ate up or destroyed the grass and consumed the water at the camp sites. The Mexicans were dressed in every variety of costume, from the embroidered jacket of the wealthy Californian, with its silver bell-shaped buttons, to the scanty habiliments of the skin-clad Indians. The horseherd contained not only horses and mules, but a few stray burros destined to pack firewood across the rugged hills of New Mexico.

The party mentioned seeing the bones of former groups who had traveled the trail and related the stories told about these travelers. Brewerton mentions also that they were continually seeing signal smoke from the Indians along the route. A group of Indians visited their camp begging for food. They were frequently meeting different groups of travelers.

Although Brewerton lost all of his drawings and field notes in the Colorado River as they were attempting to cross, he was able to reconstruct his notes from memory. This was no doubt done at a much later time as there was probably no paper or pen available before reaching Taos. However, Brewerton was turned around when it came to the Green and Colorado Rivers. One would think that possibly he was wrong, that it was the Green River where they had all of the trouble, but Kit Carson [2] also confirmed that it was the Colorado where they had lost equipment. From the description that is given by Heap in chapter eight, it is no wonder that the Colorado River proved to be such a problem for early travelers to cross. Also, the Green River, which is a tributary of the Colorado, is smaller than the Colorado.

The route that the party traveled is not entirely clear from the records left by Brewerton. It is most likely, however, that the party traveled the North Branch of the Old Spanish Trail which parallels present day Interstate Highway 70 from Green River, Utah to Grand Junction, Colorado. Then they traveled a route which parallels US Highway 50 from Grand Junction to east of Gunnison, Colorado, near the intersection of US 50 and State Road 114. From there they followed Cochetopa Creek to the top of Cochetopa Pass, then down Saguache Creek. On many of the old maps, including the Alexander de Humboldt map of 1804 of New Spain, the headwaters of the Rio Grande and the Saguache Creek of present-day maps are one and the same. They crossed the San Luis Valley to just west of the Sangre de Cristo Mountains near Rito Alto Creek. From here they followed the trail (this route was a well-worn trail documented by Wheeler in his 1873 Survey of the San Luis Valley) south to Taos which was the home of Kit Carson. On many of the older maps of the San Luis Valley, the area to the east of Saguache, Colorado (described by Anza in chapter three as the Ciénega) was part of the San Luis Lakes. Some of these old maps show the San Luis Lakes to extend from present-day Saguache, Colorado to the Great Sand Dunes. This is probably the area where the mosquitos were so bad due to the marshy nature of the area.

140

June 3, 1848

I remember celebrating my birthday, which comes in June *(the precise date I will leave the reader to guess, if he be a Yankee)*, by standing upon the banks of Grand (Colorado) River, (Brewerton was standing on the bank of the Grand or Colorado River. It was in crossing this river that they lost one raft of supplies and equipment.)[3] and looking with a most rueful countenance and many secret forebodings upon the turbid current of the swollen stream. And well I might. I have said it was in June; and one might suppose that a cold-bath in early summer was no great hardship; but in this case, I found that the association of the month with summer ended with its name; for the strong wind felt more like a December blast as it went rushing by, and the angry torrent at my feet, fed by the melting snows, was many degrees colder than the water of a mountain spring. But this formidable obstacle was to be passed, and how to overcome the difficulty I scarcely knew. Kit, however, solved the problem, by proposing a raft, and accordingly all hands went to work with a will to collect the necessary material from the neighboring woods. Kit, in his shirt sleeves, working hard himself—instructing here and directing there, and as usual, proving himself the master-spirit of the party. After much labor, a few logs were properly cut, notched, and rolled into the water, where they were carefully fastened together by binding them with our *réatas*, until this rude expedient furnished a very passable mode of conveyance for a light load of luggage.

Having freighted it as heavily as we dared with our packs and riding saddles, and placed the bags containing the California mails upon the securest portion, we next proceeded to determine who of our party should be the first to swim the stream. Five men were at length selected, and as I was a good swimmer I concluded to join the expedition as captain. So taking Auchambeau as my first mate, we two plunged into the stream; and having arranged our men at their appointed stations, only waited Kit's final orders, to trust ourselves to the waters. These instructions were soon briefly given in the following words, "All you men who can't swim may hang on to the corners of the raft, but don't any of you try to get upon it except Auchambeau, who has the pole to guide it with; those of you who can swim are to get hold of the tow-line, and pull it along; keep a good lookout for rocks and floating timber; and whatever you do, don't lose the mail bags." And now with one sturdy shove, our frail support was fairly launched, and with a farewell cheer from our comrades upon the shore we consigned ourselves to the mercy of the tide.

I have remarked that I went as captain; but once under way, I found that we were all captains; if indeed giving orders did any good where half one's words were lost amid the roaring of the rapids. In fact we mismanaged the business altogether, until at length I fancy that the poor stream, already vexed beyond endurance, determined to take the matter under its own guidance, out of pity for the nautical ignorance which we had displayed; and finally settled the thing by abandoning us in disgust upon the same side from whence we had started, but more than a mile further down. Ere this operation was concluded, however, it favored me, doubtless in consideration of my captainship, with a parting token; which but for the ready aid of Auchambeau must have finished my adventures upon the spot. I had swam out with a lariat to secure the unfortunate raft to a tree, when the current brought the heavy mass of timber into violent contact with my breast, throwing me back senseless into the channel. Just as I was performing a final feat, in the way of going down, Auchambeau got hold of my hair, which I luckily wore long, and dragged me out upon the bank, where I came to in due course of time.

Our situation was now far from pleasant, the only article of dress which we wore being our hats, the rest of our clothing having been left behind to come by another raft. To go up the rapids against the stream was out of the question; and to cross from where we were, with a considerable fall and jagged rocks just below us, equally impossible. So we had no resource but to shoulder our baggage and travel back on foot, following, as nearly as the thickets would permit, the windings of the river; and uttering more than one anathema upon the thorny plants, which wounded our unprotected feet at every step. It was high noon before we reached camp; and nearly four o'clock ere we were again prepared, and once more summoned up our resolution for a new trial.

This second attempt, after an infinite deal of trouble, proved successful, and we landed upon the opposite bank in a state of almost utter exhaustion; indeed Auchambeau, from over-exertion, and long exposure to the chilling snow water, was taken, upon reaching the shore, with cramps which convulsed him so terribly that we feared they might even destroy life itself. Our first care was, therefore, for him; and by dint of violent friction and rolling in the sand we succeeded in restoring our patient; and then turned our attention to unloading the raft, which had been partly drawn out of the river, and secured to the trunk of a fallen cotton-wood. In this labor we were assisted by a party of Eutaw Indians who had come down to meet us. In fact these fellows did the greater portion of the work, as our weary crew were as yet incapable of much exertion. I have since thought that while thus employed we must have looked like Robinson Crusoe, and his man Friday, supposing those distinguished individuals to have been multiplied by five; the wild scenery, the dashing waters, and our own singular costumes (*for we were by this time dressed in buffalo robes borrowed from our Indian friends*), all combining to carry out the delusion.

Having seen our baggage safely landed, and beheld the raft (*bad luck to it, for in this instance I could not "speak well of the bridge which carried me over"*) go down the rapids, to be dashed against the rocky cliffs below, we ascended the stream, hallooing to our companions to notify them of our safe arrival; the receipt of which information they acknowledged by hearty cheer. Both parties, with the assistance of the Indians, (The Ute Indians had been helpful in assisting the travelers in need. This happens several times in these diaries. See chapters four & eight.) then prepared to cross our caballada, who were expected to swim the river. With this view we selected a point upon our side, considerably below the position occupied by the opposite party, where the bank shelved gradually, and afforded a better footing than elsewhere. (This detail is nearly the same as that given by the Hayden Expedition, Henry Gannett's drawing, as they crossed the Colorado River on the south side of Grand Junction at about 28-1/4 Road.) Here we took our station to attract the attention of the swimming animals by shouting and whistling. Upon our signifying our readiness to receive them, one of the opposite party rode into the water upon the old bell-mare, and the frightened mules were forced to follow, urged on by the yells and blows of their drivers. In a few moments the whole caballada was under way; the old bell-mare, striking out and breasting the waves gallantly, while the mules, with only their heads and long ears visible above the water, came puffing like small high-pressure steamboats in her wake. The yelling on our side now commenced, in which concert the Indians took the thorough base, performing to admiration; while our Mexican muleteers rent the air with their favorite cry of "*anda mula,*" "*hupar mula.*" The animals, attracted by the noise, made straight for us; and we soon had the gratification of seeing them safely landed, dripping and shaking themselves like so many Newfoundland dogs.

At this point, however, our good fortune was destined to end. Kit, it is true, with a few men, and a small portion of luggage, made the passage safely; but a large raft, which carried the greater share of our provisions, was dashed against a sawyer in the stream, which separated the logs, leaving the men to save themselves as they best could; this they did with considerable difficulty; but six rifles, three saddles, much of the ammunition, and nearly all our provisions were totally lost. (Carson in his account of this expedition states that they lost their raft in the Grand or Colorado River.)[4] Under these depressing circumstances, our camp that night was anything but a lively one; the Eutaws being the only persons who seemed to feel like laughing. Indeed, I half think that our loss put them in high goodhumor, as they had some prospect of recovering the rifles, when a lower stage of water should enable them to explore the bed of the stream. The little that remained of our private mess stores, was now the only certain dependence left to us in the way of food for our whole party. These stores were equally divided by Carson himself; our own portion being the same as that of our men, and the whole would, with economy in using, furnish but three days' scanty rations for each individual. Some of our men had lost their riding-saddles, and were fain to spread their blankets upon a mule's back, and jog along as they best might—a mode of travel which, when the animal's bones are highly developed, I take to be "bad at the best," for the rider. Others of the party had lost their clothing; and I am sorry to say that the number of pairs of "nether integuments" was two less than that of the people who ought to have worn them. But this was a trifle compared with our other difficulties, for there was nobody in those regions who knew enough of the fashions to criticize our dress; and as for ourselves we were in no mood to smile at our own strange costumes. Personally, I had been more lucky than the majority of my companions, having saved my precious suit of deer-skin, my rifle, and a few rounds of ammunition; but, alas! the waters of Grand (Colorado) River had swallowed up my note-book, my geological and botanical specimens, and many of my sketches, a most serious and vexatious loss, after the labor of collecting and preparing them.

Two days' travel brought us to Green River, (Brewerton reverses the location of the Colorado and Green Rivers.[5] Carson and Brewerton were traveling from west to east and therefore would have reached the Green River before reaching the Grand or Colorado River.) where we underwent much of the same difficulty in crossing which we had encountered in the passage of Grand (Colorado) River; but we had now learned wisdom from experience, and had, moreover, little left to lose.

The dreaded "third day" which was to see us provisionless at length arrived, and, instead of breakfast, I tried to fill the "aching void" by drawing my belt a hole or two tighter; a great relief, as I can testify, for the cravings of an empty stomach.

As I rode along, reflecting, rather gloomily, I must confess, upon the position of our affairs, and considering where or in what form a supply might best be obtained, I discovered that the same feelings were occupying the minds of most of the party; and before we halted for the night it was moved, resolved, and finally determined, that the fattest of our way-worn steeds should be killed, dressed, and eaten. This idea furnished ample material for contemplation. Eat horse-meat! The very thought was revolting. But then the contemplation of horse-meat, as an edible, had been with me but an abstract idea, which I had never contemplated putting into practice. Now, however, the thing was tangible. To eat, or not to eat, became "the question," and, after due consideration, Hunger arguing the case on one side, with strong Necessity for an advocate—and Fastidiousness taking the opposite, with Prejudice for her backer, I came to the conclusion that I would not and could not eat horseflesh. In accordance with this valorous decision, although upon our arrival at camp, a horse *(lean, old, and decidedly tough)* was actually killed, cut up, and freely eaten of, I alone stood aloof, and went supperless to bed. But it was all in vain; for Starvation is a weighty reasoner, and Hunger gained the day at last. I stood out like a Trojan for eight-and-forty hours, and then "gave in" with as good a grace as possible, and for more than a week ate horseflesh regularly. Perhaps the reader would like to know how it tasted. I can only say that it was an old animal, a tough animal, and a sore-backed animal—and, upon the whole—*I prefer beef.*

During this period of scarcity, we met with several parties of Indians; but found their condition little better than our own; indeed, I believe that it would have nauseated even a frequenter of a sixpenny "restaurant," to have seen the horrible messes which their women were concocting. But I had got bravely over my squeamishness by this time, and would have dined with a Mandarin, without ever inquiring into the contents of the dishes. Really, I blush to confess it—but I actually tried to buy a fat puppy, which, truly and conscientiously, I intended to have eaten. I enticed the brute *(which, by the way, was a short-haired animal, with a stumpy tail, and a decidedly mangy look)* into the lodge of its owner, and then by means of signs, opened a negotiation for its purchase. I offered the extent of my available capital—three cartridges and five brass buttons. I said, "bow-wow," pointing first to the dog, and then to my mouth, which already watered in anticipation of the dainty; but though my proposition was comprehended, and the savage looked upon the buttons with a longing eye, he seemed unwilling to trade; and, finally, explained his reluctance, by pointing with one hand to the puppy, while he gently patted his capacious stomach with the other: thereby giving me to understand that the beast was intended for his own private eating. Finding that the dog was not to be obtained by fair means, and urged by necessity to secure him, at all hazards, I returned to camp, and dispatched "Juan" as a foraging party of one, to invade the enemy's camp and carry off the puppy, "*nolens, volens.*" But he found the animal *(who may have suspected something from the intentness with which I had regarded him)* safely housed, and abandond the enterprise in despair.

Upon reaching the borders of the Rocky Mountains, our situation, so far as food was concerned, became somewhat improved. We found this portion of the country to be by far the most pleasing and interesting which we had yet seen—every turning of the trail disclosing some new beauty of its grand and majestic scenery. Our course, except while crossing a dividing ridge, lay mostly along the mountain passes, where huge cliffs reared their rocky barriers, upon either hand crowned with various trees, the pine and a species of aspen being the most prominent. These valleys abounded in game, among which I noticed the black-tailed deer, elk, antelope, and the Rocky Mountain sheep or "big-horn," as they are sometimes called. This abundance, however, proved rather a matter of vexation than a real benefit; for the animals were so wild and unapproachable that our hunters were often disappointed in obtaining meat; so that but for the Indians, who were here better provided, we should have been obliged to return to the horseflesh.

I shall not soon forget accompanying Carson about this time, on one of our many excursions to procure venison. We had discovered a doe with her fawn in a little grassy nook, where the surrounding rocks would partially screen us from their view, while we crawled within gunshot. Dismounting with as little noise as possible, I remained stationary, holding our horses, while Kit endeavored to approach the unsuspecting deer. We were both somewhat nervous, for our supper and breakfast depended on our success; and we knew well from former experiences that if the doe heard but the crackling of a bush she would be off like the wind. Kit, therefore, advanced with somewhat more than ordinary care, using every caution which a hunter's education could suggest, and at length gained a point within rifle-shot of his prey. My nervousness was now at its height; why don't he fire? thought I. But Kit was cooler, and calculated more closely than myself. At last I saw him bring his rifle to his eye, at the same time showing himself sufficiently to attract the attention of the doe, who raised her head a little to get a look at the object of alarm, thus offering a better mark for his rifle; a moment more, and at the report of the piece, the doe made one convulsive bound, and then rolled upon the sward. To tie our horses, cut up the deer, and attach its quarters to our saddles was the work of twenty minutes more; and then remounting, we pursued our way, making quite a triumphal entry into camp, where Kit's good luck rejoiced the hearts and stomachs of every man in the party: it was really a great event to us in those days, and we had that night a right jolly time of it.

As the events here recorded took place when I was several years younger that I now am, I trust that the following incident will be regarded leniently by the readers of this off-hand, but strictly veracious, narrative. I relate it for the benefit of all romantic young ladies; and I may add, that although I consider the thing original in my own case, I have not the slightest objection to any young gentleman's doing likewise, if placed in a simmilar position.

To begin my story at the proper point, I must confess that in bidding farewell to the Atlantic coast, I left the object of a boyish flame behind me. A noble-hearted woman she was, with a very witching pair of eyes. *(At least, I thought so then—but a plague upon such descriptions, say I. I never yet attempted to get through a lover's catalogue of lips and teeth, Grecian noses and ivory necks, and all that, without breaking down, so I will leave it to my lady readers to imagine all "my fancy painted her.")* Suffice it to say, that she was a sensible woman withal, believing firmly in the old adage, "that a rolling stone gathered no moss"; and with such excellent principles it is hardly wonderful that she liked neither soldiers nor soldiering. But yet it was *one* of my first loves; a fancy of sweet sixteen; and campaigning had not altogether jolted her image out of my head. So one evening, as I stood upon a commanding height just above our camp, I thought of home and absent friends; until yielding to the duplex influences of a poetical temperament, and the solemn twilight hour, I fell into a train of romantic musings which ended in my cutting the name of my fair friend upon the barkless trunk of a gigantic pine, where it is doubtless legible at the present time, and may, for ought I know to the contrary, furnish some future traveler with a fair subject for wonderment and mystery.

The spot, moreover, had an interest about it beyond the mere fact of its lying amid the depths of a mighty wilderness, as it is said to be upon the line which divides the waters of this vast continent, those on the right hand flowing into the Gulf of Mexico, while those on the left mingle with the calmer waves of the Pacific. (The author believes, as does Hafen (Hafen pg. 336, note 12)[6] that Carson and Brewerton traveled the North Branch of the Spanish Trail. They crossed the Colorado River at present-day Grand Junction, Colorado. Brewerton does not give a great deal of geographic detail, but the detail (Brewerton pgs. 129-136)[7] that he gives about crossing the Continental Divide could fit that of Cochetopa Pass.) Were I in that region now, I think that I could almost find the identical tree, from the vicinity of a huge pair of antlers which I recollect to have seen lying near its base. If any man believes that the achievement was simply a "labor of love" unattended by any exertion, hardship, or danger on my part, I can only say that if he will stand upon the summit of an airy cliff, at the rather chilly hour of sunset, and cut three large capitals into the trunk of a very knotty pine with no better tools than a rusty jack-knife, I will give him a certificate for any amount of chivalry and devotion, and—call him a fool to boot.

From these rugged mountain paths we at length emerge, descending into the beautiful plains known as Taos Valley. (Carson and Brewerton were probably descending Cochetopa Pass into the area of the town of Saguache. The San Luis Valley was often times called the Taos Valley.) Here we had scarcely gone a day's journey, before we discovered a great increase in the amount of "Indian sign," and also a change in its appearance, which, though hardly perceptible to an inexperienced eye, was too surely read by Carson's not to beget great uneasiness.

"Look here," said Kit, as he dismounted from his mule, and stooped to examine the trail. "The Indians have passed across our road since sun-up, and they are a war party too; no sign of lodge poles, and no colt tracks; they are no friends neither: here's a feather that some of them has dropped. We'll have trouble yet, if we don't keep abright look-out."

Our camp that night was upon the borders of a stream (Referring to Ruxton's acount in the previous chapter, we know that following the East Fork of the North Branch of the Old Spanish Trail from the north end of the San Luis Valley south into New Mexico would place one at Questa, (Rio Colorado) New Mexico. To backtrack from Questa one-hundred miles north along the East Fork would place one at about Rito Alto Creek. This is where the east fork of the trail turns west to join the West Fork of the North Branch at present-day Saguache, Colorado.) which had been swollen by the melting of the snows, until the neighboring prairies had been overflown to a considerable extent. This deposit of water, now grown partially stagnant, had given birth to myriads of musquitoes, who at evening arose like a mighty cloud from their marshy beds to precipitate themselves upon our devoted camp. Talk about the plagues of Egypt! I will compromise for any amount of frogs and locusts, or even take fleas, by way of variety; but defend me from those winged torment, called musquitoes. These fellows, too, were of the regular gallinipper tribe, of which old officers who have seen service in the everglades of Florida tell such wonderous tales. To repulse this army of invasion we made smokes, and hovered over them until our eyes were literally "a fountain of water;" but though whole battalions were suffocated, and perished in the flame, millions rushed in to fill their places and renew the fight. Our poor mules, equally annoyed with ourselves, showed more sagacity than I gave them credit for, by getting together in a body, and standing in pairs, side by side, so that the tail of one was kept in motion near the head of the other, thus establishing an association for mutual protection, which kept the insects in some measure at a distance. But it certainly was a ludicrous sight to watch the long-eared crowd with their tails going like the sails of an assembly of windmills, and to observe their look of patient resignation when some musquito, more daring than his fellows, broke through their barrier, biting keenly in defiance of their precautions. Finding it impossible to remain by the camp fires, I at length rolled myself up in a Mexican blanket, covering my head so completely that I excluded not only the musquitoes but the air, and thus remained in a state of partial suffocation, listening to the shrill war song of our assailants, until the cooler winds of midnight forced them to leave the field, and take refuge in the oozy swamps.

We were up before the sun upon the following day, and continued on down the valley. Near noon Carson discovered a number of what appeared to be Indians some distance ahead, in a hollow, where a few stunted trees partially concealed them from our view. A little beyond their camp we perceived a large number of animals grazing, which betokened the presence of a party as large, or nearly as large, as our own. As these people were evidently unaware of our proximity, we called a halt, and after a moment's consultation, determined to make a charge, and as we seemed pretty equally matched in regard to numbers, to take, if necessary, the offensive line of conduct. With this view, we selected ten of our best men, and having arrayed our forces, came down, so far as determination was concerned, in very gallant style, each man with his rifle in his hand, firmly resolved to "do or die." But, alas, for the poetry of the affair, we could boast but little of the *pomp, pride, and circumstance of glorious war,*" either in our dress or accoutrements. "Falstaff's ragged regiment," so often quoted as the *ne plus ultra* of volunteerism, were regular troops when compared with our dashing cavaliers. We looked ragged enough and dirty enough in all conscience, without any extra attempt at effect, but, as if to complete the picture, the two unfortunate individuals who wanted "unmentionables" were front-rank men, and your very humble servant, the author, had a portion of an under-garment which shall be nameless tied round his head in lieu of a hat. Take us all in all, we certainly did not neglect the advice of one of Shakespeare's heroes, who bids his followers "hang out their banners on the outer wall." The mules, too—confound their stupidity!—ruined the affair, so far as it might be considered in the light of a secret expedition, by stretching out their heads, protruding their long ears, and yelling most vociferously. "Confound your stumbling body!" said one old mountaineer to his steed (a wall-eyed marcho), "maybe you'll have something to make a noise for, when you get an Apache arrow slipped into you." But our famous charge on mule-back was brought to an abrupt and inglorious close upon reaching the camp of our supposed enemies, by the discovery that they were nothing more nor less than Mexican traders, who had penetrated thus far into the wilderness for the purpose of trafficking with the Indians.

From these fellows we obtained some useful, but not particularly encouraging, information, to the effect that a party of mountaineers, larger than our own, and better supplied with arms, had been attacked by the Indians near the point at which we expected to encamp that night, defeated, and despoiled of their property. There was nothing before us, however, but to push ahead, and that evening found few in our camp who cared to sleep soundly. With a view to greater watchfulness, our guard was doubled, the sentries crawling to and from their posts; and all making as little disturbance as possible. The fires of an Indian camp—probably a part of the same band who had defeated the mountaineers—shone brightly from a hillside about half a mile distant; and having nothing to cook, we deemed it most prudent to extinguish our own, which had been lighted to drive away the musquitoes. During the night great uneasiness among the animals betokened the presence or close vicinity of lurking Indians; and Kit, whose long acquaintance with the savages had taught him a perfect knowledge of their modes of warfare, believing that they would attack us about daybreak, determined to steal a march upon the enemy. In pursuance of this object, we saddled our beasts at midnight, and departed as noiselessly as possible, traveling by starlight until the first glimmer of the dawn, when we paused for a few moments to breathe our tired animals, and then continued on.

We had, upon leaving our last night's camp, nearly one hundred miles to travel before reaching the first settlements in New Mexico, the nearest place of safety; (In 1846 George Frederick Ruxton traveled the East Fork of the North Branch of the Old Spanish Trail. He stated that "Rio Colorado (Red River) is the last and most northern settlement of Mexico". See chapter five.) and it was now determined to make the distance without delay. Accordingly we pressed on as rapidly as the condition of our cattle (?) would permit, stopping only to shift our saddles to one of the loose animals when those we rode showed signs of giving out. Late in the afternoon we had, by the free use of whip and spur, reached a point some eighteen miles distant from the first Mexican habitations. (This was probably near the location of the Colorado/New Mexico state line.)

I was just beginning to feel a little relieved from the anxious watchfullness of the last few days, and had even beguiled the weariness of the way by picturing to myself the glorious dinner I would order upon reaching Santa Fé, when Carson, who had been looking keenly ahead, interrupted my musings, by exclaiming: "Look at that Indian village; we have stumbled upon the rascals, after all!" It was but too true—a sudden turning of the trail had brought us full in view of nearly two hundred lodges, which were located upon a rising ground some half a mile distant to the right of our trail. At this particular point the valley grew narrower, and hemmed in as we were upon either hand by a chain of hills and mountains, we had no resource but to keep straight forward on our course, in the exception that by keeping, as sailors say, "well under the land," we might possibly slip by unperceived. But our hope was a vain one; we had already been observed, and ere we had gone a hundred yards, a warrior came dashing out from their town, and, putting his horse to its speed, rode rapidly up to Carson and myself: he was a finely formed savage, mounted upon a noble horse, and his fresh paint and gaudy equipments looked anything but peaceful. This fellow continued his headlong career until almost at our side, and then, checking his steed so suddenly as to throw the animal back upon its haunches, he inquired for the "capitán" *(a Spanish word generally used by the Indians to signify chief)*; in answer to which, I pointed first to Carson and then to myself. Kit, who had been regarding him intently, but without speaking, now turned to me, and said: "I will speak to this warrior in Eutaw, and if he understands me it will prove that he belongs to a friendly tribe; but if he does not, we may know the contrary, and must do the best we can: but from his paint and manner I expect it will end in a fight anyway."

Kit then turned to the Indian, who, to judge from his expression, was engaged in taking mental but highly satisfactory notes of our way-worn party with their insufficient arms and scanty equipments; and asked him in the Eutaw tongue, "Who are you?" The savage stared at us for a moment; and then, putting a finger into either ear, shook his head slowly from side to side. "I knew it," said Kit; "it is just as I thought, and we are in for it at last. Look here, Thomas!" added he *(calling to an old mountain man)*—"get the mules together, and drive them up to that little patch of chaparral, while we follow with the Indian." Carson then requested me in a whisper to drop behind the savage (who appeared determined to accompany us), and be ready to shoot him at a minute's warning, if necessity required. Having taken up a position accordingly, I managed to cock my rifle, which I habitually carried upon the saddle, without exciting suspicion.

Kit rode ahead to superintend the movements of the party who, under the guidance of Thomas, had by this time got the pack and loose animals together, and were driving them toward a grove about two hundred yards further from the village. We had advanced thus but a short distance, when Carson *(who from time to time had been glancing backward over his shoulder)* reined in his mule until we again ride side-by-side. While stooping, as if to adjust his saddle, he said, in too low a tone to reach any ears but mine: "Look back, but express no surprise." I did so, and beheld a sight which, though highly picturesque, and furnishing a striking subject for a painting, was, under existing circumstances, rather calculated to destroy the equilibrium of the nerves. In short, I saw about a hundred and fifty warriors, finely mounted, and painted for war, with their long hair streaming in the wind, charging down upon us, shaking their lances and brandishing their spears as they came on.

By this time we had reached the timber, if a few stunted trees could be dignified with the name; and Kit, springing from his mule, called out to the men, "Now, boys, dismount, tie up your riding mules; those of you who have guns, get round the caballada, and look out for the Indians; and you who have none, get inside, and hold some of the animals. Take care, Thomas, and shoot down the mule with the mail bags on her pack, if they try to stampede the animals."

We had scarcely made these hurried preparations for the reception of such unwelcome visitors, before the whole horde were upon us, and had surrounded our position. For the next fifteen minutes a scene of confusion and excitement ensued which baffles all my powers of description. On the one hand the Indians pressed closely in, yelling, aiming their spears, and drawing their bows, while their chiefs, conspicuous from their activity, dashed here and there among the crowd, commanding and directing their followers. On the other side, our little band, with the exception of those who had lost their rifles in Grand (Colorado) River, stood firmly round the caballada; Carson, a few paces in advance, giving orders to his men, and haranguing the Indians. His whole demeanor was now so entirely changed that he looked like a different man; his eye fairly flashed, and his rifle was grasped with all the energy of an iron will.

"There," cried he, addressing the savages, "is our line, cross it if you dare, and we begin to shoot. You ask us to let you in, but you won't come unless you ride over us. You say you are friends, but you don't act like it. No, you don't deceive us so, we know you too well; so stand back, or your lives are in danger."

It was a bold thing in him to talk thus to these blood-thirsty rascals; but a crisis had arrived in which boldness alone could save us, and he knew it. They had five men to our one; our ammunition was reduced to three rounds per man, and resistance could have been but momentary; but among our band the Indians must have recognized mountain men, who would have fought to the last, and they knew from sad experience that the trapper's rifle rarely missed its aim. Our animals, moreover, worn out as they were, would have been scarecely worth fighting for, and our scalps a dear bargain.

Our assailants were evidently undecided, and this indecision saved us; for just as they seemed preparing for open hostilities, as rifles were cocked and bows drawn, a runner, mounted upon a weary and foam-specked steed, came galloping in from the direction of the settlements, bringing information of evident importance. After a moment's consultation with this new arrival, the chief whistled shrilly, and the warriors fell back. Carson's quick eye had already detected their confusion, and turning his men, he called out, "Now, boys, we have a chance, jump into your saddles, get the loose animals before you, and then handle your rifles, and if these fellows interfere with us we'll make a running fight of it."

In an instant each man was in his saddle, and with the caballada in front we retired slowly; facing about from time to time, to observe the movements of our enemies, who followed on, but finally left us and disappeared in the direction of their village, leaving our people to pursue their way undisturbed. We rode hard, and about midnight reached the first Mexican dwelling which we had seen since our departure from the Pacific coast. This town being nothing more than a collection of shepherds' huts, we did not enter, but made camp near it. Here also we learned the secret of our almost miraculous escape from the Indians, in the fact that a party of two hundred American volunteers were on their way to punish the perpetrators of the recent Indian outrages in that vicinity; (Perhaps an interested researcher at a future date might research military records and find the necessary proof to end the mystery of the route used by Carson and Brewerton!) this then was the intelligence which had so opportunely been brought by their runner, who must have discovered the horsemen while upon the march.

It is almost needless to say that we slept the sleep of tired men that night. I for one did not awake with the dawn. Our tired animals too appeared to require some repose ere they renewed their labors; and it was therefore decided that we should take a holiday of rest before departing for Taos, now distant but one day's journey. I remember celebrating this occasion by visiting one of the Mexican huts, where I ordered the most magnificent dinner that the place afforded, eggs and goat's milk, at discretion—if discretion had anything to do with the terrible havoc we made among the eatables, a thing which on reflection appears to me more than doubtful.

Early upon the following day we resumed our march, and that evening terminated our journeyings for a season, by bringing us to the Mexican village of Taos, (Since Taos was the home of Kit Carson, it would make sense to the author that the North Branch of the Old Spanish Trail would have been the route that they used.) where I was hospitably entertained by Carson and his amiable wife, a Spanish lady, and a relative, I believe, of some former Governor of New Mexico.

The Kit Carson Home as it appears in 1997. The house was built in 1825 and later purchased by Carson who lived in Taos, New Mexico from 1843-1863.

And now, as our good parsons say, "a few words more and I have done," and I most sincerely hope that these farewell lines may not bring the sensation of weariness to the reader which I have sometimes felt upon hearing the foregoing announcement from the pulpuit. What I have written is simply a plain, unvarnished statement of facts as they occured. While I grant that the capital "I" has come in more frequently than I could have wished, I must disclaim all title to the hero-ship of my story. I was but a looker-on, "a chiel," who, though "takin' notes," did not then mean to "prent 'em."

Since writing a portion of the foregoing narrative, Mr. Christopher Carson has been nominated by our President to the Indian Agency of the Territory of New Mexico, a highly responsible office, requiring great tact, much common sense, and a fair amount of judgment. This excellent selection has been ratified and confirmed by the Senate, and I am free to say, that Kit Carson has no friend, among the many who claim that honor both east and west of the Rocky Mountains, who congratulates him more sincerely than myself. He is eminently fitted for the office; and all who know him will agree with me when I declare that I believe him to be "An honest man, the noblest work of God."

As those who have followed me in my wanderings through the wilds of the Rocky Mountains, and amid the sands of the Great American Desert, may not feel altogether uninterested in the continuation of my journey to the frontiers of Missouri, I will resume the thread of my narrative from the point where it was interrupted by our arrival at the village of Taos, in the Territory of New Mexico.

I have already stated that the way-worn condition of our animals, as well as the weariness of the men, caused a day's delay at the rancho at which we encamped before entering Taos, where we were again detained for similar reasons from Saturday until the Tuesday morning following. During our sojourn there I visited most portions of the town, which, beyond the fact of its having suffered in former days from the chances of intestine warfare or foreign invasion, has little to commend it to the notice of the traveler. Its inhabitants exhibit all the indolent, lounging characteristics of the lower order of Mexicans, the utter want both of moral and mental culture making itself everywhere apparent. These people, who know no higher duty, and acknowledge no purer rule of conduct than a blind compliance with the exactions of a corrupt priesthood, regard honest labor as a burden, and resort to it only when driven by their necessities. Sleeping, smoking, and gambling consume the greater portion of their day; while nightly fandangos furnish fruitful occasions for murder, robbery, and other acts of outrage. I speak of the country as it impressed me at the period of my passage through it, some years ago, when these remarks were applicable to a large majority of its male population. It is but just, however, to state, that the women of New Mexico toil harder, and in this respect are more perfect slaves to the tyranny of their husbands, than any other females, if we except the Indians, upon this continent. They are literally "hewers of wood and drawers of water," but, unlike their cowardly and treacherous lords, their hearts are ever open to the sufferings of the unfortunate. Many have borne witness to the fact; for the wounded mountaineer, the plundered trader, and fettered prisoners dragged as a triumphal show through their villages by men who never dared to meet their captives upon equal terms in the field, have experienced sympathy and obtained relief from these dark-eyed daughters of New Mexico.

The houses of Taos, like those of Los Angeles in California, are for the most part built of *adóbes*, with walls of great thickness, the windows being narrow, and strongly barred with iron rods, which, while they afford a greater degree of security to the residents in times of danger, give the place a gloomy, prison-like appearance, which is far from agreeable. In the arrangement of the interior of their dwellings, as well as in the character of the furniture which they contain, the New Mexicans differ greatly from any of the Spanish race whom I have hitherto seen. The sides of their rooms are provided with huge rolls of *serapes (a kind of coarse blanket, which forms one of their principal articles of trade with the adjoining provinces, being largely manufactured by the women of the country).* These rolls answer the double purposes of beds by night and lounges by day. With the exception of these changeable conveniences, the one apartment, which serves as kitchen, parlor, and bedroom for a whole family, boasts no other movables, unless, indeed, some aristocratic *rico* indulges in the luxury of a bench or table fashioned of native wood, so rudely carved and put together that it would have done no great credit to skill of our friend Robinson Crusoe, if found in his island habitation.

Both rich and poor, however, agree in appropriating one end of their dwellings to a sort of family altar or chapel, where rude engravings of saints, images intended to represent the Saviour, or "La Madre de Diós," sacred relics, and consecrated rosaries, are displayed around a huge crucifix, which occupies the centre of the wall on that side of the apartment. These images, particularly upon high fiestas and holidays, are decked out by the females of the family with all sorts of tawdry ornaments; and on such occasions it is by no means uncommon to see a doll representing the Virgin Mary arrayed in a muslin frock, trimmed with artificial roses, and festooned with ribbons of gayest hues.

The concluding paragraphs of my Rocky Mountain narrative chronicled the fact that my friend Carson had a wife who was then residing in Taos. Now it was evident that Kit felt disposed to linger by his own fireside to the last moment which duty would permit; and when we remember the long and weary days of peril and fatigue which our adventurous mountaineer must necessarily undergo before revisiting his home, few of our lady readers will wonder at the wish, however strange it may appear to those unfortunate Benedicts who have found the silken chains of matrimony grow heavier in the wearing. To carry out his design, it was mutually agreed that I should depart for Santa Fé with the greater number of our men, and there await the arrival of Carson, who, with fresher animals, purposed accomplishing the distance—upward of seventy-five miles—in about one third of the time which would be consumed by our tired and foot-sore beasts in reaching their destination.

It was a pleasant morning in the month of June, at about ten o'clock—judging by the shadow of an old *adóbe* church, which serves as a sort of town clock or sun-dial to the denizens of Taos—when I bade Kit a final good-by, with a hearty shake of the hand, flung myself into the saddle, and turned the face of my "little gray," and mine own in consequence, toward that portion of our party who had already lessened the distance between themselves and "La Ciudád de Santa Fé" by a good Mexican league—which I take to be the longest in the world.

It was nearly sunset, when the close of our first day's travel brought us to the banks of a clear but rapid brook, which wound its way through the narrow street of a

The church of San Francisco de Asis at Ranchos de Taos is probably the church mentioned by Brewerton. This massive and beautiful adobe structure was completed in 1815.

little Mexican village. Here we encamped; and while still engaged in removing the saddles from our weary beasts, we recieved a deputation of the inhabitants, who sent a *fair* representation, in the shape of some half a dozen *señoritas*, who brought eggs, goat's milk, and *tortillas*—the sum total of the products of the place. Each and all of these they were willing to dispose of to their "*amígos,*" *Los Americanos*, for a pecuniary consideration. But, as their "American friends" were just then decidedly deficient in funds—five silver dollars being a large estimate of the amount of "circulating medium" in the hands of our party—and, moreover, as we confidently expect that the same state of things would continue until relieved by the pay-master, their traffic prospered poorly.

The bill of fare at breakfast was—thanks to the kindness of my reverend friend, the Padre, who came down to share it—considerably, improved by the addition of some of the odds and ends of our last night's entertainment, to say nothing of half a gallon of goat's milk, and a couple of dozen of new-laid eggs, sent in by "particular request."

Our journey for the day was marked by no particular incident, except that many of our mules showed symptoms of giving out; and even my indefatigable little gray, who had borne up amid all the privations of hard travel and short rations, threatened momentarily to drop down upon the road. But as we expected to reach Santa Fé upon the evening of the morrow we felt anything but despondent; and good stories, sly jokes, and pleasant allusions to our adventures by the way seemed the occupation of all.

Having completed our alloted distance, we encamped for the night at a rancho where a Mexican "Alcalde"—a very different sort of person from my friend the Priest—gave me a crusty invitation to supper, and nearly compassed the destruction of my digestive organs through the medium of over-done eggs and raw *aguardiénte*. I was the gainer, however, by his surliness, for it induced me to make a virtue of necessity, and retire at a seasonable hour. As I pronounced a benediction upon the servant of the Church, so will I record my malediction against the representative of the civil authority. That he may fall a victim to the miseries of his own society is the very worst evil which I could wish *Señor Alcalde Don Antonio Guerrara*.

Our start upon the third, and, we hoped, final day's travel between Taos and Santa Fé, was an early one. It was just sunrise by the luminary in question; not to mention an authority which, as threatening clouds were darkening the eastern horizon, might have been considered an equally reliable sign—I refer to the Alcalde's chicken-yard, a preserve well stocked with fowls, as I am inclined to suspect my unscrupulous follower Juan had ascertained during the night, or else whence came the raw material for the stew on which we breakfasted?

By noon we had reached a Mexican village, where, as Little Gray, my "ultimatum" in the way of transportation, was now upon her last legs, being scarcely able to carry herself, to say nothing of a rider, I concluded to tarry and dine, intending to push on and overtake the party, or, at all events, reach Santa Fé that night.

Once more upon the road, I experienced so much of that chilly uncomfortable feeling which is connected with a departure from pleasant quarters, and the undertaking of a long and lonely ride, that I determined to shorten its duration, if it were possible, and with this intention halted to consult a peasant who was lazily working upon one of the numerous irrigating ditches which are the inseparable assistant of New Mexican agriculture. This fellow, upon understanding that I was in haste, recommended *el señor* to take a certain by-road, which he pointed out, assuring me that it would be the nearest by more than a league. It was in an evil hour that I listened to his advice, and departed from the beaten track to follow an almost unused bridle-path, which the gathering shadows of evening rendered yet more indistinct. But, buoyed up by hopeful anticipations of rest, and gay time in Santa Fé, I kept jogging on while daylight and twilight, and the pale radiance of a cloudless moon worked their changes in the aspect of earth and sky; changes which succeeded each other with a rapidity best accounted for by my own impatience and solitary weariness of the way.

It was not far from noon when, as we emerged from the pine-clad hills, I beheld for the first time our long-desired haven, "La Ciudád de Santa Fé."

8

1853/GWINN HARRIS HEAP

Lieutenant Edward Fitzgerald Beale, the expedition leader, was born in Washington, D.C., on February 4, 1822. He was reared in a military atmosphere since his grandfather and father both served in the United States Navy.

In making up his party, Beale invited his cousin, Gwinn Harris Heap, to serve as journalist for the expedition. Heap was born in Chester, Pennsylvania, on March 23, 1817, the son of Dr. Samuel Heap and Margaret *Porter* Heap. His journals were published in the book, *Central Route to the Pacific* in 1854.

The expedition left Westport on the Missouri frontier on May 15, 1853 at 3 P.M. A group of women and men accompanied them a few miles out onto the prairie where they drank champagne to the success of the journey. They traveled west on the Santa Fe Trail as far as the ruins of Bent's Old Fort which they reached on May 30, then continued west up the Arkansas River to the Huerfano River. From the Huerfano they traveled south down the Taos Trail which left the Huerfano River, up South Oak Creek and then crossed Sangre de Cristo Pass to Fort Massachusetts. Upon reaching the fort it was found that both men and animals could not to be obtained. Beale and Major George Blake, the commander of the fort, traveled south toward Taos in search of a guide and additional animals. They returned with a guide and a muleteer. No mention is made if they were able to obtain additional animals.

Leaving Fort Massachusetts, the party crossed the East Fork of the North Branch of the Old Spanish Trail. This was referred to by Heap as "the trail of Roubideau's wagons from the upper Arkansas settlements, which entered through Roubideau's Pass in the Sangre de Cristo."

Ron Taylor and the author flew around Mount Blanca on August 21, 1995. We located a wagon road heading northwest from the town of Blanca. The author believes that this is the wagon road that Heap saw on June 15, 1853.

After crossing the Trail the Beale/Heap expedition continued west about the same route as the railroad tracks of today where they joined the Rio Grande and camped near present-day Alamosa, Colorado. They traveled along the north side of the Rio Grande until reaching the West Fork of the North Branch of the Old Spanish Trail. Here they turned north following the West Fork to Russell Spring. At Russell Spring they left the Main Fork of the Trail and followed a lesser-used trail up Tracy Cañon. They crossed the ridge north of Tracy Mountain and continued on to descend Hodding Creek to the Saguache Valley. At this point they joined the main North Branch which they followed until reaching Cochetopa Creek. Leaving the main North Branch, they struck across country to the Lake Fork of the Gunnison River. There they again joined the main North Branch of the Old Spanish Trail. From Grand Junction the Beale/Heap expedition probably followed the Colorado River to its confluence with the Dolores River. The party left the Colorado and followed what later was to become known as the Old Salt Lake Wagon Road to Green River, Utah. Before continuing on from the ruins of Fort Uncompahgre, Heap returned to Taos to replace supplies lost in attempting to cross the swollen Gunnison River. His relief party returned to the Cochetopa Pass area by way of a different route. They traveled from the Lake Fork of the Gunnison across country to the area of the Los Pinos Ute Indian Agency and returned by the same route.

May 31, 1853

Swarms of mosquitoes prevented much sleep. Thunder and lightning north and south of us all night. Started at sunrise; the sky was clear and weather cool, with a bracing wind from the northwest; in a few hours it veered to the southwest. At ten o'clock, we had our first view of the Spanish Peaks, distant about seventy miles. (The Arkansas River from 1803-1846 was the north boundary of New Mexico. The Spanish Peaks were landmarks of travel in New Mexico.) Travelled up the left bank of the Arkansas, and obtained at times several picturesque views of the river, which is occasionally hemmed in by rocky cliffs. The country was more rolling, stony, and dry than on the preceding day. Saw many deer and antelopes. At ten o'clock, we passed the mouth of Purgatoire River, flowing into the Arkansas from the southwestward. Beds of excellent coal have been discovered on this stream, which will be of inestimable value hereafter. At twelve, encamped on "Lower Dry Creek," where we found scanty dry grass and water in pools. The Delaware brought in two fine antelopes. Travelled ten miles in the afternoon, and encamped three miles above Bent's Fort.

This is a reconstruction of Bent's Old Fort which was built by Cerán St. Vrain, Charles & William Bent about 1833. It was destroyed by William Bent in 1849 after the U.S. Army refused to buy the fort.

We rode all through the ruins, (About 1849 William Bent moved east near the area of present-day Lamar where he built a stone Trading Post.)[1] which present a strange appearance in these solitudes. A few years ago this post was frequented by numerous trappers and Indians, and at times exhibited a scene of wild confusion. It is now roofless; for when the United States refused to purchase it, the proprietors set it on fire to prevent its becoming a harbor for Indians. The adobe walls are still standing, and are in many places of great thickness. They were covered with written messages from parties who had already passed here to their friends in the rear; they all stated that their herds were in good condition, and progressing finely. Day's march, 35 miles; distance from Westport, 550 miles.

June 1

The weather in the morning was pleasant, and the wind from the northwest cooled by passing over the snow-clad peaks of the Rocky Mountains. According to our maps, we were now within an easy day's travel of the mouth of the Huerfano *(Orphan's River)*, and were impatient to reach that point, as we there intended to diverge from the beaten track, and, leaving the Arkansas behind us, traverse the plains lying between that river and the base of the Spanish Peaks, Sangre de Cristo Mountains, and the Sierra Mojada (Wet Mountains).

Started before sunrise; the road leading occasionally on the Arkansas bottom, but more frequently over the upper plain. The bottom was covered with an abundance of coarse grass, whereas, on the plain, it was scanty, and in bunches. Proceeding four miles we crossed Upper Dry Creek, which is seven miles from Bent's Fort; and in twelve more, passed a large pond. Many large bands of antelope and deer bounded away on either side as we advanced. At half-past twelve we ascended a remarkable spur, which projects into the river-bottom, and can be seen for fifteen miles below; it bears northeast from the Spanish Peaks. From this point we could mark the course of Timpas Creek from the mountains to its junction with the Arkansas. On the right bank of the Timpas, near its mouth, are several singular buttes, two of which are conical, and the remainder flat-topped. Our noon camp was two miles below the Timpas, and about twenty-eight above Bent's Fort. As this was the distance from Bent's Fort at which the mouth of the Huerfano was placed on our maps, we expected to reach it before dark; but found that we would have to travel sixteen or seventeen miles farther up the Arkansas. In fact, from this point until we reached the Mormon settlement on Little Salt Lake, we could place no reliance on the maps. Crossed the Arkansas one mile above the mouth of the Timpas, and had no difficulty in fording it, though, without due caution, animals are liable to get entangled in quicksands. The grass on the plains west of the Arkansas was more abundant and of a better quality than that on the side we had just left; there was also much grama grass and cactus. The water of the Timpas, which was found in holes only, was cool, but slightly brackish. The night was bright and starry, and illuminated during part of the evening by a beautiful aurora borealis. Day's travel, 30 miles; distance from Westport, 580 miles.

June 2

Left the Timpas at early dawn, and discerned at a distance of fifteen miles several high buttes, bearing due west, in a line with the southern end of the Sierra Mojada (Wet Mountains); towards these we now directed our course. The country was gradually rolling towards the buttes, and covered with abundant bunch grass; the prickly pear, or cactus, which grows in clusters close to the ground, was at times very distressing to our mules; their constant efforts to avoid treading on this annoying plant gave them an uneasy, jerking gait, very harassing to their riders during a long day's march. Upon reaching the summit of the buttes, a magnificent and extensive panorama was opened to our view. The horizon was bounded on the north by Pike's Peak, northwest and west by the Sierra Mojada (Wet Mountains), Sangre de Cristo Mountains, and Spanish Peaks; to the south and east extended the prairie, lost in the

162

The Badito Cone near the crossing and a popular camp site on the Huerfano River was a land mark used by travelers.

hazy distance. On the gently undulating plains, reaching to the foot of the mountains, could be traced the course of the Arkansas and Sage Creek by their lines of timber. The Apispah (Apishapa), an affluent of the Arkansas, issuing from the Sierra Mojada (Wet Mountains), was concealed from sight by a range of intervening buttes, while the object of our search, the Huerfano, flowed at our feet, distant about three miles, its course easy to be distinguished from the point where it issued from the mountains to its junction with the Arkansas, except at short intervals, where it passed through cañons in the plain. Pike's Peak, whose head was capped with eternal snows, was a prominent object in the landscape, soaring high above all neighboring summits.

Descending the buttes to the Huerfano, we encamped on it about five miles above its mouth. A bold and rapid stream, its waters were turbid, but sweet and cool; the river-bottom was broad, and thickly wooded with willows and cottonwoods, interlaced with the wild rose and grape-vine, and carpeted with soft grass—a sylvan paradise. This stream was about twenty-five yards in breadth, and five feet deep close to the bank. Bands of antelope and deer dotted the plain, one of which served us for supper, brought down by the unerring rifle of Dick, the Delaware.

This camp was to us a scene of real enjoyment; a long and tedious march, over plains of unvarying sameness, was over, and we were now on the eve of entering upon a new and unexplored country, which promised to the admirers of nature a rich and ever-varying treat. The hunters of the party also looked forward with impatience to reaching the mountains, where game of every description was said to abound, and where it would not be necessary to exercise the great patience and perseverance, without which it is difficult to approach deer and antelope on the plains; the Delaware possessed both these requisites in perfection, and gave us daily proofs of his skill. We noticed, whilst traveling along the same route with emigrants, that although game was at times comparatively scarce near the road, it was not owing to the number they destroyed, but rather to the constant *fusillade* which they kept up on everything living, from a buffalo to a goffer, and from a grouse to a blackbird.

In the afternoon, we continued up the Huerfano about a mile, and crossed over to the left bank; the ford was good and but three feet deep. Fine grama grass grew on the upper plain on each side of the river, and an abundance of rich grass on the bottom land. A large growth of cottonwoods line the banks of this stream for twelve miles above its mouth, though higher up it is not so heavily timbered. It is hemmed in at intervals by picturesque bluffs of sandstone.

The following are the bearings of the mouth of the Huerfano; Pike's Peak, northwest; northern Spanish Peak, south-southwest; southern Spanish Peak, south by west. General course of the river, from southwest to northeast. Day's journey, 28 miles; total, 608 miles.

June 3

Our camp the preceding night was a mile below the lower end of the cañon through which the Huerfano forces a passage; this chasm is about ten miles in length, and the ground on each side is much cut up by deep and rocky ravines running into it. I rode up to its entrance to sketch; the scenery was wild and beautiful; wild turkeys flew away at my approach, and the startled deer rose from their beds in the grass at the bottom of the cañon, making their escape up a ravine to the plain. A line of bluffs runs parallel to the Huerfano on the west from two to five miles distant, and wagons should travel at their base to avoid the broken ground nearer the stream; a thick growth of dwarf pine and cedars covers their summits. The wagon trail from the Greenhorn and Hardscrabble settlements on the upper Arkansas approaches the Huerfano below this cañon, leaves it there, and returns to it above. (The wagon road that led to the Greenhorn settlement followed the east side of the Greenhorn Mountains.)

After a ride of twenty-four miles up the left bank we encamped to noon on a gully where we found water in rocky hollows; the pasturage was excellent, as in fact it had been since reaching the Huerfano, for we had not seen better since leaving Council Grove. The scenery, as we approached the country between the Spanish Peaks and the Sierra Mojada (Wet Mountains), was picturesque and beautiful; mountains towered high above us, the summits of some covered with snow, while the dense forests of dark pines which clothed their sides, contrasted well with the light green of the meadows near their base. All day, heavy clouds had been gathering on the mountain-tops, portending a storm; at noon it broke, covering them with snow, and soon after swept over the plain. Here it rained in torrents, accompanied by westerly wind, which blew with such fury as to render it impossible for man or beast to face it; at the crossing of Apache Creek, a small affluent of the Huerfano, we were compelled to turn our backs to the gale and wait patiently for its subsidence. Long before the rain had ceased on the plains, the mountain tops were again glittering in the setting sun, the newly fallen snow sparkling in his beams, tinged with a rosy hue. Soon after dark we encamped on the Huerfano, in the midst of luxuriant grass. Our packs and bedding had got wet, the ground was spongy and boggy, and, although the rain had ceased, a heavy dew fell during the night, which completely saturated us; we made our beds in deep mud. About a mile beyond our camping place stood the Huerfano Butte, which is so prominent a landmark. Day's march, 34 miles; total distance from Westport, 642 miles.

June 4

I rode ahead of camp, to Huerfano Butte, a remarkable mound, bearing north from the southernmost Spanish Peak, and about fifty yards from the right bank of the river; its appearance was that of a huge artifical mound of stones, covered half-way up from its base with a dense growth of bushes. It is probably of volcanic origin, and there are many indications in this region of the action of internal fires.

Our ride to-day was full of interest, for we were now approaching the Sangre de Cristo Pass, (Sangre de Cristo Pass was used by several of the people included in these diaries. See chapters three, five, six, eight, nine, ten, & fifteen.) in the Sangre de Cristo Mountains. We had been traveling for eighteen days, over an uninterrupted plain, until its monotony had become extremely wearisome. The mountain scenery, which we entered soon after raising camp this morning, was of the most picturesque description. We crossed the Huerfano seven miles above the Butte; at this point it issues from a cañon one hundred and fifty yards in length; above it the valley, watered by the Huerfano, forms a beautiful plain of small extent, surrounded by lofty and well-wooded mountains; numerous rills trickle down their sides, irrigate the plain, and join their waters to those of the Huerfano, which are here clear and cold. We did not enter this valley, but left the H. after crossing it, and followed up the bed of one of its tributaries, the Cuchada (South Oak Creek), a small brook rising near the summit of the Sangre de Cristo Pass. This small valley of the Huerfano contains about six hundred acres, and forms a most ravishing picture; it would be a good place for recruiting cattle after their weary march across the plains, as they would be perfectly secure and sheltered, and the pasturage is excellent. This, however, is the case all through these mountains, for waving grass, gemmed with flowers of every hue, covers them to their summits, except in the region of snow. The Cuchada (South Oak Creek) led us up a succession of valleys of an easy grade. We were now traveling on an Indian trail; for the wagon trail, which I believe was made by Roubideau's (Robidoux) wagons, (Although the road was called Robidoux's Road, it was originally traveled by wheeled vehicles in 1787 as Manuel Segura traveled to San Carlos de los Jupes to build this farming community for the Jupe Comanche.)[2] deviated to the right, and went through the pass named after him. This pass is so low that we perceived through it a range of sand hills (These sand hills/Great Sand Dunes National Monument can not be seen until you have descended Robidoux's/Mosca Pass for some distance.) of moderate height, in San Luis valley; to have gone through it, however, would have occasioned us the loss of a day in reaching Fort Massachusetts, through it is the shortest and most direct route to the Coochatope (Cochetopa); and Mr. Beale's views constrained him to take the most direct route to Fort Massachusetts, where he expected to obtain a guide through the unexplored country between New Mexico and Utah, and also to procure some mules. We were therefore very reluctantly compelled to forego the examination of Roubideau's (Robidoux) Pass.

Encamped at noon at the foot of a remarkable rock, watered at its base by the Cuchada (South Oak Creek); it resembled the ruined front of a Gothic church. (The ruined front of a Gothic church is what Gwinn Harris Heap perceived, but George Frederick Ruxton describes it as a ruined castle. See chapter six.) Encamped for the night six miles farther up the valley, and near the summit of the Sangre de Cristo Pass. An excellent wagon road might be made over these mountains, by the Sangre de Cristo Pass, (The wagon road was not built until later in the summer. See chapters nine, ten, & fifteen.) and still better one through Roubideau's (Robidoux).

The grass around our encampment was really magnificent; it was in a large mountain meadow, watered by numerous springs and girt in by dark pines. Through an opening in the mountains, to the eastward, we could see the sunny plains of the Arkansas and Huerfano, with its remarkable *butte*, whilst around us heavy clouds were collecting, giving warning of a storm and wet night. We made ourselves shelters and beds of pine boughs. The Delaware had killed a fat antelope, which furnished us a hearty supper; and we sat around our fire, until a late hour, well pleased with having accomplished in such good time and without accident the first stage of our journey, for we expected to reach Fort Massachusetts at an early hour next day. Day's march, 26 miles; total distance, 668 miles.

June 5

The rain fell at intervals all night, but the clouds dispersed before dawn, and the sun rose in a bright and clear sky; the plains, however, were concealed under a sea of snowy mist.

Continued our course to the southwestward through thick pine woods, and in one mile we reached the head waters of Sangre de Cristo Creek, flowing into the Del Norte after its junction with the Trinchera. The Sangre de Cristo mountains, and the Sierras Blanca and Mojada, were covered with snow. We followed down the Sangre de Cristo, which every moment increased in size, its clear and icy water leaps over rocks, and the mountain sides were covered with tender grass, strawberry blossoms, and violets.

On our maps, the Sangre de Cristo is improperly named Indian Creek, which is a fork of the Sangre de Cristo, and is not named at all on them. Up Indian Creek, I am informed, there exists an excellent pass from San Luis valley to the plains on the eastern side of the mountains.

After crossing Indian Creek, we halted a few minutes to make our toilets previous to our arrival at Fort Massachusetts; and, although our hunter had just ridden into camp with a haunch of fat venison behind his saddle; and our appetites, which were at all times excellent, had been sharpened by a long mountain ride without breakfast, we were too impatient to reach the fort to lose time in camping. We arrived there late in the afternoon, and received a warm and hospitable welcome from Major Blake, the officer in command, Lieutenants Jackson and Johnson, and Dr. Magruder. An incipient rain-storm made us feel sensible that we were still in the vicinity of the Sierra Mojada *(or Wet Mountains)*, which well merit the name, for rain fell every day that we were in or near them; on the highest peaks in the form of snow, and lower down in hazy moisture, alternating with drenching showers. This humidity gives great fertility to this region, and the country bordering on the sides of these mountains, as well as the valleys within their recesses, are unequalled in loveliness and richness of vegetation. To the settlers, they offer every inducement; and I have no doubt that in a few years this tract of country will vie with California or Australia in the number of immigrants it will invite to it. It is by far the most beautiful as well as the most fertile portion of New Mexico, and a remarkably level country unites it with the western frontier of the Atlantic States. As soon as this is thrown open to settlement, a continuous line of farms will be established, by which the agricultural and mineral wealth of this region will be developed. Communication will then be more rapid, and instead of the mail being, as it is now, thirty days in reaching Fort Massachusetts, (Fort Massachusetts was built in 1852 to protect the settlement of San Luis which was built in 1851.)[3] it will be carried through in eight or ten.

Messrs. Beale, Riggs, Rogers, and myself quartered at the Fort; the men encamped two miles below on Utah Creek, in a beautiful grove of cottonwoods. A tent was sent to them, and with fresh bread and meat they were soon rendered perfectly comfortable. There was excellent pasturage around their encampment, on which the mules soon forgot the hard marches they had made since leaving Westport. Day's travel, 25 miles; total distance from Westport to Fort Massachusetts, 693 miles.

June 14

As it was found impossible to obtain here the men and animals that we required, and that it would be necessary to go to Taos, and perhaps to Santa Fé, for this purpose, Mr. Beale and Major Blake left for the former place on the morning after our arrival at the fort. Taos is about eighty, and Santa Fé about one hundred and forty miles to the southward.

During our detention at Fort Massachusetts, I took frequent rides into the mountains on each side of it.

This post is situated on a narrow gorge through which the Utah rushes until it joins the Trinchera, and is a quadrangular stockade of pine log pickets, enclosing comfortable quarters for one hundred and fifty men, cavalry and infantry. Lofty and precipitous mountains surround it on three sides; and although the situation may be suitable for a grazing farm on account of the pasturage, and the abundance of good timber may render this a convenient point for a military station, it is too far removed from the general track of Indians to be of much service in protecting the settlements in San Luis valley (Fort Massachusetts probably served more to protect San Luis from the more aggressive Indians that entered the San Luis Valley from the plains.) from their insults and ravages. The Utahs, who infest the Sahwatch (Saguache) mountains, enter San Luis valley by the Carnero and Coochatope (Cochetopa) Passes from the westward, and by those of Del Punche, Del Medino, and Del Mosque from the northward and northeastward, and a post established at the head of the valley of San Luis would be much more effective in keeping these marauders in check, as it would there be able to prevent, if necessary, their descending into the valley in large numbers, and completely cut off their retreat with their booty. The valley of the Sahwatch (Saguache), so rich in pasturage, so well adapted to tillage, and so abundantly watered and timbered, appears to offer the best possition for a fort, and it would be as accessible from Taos as the post on the Utah, although the distance would of course be greater.

The cavalry at Fort Massachusetts numbered seventy-five men of whom forty-five were mounted. Though their horses were excellently groomed and stabled, and kept in high condition on corn, at six dollars a bushel, they would soon break down on a march in pursuit of Indians mounted on horses fed on grass, and accustomed to gallop at half speed up or down the steepest hills. Corn-fed animals lose their strength when they are put on grass, and do not soon get accustomed to the change of diet. Of this fact the officers at the fort were perfectly sensible, and regretted that they were not better prepared for any sudden emergency.

The weather during our stay at the fort was cool and bracing; wind generally from the southwest, with frequent showers of rain.

Mr. Beale returned from the southern country late in the afternoon of this day, and brought with him a guide, and a Mexican *arriero (muleteer)*; they were cousins, and both named Felipe Archilete. Jesus Garcia was discharged here, and Patrick Dolan, a soldier who had served out his time, hired in his place. Our party now numbered fourteen.

The guide, Felipe Archilete, or "Peg-Leg", for it was by this *sobriguet* that he was commonly known to Americans, deserves particular mention. He had spent the greater part of his life trading and trapping in the Indian country, and his accurate knowledge of the region between the Arkansas and Sevier River in Utah Territory, as well as his acquaintance with the Utah tongue, promised to render him of great service to us in the absence of Mr. Leroux. A few years ago, in a skirmish with the Utahs, he was wounded in the left ankle with a rifle ball, which completely crippled his foot, and compelled him to use at times a wooden leg, which he carried suspended to his waist. Notwithstanding his lameness, he was one of the most active men of the party, and was always the foremost in times of difficulty and danger.

During Mr. Beale's absence, I replenished our provisions from the sutler's store, and had a small supply of biscuit baked; a bullock which I purchased from the quartermaster, was cut up and jerked by the Delaware, and the mules were reshod, and a supply of spare shoes and nails obtained. They were completely rested, and in even better condition than when we started from Westport; after a general overhauling of the camp equipage by the men, everything was put in order for resuming our journey, as soon as Mr. Beale should return.

June 15

Bidding adieu to our kind friends at the fort, we resumed our journey at noon, and traveled down Utah Creek south-southwest, until it debouched in the valley of San Luis, when we altered our cource to west by north. In six miles from Fort Massachusetts, we crossed the trail (This trail which they crossed is the East Fork of the North Branch of the Old Spanish Trail. It passes through the present-day town of Blanca and continues around the west side of Mount Blanca. The D & R G W Railroad crossed this road going west in 1878. This crossroad developed into the town of Blanca.) of Roubideau's wagons from the upper Arkansas settlements; they entered through Roubideau's Pass in the Sierra Mojada *(Sangre de Cristo)*. After crossing it, our route led us over a level plain covered with artemisia, cacti, and patches

169

of the nutritious grama. A ride of twenty-five miles brought us at dark to a slough of the Rio del Norte, (This is near the present-day town of Alamosa, Colorado.) where we encamped. Day's march, 25 miles; total distance from Westport, 718 miles.

June 16

Our animals were inclined to stray back to the fort, but by constant watchfulness during the night they were prevented from wandering too far from camp. We never hobbled nor picketed our mules, unless compelled to do so by circumstance, for it was noticed that when thus confined they did not eat as heartily as when allowed to range freely in search of the grass they preferred. It was the duty of the men on guard to prevent their straying, and this added much to our fatigue,

Having ascertained that our supply of lead was insufficient, Mr. Rogers and myself started at 4 A.M. to return to Fort Massachusetts to procure more. We crossed a spur of the mountains in a direct line to the fort, instead of going round by their base, thereby saving four or five miles of the distance. The trail was much obstructed by trees and brush; but we reached the fort at an early hour, and also avoided a very troublesome march, where some of our mules were mired the day before.

At the fort, we engaged Juan Lente as arriero *(muleteer)*, and bought a mule for him. On returning to our last camping place, Lieut. Johnson gave us an escort of two dragoons. The weather was cool and pleasant in the morning, but warm in the afternoon. Having started from the fort at 2 P.M. we did not reach the slough on the Del Norte until 8½ P.M.

The camp had left in the morning, and had crossed the bottom lands of the Del Norte, (They traveled west along the north side of the Rio Grande much the same as the early day stage coaches.) eighteen miles in breath; this crossing is at times difficult and dangerous on account of the numerous sloughs and marches, which can be altogether avoided, however, by a circuit of a few miles.

Midway to the river they fell in with some Utah Indians, hunting wild horses; the Indians were the first to discover our party, and the foremost stood upright on his horse, in order to obtain a better view; he counted their number, and signalized his discovery with his gun to his comrades, who thereupon approached at full speed. They had their squaws with them and some children, all mounted on good horses, and were quite friendly. In the course of the day they lassoed a mustang, but strangled him in their eagerness to secure their prize. 18 miles; 736 miles.

June 17

Mr. Rogers and myself started at 3 A.M., and overtook our party at 8:30 A.M., as they were preparing to raise camp. We proceeded immediately on our journey, and coasting up the left bank of the Del Norte about ten miles, left it where it made a bend to the westward, (At this location Heap and Beale reached the West Fork of the North Branch of the Old Spanish Trail.) directing our course north by west to the Sahwatch (Saguache) valley the commencement of the Coochatope (Cochetopa) Pass. Before leaving the Del Norte, the Indians were asked whether there was water in the direction in which we were going; for the commencement of the Sahwatch (Saguache) valley was about thirty miles distant. They replied that we should find water and grass by going around by the foot of the mountains, but none by going direct. The circuitous route they recommended would have occupied us two days, whilst we hoped to accomplish the distance direct before night. Our red friends were unwilling to venture with us, and bade us farewell; we parted with them on friendly terms; they had spent the night in our camp, shared our supper and breakfast, smoked our pipes.

 The plain was as level as the sea to the foot of the mountains, which inclose San Luis valley. A low spur of hills to the northward, indicated the entrance to the valley of the Sahwatch (Saguache). In fourteen miles from the point where we left the river, we crossed a fine brook of clear and cool water-the Rio de la Garita, (From the Rio Grande to La Garita Creek the Old Spanish Trail travels nearly due north. At La Garita Creek the trail takes a northeasterly course. On the south bank of La Garita Creek, Spanish or Mexican Traders built the adobe Torrez Trading Post about 1858.)[4] which rises in the Sahwatch mountains, and, flowing east, discharges itself into a large lagoon at the base of the Sierra Mojada (Sangre de Cristo not the Wet Mountains or Sierra Mojada), in the northern part of the valley of San Luis. Its banks were swampy, and, although later in the season this inconvenience probably does not exist, wagons would do well to cross it nearer to the mountains on the left. Our course was in the face of a breeze which raised clouds of dust wherever the soil was loosened by our animals' feet, and those riding in the rear suffered much inconvenience from it. In ten miles from the Rio Garita, we came to an abundant spring, (Russell Spring.) surrounded by good grass, where we rested but a moment to drink, though we had travelled steadily since morning without eating. Mr. Beale was anxious to reach the entrance of the Sahwatch (Saguache) valley before evening, and to regain some of the time which had been unavoidably lost at Fort Massachusetts. At the spring we found a trail (This trail can best be seen today from an airplane. It continued to be the road from Del Norte to Saguache, Colorado until in the late 1930s, when the North Gunbarrel Road/US 285 was built up, thus ending the boggy two track road that led from Monte Vista to Saguache.) leading to the Sahwatch (Saguache) valley, and as soon as our mules struck it they stepped out with fresh spirit. The valley of San Luis, to the commencement of the Sahwatch (Saguache) is singularly level, the smooth ground seeming only to have the natural curve of the earth. The only vegetation, excepting in the vicinity of water, was artemisia, cactus and occasionally grama grass.

The valley of the Sahwatch (Saguache) has two entrances from that of San Luis. The one which we selected, on account of its being the nearest, is called by the Spaniards El Rincon del Sahwatch (El Rincon del Sahwatch or the corner of the Saguache is a route that would travel approximately Forest Service Road 704 up Tracy Cañon, crossing the ridge north of Tracy Mountain to Houselog Creek/ Hodding Creek.) *(the corner of the Sahwatch)*, as it forms a cut-off into Sahwatch (Saguache) valley proper. The main entrance is a few miles farther on. We went three miles up the Rincon, and encamped at sunset at a spring (There is a spring lying in Tracy Cañon about three miles from the base of the hills. Its at 8368 feet elevation.) of excellent water, where our mules found fine pasturage. Mr. Rogers and myself rode sixty-eight miles this day, and fifty the day before; which I mention to show the facility of travelling in this region. Day's march, 50 miles; whole distance, 786 miles.

June 18

Mosquitos allowed us little rest. As our animals had rather along march the day before, camp was not raised until 8 A.M. For two and a half miles our course was west by north; we then turned to the northward over some steep hills, and, upon reaching their summit, (The saddle of the ridge north of Tracy Mountain is 9866 feet in elevation and lies about two miles from the spring.) obtained a glorious view of the valley of the Sahwatch (Saguache). It was quite level, and from two to five miles in breadth, gradually narrowing to the westward; the rise was imperceptible, appearing like a continuation of the plain of San Luis. An abundant stream, the Sahwatch (Saguache), nearly as broad as the Huerfano, but deeper, flows through its centre, and empties into the lagoon in San Luis valley. (Early day maps show the Lagoon/San Luis Lakes extending nearly to the town of Saguache.) Its surface was clothed with nutritious grasses, and the hills and mountains by which it is hemmed in were covered with a thick growth of firs, aspens, and pines.

We proceeded fourteen miles farther up, and encamped at noon in a small valley (Hodding Creek) running into the main one. There is an abundance of water in all the lateral valley, as well as grass; in the main one, I noticed a superior quality of sandstone. The weather was clear and pleasant, and wind west.

On resuming our march in the afternoon, we ascended the small valley, as it shortened the distance a couple of miles, and re-entered that of the Sahwatch (Saguache). After a ride of eight miles we crossed Sahwatch (Saguache) Creek, (This was known as the upper crossing of Saguache Creek before the road was deviated to the west of the hill at the Buffalo Gate.) its waters reaching to our saddles, and encamped, as the sun was setting, at the entrance of the celebrated COOCHATOPE (Cochetopa) PASS.

Sahwatch (Saguache) valley maintains its level character to this point, and for several miles above, where it was shut from view by a curve. The entrance to the Carnero Pass is about a mile above the Coochatope (Cochetopa), and we regretted that we had not time to examine it.

A military post placed in Sahwatch (Saguache) valley, between these two passes, would do important service in holding the Utahs in check. These Indians most frequently enter San Luis valley through these passes, and it is here that a fort would be best placed to prevent their incursions, or to intercept their retreat with booty. The mountains are clothed with timber from their base to their summit, the valley with luxuriant and nutritious grasses, and clear, brawling mountain streams pour into them on every side. The distance to the nearest New Mexican settlements is about one hundred and twenty miles, and the intervening country is a dead level. If undisturbed by the incursions of Indians, these valleys would soon be settled and cultivated; for it is only of late, since the establishment of a military post on Utah Creek, that settlements of any consequence have been made on Costilla and Culebra creeks. (Costilla, Costilla Creek, was settled in 1849 and San Luis, Culebra Creek, in 1851.)

COOCHATOPE (Cochetopa) PASS is a wonderful gap, or, more properly speaking, a natural GATE, as its name denotes in the Utah language. On each side, mountains rise in abrupt and rocky precipices, the one on the eastern side being the highest. We climbed up the one on the left, which is but a confused mass of rocks, but in their crevices were many beautiful and sweetscented flowers. The bottom of the Pass was level and at right angles with Sahwatch (Saguache) valley; and we had thus far reached twenty-five miles into the mountains, from San Luis valley, without any apparent change of level. Singular as it may appear, it is nevertheless a fact that, notwithstanding the distance that we had penetrated into these mountains, had it not been for the course of the waters, it would have been difficult to have determined whether we were asending or descending.

A stream (Sheep Creek) issues from Coochatope (Cochetopa) Pass and joins the Sahwatch (Saguache); it is called *Coochumpah* by the Utahs, and *Rio de los Cibolos* by the Mexicans: both names have the same signification—*River of buffaloes*. *Coochatope* (Cochetopa) signifies, in the Utah language, *Buffalo gate*, and the Mexicans have the same name for it, *El Puerto de los Cibolos*. The pass and creek are so called, from the large herds of these animals which entered Sahwatch and San Luis valleys through this pass, from the Three Parks and Upper Arkansas, before they were destroyed, or the direction of their migration changed, by the constant warfare carried on against them by Indians and Mexicans. A few still remain in the mountains, and are described as very wild and savage. We saw a great number of elk-horns scattered through these valleys; and, from the comparatively fresh traces of buffaloes,

173

Buffalo Gate or old entrance to Cochetopa Pass.

it was evident that many had visited the pass quite recently. The abundant pasturage and great shelter found here, even in the severest winters, render them a favorite resort at that season for game of every description. Coochatope (Cochetopa) Pass is traveled at all seasons, and some of our men (This indicates that the North Branch was frequently used by travelers from New Mexico.) had repeatedly gone through it in the middle of winter without meeting any serious obstruction from snow. Many Utahs (Utes) winter in the valleys lying within the Sahwatch (Saguache) mountains, where Mexican traders meet them to barter for buckskins and buffalo robes.

Our Delaware, in commemoration of our arrival at this point, killed a mountain sheep, and soon a dozen sticks were around the fire, on which were roasting pieces of this far-famed meat; but this was a bad specimen, being both old and tough. Day's travel, 22 miles; total distance, 808 miles.

June 19

We resumed our journey at 5:30 A.M., and having travelled two miles, reached the forks of the Coochumpah (East Pass Creek), (The distance to the north does not fit but the remainder of the description does fit that of East Pass Creek.) taking the west fork up the valley, which here commenced to ascend at an easy grade. The mountain sides were clothed with fine timber, among which were pines, firs, and aspens, and the valley with the most luxuriant grass and clover, this being the first clover we had seen. Around us were scattered numerous elk-horns and buffalo skulls. Eight miles brought us to a remarkable cliff, about one hundred feet in height, which beetled over the trail on our left; nine miles from the "Gate," we saw the last water flowing east to Atlantic; in five minutes we were on the culminating point of the pass, and in ten more crossed the first stream flowing west to the Pacific. It was almost as if we were standing with one foot in waters which found their way to the Gulf of Mexico, and the other in those losing themselves in the Gulf of California.

In our eagerness to explore this pass to its western outlet, Mr. Beale and I rode far ahead of the remainder of the party. The scenery was grand and beautiful beyond description. Lofty mountains, their summits covered with eternal snow, lifted their heads to the clouds, whilst in our immediate vicinity were softly rounded hills clothed with grass, flowers, and rich meadows, through which numerous rills trickeled to join their waters to Coochatope (Cochetopa) Creek.

At noon we encamped on this stream, where it had already swollen to a considerable size. It is a tributary to Grand (Gunnison) River, east fork of the Great Colorado. Near camp was a lofty and steep hill, which I ascended to obtain a better view of the country; one of its principal features was the Coochatope (Cochetopa) Mountain to the southeast; high, round, and dark with pines.

We were here compelled, by the necessity that we were under of selecting the shortest route, to go by the trail which takes the most direct course to Grand (Gunnison) River, though there was a more circuitous route to the right, leading over a level country, but which would have lengthened the journey by two days. (The Heap/Beale expedition now leaves the main fork of the North Branch and takes a short cut.) Travelled ten miles in the afternoon over a rich rolling country, well timbered and watered, and covered with luxuriant grasses. Saw many deer, antelopes, and mountain sheep. Day's travel, 34 miles; whole distance, 842 miles.

June 20

The usual cry of "catch up," set the camp in motion at 5:45 A.M. We travelled twenty-two miles over a rolling country, more hilly than our route of the previous day, and encamped on a rivulet at noon. Our course was south by west. The hill-sides and mountains were still covered with a thick growth of pines and aspens; wild flowers adorned the murmuring stream, and beautified the waving grass. Every few hundred yards we came to one of these purling brooks, the haunt of the timid deer, who bounded away at our approach. To the westward, the Eagle Range (La Sierra del Aguila), towered high above the surrounding mountains, its summits capped with snow, some patches of which we passed near our trail. Mr. Beale shot a species of grouse, larger than a prairie hen, and caught one of her young. At 5:30 P.M., in five milcs from our noon camp, we crossed the two forks of the Jaroso *(Willow Creek)*, a strong stream running into Grand (Gunnison) River, not laid down on any map. At 7 P.M. we rested for the night in a valley watered by a small shallow brook, very marshy, and swarming with mosquitos. Our general course this day was southwest. Numbers of deer and antelopes were seen; indeed, these sheltered valleys seem expressly intended as coverts for these gentle animals.

About a mile before reaching the Jaroso, we crossed a valley where a party of Americans were cruelly murdered by the Utahs, in the spring of this year. Five Americans, and a few Mexicans, were driving sheep to California by this route, and, from some cause which I did not ascertain, a disagreement arose between them and a band of Utahs, who were still here in their winter-quarters. The latter forbade their passing through their country, and, placeing a row of elk-horns across the valley, threatened them with instant death if they crossed that line. The whites deeming this a vain threat, attempted to force their way through, were attacked, and all killed. The elk-horns were still in the position in which the Indians had placed them. Our guide, Felipe, had an account of this affair from Utahs who had been actors in the affray. At this point the trail from the Del Norte through the Carnero Pass joins that through the Coochatope. Traders from Abiquiú come by it into these mountains to barter for peltries with the Utahs. Day's travel, 34 miles; total, 876 miles.

June 21

Raised camp at 4:45 A.M. and travelled five miles west by south, crossing a steep and rocky hill covered with pines, and in five miles entered a small valley watered by the Rio de la Laguna *(Lake Creek)*. This creek issues from a lake near the summit of the Sierra de la Plata *(Silver Range)*, about twelve acres in area; we found it unfordable on account of its swollen condition from melting snows. Its current was swift and waters turbid, rolling with a loud roar over a rocky bed. It both enters and leaves this valley through narrow and rocky cañons; above the upper one it flows through another valley of larger extent and of great beauty.

It became a question with us, how our packs were to be transported over the laguna without getting them wet or lost, and we at first attempted to make a bridge by felling a tall pine across the stream, but it fell partly into the water, and the current carried it away, tearing it into pieces. This plan having failed, another was adopted, suggested by what Mr. Beale had seen in his travels in Peru, and the mode of crossing the plunging torrents of the Andes, which was entirely successful.

Mr. Rogers selected a point where the stream was for some distance free from rocks, and succeeded, after a severe struggle, in swimming across; and one of the men mounting a stray Indian pony, which we found quietly grazing in the valley, dashed in after him, and also effected a landing on the opposite side. To them a light line was thrown, and having thus established a communication with the other side, a larger rope was drawn over by them, and tied firmly to a rock near the water's edge. The end of the rope on our side was made fast to the top of a pine tree; a backstay preventing it from bending to the weight of the loads sent over. An iron hook was now passed over the rope, and by means of a sling our packs were suspended to it. The hook slided freely from the top of the tree down to the rock; and when the load was taken off, we drew the hook and sling back to our side by a string made fast to it. The last load sent over was our wearing apparel, and just after parting with it, a violent hailstorm broke over us, making us glad to seek shelter from its fury under rocks and trees. Most of the day was thus consumed, and it was not until 5 P.M. that we mounted our mules and swam them across. The water was icy cold, and some of the animals had a narrow escape from drowning. We, however, saddled up immediately, and, proceeding four miles from the creek, encamped for the night in a small hollow. On leaving the Rio de la Laguna, the road ascended a high and steep hill. The country travelled over this day was abundantly grassed, the hills timbered with firs, pines, and aspens, and the streams shaded with willows. Day's travel, 9 miles; total, 885 miles.

June 22

We started soon after sunrise and travelled west by south over steep hills, well timbered and covered with rich grasses. The weather was clear and cold, and wind fresh from the west. Crossed three streams swollen by melting snow: the Rio Hondo *(Deep River)*, the Savoya, and the Pentacigo *(Leek Creek)*. At 10 A.M., in twenty miles from the Rio de la Laguna, we crossed the two forks of the Nawaquasitch *(Sheep-tail Creek, Utah language)*. The Mexicans call it Los Riitos Quartos *(Twin Creeks)*, and the Cola del Carnero *(Sheep-tail Creek)*. We forded it immediately above the junction of the forks. Both were much swollen, and we had some difficulty in crossing the packs, some of which got wet. A pair of saddle-bags containing many articles of value to us were lost in this crossing. All these streams are mere rivulets a month or two later. Encamped at noon on the left bank of the western fork of the Nawaquasitch.

Started again an hour before sunset, and following down the left bank of the Nawaquasitch until it turned to the northward through a deep cañon, left it and directed our course to the westward. The Nawaquasitch empties into Grand River *(east fork of the Colorado)*, not far beyond the outlet of this cañon. All the streams that we passed this day are tributaries of Grand (Gunnison) River, and are not laid down on any map.

We were now approaching the western limits of the Sahwatch Mountains, and continued down a rivulet until it gave out, as it reached the base of the hills. Upon reaching the plain which extends from the foot of the Sahwatch Range to

177

Grand (Gunnison) River, (The expedition reaches the Gunnison River and returns to the main fork of the North Branch of the trail.) we encamped for the night, having made twenty miles since noon. There was grass in small patches on the brook down which we travelled, and it grew scantier as we approached the plains. This stream dries up entirely in a month or six weeks from this time.

The Pareamoot Mountains *(Elk Mountains, Utah tongue)*, a range of whose unexplored beauties much had been related to us, loomed up darkly between us and the setting sun. Day's march, 38 miles; total distance, 923 miles.

June 23

At an early hour in the morning, Mr. Beale, Felipe Archilete, the Delaware, and I, taking the lead, arrived at the River Uncompagre at 11:10 A.M. We travelled about twelve miles parallel with this river, and found it everywhere a broad rapid stream, entirely too rapid and swift to ford with safety; we therefore continued down its right bank until we reached Grand (Gunnison) River.

We had been prepared to find Grand (Gunnison) River swollen, for its tributaries which we had crossed were all at their highest stage of water; but we had not anticipated so mighty a stream. It flowed with a loud and angry current, its amber-colored waters roaring sullenly past, laden with the wrecks of trees uprooted by their fury. Sounds like the booming of distant artillery, occasioned by the caving in of its clayey and sandy banks, constantly smote our ears. This fork of the Colorado rises in the Middle Park, and gathers all its head waters in that inclosure, and is described by Frémont, who crossed it there, as being a large river, one hundred and thirty yards wide where it breaks through its mountain rim and flows southwest. Between that point and where we approached it, numerous streams contribute their waters to increase its volume; and where we now stood, anxiously gazing at its flood, it had spread to a breadth of over two hundred and fifty yards.

As it was evident that this river was nowhere fordable, it was determined to commence at once the construction of a raft. A place where dead wood was found in abundance was selected for our encampment, and to reach it, it was necessary to cross a broad slough, where the mules sank to their bellies in the mud; the packs were carried over on our heads. This brought us to an island of loose, rotten soil, covered with grease wood and some coarse grass. We had no shelter from the sun, which was intensely hot, and the mosquitos and gadflies were perfectly terrific.

From this point, the Pareamoot Mountains were in full view; they ranged from the north, and terminated in an abrupt declivity on the western side of Grand (Gunnison) River, opposite to the mouth of the Uncompagre. They were described to me as abounding in game, and well timbered; on their plateaux, are fine lakes filled with excellent fish, rich meadows, abundant streams, every natural attraction, in fact, to induce settlement.

Our guide, Felipe, had spent three years in them, trapping and hunting, and said that there is no richer country on the continent. These mountains are not laid down on any map. Day's travel, 28 miles; total distance, 951 miles.

June 24

Whilst most of the party were busily occupied in collecting and cutting logs, constructing the rafts, and transporting the packs, saddles, &c., to the point of embarkation, which had to be done in deep mud, and under a scorching sun, others explored the banks of the river, to ascertain whether a place could be found where the *cavallade* could be crossed over. The river was examined several miles above our encampment, but its banks on our side were everywhere so marshy as to prevent the approach of the mules to the water's edge. At the encampment, the ground was firmer, but we feared to drive them into the river at this point, as it was here not only very rapid and broad, but its opposite banks, as far down as we could see, were marshy and covered with a thick jungle, from which our mules, after the exhaustion of swimming across so swift a current, would have been unable to extricate themselves.

Towards noon the raft was completed, but we were far from feeling confident about crossing at this point. Archilete, who was well acquainted with all the fords and crossing-places, stated that perhaps a better point might be found a few miles below the mouth of the Uncompagre, which flowed into Grand (Gunnison) River a short distance below us. As it was evident that it would be risking the entire loss of our animals and packs to attempt to cross them here, it was determined to abandon the raft and to move camp farther down without delay. Everything was again transported to the main shore across the slough. The animals had much difficulty in crossing this place, even without loads; with them, they sank hopelessly into the mud, from which it was very difficult to drag them out.

A more dirty, begrimed, and forlorn looking party was never seen; we were covered with mud to our waists; wherever the mosquitos and gadflies could reach our skin they improved the opportunity most industriously, and most of the men were covered with blisters and welts. All cheerfully took a share in this labor, but a volley of execrations was poured on this quagmire, which was appropriatly christened the "Slough of Despond."

Having transported everything to dry land and got the animals through the mud, we once more packed them and resumed our journey down the left bank of Grand (Gunnison) River until we came to the Uncompagre, a short distance above its mouth.

The largest animals were here selected to carry the packs across, their feet barely touching the bottom, whilst the strenth of the current drove the water over their backs. Some of the men, mounted on horses, led the pack mules, and prevented their being carried down the stream where the water was deeper. One mule, with a valuable pack, having gone in of her own accord, was carried away, lost her foothold and sank, the weight of the pack being too great to allow her to swim; she was swept down the stream with great rapidity, rolling over helplessly until entirely lost to our sight by a bend of the river. Some of the party swam across, and one, benumbed by the coldness of the water, and exhausted by struggling against the stream, would have been drowned had he not been providentially seized just as his strength had entirely failed him.

We encamped a few miles below the Uncompagre, on the left bank of the Grand (Gunnison) River, upon a bluff from which we had a fine view of its course, and of the Pareamoot Mountains opposite. Our tormentors, the mosquitos, did not fail to welcome us with a loud buzz, whilst the drone of the gadfly, which might with truth be termed the *furia-infernalis* of the plains, gave notice that he was about, thirsting for our blood. Wherever he inserted his proboscis, the sensation was like that of a redhot darning needle thrust into the flesh, and was followed by streams of blood. The mules and horses suffered terribly by these flies.

Our provisions, by losses in the river and damage by water, were fast diminishing, and it was deemed prudent at this time to put ourselves on a limited allowance, for it was uncertain how long we might be detained in crossing this river, the Avonkaria, and Upper Colorado.

The pack lost with the mule drowned in the Uncompagre contained many articles of importance to us, besides all our pinole *(parched cornmeal)*, and some of the men lost all their clothing.

It was late when we got to camp, and after a day of toil, exposure, and annoyance, nothing more could be done than to select the tree out of which to make a canoe, and the place to launch it; for all idea of crossing on a raft was abandoned. A few miles below the encampment the river was shut in by a cañon, towards which it dove with great swiftness; a raft carried into it would have been torn to pieces in a moment, without a chance for the men on it to save their lives. Day's travel, 5 miles; total, 956 miles.

June 25

At early dawn most of the party commenced working on the canoe; their only tools were two dull axes and two hatchets. A large cottonwood tree was felled for this purpose, and it was hoped to have the canoe finished the next day. The wood, being green and full of sap, was hard to cut, and so heavy that chips of it sank when thrown into the water.

The river still maintained the same level, and the bottom land was overflowed and marshy. The high lands on which we were encamped were composed of a loose, rotten soil, producing no vegetation except stunted sage bushes. The only game we had seen for two days was an occasional sage rabbit, so called from its flesh having a strong flavor of the wild sage *(artemisia)*, on which it feeds. The sun was very hot and mosqiutos tormenting; we removed our camp to the bluffs in the hope of avoiding them, but with little success. At this point, the general course of the river was parallel with the Pareamoot Mountains, from northeast to southwest. The latter appeared to rise in terraces, upon which much timber could be seen.

The work on the canoe was continued steadly all day, though some of the party entertained grave doubts about crossing in it; besides, the two rivers beyond Grand (Gunnison) River were said to be larger and their current swifter than this. Archilete stated that he had never seen the river so high, and that it was owing to the unusual quantity of snow which had fallen in the mountains during last winter. The wind rose at ten o'clock and blew with violence until sunset, which relieved us in a measure from the torment of mosquitos, but they returned in fresh swarms as soon as it lulled.

June 26

Opposite to our encampment was old "Fort Roubideau," (Robidoux) now

This is a recreation of Fort Uncompahgre built by Antoine and Louis Robidoux in 1828 at a site west of this location.

abandoned and in ruins. It was formerly a trading post belonging to the brothers Roubideau (Robidoux), (Fort Robidoux was built about 1828 by Antoine and Louis Robidoux and flourished until 1844.)[5] of St. Louis, Missouri, who carried on a lucrative trade with the Utahs for peltries.

Beavers are quite numerous on all these rivers, and have greatly multiplied of late years since the demand for their furs has diminished.

The canoe was completed at noon, and a fire was kindled in and around it to dry it. At 4 P.M., the first load went over with the Delaware and Archilete. Everything had to be carried to the water's edge through a thick jungle, knee deep in mud, and under a broiling sun.

They reached the opposite side safely, although the current carried them some distance down the stream. The canoe was found to be very heavy, and easy to upset. Archilete, Juan Lente, and myself went with the second load, reached the other side, and, after unloading, dragged the canoe some distance up stream to enable Archilete, who was to take it back, to make a landing at the point where the packs were deposited. Two more of the men crossed with the next load, and Archilete returned in the canoe to the left bank for the night.

We were now four persons on the right bank of the stream, with the prospect of getting the rest of the party and packs across at an early hour the next day. We retired to some dry land about half a mile from the river, and carried to it the few things that had been brought over. Just before dark, Dick, the Delaware, made his appearance in camp, dripping wet, and reported that he had just swam across with some of the mules; that after getting all into the water most of them had turned back, while three mules and one horse, having reached the right bank, had sunk into the mud, from which he had been unable to relieve them. We immediately went down to the water's edge with ropes, and with great difficulty got the horse out of his bed of mud, but found it impossible to extricate the mules. We were compelled to leave the poor animals in their forlorn situation until the morning, when we hoped to get them on dry land.

June 27

Rose at dawn, and our first business was to get the mules out of their dangerous predicament, by cutting bushes and spreading them around the mired animals, thus rendering the ground sufficiently firm to support their weight.

At an early hour, a signal was made to us from the other side that the canoe was about starting to cross. We therefore went down to the river side to receive its load. In a few minutes she made her appearance, driving rapidly down the stream. She was heavily loaded, barely four inches of her gunwale being above the water's edge. Felipe Archilete, a strong and active fellow, was paddling, whilst George Simms was crouched in the bow of the boat. They were unable to reach the point where previous landings had been effected, and were soon shut from our sight by trees and tangled bushes, growing close to the water. In a few seconds we heard the most alarming cries for help, and upon rushing to the spot from which these cries proceeded, found Archilete and George just emerging from the water, nearly exhausted with their struggles.

It appears that upon approaching the bank and grasping some small limbs of trees overhanging the water, the latter broke, whereupon one of the men, becoming alarmed, attempted to jump from the boat to the shore, causing it immediately to upset. They were both thrown into the stream, which here ran with a strong current, and it was with difficulty that they reached the shore. I immediately called to one of the men who was standing near the horse, to gallop down the river's edge, and by swimming him into the middle of the stream to endeavor to reach the canoe should it make its appearance. But it was never seen again, nor did we recover any of the articles with which it was loaded. We lost by this accident seven rifles, nearly all our ammunition, pistols, saddles, cornmeal, coffee, sugar, blankets, &c.

With broken axes and dull hatchets it would have been difficult if not impossible to have constructed another canoe; and, besides, the men were too much discouraged by this loss to undertake the labor with the spirit necessary to carry it through.

Our party was equally divided; we were seven on each side. Some of the gentlemen on the left bank were now anxious to return to New Mexico to proceed to California by some other route; but Mr. Beale would not listen for a moment to such proposition. He hailed me at eight o'clock, and told me that as soon as he could construct a raft, and get the few remaining things and animals over, we would push on for the Mormon settlements near the Vegas de Santa Clara. Expedition was necessary, for we had provisions for only four or five days.

The Delaware swam back to Mr. Beale's side to assist him to construct a raft or canoe. He was a splendid swimmer, and went through the water like an otter. They immediately commenced the construction of another canoe, but both axes being broken, they soon had to relinquish the task as hopeless.

An inventory was made of the provisions, and it was found that we had twenty-five pounds of biscuit, mostly in dust, twenty-five pounds of dried venison, and ten pounds of bacon. Although this was but slender provision for fourteen hungry men, we had no fear of starvation, or even of suffering, as long as we had the mules. I also discovered in an old bag a small supply of powder and lead, and some chocolate and tobacco. A canister of *meat-biscuit*, upon which we had depended in case of an emergency of this sort, had unfortunately gone down with the canoe.

At an early hour in the morning, we saw flying from a tree on the left bank, the preconcerted signal to "come down for a talk." To reach the river, we had to wade for half a mile through a deep marsh, into which we sank to our knees, and the air was thick with mosquitos.

Mr. Beale informed me that it had been decided to return to Taos for supplies, and inquired whether we could get back to the left bank. As two of the men on my side stated that they could not swim, it was decided to make a raft, and, if possible, to save the articles we had with us. Before this was determined upon, however, Mr. Beale ordered Archilete to swim over to his side, which the latter did at once, taking his timber leg under his arm; and in the afternoon they made another ineffectual attempt to get the animals across. There was but one point where it was possible to drive them into the river, and here they crowded in on each other until those underneath were near drowning. Mr. Beale and one of the men, who were riding, went into the river to lead the band across. The mules fell on them from the bank, which was at this place about three feet high, and for a moment they were in imminent danger of being crushed. An old horse alone struck boldly over, but none of the other animals followed his example. They all got out on the same side, and could not be again driven into the water.

Mr. Beale now desired me to make arrangements for returning to his side of the river, and while preparing the animals to move down to our camping ground, I thought I heard a faint shout, and at the same time perceiving two dark objects moving in the water, some distance up the stream, I suspected that they were men from the opposite shore endeavoring to reach land on our side. The current was carrying them swiftly on towards a high bank overhanging the stream, where, without help, to have effected a landing would have been impossible.

Hastily seizing a rope, and calling to the men to follow, I ran to the top of the cliff. In fact, they were our two best swimmers, Dick and Felipe, who were scarcely able to keep their hold until ropes could be led down to them. We drew them up half perished, and it required a good fire and something stimulating to restore circulation to their limbs, benumbed by the icy coldness of the water. Although we had no sugar, some coffee, that the Delaware had brought, tied in a hankerchief on his head, cheered the men, and we passed a good night, happy in any rest after such a day of toil.

June 29

At an early hour in the morning, I commenced throwing into the river everything that we could possibly dispense with, such as clothing, &c. I allowed each man to select sufficient clothing from the general stock to make up one suit, and it was singular how soon their wants increased. Some of the Mexicans, who heretofore had been satisfied with one shirt and a pair of pants, now arrayed themselves in as many breeches, drawers, shirts, and stockings as they could force themselves into. I *cachéd*, under a thick bush, a few Indian goods that we had brought with us as presents.

The three mules and two horses were passed over to the left shore without much difficulty by pushing them into the water from a bank, whence the eddy immediately carried them into the middle of the stream. They got out safely on the other side, and we at once commenced constructing the raft.

It was completed at 1 P.M., and, although it was twelve feet in length by eight in breadth, the weight of seven men, with the saddles, arms, and provisions we had saved, caused it to sink eighteen inches under water. It drifted rapidly down the stream, the men whooping and yelling, until one struck up the old song of "O Susannah!" when the rest sang the chorus. In this style, we fell upwards of two miles down the river, propelling ourselves with rough paddles. Mr. Beale and others of the party stood on a hill on the opposite side cheering and waving their hats. Having approached within ten yards of the left bank, our tritons, Dick and Archilete, sprang into the water, with ropes in their teeth, and reaching the shore soon dragged the raft to the bank, upon which the remainder of the crew landed. (Gwinn Harris Heap was chosen to return to Taos, New Mexico to purchase new supplies. He traveled the Old Spanish Trail to the junction of the Gunnison River and Lake Fork. Here his group took a different route. They met a group of Utes who were herding a large flock of tame goats. The Utes, upon finding that the men had not eaten for some time, fed them and supplied them with enough food to make it to Taos. At Taos, Heap purchased supplies as well as hide boats to be used to cross the rivers. He also hired Thomas Otterby (Tom Toben), José Galliego and Juan Cordova to replace the seven men who stayed in Taos to travel to California by another route. The five men returned to the Sawatch Valley by way of Carnero Pass and the same route as on the trip to Taos.)

July 17

We were now again united, (Gwinn Harris Heap returned to the area of present-day Montrose on July 17, 1853, having been gone since June 29.) and freed from the anxiety for each other's safety which had been weighing on us since the day of our separation. We resumed our journey at sunrise, with the hope of soon overcoming all difficulties. Although the sun rose in a cloudless sky, yet before noon the rain commenced falling in heavy showers. Mr. Beale and myself, having much to relate to each other, rode several miles ahead of the men. We descended to the plain at the foot of the Sahwatch (Saguache) mountains by the same trail over which we had already twice traveled, and which was now familiar to us. On approaching the Uncompagre, we traveled parallel with its course towards Grand (Gunnison) River, keeping on the trail of the two men sent ahead the day before with the hides to construct the boat. At noon, we noticed two recumbent figures on a distant butte, with horses standing near them; when we had approached within a mile they sprang to their saddles and galloped towards us at full speed. They were Utah (Ute) Indians, on a scout, and evinced no fear of us, but, approaching, frankly offered us their hands. We conversed with them partly by signs and partly by means of the few Utah (Ute) words which we had picked up, and their scanty knowledge of Spanish, which extended only to the names of a few objects and animals. They told us that large numbers of their tribe were encamped a few miles below, on the Uncompagre, and, bidding them farewell, we went on to meet our train.

Soon after parting with them, we saw on the hill-sides and river bottom, a vast number of gayly-colored lodges, and numerous bands of Indians arriving from the northward. Upon approaching, we were received by a number of the oldest men, who invited us to ascend a low, but steep hill, where most of the chiefs were seated. From this point we had a view of an animated and interesting scene. On every side fresh bands of Indians were pouring in, and the women were kept busy in erecting their lodges in the bottom near the Uncompagre, as well as on the higher land nearer to us. Horses harnessed to lodge poles, on which were packed their various property, and many cases their children, were arriving, and large bands of loose horses and mules were being driven to the river side to drink or to pasture. Squaws were going to the stream for water, whilst others were returning with their osier jars filled, and poised on their heads. Some of the young men were galloping around on their high-mettled horses, and others, stretched lazily on the grass, were patiently waiting until their better halves had completed the construction of their lodges, and announced that the evening meal was prepared. All the males, from the old man to the stripling of four years, were armed with bows and arrows, and most of the men had serviceable rifles. We almost fancied that we had before us a predatory tribe of Seythians or Numidians, so similar are these Indians in their dress, accoutrements, and habits, to what we have learned of those people.

An old chief, who, we were told, was one of their great men, addressed us a discourse, which very soon went beyond the limits of our knowledge of the Utah tongue, but we listened to it with the appearance of not only understanding the subject, but also of being highly interested with it. Our men, with Felipe Archilete, the guide and interpreter, were many miles in the rear, and we waited until their arrival, for Mr. Beale wished to take advantage of this opportunity to have a conversation with these chiefs, two of whom were the highest in the nation.

When Felipe came up, Mr. Beale and the capitanos, as they styled themselves, engaged in a long "talk." Mr. Beale told them that many Americans would be soon passing through their country on their way to the Mormon settlements and California, with wagons and herds, and that, if they treated the whites well, either by aiding them when in difficulty, guiding them through the mountains, and across the rivers, or by furnishing them with food when they needed it, they would always be amply rewarded. They appeared much gratified to hear this, and by way, no doubt, of testing whether his practice coincided with his preaching, intimated that they would be well pleased to receive, then, some of the presents of which he spoke; remarking, that as we had passed through their country, used their pasturage, lived among their people, and had even been fed by them, it was but proper that some small return should be made for so many favors. This was an argument which Mr. Beale had not forseen; but having no presents to give them, he explained how it was; that, having lost everything we possessed in Grand (Gunnison) River, it was out of his power to gratify them. This explanation did not appear at all satisfactory, nor did they seem altogether to credit him. They were very covetous of our rifles, but we could not, of course, part with them. The old chief became taciturn and sulky, and glanced towards us occasionally with a malignant expression.

We took no notice of his ill-temper, but lit our pipes and passed them around. In the meanwhile, our men had, in accordance with Mr. Beale's directions, proceeded to Grand (Gunnison) River, where they were to seek for Wagner and Galliego, and encamp with them. Felipe, whose quick and restless eye was always on the watch, dropped us a hint, in a few words, that it was becoming unsafe to remain longer in the midst of these savages, for he had noticed symptoms of very unfriendly feelings.

We were seated in a semicircle on the brow of a steep hill, and a large crowd had collected around us. Rising without exhibiting any haste, we adjusted our saddles, relit our pipes, and shaking hands with the chiefs who were nearest to us, mounted and rode slowly down the hill, followed by a large number of Utahs, who, upon our rising to leave them, had sprung to their saddles. The older men remained seated, and our escort consisted almost entirely of young warriors. They galloped around us in every direction; occasionally, a squad of four or five would charge upon us at full speed, reining up suddenly, barly avoiding riding over us and our mules. They did this to try our mettle, but as we took little notice of them, and affected perfect unconcern, they finally desisted from their dangerous sport. At one time, the conduct of a young chief, the son of El Capitan Grande, was near occasioning serious consequences. He charged upon Felipe with a savage yell, every feature apparently distorted with rage; his horse struck Felipe's mule, and very nearly threw them both to the ground. The Indians then seizing Felipe's rifle, endeavored to wrench it from his hands, but the latter held firmly to his gun, telling us at the same time not to interfere. We and the Indians formed a circle around them, as they sat in their saddles, each holding on to the gun, whose muzzle was pointed full at the Indian's breast. He uttered many imprecations, and urged his followers to lend him their assistance. They looked at us inquiringly, and we cocked our rifles—the hint was sufficient—

they declined interfering. For some minutes the Utah (Ute) and Felipe remained motionless, glaring at each other like two game-cocks, each watching with flashing eyes for an opportunity to assail his rival. Seeing that to trifle longer would be folly, Felipe, who held the butt-end of the rifle, deliberately placed his thumb on the hammer, and raising it slowly, gave warning to the young chief, by two ominous clicks, that his life was in danger. For a moment longer, the Utah (Ute) eyed Felipe, and then, with an indescribable grunt, pushed the rifle from him, and lashing his horse furiously, rode away from us at full speed. Felipe gave us a sly wink, and uttered the highly original ejaculation—"Carajo!"

We crossed the Uncompagre about twelve miles above our former fording-place. (The usual crossing place on the Uncompaghre River was at Johnson Ford in present-day Montrose, Colorado. It would appear that the expedition crossed in the vicinity of Olathe, Colorado.) The rain, which had been falling at intervals all day, now descended in torrents, and the river soon became so deep and rapid, that our return was entirely cut off. Our object in crossing it was to ascertain the condition of Grand (Gunnison) River, where we had previously been balked by the loss of the canoe. We travelled until nine o'clock, when we met some Utahs sent by Wagner to inform us that he had found a ford, which would dispence with the necessity of building a boat. The rain not abating, and having ridden since morning upwards of fifty miles, we concluded to accept the hospitality of our Indian friends, who offered us a lodge in an encampment, which we soon after reached. It consisted of six large deer-skin lodges on the brow of a hill overlooking in front the angry current of the Uncompagre, whilst on the left was Grand (Gunnison) River, about a mile distant. From this point we saw numerous fires dotting the opposite shores of the Uncompagre, amongst which shone a larger one lit by our men, for the purpose of guiding us through the storm to their encampment. Before we entered the lodge, a number of squaws and children issued from it, to make room for us, and scattered themselves among the other lodges; the men remained, squatting closely together on one side, while Mr. Beale, myself, and Felipe, spreading our saddleblankets near the fire, threw ourselves, in utter weariness, upon them. At this moment we would willingly have sold our birthrights for a mess of pottage, for we had tasted nothing since dawn.

We soon lit and passed around the friendly pipe, and made ourselves as comfortable and as much "at home" as circumstances would permit. The flickering blaze of the fire fell on the wrinkled visage of two or three old squaws, who had quiely crept near the door for a view of the "Mericanos," while outside, and peering over each other's shoulders, were a group of girls, whose bright eyes and laughing faces disclosing their pearly teeth, formed an agreeable contrast with the serious and even surly countenances of the men, and haggard appearance of the older squaws. Knowing that our men would feel anxious on account of our prolonged absence *(for having left us in the midst of the Indian encampment they had good reason to fear for our safety)*, Mr. Beale inquired whether there was any one who would undertake to carry a message to them across the river. A handsome young Indian volunteered to go, and Mr. Beale liberally promised to reward him on his return with a plug of tobacco, which he exhibited, to prove that he was in earnest. This generosity was duly appreciated; and it is probable that, with the offer of a few more plugs, the whole band might have been sent over as attachés to the embassy. Mr. Beale wrote to Young, to send us coffee, sugar, and biscuits; and our messenger, having stripped to the buff, rolled the paper up, and carefully thrust it through the lobe of his ear, which was pierced with large holes. Mounting a powerful horse, he disappeared in the darkness, towards the Uncompagre.

Much sooner than we had anticipated, he returned—his horse as well as himself—dripping with moisture, and brought, safely tied on the top of his head, the articles Mr. Beale had written for. He also carried in his ear a note from Young, stating that the Indians were quite peaceable and well-disposed, and had indicated a ford near which our men were encamped.

All uneasiness, on their account, being set at rest, we gave ourselves up entirely to the enjoyment of our novel situation. Knowing that nothing, not excepting music, "hath such charms to soothe the savage breast" as a good *feed*, Felipe asked for a large kettle, which was soon produced, and suspended from three sticks, over the fire. This he filled with coffee, well sweetened, and threw in also the bisquit. Affairs were now assuming an aspect which our hosts appeared to consider of intence interest. Their eyes did not wander for a moment from the magic kettle; and their half-opened mouths actually watered as the delicious aroma of the coffee filled the lodge. Felipe now called for our cups, which we carried suspended to our saddles, and for every other utensil in the camp, and served the delicious beverage around. The redskins sipped it scalding hot, accompanying each sip with a deep *ugh*! signifying their great enjoyment; and, having drained their cups to the dregs, they rubbed their stomachs, in token of its having done them infinite good. Fatigued as we were we soon stretched ourselves out to sleep, and though the wind howled around us, and the rain fell all night, we slept soundly and comfortably, the fire in the centre keeping the lodge quite warm, whilst an aperture in the top allowed the smoke to escape freely. Days travel, 50 miles; distance from Taos, 326 miles.

July 18

We saddled up at early dawn, swam our mules across the Uncompagre, and rejoined our men. They informed us that Juan Cordova had deserted the day before, and returned to Mr. Beale's encampment on the Savoya in company with the two

Indians we had met in the morning, and who were going that way.

We found camp filled with Indians, who, however, behaved in a friendly manner, and had even supplied the men with a bucket-full of goat's milk. No time was lost in preparing to ford Grand (Gunnison) River, (On the Wheeler Map this is known as the Robidoux Ford.) and some Indians went ahead to show us the way. On reaching the stream we found that it had fallen about six feet, and under the guidance of the Indians had no difficulty in getting over. The water reached nearly to the mules' backs, but the packs had been secured so high as to prevent their getting wet.

The Indians followed us across in large numbers, and at times tried our patience to the utmost. They numbered about two hundred and fifty warriors, and were all mounted on fine horses, and well armed with bows and arrows, having laid aside their rifles, which Felipe considered a sign that their designs were unfriendly, as they never carry them when they intend to fight on horseback. Their appearance, as they whirled around us at full speed, clothed in bright colors, and occasionally charging upon us with a loud yell, made a striking contrast with that of our party, mounted as we were upon mules, in the half-naked condition in which we crossed the river *(for it was dangerous to stop for a moment to dress)*. They enjoyed many laughs at our expence, taunting us, and comparing us, from our bearded appearance, to goats, and calling us beggarly cowards and women. Most of these compliments were lost to us at the time, but Felipe afterwards explained them. The old chief, the same who had given us such a surly reception on the preceding day, and his son, who had made a trial of strength with Felipe for his rifle, soon joined us, and behaved with much insolence, demanding presents in an imperious manner, and even endeavored to wrench our guns from our hands, threatening to "wipe us out" if we refused to comply with their wishes. They frequently harangued the young men, and abused us violently for traversing their country, using their grass and timber without making them any acknowledgment for the obligation. The latter listened in silence, but most of them remained calm and unmoved, and evinced no disposition to molest us. The chiefs then changed their tactics, and endeavored to provoke us to commence hostilities. Mr. Beale calmly explained to them that, having lost everything in the river, he was unable to make them such presents as he would have desired, and added *(addressing himself to the chiefs)* that he clearly saw that they were evilhearted men; for, after treating us as brothers and friends, they were now endeavoring to make bad blood between us and their people. He ended by telling them that we had a few articles which he would have distributed to them, had they not behaved in so unfriendly a manner; but that now, the only terms upon which they could obtain them was by giving a horse in exchange. Mr. Beale's motive for not giving them presents was our inability to satisfy the whole party, for all we possessed was a piece of cloth, a calico shirt, and some brass wire, and these articles, valueless as they were, if given to a few, would have excited the jealousy and ill-will of the less fortunate, and thus made them our enemies. The Indians, however, declined giving a horse in exchange for what we offered, saying that it would not be a fair bargain. Mr. Beale then said: "If you want to trade, we will trade; if you want to fight, we will fight;" requesting those who were not inclined to hostilities, to stand aside, as we had no wish to injure our friends.

The chief's, finding themselves in the minority as regarded fighting, finally consented to give us a mare for our goods; and after the trade was made we parted, much relieved at getting rid of such ugly customers.

The Utahs had been in company with us for several hours, and had often separated our party. During all this time our rifles were held ready for use, not knowing at what moment the conflict might commence. Had we come to blows, there is no doubt that we should have been instantly overwhelmed. The Delaware had kept constantly aloof from the party, never allowing an Indian to get behind him; and although he silently, but sullenly, resisted the attempts that were made to snatch his rifle from his gasp, he never for a moment removed his eyes from the old chief, but glared at him with a ferocity so peculiar, that it was evident that feeling even stronger than any that could arise from his present proceedings, prompted the Delaware's ire against the rascally Utah. Dick subsequently told us that, when he was a boy, he had fallen into the hands of this same old chief, who had been urgent to put him to death. Dick had nursed his revenge with an Indian's constancy, and upon the first blow, intended to send a rifle ball through his skull.

Several times Felipe warned us to be on our guard, as the attack was about to commence, and Mr. Beale directed all to dismount upon the first unequivocal act of hostility, to stand each man behind his mule, and to take deliberate aim before firing.

Travelling down Grand (Gunnison) River, at some distance from its right bank, we came to where it flowed through a cañon. The ground on either side of the river was much broken by ravines. The country, about a mile from the river, was barren and level, producing nothing but wild sage and prickly pear. After a harassing day we encamped on a rapid, clear and cool brook, with good pasturage on its banks, called in the Utah (Ute) language, the Cerenoquinti; it issues from the Pareamoot Mountains and flows into Grand (Gunnison) River. Day's travel, 25 miles; whole distance from Westport, computed from June 23, 976 miles.

July 19

Resumed our journey at 5:30 A.M., and travelling twelve miles southwest over a level and barren country, encamped on the Avonkarea *(Blue* (Colorado) *River, Utah tongue)*. Our encampment was on a high rocky bluff overhanging the stream, and offering a beautiful view of its course. (The crossing on the Colorado descended the bluffs by way of an arroyo located at 28-1/4 Road.) The scenery was grand beyond description; the fantastic shapes of the mountains to the northward resembled in some places interminable ranges of fortifications, battlements, and towers, and in others immense Gothic cathedrals; the whole was bathed in the beautiful colors thrown over the sky and mountains, and reflected in the stream by a glowing sunset.

This river was broader and more rapid than Grand (Gunnison) River, and as we had anticipated, entirely too deep to ford. At the point where we encamped, it was about three hundred yards in breadth, and it had evidently recently been much wider. It frothed and foamed as it rushed impetuously past the rocks, bearing on its bosom huge trees, which rolled and writhed like drowning giants. The men immediatly commenced making a frame for the boat, the qualities of which we were about to test. The keel and longitudinal ribs were made with saplings, and the transverse ribs with small limbs of willows, which bent easily to any shape required. The hides—two of which had been closely sewed together—were softened by soaking in the river, spread under the frame; and the edges, perforated with holes, were brought up its sides and tightly laced to them with thongs. The boat was finished by sunset, and although neither as light nor as graceful as a birch-bark canoe, it promised to carry us and our packs over safely.

Soon after arriving at the Avonkarea (Colorado), we were hailed from the opposite shore by a Mexican, who informed us that he and his party had been waiting twenty days for the waters to fall, being unable to cross over.

He stated that they had left the Mormon settlements at the Vegas de Santa Clara on the 20th of June, and had lost two of their men by drowning in Green River. Mr. Beale promised to assist them over.—12 miles; 988 miles.

July 20

Commenced crossing at an early hour. The boat answered admirably; it was buoyant, easily managed, and safe. Before sunset most of the train had crossed, and the Delaware had succeeded in swimming the mules over, by following in their wake, and heading off those that tried to turn back. It took us longer than we had anticipated, to get our effects across, as it was necessary at each trip to tow the boat some distance up the right bank, in order to make our encampment on the left, without drifting below it. The current was very rapid, and the work of towing the boat up through the bushes which overhung the stream, very laborious. Some of the Mexicans and a few of their packs were carried in safely to the left bank. It rained heavily during the afternoon, and we passed a wet night under our blankets. The camp was crowded with Indians, who were anxious to trade, but were not troublesome. As some of them passed the night with us, we allowed our animals to run with theirs.

Henry Young was at one time in a very precarious position, from which he was relieved with difficulty. One of the mules had stubbornly resisted every effort to get her over, and had finally made a landing under a high precipice on the left shore, from which it was impossible to dislodge her, without going into the water and swimming to the spot. This was attempted by Young, and as the current here swept down with tremendous velocity, he was on the point of drowning, when forunately he seized a rock, upon which he landed. It was now dark, the rain falling fast, and to have passed the night in this situation was certain destruction, for he was under a precipice, and in front of him roared the Avonkarea. No one knew that he had gone into the water, and we were not aware of his distress until he had attracted our attention by his shouts, and a flash of lightning revealed him to us. The boat was got down to him after more than an hour's work, and he was finally brought into camp nearly frozen.

July 21

The remainder of the packs and men crossed in the morning, and the day was consumed in sending the rest of the Mexicans and their luggage to the opposite side. They were also assisted in crossing over their animals. These men reported that they had been badly treated by the Mormons at the Vegas de Santa Clara, and that two of their number had been put in jail. They warned us to be on our guard, when we arrived in Utah Territory, as they *(the Mormons)* had threatened to shoot or imprison all Americans passing through their country. (The Mormon hostilities continued until coming to a head in 1858. This was after they burned U.S. Army supply wagons in 1857.) Notwithstanding their plausible story, the Mexicans only impressed us with the belief that, having misbehaved, they had received the chastisement they deserved, for it was well known to us that the Mormons strickly prohibited the practice of the natives of New Mexico of bartering firearms and ammunition with the Indians for their children.

We wrote many letters by these men, which they promised to deliver to Mr. Leroux, in Taos.

The hides were removed from the frame of the boat and reserved for future use, and having got our animals together we resumed our march at 7 P.M.

The Avonkarea (Colorado) joins Grand (Colorado) River (The Gunnison River enters the main branch of the Colorado River a few miles below the crossing. The names of these rivers have been adapted as they have today to avoid the confusion seen in this diary.) five or six miles below where we crossed it. We travelled down the last-mentioned stream, our course being southwest, and encamped at 11 P.M. at Camp L'Amoureux, so called after a French trapper who trapped here for several years, until drowned in Grand (Colorado) River. Our road lay over a level plain, whose loose, rotten soil was covered with a thick growth of artemisia, cactus, and greasewood. At this camp, both grass and timber were abundant, but the mosquitos allowed no rest to man or beast. A plain extends on this side of the river about twelve miles in breadth, bounded on the northwest by a range of steep, bald, and deeply furrowed mountains. Day's travel, 16 miles; total distance from Westport, 1,004 miles.

July 22

We were in the saddle at 7:30 A.M., and in ten miles reached the Rio Salado *(Salt Creek)*, and following down its bed, which only contained water in holes, encamped on Grand (Colorado) River, near where it *(Salt Creek)* discharges itself. This creek is a running stream in winter, and its water is then drinkable; but it ceases to run in summer, and its water, which is then only found in hollows, is very brackish. Wherever the main river *(Grand* (Colorado) *River)* can be reached, which is practicable at some points, there are good camping places, where grass and timber are abundant.

The face of the country, as on the previous day, was an arid plain, with scanty vegetation. To the northwest, at a distance of eight miles, was a range of steep bluffs, and Grand (Colorado) River, on our left, was shut from view by naked hills.

A few Indians visited camp, and partook of our dinner. We obtained from them some beautiful buckskins, which the Utahs have a skilful mode of preparing. They told us that the river abounded with large fish, and one of the men immediatly manufactured a hook with a horseshoe nail. We had satisfactory evidence of the weight of the fish, for the first that bit carried away "hook and line, bob and sinker."

Travelled twenty miles in the afternoon, and encamped again late at night on Grand (Colorado) River. To avoid the mosquitos, some slept on the top of a lofty rock, and were tolerably free from their annoyance; but those who made their beds below were allowed no rest. From the Rio Salado, our route lay over arid hills of sand and sandstone. 30 miles; 1,034 miles.

July 23

Raised camp at sunrise, travelling over rough and barren hills near the river, and at 10 A.M. rested for the last time on its banks. The scenery here was pictureesque. On our side, the stream was overhung by high cliffs of dazzlingly white sandstone, against which it dashed with violence; whilst on the left shore were extensive meadows, ornamented with numerous clusters of trees. All hands bathed in the river, and found its waters cool and refreshing. The heat of the weather was intence, until a distant thunderstorm refreshed the air.

Resuming our journey, we left Grand (Colorado) River, and, directing our course west-southwest across a sandy and parched plain towards Green River, stopped for the night at 10 P.M., at a place where there was scanty grass and no water; but we had brought a supply for our own use, and had watered the mules before starting. Day's travel, 36 miles; total distance, 1,070 miles.

July 24

The men passed a refreshing night, perfectly free from the mosquitos, which had been a source of such serious annoyance since leaving the settlements in New Mexico. Started at 5 A.M., and, travelling thirty-five miles, encamped on Green River Fork of the Great Colorado at 1 P.M.

The country we traversed was stony and broken by dry watercourses. On every side, and principally to the north and northeast, extended ranges of rugged hills, bare of vegetation, and seamed with ravines. On their summits were rocks of fantastic shapes, resembling pyramids, obelisks, churches, and towers, and having all the appearance of a vast city in the distance. The only vegetation was a scanty growth of stunted wild sage and cacti, except at a point known as the Hole in the rock, where there were willows and other plants denoting the vicinity of water, but we found none on our route. The sun was exceedingly hot, and we, as well as our mules, were glad to reach the river, where we could relieve our thirst. Saw four antelopes near Green River, to which the Delaware immediatly gave chase, but was unable to get within gunshot.

Green River was broader and deeper than either Grand (Gunnison) River or the Avonkarea (Colorado), but its current was neither so rapid nor so turbulent. The scenery on its banks was grand and solemn, and we had an excellent view of it from our camping place on a high bluff.

The frame of the boat was commenced at once. Some Indians made their appearance on the opposite shore, and one of them swam over to our side, assisted by a log, on which he occasionally rested. Day's travel, 35 miles; total distance, 1,105 miles.

July 25

At an early hour the men resumed their work on the boat; the hides were found to be rotten and full of holes, as we had neglected to dry them after crossing the Avonkarea; but by dint of patching with pieces of India-rubber blankets and sheepskins, and smearing the seams with a mixture of tallow, flour, soap, and pulverized charcoal, the boat was made sufficently tight, that with constant bailing, all the men and packs were carried over in four trips. I went with the first load to guard our packs, as Indians were on the left bank watching our proceedings.

Mr. Beale made great exertions to hurry the train over this river. He went across at every trip, jumping into the river where it was shallow, and taking the boat in tow until he was beyond his depth. He was thus for many hours in the water, encouraging the men by his example. We had now an excellent party; the men were daring and adroit; they exhibited no fear when we were so hard pressed by the Utahs, and when exposure or toil was required of them, not one flinched from his duty. Some appeared almost to rejoice whenever there was a difficulty to overcome, and we never heard the Delaware's wild shout and laugh without suspecting that either he or his mule had got into some predicament, either by sliding down a bank, or getting into the mire, or entangled in a jungle. He never asked for help, and rejected all assistance, relying on himself in every emergency.

At sunset, the crossing of Green River was effected, and we gladly gave the boat to the Indians, who ripped it to pieces to make moccassons soles of the hides. We proceeded a mile up the stream, and encamped in the midst of luxuriant grass. A band of twenty-five mounted Utahs accompanied us and passed the night in our camp; we gave them to eat, and they seemed quite friendly. Their accounts of the Mormons corroborated what the Indians and Mexicans on the Avonkarea (Colorado) had told us. Day's travel, 1 mile; whole distance, 1,106 miles.

9

1853/JOHN WILLIAMS GUNNISON

John W. Gunnison's expedition was one which left a record of travel on what was to become known as the East Fork of the North Branch of the Old Spanish Trail. This was from Gunnison's daily log. Their travels took them from Fort Massachusetts to Taos then back to the Fort, before continuing on to the Green River in Utah.

The Gunnison party left Westport on the Missouri frontier, on June 23, 1853. The expedition was made up of Captain John W. Gunnison, topographical engineer, commander; First Lieutenant E.G.Beckwith, third artillery, assistant; Richard H. Kern, topographer and artist; Sheppard Homans, astronomer; Dr. James (Jacob) Schiel, surgeon, geologist; Frederick Creutzfeldt, botanist; J.A. Snyder, assistant topographer; Charles Taplin, wagon-master; Brevet Captain R.M. Morris, First Lieutenant of this expedition; and L.S. Baker, Second Lieutenant; with some thirty noncommissoned officers and men of the regiment of mounted riflemen. Instruments used consisted of: two sextants, two artificial horizons, one theodolite, two small surveyors' compasses, two reconnoitering spy-glasses, two surveyors' chains, two Bunten's barometers, two aneroid barometers, two thermo-barometers, one hygrometer, one box chronometer, one compensating balance watch, two viameters, and one grade instrument; besides thermometers and small pocket-compasses. The expedition included eighteen wagons; sixteen of which were pulled by six mules each, an instrument carriage drawn by four mules, and an ambulance pulled by two horses which were changed for four mules before crossing the mountains. The wagons were used to demonstrate that this was, in fact, a practical route to be used as a wagon road. Hayden in his report in 1870s claimed that Gunnison was foolish to have taken wagon from Gunnison, Colorado to Grand Junction. Gunnison was not the last to have taken wagon through the area of the North Branch and this route though believed to be impractical by some has become our modern highway fifty.

The purpose of Gunnison's expedition was to explore and survey the route to see if it was practical and economical as a railroad route for the Central Pacific, which was to run from the Mississippi River to the Pacific Ocean.

Gunnison's difficulty in obtaining broke or trained animals in Missouri indicates the importance of the Old Spanish Trail. If it had not been for the thousands of horses and mules that traveled along this trail to the east, would there have been even the untrained animals available? In 1820 a team of mules in Missouri sold for $20. By 1850 a team of mules was selling for $200[1]

Gunnison and his party traveled from Westport, Missouri on the Santa Fe Trail as far as Bent's Fort. Then they ascended the Arkansas River to the Huerfano River. After leaving the settlement at Greenhorn, the party followed the Taos Trail southwest to Sangre de Cristo Pass, crossing it to Fort Massachussets, then traveled south to Taos. Marcelino Baca was to guide them only as far as the Fort. At Taos they obtained the services of Antonie Leroux, who was to guide them to the Green River.

The road from Fort Massachusetts to Taos was the East Fork of the North Branch of the Old Spanish Trail. The trail followed along the west side of the Sangre de Cristo Mountains from Santa Fe, New Mexico to Saguache, Colorado.

After returning to the fort with his guide Captain Gunnison traveled around Mount Blanca and explored three-fourths of a mile up Medano Pass which he called Williams Pass. He stated that it was less favorable than Robidoux's Pass, and that it was followed by a large Indian trail. From here they skirted the western base of the Sand Dunes, then struck off across the sandy plain which extends far into the San Luis Valley, soon arriving on Sand Creek. In this area Gunnison's party saw a herd of wild horses which apparently frightened their horses. It took until dark to recover them.

Captain Gunnison had traveled along the west side of the Sangre de Cristo Mountains following the East Fork of the North Branch of the Old Spanish Trail. He camped on White (Blanca) Creek, Medano Creek, Sand Creek, Chatillon's (Deadman) Creek, Crestone Creek, Leroux (Rito Alto) Creek, Homans (San Luis) Creek, at Sawatch Spring & Sawatch Butte (Hunts Spring & Rattlesnake Hill), and east of the present-day town of Saguache, Colorado.

Gunnison and his party explored some of the side cañons as they crossed Cochetopa Pass, cutting down or removing downed trees from their path. They descended Cochetopa Creek staying to the higher ground to the east of the creek. They crossed the Gunnison River at the present day town of Parlin. They followed the Gunnison River to the Colorado River. After crossing the Colorado River near the present-day town of Grand Junction, Colorado, they followed the Colorado River to its confluence with Westwater Creek. Gunnison camped near the confluence for three days to give his animals time to build up their strength before crossing the dry section ahead. From here Gunnison turned northwest leaving the Colorado River and traveling two or three miles from the book Cliffs. Gunnison hoped to find water in the mouth of the cañons as he crossing the dry section to near Crescent Junction. There he joined the South Branch of the Old Spanish Trail upon which he continued to the Green River which they crossed about three miles north of the present-day town of Green River, Utah.

August 6, 1853

Our course from camp was W.N.W., in a direct line for the Wet mountains, crossing the Cuchara at the point at which we had visited it the previous evening. The banks were here vertical walls of clay, twenty feet in height, resting on a stratum of shale. We descended through a break in the bank, and following the bed of the stream for some distance, ascended the opposite bank through a similar opening. The borders of the river are here entirely destitute of grass. A few miles below us, plainly in sight, the river enters a cañon; the hills about it, and an unusual extent of rolling country, being covered with a thick growth of low cedar. On the table-land beyond this river we passed innumerable prairie-dog towns, herds of deer and antelope, and several bands of beautiful wild horses, which came circling round us in all the pride of their native freedom, at a distance of fifty or eighty yards, and at the report of a rifle dashing wildly away over prairie, hill, and valley, exciting our admiration. On this table-land we also passed basins of rain-water some hundred yards in diameter, which in dry seasons are themselves doubtless dry. Ten miles from the Cuchara we descended from the table-land to the valley of a stream evidently rising in the position laid down on some maps for the Huerfano, and on whose southern bank we had an hour before had a fine view of an isolated butte in its bottom—a feature of this valley marked and unmistakable. It is from this butte, from its isolation known as the Huerfano or Orphan butte, that this river derives its name. This stream we crossed as we had the Cuchara; its volume of water being less than that of the latter stream, and its clay banks, overlying the shale of the bed, of less height. The Huerfano between this point and the head of its cañon, seen a few miles distant on our right, and which is said to be the longest in this part of the country, has but little timber on its banks. The Cuchara enters the Huerfano in this long cañon, and the river for eighteen miles between the mouth of its cañon and the Arkansas, it is said, has a large border of cotton-wood. We next came to the Apache creek, whose sources in the Wet mountains had been visible during our morning ride. It is a small mountain stream, with water at this time only in pools. Willow, plum, thorn, and cherry bushes, with a few cotton-wood trees, grow densely thick on its borders, and we were detained an hour in making a passage through them. Beyond this creek we entered upon a wide open valley of weeds, prickly-pears, and sand, and I changed my course a little more to the north, hoping to strike the trail from Taos to the Greenhorn (The Taos Trail/Trappers Road stretched from Pueblo, Colorado to Taos, New Mexico. From Pueblo it followed the north side of the Saint Charles River southwest to the Greenhorn Mountains. The road then traced the east side of the Greenhorn Mountains to the southwest crossing the Huerfano at Badito. Following South Oak Creek to the southwest, the road crossed Sangre de Cristo Pass to Sangre de Cristo Creek, then followed the west side of the Sangre de Cristo Mountains to Taos.) near the base of the mountain, which we reached after a ride of four miles, and found the trail as anticipated. Following this trail we rose over a hill and descended into a rough narrow ravine, which we followed in a northeast direction for a mile and a half, and then passed over a high ridge—a spur of the Wet mountains—covered with oak bushes, to another ravine, on the sides of which we were gladdened by the sight of a herd of cattle and horses feeding, and were soon in the camp of a trader from New Mexico returning from Fort Laramie. From him we learned that the two streams and ravines are called the Granaros by the Spaniards. Passing over another sharp ridge, we descended in two miles to the fine little valley of the Greenhorn, a stream of two feet in width and three or four inches in depth, which is now, entirely diverted from its natural channel and employed in irrigating the lands of the six New Mexican families who reside at and constitute the present population of the place. They plant a few acres of corn and of wheat, of beans and of water-melons—in all, an area equal to that of a small eastern farmer, who cultivates his own fields. Two hundred fanegas of wheat and fifty of corn, with the requisite amount of beans and melons, constitute the largest total crop of this valley. They have a few cattle and horses—the latter very poor. The houses are built of adobe or sun-dried bricks, without windows or other openings than a single door, in entering which a man of six feet in stature must bow very low. In front of each house is enclosed a small space of ground, twenty yards in width, by poles planted in the earth and lashed to horizontal strips by rawhide thongs. These picketed yards are intended as a protection against Indians—the Utahs having killed some of their cattle last year, destroyed their grain, and stolen their horses. Corrals are attached to the backs of their houses, built in all respects like the front enclosures. With one exception all the houses of this settlement are joined, and a tall man can reach to the roof, on which the whole population, not absent in the fields, assembled on the approach of my party, not knowing whether to expect friends or foes. I enjoyed the hospitality of the smaller mansion, being invited to a seat on the only article of furniture in the room, a board against the wall, spread with a blanket and furnished with a pillow. On the earthen floor, at the sides of the room, were two or three narrow beds on wool mattresses. I soon found the guide I wanted, and engaged his services hence to Fort Massachusetts, in the San Luis valley of New Mexico. Mossalino (Marcelino Baca) is, by birth, of the Spanish New Mexican race, of about forty-five years of age; having spent it entire in the wild life of a mountaineer—by turn a hunter, a trapper, a trader, a voyageur, a fighter, a farmer, and a guide—he is familiar with the country westward to the Pacific. Last year he lived at this place with his Pawnee squaw; but his losses by the Utahs were considerable, and he removed to the pueblo of the Arkansas, where he is, with his family, the sole occupant of the place. He had this year planted a little corn there, but the high water of the river destroyed it, and he has no crop now growing. "I have lived," said he, "nine years on meat alone, at one time, in these mountains, without tasting bread or salt. I can now live well enough for me with coffee and the little meat I can kill." He is reputed a fine hunter. "I never see a grizzly bear but I give him a shot. I try to hit in the right spot; but if I miss it, I have to run. We will have," alluding to our trip, "a fine chance for fun;" and his dark liquid eyes flashed as he looked towards the mountains, and visions of his grizzly friends appeared to his imagination. But few men of experience are bold enough to attempt to shoot these animals unless accompanied by a friend well armed. The mistress of the house very courteously inquired where I would have my bed prepared, which I preferred leaving to her own convenience. I should, however, have been a little surprised, had this been my first visit to a New Mexican residence, at the place selected—in the yard, just in front of the door, under the broad, bright, blue canopy of heaven, brilliant with stars. I enjoyed the matronly grace and dignity of the mistress as she brought forth the pallet and spread the necessary blankets to exclude the chilly night winds from the mountains. There, too, were spread the beds for the family, the open air being preferred to the house during pleasant weather. I could, of course, procure no supplies at this place at this season of the year.

August 7

I returned this morning by a route somewhat to the west of that followed yesterday; and after passing the Geanaros (Graneros), crossed the Huerfano at the butte, and soon after reached camp, which had remained on the Cuchara.

August 8

We crossed immediately over to the Huerfano Butte by the route which I had followed the previous day. This butte is one hundred and fifty feet in height, as determined by Mr. Homans, standing in the river bottom quite detached from the adjacent hills. Its diameter at the base is equal to twice its altitude, sloping up to its summit, which is about twenty-five by forty feet across. Its base is strewn around with prismatical blocks of granite rocks, of from one to six feet across, and its surface is also covered with these prisms, which are very dark—containing iron, perhaps, as a coloring matter. A narrow way, leading over the summit from the southeast, is nearly destitute of these rocks, on either side of which they are arranged in regular order, presenting a trap-like appearance. Latitude of this butte, 57° 45' 03." Captain Gunnison remarks in his journal,that our line of travel since leaving the Arkansas should not be followed; "but, striking up a valley or plain ten miles from the mouth of the Apishpa, in a course for the Spanish Peaks, cross the Cuchara near our camp of August 5th, and continue over to the Huerfano, which gives a direct line of travel on a fine plain. But if we undertake to ascend the Apish(a)pa, or the Huerfano, by following their valleys, we meet with cañons on the former, as we have described— and on the latter, we are informed, eighteen miles above its junction with the Arkansas. And the whole country having been under our eye as we travelled on the higher land to the south of this indicated route, we can say that no obstruction of any magnitude exists, thus far, to the successful construction of a railroad."

August 9

The river here is eighteen feet wide, by one deep,with a rapid current. The soil is light, and would produce, if irrigated, fine crops. Stone for bridges and building purposes may be readily had. We moved up the river for several miles on its southern bank, and then crossed to the north side, and a mile above recrossed by the ford on the Taos trail to the southern shore, but only to recross again and again, five or six times, the river here coming through a narrow passage formed by the Greenhorn mountains, or Sierra Mojada, on the north, and spurs from the Sierra Blanca on the south, of some six hundred feet in width in its narrowest part, but still good for a wagon or a rail road, with a little labor. The Taos trail of which I have spoken leaves the river at this gorge, leading directly to El Sangre de Cristo Pass. Captain Gunnison finding a better route, however, kept up the river, encamping on its northern bank, where the hills are covered by small cedars and pines. Day's march, 14.54 miles.

August 10

We crossed the Huerfano this morning, and pursued a fine valley between two spurs from the main chain, luxuriant with grass, from one-half to one mile in width, to the base of the mountain five miles to the south: and then turned east by the same valley depression into an adjacent valley, and encamped at its head, as it began to rain, after a march of seven miles. Narrow ridges of sand and limestone of considerable height, covered with wide branching cedars, suitable only for fuel, and a few dwarfed pines, extended from the base of the mountain north to the Huerfano, along the summits of which a road could easily be constructed, diminishing the ascent to the pass. Ours was to-day literally a pathway of flowers, among which the helianthus, a verbena, a lupine, and the blue flowering flox, were brilliant and showy. Magpies flew around us, but escaped our shots uninjured. Bears were seen on the Huerfano, and our hunters supplied us abundantly with venison.

August 11

We left the valley of our camp by ascending a giant mountain spur, along the top of which we followed to the south for some assistance, ascending as we approached the main mountain, and then descending into the next eastern ravine or valley, through which flows a little rill, entering the Huerfano at the gorge which we passed two days ago. This descent was difficult, and so sidling that we were obligated to hold the wagons by hand-ropes to prevent their being overturned. By following the rivulet from the river this difficulty would be avoided. We ascended it for some distance through waving fields of grass quite up to our saddle-girths; and, cutting a road for a short distance through a forest of quaking-asp as we turned to our left, encamped, in a shower of rain, amidst the luxuriant fields of blue grass *(of the mountain men)* and flowers. Quaking-asp covers the mountain around us, interspersed with small pines. Fire, however, swept over these mountains two years ago, destroying much of the timber. Sandstone, an impure limestone, and porhyrite rocks, are among the most common of this part of the mountain. Distance marched, 5.12 miles.

August 12

A working party was engaged during yesterday afternoon in opening a road through the forest to the summit of the (Sangre de Cristo) (Note in this and in chapter eight that the existing wagon road went up the Huerfano River. Gunnison was building a wagon road up South Oak Creek and across Sangre de Cristo Pass.) pass, and much of to-day has been spent in the same manner and in working on the opposite side-hill, along which it is necessary to descend from the pass. The teams, too, were engaged all day in making the ascent as the road advanced, and at dark the most of them had reached the summit, and a few had descended some distance to El Sangre de Cristo creek: and all were obliged to encamp where night overtook them. on a line of two or three miles, on the summit and either side of the pass. The examination of the various depressions in the mountains also went on to-day, to ascertain their elevations and practicability for roads. The scenery around us is very fine—the views from various points extending far back over the plains, buttes, ridges, and streams, on which we have for so many days laboriously pursued our march. The bold, rocky mountain peaks tower loftily above us—whitened here and there with lines of snow—round which, at mid-day, dark masses of clouds gather and the lightning plays, while torrents of rain pour down their sides with irresistible fury. The valleys of the mountain are small, but unsurpassed in luxuriant grass; the mountain sides are plentifully supplied with aspen and small pine, and all around us, and under our feet, covered with exquisitely beautiful flowers. Here, too, the geologist finds an interesting field, and sportsmen's spirits are excited by grouse and pheasants, deer and grizzly bear, in every valley and glen, and the streams are alive with the finest mountain trout.

The wagon tracks descending from Sangre de Cristo Pass. John W. Gunnison, in 1853 was the first to bring wagons across this pass.

August 13

The labor of crossing the ridge was completed this morning, and just in advance of the 1 o'clock shower we encamped in but near the head of the southern descent of this pass, on the Sangre de Cristo, which is a small stream of clear, cold water, in a beautiful little park or valley. (Ruxton says that the Indians and Mexicans called this little valley El Vallecito. See chapter six.) The labor of crossing this ridge has been very considerable, which is partly owing, however, to the rarified atmosphere at so great an elevation. Both men, and animals were soon exhausted and obligated constantly to stop and rest, where at a lower altitude no rest would have been required. Our teams were all doubled, without being then able to do the ordinary work of a single one, and the strongest men sat down out of breath after a few moments' exertion. Astronomical observations gave us for the latitude of this camp, which is $2^1/_2$ miles from the summit passed by wagons, 37° 36' 56" N.

From the Arkansas river, at the mouth of the Apish(a)pa, it is eighty miles by the route we travelled to the Huerfano butte; but this distance is at least one-fourth greater than is necessary in the construction of a railroad between these points. Taking the shorter distance our ascent was 28 feet 10 inches, in whole numbers, to the mile, the elevation of the butte being 6,099 feet above the sea. We ascended the Huerfano river $14^1/_2$ miles above this point, ascending nearly 52 feet 10 inches per mile. The ascent during the first day's march from the Huerfano river to the base of the Sierra Blanca, 7.59 miles, was 603 feet, or 79 feet 5 inches per mile. On the following day we advanced 5.12 miles, ascending in that distance 1,289 feet, or over 251 feet per mile; and from thence to the summit of El Sangre de Cristo Pass, seven-tenths of a mile, the ascent was 647 feet, developing a line entirely impracticable for a railroad. Huerfano river west of the gorge through which we passed on the 9th instant, drains a large circular amphitheater, surrounded on the north, west, and south, and partly on the east, by elevated mountain ranges, with large, irregular spurs extending into this valley, and sending down numerous tributaries to the river. Twelve miles above this gorge stands the Black Butte, an immense mass of rocks with irregular points shooting up 100 and 200 feet. Here comes in a fine stream from the northwest, two miles beyond which another enters from the west from near William's (Medano) Pass. At this point the Huerfano, whose general course from the gorge is N. 70° W., bends towards Roubideau's (Mosca) Pass on a curve for some three miles, where it receives the waters of Gunnison's creek, a small stream from the south, but which towards its source descends more from the east. This little creek continues the curve, until it reaches the point whence it issues from the mountain at the foot of the declining ridge, near which, but on the opposite side, our wagons passed, at the head of a small valley, on leaving the Huerfano. Following this stream above this point, it is, by chain, five and one-fourth miles to the summit, the water descending on an inclined plane without falls, with an equable, swift current. Four miles and a half from the summit the creek flows through a narrow passage in the rocks, which slope up to the top at a small angle from the vertical, the width at bottom being one hundred and fifty feet, affording abundant room for the stream and a road. Above this gorge or cañon there is a small park, such as are found on the heads of many of the streams in this part of the country, abounding in deer, elk, and bear, and affording luxuriant pasturage for thousands of head of cattle: indeed, few more inviting spots for grazing can anywhere be found. Two miles and a half from the summit is Turret Rock, a pillow-like cone of stone, divided in the centre from the apex, with one face a plane, against the base of which the stream strikes and is deflected a little to the left. Above this, numerous small streams join the main one from the southeast, and that from the summit descends at the foot of the grassy slopes which extend up to the base of the crowning peaks of the Sierra Blanca. A railroad or any judiciously chosen wagon road would cross the summit-level near the base of these peaks, and, taking advantage of the winding slopes, pass down the right of the creek to Turret Rock, to where the park becomes a gorge, and thence be confined to the little valley, from one hundred and fifty to three hundred feet in width, where it could be constructed along the foot of the hills with great ease, and issue with the stream from the mountain upon a broader valley, and, swinging around the base of the hills that set off from the great mountain masses reaching to within a short distance of the Huerfano river, pass through the gorge of that stream, and taking choice of the great plains, to and along the Arkansas and Kansas rivers to the Missouri. The supposed distance *(for it was not measured)* from our last camp, of August 8, on the Huerfano, to the summit of the Sangre de Cristo Pass, by the circuit just indicated, is from twenty-four to twenty-six miles, and the ascent to be overcome, two thousand three hundred and fifty-four feet—an average of ninety-eight feet and one inch to the mile for twenty-four miles, or of ninety feet six inches per mile for the longer distance. On the 13th of August the day was bright and clear, and the mean of five hourly barometrical observations gave us an altitude for this pass above the sea, of nine thousand two hundred and nineteen feet, which I have used in the estimated elevation to be overcome. "A single grade," says Captain Gunnison, from whose notes I have derived the data for the description of this pass, "could easily be carried from the summit to the gorge of the Huerfano river; but two, one along Gunnison's creek and one on the river, would probably be preferable. Spruce-pine in abundance is at hand on the mountain sides, to supply ties for hundreds of miles of railroad, especially if that which the great fire of 1851 swept over and left standing, killed and blackened, be not left to decay." The small stream called El Sangre de Cristo rises near the summit of the pass, and runs in a general southwestern direction to the valley of San Luis. The valley of this stream is narrow, the stream being lined with thickets of willow bushes, and, winding from side to side, impinges against the base of the hills, forcing us frequently to cross it, or, where it was practicable, to pass over the foot of the hills. The labor of preparing the road for twelve miles was considerable, employing a large force, of which Captain Morris took charge, for four days. (It took Gunnison's men a total of six days to build a road through Sangre de Cristo Pass. This would indicate as Heap and Gunnison said, that to this point there had only been a trail through this route.)

We descended from the summit of the pass during the first mile and three-fourths, 178 feet, or about 101 feet per mile; and 549 in the next 5.34 miles, or nearly 103 feet per mile. Six miles from this point we left the Sangre de Cristo, and rose to a plain extending along the base of the mountain spur, which we follow for 4.57 miles, encamping on Utah creek, a short distance below Fort Massachusetts. (Gunnison was traveling down Sangre de Cristo Creek while Fort Massachusetts was on Ute Creek. Gunnison's Road and the later supply road connecting these two creeks can still be seen by flying in an airplane across the elevated plain which connects the two.)

After completing the examination of the Sangre de Cristo Pass, Captain Gunnison made an examination of the mountains to the south of the Spanish Peaks, by ascending Gold Branch from its junction with El Sangre de Cristo, to near its head. It is a very crooked stream, coming into the Sangre de Cristo from north 55° east for three miles, then east for one mile, thence winding from the southeast near the mountains beyond Indian and Culebra creeks, and near one of the head branches of the Cuchara. Becoming satisfied, after a long ride, of the exaggeration of the guide, who had represented this route as" without a hill," the party ascended a high peak and looked down upon the extended plains, over which, for a month, we had wound our way. The view was majestically beautiful, with the Huerfano, Cuchara and Apishpa at their feet, and towering mountains to the north and south, with the valley of San Luis to the west. (On November 15, 1993 the author flew across La Veta Pass at 38,000 feet. This gives a much better view than Gunnison saw but one can certainly get a feel for what he describes.) Descending again to the stream they had left, and finding that about ten miles from its head they were, by barometer, higher than on the Sangre de Cristo Pass, and that the gorge was very winding and narrow, they turned back from their southern course for two miles, and then rode up hill for two hours, much of the way steep and stony, and arrived at the summit of the ridge, "where one could look almost vertically down on the heads of creeks of the Cucharas—one of which winds under Bald mountain, considerably to the south of the Spanish Peaks, where there is a not inviting depression, entirely impracticable for a road." The party passed over fine grassed slopes, and through groves of branching pine and aspen. In descending they came upon a fresh trail, which had been made by a party of hunters from Taos, who had crossed by the Culebra Pass to the head of the Cuchara, and obtained pack-loads of venison. These men travel a hundred miles, kill the game and pack it on asses, taking from ten to twelve days to procure the load, and four to return to market. They use no salt, only cover the meat to keep it from the flies. At night they spread out the quarters and saddles on the ground, and lie down among them to protect them from the dogs and wolves. And notwithstanding the daily occurrence of showers about the highest peaks of the mountains, the dryness of the atmosphere is such that the meat is well preserved."

At a late hour, after a fourteen hours' ride, the party arrived at Mr. William's herd-grounds on the Sangre de Cristo, Captain Gunnison being quite ill. They dined with the master of the rancho on milk and tole, or parched corn-meal pudding, and slept under his awning on buffalo-robes. Captain Gunnison was quite restored by the kind attentions of Mr. Taplin and his host, from a severe attack of inflammatory rheumatism, which had been greatly aggravated by sleeping out at night with the gentlemen of his party, in exploring the Sangre de Cristo Pass. The information gained in regard to the snow which falls in El Sangre de Cristo Pass and valley of San Luis, is conflicting. Massalino, our guide through the pass, states that he crossed it in February last, a winter of unprecedented severity and great fall of snow; that he was seven or eight days in making the crossing, which is usually made in two—the dry snow being ten feet deep in the ravines, while the ridges were nearly bare. Antoine Leroux, on the contrary, represents it generally as unusually free from snow for a mountain pass, which can be crossed with facility during the severest storms.

The officers of the army stationed at Fort Massachusetts, which is situated just under the Sierra Blanca, in a sheltered valley on Utah creek, about seventeen miles from the summit of the pass, represent the snow, which is usually very dry, to have been in the valley about them, during the past winter, about two feet in depth. Once during our stay in this vicinity, during a thunder-storm on the lower peaks, those more elevated were covered with a beautiful mantle of white. There are no evidences of snow-slides or avalanches about the pass.

Our recent experience in exploring a wild mountainous country without guides, was such as to show the necessity of profiting by the practical lessons in geography gained in the school of the trapper and hunter, by that useful class of mountaineers who have spent so many years of their lives in encountering the hardships and imminent dangers hourly incident to their occupation in these fields of savage barbarity, short-lived gratitude and native grandeur, which are annually stained by the sacrifice of some of their number, as victims to unbridled ferocity. Accompanied by Lieutenant Baker, I accordingly started on the 15th instant from our camp at the head of El Sangre de Cristo, for Taos, in New Mexico, the headquarters of many of the most reliable and experienced of these mountain men. Leaving camp, we passed rapidly down the Sangre de Cristo (Mountains) for ten miles, and entering the broad and extensive valley of San Luis, hemmed in on either side by high mountains, and traversed by the Rio Grande del Norte and its mountain tributaries, skirted with bushes and a little timber, soon reaching the Trenchara which comes in from the mountains to our left, and is joined a few miles to our right by the Sangre de Cristo, whence it flows on to the Rio Grande. A ride of twenty miles further brought us to the Culebra, or Snake creek. (About seven miles north of San Luis, Colorado, which lies on Culebra Creek, one can reach the East Fork of the North Branch of the Old Spanish Trail coming from the west side of Mount Blanca. It was here that the trails from Pueblo and Fort Massachusetts joined the Old Spanish Trail.) There is a small settlement five miles to the east of the point where we crossed this stream, near the mountains; but without visiting it we continued our journey, and arrived a little after dark, after a ride of sixty-five miles, at the Costilla, (The settlement of Costilla was established about 1849. See chapters six & fifteen.) a stream similar to the last, on which a new settlement is opened and a few fields are already covered with crops of corn, wheat, oats, and the other usual crops of a New Mexican farm. But the settlement contained no grass, and our Indian bred mules, not knowing the taste of corn, disdained it, much to our regret, for we deemed so long a ride inhuman enough to our animals, without consigning them to a night of abstinence, with a fifty-mile ride before us for the following day. We therefore negotiated for the corner of a wheatfield, the kernels being still soft, and were gratified with the avidity which our Comanches exhibited in feeding on this grain. During the day's ride we had occasionally seen the smokes from the signal-fires of the Indians in the mountains; but they did not molest us, although we subsequently learned that a party of New Mexicans had been robbed by them, near where we saw their smokes just as we were passing them. The night was lovely and beautiful, succeeded by a bright, clear day. Resuming our way southward in the early morning, at 10 o'clock we passed settlements on streams near the base of the mountains, and at noon arrived at the Rio Colorado, or Red River of the Rio Grande del Norte, where there is a considerable settlement, surrounded by fields of grain. At 3 o'clock we crossed this stream a short distance from the village, and ascended the low, stony, mountain range, which here extends across the broad valley of the Rio Grande, separating the valley of San Luis from that of Taos.

The Rio Grande passes this low range in one of the most formidable cañones existing in this part of the country. Our pathway was thickly shaded by a forest of pines; and the landscape views of the valleys and near and distant mountains, during our afternoon's ride, were among the finest I have ever seen. Fifteen miles from the Rio Colorado we crossed the Arroyo Hondo, or Deep arroyo, from one hundred and fifty to two hundred feet in depth, with fine streams carried in irrigation trenches along its sides to the cultivated fields of the valley, which, from the crest in all directions, appeared by twilight covered with fields of grain; and, to shorten our evening ride, we followed on the banks of the irrigating ditches for some distance, until we reached the road leading to Taos, where we arrived at 10 o'clock at night. The valley of Taos is large, and for New Mexico, extensively cultivated, containing several small villages, of which the principal is San Fernando de Taos, (San Fernando de Taos was located about two miles southwest of the Indian Pueblo.) and many farms. It is on all sides surrounded by high mountains, the Rio Grande entering it through a gigantic cañon, and also leaving it through one. The water of the river is but little if at all used for irrigation, the mountain streams being large and more favorably situated. In our ride of over a hundred miles from El Sangre de Cristo to this place, we saw no grass in the valley worth naming; the vegetation being confined almost exclusively to artemisia and a few varieties of cacti, but chiefly the prickly pear—the pine of the mountains at times extending well down to the plains. In the high small valleys of the mountains the grass is luxuriant and the flowers beautiful. Here, too showers are of daily occurrence, whilst in the broad valley but little rain falls and nothing can be cultivated except by irrigation. Procuring what information we could of the country westward over which we were to pass, and the services of a guide, we returned in thirty hours to our camp, *(which in our absence had been moved but fifteen miles,)* by nearly the same route we had followed in leaving it, arrived at noon on the 19th of August. On the following day we were joined by the experienced and well-known guide, Antoine Leroux. Here some half-dozen men came to ask for their discharge, refusing to perform further duty. One who had refused to guard the animals, while grazing in the early part of the day, was discharged, forfeiting arrearages of pay for a violation of his contract. Two others preferred their discharge on the same terms, which was granted; the others returning to their duty.

August 23

We were detained in making necessary repairs, and in obtaining supplies at Fort Massachusetts, until this morning, when we took leave of the officers of the post, from whom we received much courteous hospitality; and following down Utah creek for three miles and a half, crossed it, and passed along the base of the gravelly hills which lie directly at the foot of the Sierra Blanca, southwest and opposite the sharpest peak of which we encamped, at White Mountain spring, seven miles from Utah creek, and in a direct line over the gravel hills not more than that from Fort Massachusetts. These gravel hills are a confused set of elevations from fifty to one hundred feet in height, resulting from the washing away of a former deposit and the crumbling of the higher mountain masses. The mountain torrents have washed among them deep channels, and occasional dykes, like vertical walls laid up in regular masses many feet thick, are left exposed. These hills are covered with branching cedars and pines, seldom exceeding twenty feet in height. A few wild hops were observed growing luxuriantly at the crossing of Utah creek.

August 24

Following the base of the Sierra Blanca on our right, with the broad valley of San Luis on our left, we encamped, after traveling fourteen miles, on a small stream from the mountain, which soon sinks in the plain. The grass along our path was scattered, and we experienced considerable difficulty in driving over the thick masses of sage which cover almost the entire surface of this immense valley. We were here nearly opposite to Roubideau's (Robidoux) or Musca (Mosca) Pass. Captain Gunnison immediately proceeded to examine it. It was found impracticable to ascend it with horses, in consequence of one of those great mountain torrents to which all mountain countries are subject having swept down it, depositing trees and rocks in every direction, and tearing the bed of the creek, over which two light wagons crossing from the Greenhorn settlement to Taos had descended but a few days before, into holes and gullies ten and twelve feet in depth. No apparent obstacle presents itself from the summit to descending with facility from this pass to the Huerfano river to the north and east; but the western descent having proved so difficult, no further examination of it was made. Our guide informs us that to the west of our trail, along the banks of the Rio del Norte to where it enters a plain through a cañon from the San Juan mountains, bearing west from our present camp, and thence above on its tributaries, the valley of San Luis, which in this part of it is known to many as the valley of San Juan, is rich and fertile, covered with extensive meadows of grass, and abounding in game and wild horses. The narrow line of timber, thirty-five miles distant upon the Rio del Norte, is plainly seen from our trail; (The trail that they were traveling is the East Fork of the North Branch of the Old Spanish Trail, which followed the west side of the Sangre de Cristo Mountains.) but it is represented to be difficult to cross the valley with wagons on account of the marshes along the river and the miry banks of the sunken creeks, and we have therefore followed the base of the Sierra Blanca, which extends from the Sangre de Cristo to Gunnison's Pass. To the north of this range, but partially connected with it, a broken range of mountains extends towards the Arkansas river, called the Sierra Mojada or Wet mountain, from the constant rains which fall upon it. Opposite to the first-named mountain, on the west of the San Luis valley, the Indian name of the mountain is Sahwatch, but it is more generally known by the Spanish name of San (The San Juan Mountains were known as the Sierra de las Grullas by the early day Spanish. See chapters two & three.) Juan. The San Luis valley is from 40 to 70 miles in width, and still more in length, and so level that trees are seen in any direction growing on the stream, as far as the eye can discern them.

August 25

The examination of Roubideau's (Robidoux) Pass being completed this morning, the main body of the party proceeded up the valley, under the command of Lieutenant Baker, while Captain Gunnison, Captain Morris, and myself, after leaving this pass, rode to William's (Medano) Pass, the approach to which from the San Luis valley is through a grove of pitch-pine, behind most gigantic sand-hills (Great Sand Dunes National Monument), rising above the plain to half the height *(apparently)* of the adjacent mountain, and shaped by the winds into beautiful and fanciful forms with waving outlines, for within certain limits this sand drifts about like snow. These immense hills are from eight to ten miles in length, lying along the base of the mountains, and four or five in width, and therefore constitute a great barrier to the western approach to William's (Medano) Pass, directly before which they stand. The stream (Medano Creek) which flows from it is turned immediately southward, and soon sinks in the sand plain. These hills are so steep and smooth on the side towards this creek, that the smallest pebbles started at their summits roll uninterruptedly into the creek, leaving their paths distinctly marked from the summits to the passes. High up on the sides are seen, at half a dozen points, single bushes of artemisia—the only vegetation seen upon them, and the only change discoverable since they were visited by Captain Pike, fifty years ago, when they were entirely destitute of vegetation, and "appeared exactly like the sea in a storm, except in color."

The course of William's (Medano) Pass as we entered it is N.58°E., but it soon bends to the left to N. 27°E. We passed up it only about three-fourths of a mile. Its width is about two hundred and fifty yards, rising gradually as far as we could see. Its walls of rock rise on either side to a height of some hundreds of feet, and are nearly vertical. Our guides represent it as continuing for fourteen miles, both in character and direction, as here described; beyond that it is more abrupt, terminating at its summit less favorably for a road than Roubideau's (Mosca) Pass. It is followed by a large Indian trail. Captain Gunnison did not deem it necessary to pursue the exploration further, and we left this pass, having only made our entrance and exit at its western portal. Turning the southern base of the sand-hills (Great Sand Dunes), over the lowest of which we rode for a short distance, our horses half burying their hoofs only on the windward slopes, but sinking to their knees on the opposite, we for some distance followed the bed of the stream from the pass, now sunk in the sand, and then struck off across the sandy plain, which here extends far into the valley, and is very uneven, the clumps of artemisia fixing in place large heaps of sand, while the intermediate spaces are swept out by the wind. As we rose a sand-knoll a few miles from camp, we were made aware of its position on Sand creek, by a light cloud of dust raised by the furious charge of frightened horses dashing over the plain; and before we reached it, at dark, we came up with Lieutenant Baker, who had succeeded in recovering all his stampeded horses. Distance 10 miles.

August 26

Our route lay over the sandy plain to the north of Sand creek, which flows around the north base of the sand-hills (Great Sand Dunes), sinking in the plain near our camp. The sand was so heavy that we were six hours and a half in making ten miles—the sand being succeeded, on the last two miles, by a light, friable soil, and heavy growth of artemisia. We camped on Chatillon's (Deadman) creek, in which we could only obtain water by digging in its sandy bed. A few scattered cottonwoods are the only trees upon these streams, on which willow bushes also flourish. The mountain sides and ravines are dark with low branching cedar and pine; but they are generally of too small a size to be of any use except for fuel.

August 27

In our course to-day we approached nearer the base of the mountains on the eastern line of the valley, the soil being still sandy, but much less so than for the last two days. The sage, however, being no less luxuriant, forced us constantly to wind about to avoid the thickest patches. A few small spots of prairie-grass were passed, and marsh grass grew luxuriantly for a few hundred yards on either side of two small (North & South Crestone) creeks which we crossed, one of which, Trois Tetons, deriving its name from the peaks whence it descends, was so miry that it turned us a mile directly towards the mountains before we could affect a crossing. To our left we could see fine prairie-grass fields, directly in the course to Coochetopa (Cochetopa) Pass, for which we were traveling around the valley; but the guide warned us of marshes, and the attempt was not made to cross them. Thirteen miles from camp we reached a fine meadow of bottom-grass a mile in width, extending from the base of the mountains far out into the plain, through the center of which winds a fine stream of mountain water, named, after our guide, Leroux (Rito Alto) creek. A few grouse and sand-hill cranes were frightened from their retreat as we came to camp. Deer also were seen here and on the mountain bases a few miles distant. Our hunter supplies us with venison; but while pursuing a wounded buck, an hour ago, was driven in by a bear, which disputed the passage to the prey. The sharp edges and needle forms of the summits of the Sierra Blanca, rising 3,000 feet above the valley, attract much admiration at our camp to-night; and the promising opening in the Sierra San Juan, to the southwest, which allured Colonel Fremont to the disaster of 1848-'49, attracts its full share of attention and comment, some of the gentlemen of our party having participated in that misfortune. The pea-vine and barley-grass grow here, thinly scattered on favorite spots; but the surface of the ground, over large spaces, is often covered with effloresced salts.

August 29

Our course bore strongly to the west to-day in nearly a direct line for the entrance to the Coochetopa (Cochetopa) Pass—keeping, however, somewhat to the north to secure a good crossing at Homan's (San Luis) creek, on which we are encamped; there being large marshes further to the south, and the dams of the beaver, which are numerous, flowing the water back to some extent. Our march was only six miles to this fine little stream, with a meadow of grass on each side, of a mile in width. Two varieties of currants, a black and a beautiful yellow, grow in and around our camp on great abundance, and are thought very delicious by the party.

August 30

Leaving camp we reached Sawatch (Hunt) spring and (Rattlesnake Hill) butte, (Hunt Spring has been an important site. It was visited by Anza in 1779 and in 1939 became the site of CCC Camp #3888. See chapter three.) by a very direct course across the valley, in ten miles and a half. This (Hunt) spring of pure cold water bursts from the base of the granitic (Rattlesnake Hill) butte which is immediately west of it, but detached from the Sahwatch (Saguache) mountains, to which it properly pertains. Captain Gunnison observed, on the 31st of August, large volumes of air at intervals escaping with the water of this spring. *(latitude 38o 07' 46")* The butte is not high, but its isolation makes it a prominent feature, standing as it does at the puerta or gate of the Coochetopa Pass. It is formed of coarse, gray granite rock. The spring sends out a fine little stream, winding south and east along grassy fields until it joins the Sahwatch creek, which we reached five miles from the butte in the broad opening leading to the Coochetopa (Cochetopa) Pass. (The location of present-day Saguache, Colorado is where the West and East Forks of the North Branch of the Old Spanish Trail join.) This stream, which is said to sink before reaching the Rio Grande, flows past our camp over a pebbly bed. It is one foot in depth and eighteen in width, with a rapid current. Its valley at this point is five or seven miles in width, growing narrow towards the west; and there are several isolated buttes standing in it, but none of them of considerable height. A few cotton-wood trees and margin of willow bushes line the stream. The soil passed over to-day was unusually light and dusty, our horses sinking hoof-deep in it over large spaces.

We here leave the immense valley of San Luis, which is one of the finest in New Mexico, although it contains so large a portion of worthless land—worthless because destitute of water to such an extent where irrigation alone can produce a crop, and because of the ingredients of the soil in those parts where salts effloresce upon the surface. Its lower portion is adapted to the cultivation of grain, as we have seen at the Costilla and Rio Colorado; and if its upper parts should prove too cold for cereals, its fine fields of grass on and above the Rio Grande del Norte must make it valuable for grazing. Elevation above sea 7,567 feet.

August 31

Five miles from camp the valley narrows to a few hundred yards in width, and continues so for most of the day's travel of twelve miles. At our camp this evening it is half a mile wide, covered with fine grass, fine bottoms of which we passed several times during the day. When ten miles from our morning camp the sand-hills (Great Sand Dunes) in front of William's (Medano) Pass lay plainly in sight directly down the valley. We then turned to our left, taking a course for a short distance south of west, on which we are encamped. The hills and mountains enclosing this thus far beautiful valley, vary in height from two or three hundred to twelve or fifteen hundred feet, covered with a scanty growth of small pine. No mountain pass ever opened more favorably for a railroad than this. The grouse at camp are abundant and fine, as are also the trout in the creek, several having been caught this evening weighing each two pounds.

September 1

On the crest of the mountains at day-light—some six or eight hundred feet above us—were a fine band of mountain sheep, some of them large, majestic fellows; but they did not tempt the spirit of the sportsmen among us. We continued on the southern course, on which we encamped last evening, for about two miles, and then turned west, following the Sawatch (Saguache) creek for six miles, where we crossed it for the last (Upper Saguache crossing) time, and left the main Indian trail which still follows that creek, which rises considerably to the south. This main trail is said to lead through thick forests of timber, through which it would require much labor to open a wagon road to Carnero Pass, equal if not superior to that of our route. We pursued for three miles a line branch (Sheep Creek) of the Sahwatch (Saguache), coming in from the north, when we left it, and, turning west followed a branch of this (East Pass) creek, and after a march of fifteen miles, encamped where a low opening in the mountains to our left afforded a small supply of grass, and enabled us to enter and encamp with our train. The valley of the Sahwatch (Saguache) to-day continued narrow, as at our camp last evening, and the travelling in it very fine, at this dry season. The valley of the next branch was still narrower, ranging from 130 yards to 150 feet, and the travelling equally fine; and in the succeeding valley, often narrowed until the huge, fallen rocks from either side had passed each other and lay scattered over the bottom, the road was still good, although we had constantly to wind around these rocks, and cross and re-cross the creek, here, as almost always under similar circumstances, with soft, springy banks. The pines are confined to the mountain tops and sides, and but few are of respectable size. Surrounding our camp they are small but numerous, extending from our camp-fires quite to the mountain tops. The rocks of the cliffs on all these creeks were porphyritic and pudding-stone, and igneous rocks of various kinds, The precipitate escarpments of the narrow ravines are of the former stone, very porous, and of a red cast, not unlike, but a shade lighter than the common red sandstone, in formations of from twenty to sixty and eighty feet in thickness. The crest of these bluffs are covered with earth a few feet in thickness, some terminating in larger or smaller plains of table-land, while others are rounded off into points and ridges. In the dry bed of a stream near camp we passed over a sedimentary stratum of coarse sandstone, much water-worn.

September 2

Captain Morris and myself went forward with working parties, to make practicable crossings for the wagons at various points where, from the winding of the streams and narrowness of the (north) pass, it should be necessary, and to cut out the timber which at various points quite filled the pass as it covered the ridge, which at this point divide the waters of the continent; those of the eastern slope flowing by the channels up which we have travelled for several days, to the Rio Grande del Norte, and thence to the Gulf of Mexico; while those from the western slope flow

Part of the old wagon road east of Cochetopa Pass. Sally Crum Photo taken in 1990.

216

into the Rio Grande, or Grand (Gunnison) river, one of the main branches of the Colorado of the West, reaching the Pacific through the Gulf of California.

We found little difficulty on the banks of the creek, but were detained some hours from the dense growth of quaking-asp, from the size of saplings to a foot in diameter, among which, fallen in every direction, was an equally large growth of dead aspens. At 11 o'clock, however, we were progressing rapidly towards the summit of the pass, which we soon reached, and, as we enjoyed the prospect before us, a slight thunder-shower was not a disagreeable accompaniment. The elevation of this pass is not enough to give an extensive view, but the numerous small, grassy valleys, and pine and aspen groves of the mountain sides to the west, afforded us a pleasant prospect, the more so as it gave hope of an easy prosecution of our future labors, at least for a time. After cutting away trees for a quarter of a mile down the western slope, we entered an open prairie, at a spring which sends out a fine little creek, which we followed for a mile, without obstruction, and encamped, at half-past 1 o'clock p.m., in a fine field of grass, where two or three mountain rills, coming from as many small valleys, unite. Distance, five miles and a quarter. Latitude, by observation, 38° 12' 34".7.

The width of this pass at the summit does not exceed six hundred yards, but the slopes to the low peaks rising above it are not abrupt. The ascent from the valley of San Luis, by which we reached the summit, was very gradual, increasing with considerable uniformity until we approached it within a short distance, where the ravine of the stream was narrow and thickly timbered; and we left it with the wagons, making an abrupt ascent to the right to the level of the summit, "which we could have reached by a easier grade," Captain Gunnison says in his notes," by keeping to the left of our track, where the ravine winds gently round to the summit-level," The approximate elevation above the sea of our camp at the Puerta, as we left the valley of San Luis, was 7,567 feet. To our next camp, twelve miles and twenty-seven hundredths above the Puerta, on the Sahwatch creek, we ascended slightly over thirty-nine feet to the mile; and in the next fifteen miles to our camp, four miles east of the summit, we ascended 913 feet, or nearly sixty-one feet to the mile; our altitude at this camp being 8,960 feet, while the indicated height of the summit itself is 10,032 feet, giving an ascent of 279 feet 9 inches per mile for 3.83 miles; and of our camp on Pass creek, one mile and thirty-three hundredths west of the summit, 9,540 feet—a descent of 492 feet in that distance, or in whole numbers, 370 feet per mile. Captain Gunnison describes the system of barometric leveling which he employed on several sections of the route explored, as follows: The instruments are kept one hour's distance apart, and record simultaneous readings at the different points of the route. The barometers being first read in camp for comparison, say at 7 o'clock a.m., the party which goes in advance moves forward at once for one hour. At 8 o'clock the barometers are read for altitudes, and the odometers for distances, and the necessary bearings by compass are taken. A small flag is then numbered and planted at this point, when the advance party again moves forward, and at 9 o'clock performs like operations; while the rear readings are made in camp at 8 o'clock, and at 9 at station No. 1, and so on at 10, &c." By this method of leveling we ascended from our camp east of the summit, 154 feet 4 inches per mile for the first mile and sixty-two hundredths; 215 feet 9 inches per mile for the next mile and thirty-nine hundredths; 396 feet 6 inches per mile for the following fifty-eight hundredths of a mile; and 292 feet on the last twenty-four hundredths of a mile at the summit, or nearly 1,200 feet to the mile. Observations taken for the purpose of ascending what extent of deep cutting could be easily effected, gave a descent of 94 feet in the first 350 feet on the eastern slope; and, allowing fifty yards for the length of the summit, an equal distance gave a descent on the western slope of forty-seven feet. But in constructing a railroad, the level of our camps and paths would be disregarded wherever it could be best effected by ascending the hill-sides along the pass, distributing the elevation to be overcome over a longer and more uniform grade. But the ravine character of the pass is such, narrow and direct, *(with sides broken by numerous lateral ravines,)* rising to no considerable height above the stream, that the elevation to be thus gained would be thrown entirely upon the last few miles preceding our camp, 3.83 below the summit, and could not probably exceed 200 feet. If, therefore, this pass be deemed desirable for a railroad, it will be necessary, after having gained this elevation at this camp, to pass the summit with a grade of 124 feet to the mile, which will require a tunnel, including a deep approach from the west, of not less than two miles in length, entering the hill three-fourths of a mile below the summit on the east, and a short distance above our camp, 1.33 mile west of the summit—diminishing the elevation to be overcome by 490 feet. Below this camp the natural grade again becomes practicable for a railroad; for a wagon-road this pass is already practicable. In the Sahwatch mountains, to the north of this pass, another pass exists, leading from one of the numerous little branches which we passed after leaving the Sahwatch spring, to the head of the Coochetopa creek, but it is not favorably represented. Captain Gunnison concludes his notes upon and made the passage of this ridge—the men working hard; and Captain Morris deserves great credit for the manner of executing the labor and selecting the route."

September 3

We proceeded down the valley of Pass creek in a westerly course, the hills on each side being cut by small rills, deep back towards their summits, which will render a winding route and much cutting and filling necessary in constructing a railroad, for which the southern side of the creek is the most favorable. Four miles from camp we passed a broad valley extending several miles to the left towards the Sierra San Juan, whose northern slope are still covered with large fields of snow. Opposite this valley that of Pass creek widens considerably, and we passed easily down it for six miles further to where another valley sweeps off to the south, through which a fine creek descends, and, uniting with that of our path, enters a broken cañon. The valley from this point extends to the south towards the snowy peaks of the Sierra San Juan, near which the Sahwatch creek is said to rise, flowing north and east along the base of the mountain to the left of this and the preceding valley, looking south, where its waters approach nearer those flowing into the Pacific than at any other point. The Carnero Pass leads from that creek over this ridge, and its summit does not appear more elevated than that of the Coochetopa (Cochetopa), and its western descent much more favorable for a road. Our guide, Leroux, represented its approach from the east, however, as more abrupt than that of the Coochetopa Pass, and did not think it practicable for our wagons to pass through the rocks and timber which obstruct it, without more labor than our limited time and the season of the year would warrant us in stopping to bestow upon them; and for the same reasons, no delay was made to examine it. The descent from our morning camp for the first 2.24 miles was *(in whole numbers)* 108 feet to the mile; 68 feet per mile for the next 2.15 miles; 93 feet per mile for the following 2.05 miles, and 42 feet per mile for the succeeding 3.47 miles.

Captain Gunnison says, "the disposition of the mountains indicates that a line can be carried from the Coochetopa (Cochetopa) Pass southwesterly for some distance, passing behind the hills which divide the two southern valleys described above, and descending the most western one, securing a better grade than by following Pass creek." This creek here inclines more to the north, and enters a small cañon which sends out several side branches, and we were forced, in turning it, to cross a ridge to the N. N. E. to another branch of the Coophetopa (Cochetopa) creek. This ridge was rough and thickly covered with several varieties of artemisia—the sage so large and stiff that our animals were very reluctant to pass through it. Distance marched 20 miles.

September 5

Following for three miles the narrow valley of the little creek on which we had encamped, either side of which is lined with ledges of sandstone, through which numerous small rivulets have cut deep channels, it is joined by other valleys and spreads out a mile or two in width, and is, whether wide or narrow, covered with abundant grass. On our right we passed a very large, elevated, and remarkably round butte, standing quite detached from the mountain beyond it. Eight miles brought us to the Coochetopa (Cochetopa) creek, a fine, rapid little stream of twenty feet in width, which we were repeatedly obliged to cross and recross as the valley narrowed in to gorges, and the stream impinged against its banks, while to avoid this at other points we passed over the artemisia bluffs. A few cotton-woods were scattered along the creek, but it was generally lined only with willow bushes. At one point where we crossed it, ledges of coarse and crumbling feldspathic granite were observed; but the rocks were generally sandstone, the light-colored argillaceous frequently overlying the red ferruginous. Conglomerate rocks, but slightly cemented, also prevailed, and a few trap-rocks were seen.

Captain Gunnison ascended a hill one mile W.N.W. from our morning camp, from which he had a fine view of the snow-clad range of mountains from which the Puncha and Coochetopa (Cochetopa) creeks descended. This mountain extends round by the north to northwest *(magnetic,)* where Grand (Gunnison) river passes between it and Elk mountain. From this point also he had a view of a snowy peak of the mountains at the head of the Arkansas river, distant in a course N.N.W. perhaps one hundred miles. From this hill he passed over the broken, barren and slightly elevated country along Pass creek, which receives many small cañones from the left, over which it would require considerable labor to construct a road; "but it could be carried over this elevation by rising below gradually for some distance." Numerous elk-horns and buffalo-skulls lay scattered whitening on the hills, attesting the former range of the latter animals to these pastures, where the small variety of artemisia with a camomile odor, of which they are said to be more fond in winter than of any of the grasses, flourishes. Reaching the mouth of Pass creek, we encamped in a meadow of half a mile in diameter, having travelled 15.88 miles. Several times during the day we experienced very sensibly the sudden changes of temperature to which high altitudes in mountain regions are subject from a passing storm or a change of wind—our thick coats being at one moment necessary to our comfort, and the next oppressive. At this season of the year, rain-storms are here always accompanied by thunder and follow the mountain ranges, or gather about their summit, which act, by their icy coldness, as natural condensers. And while I am writing this evening it is snowing on the higher peaks in sight, and a slight shower of rain, accompanied by violent thunder, is falling on the lower ranges. At this camp our altitude was 7,681 feet above the sea—a descent of 1,134 feet from the head of the cañon on Pass creek, sixteen miles distant, or of seventy-one feet per mile.

September 6

Seven miles from camp the valley of the Coochetopa, (From the point where Cochetopa Creek enters the cañon, Gunnison traveled to the right of the creek upon the higher and more easily traveled ground to arrive at the location of Parlin, Colorado.) which we experienced the same difficulty in following to-day as yesterday, and which was here and there lined with bluffs of coarse pebbles and boulders, slightly

cemented and crumbling, opened into that of Grand (Gunnison) river, on the opposite side of which are high ledges of red sandstone—the base of the Elk mountains.
This valley for eight miles after we entered it, is from one-half to one mile and a
quarter wide, covered abundantly with grass, the (Tomichi) stream being lined with
willow and cotton-wood. The bottom is very level, and is evidently annually overflowed at the season of the melting of the mountain snows, the drift of the present
season lying scattered in the grass to the base of the hills. Elk mountain towers high
above us to the west, the hills immediately along the valley being high and more or
less of a table character, or what the mountain men, of Spanish descent, term mesas—elevated level spaces of land, terminated on one or more sides by precipices and
lower levels. Grand (Gunnison) river is at present a fine, clear (Tomichi) stream of
cold water, one hundred feet wide and three feet deep, flowing rapidly over a paving-
slope bed. Our guide states that its main branch rises in the Elk mountains to the
northwest. This is joined by a large (Gunnison) branch from the north which rises in
the range of mountains to the west of the headwaters of the Arkansas river, and
drains the western slope of that range, and of the Sahwatch mountains. Following
the eastern slope of Elk mountain to its termination, Grand (Gunnison) river passes
to the south and west of it, where it joins the Nah-un-kah-rea, or Blue (Colorado)
river of the Indians and mountain men, which raise in the Middle Park, and is erro-
neously called Grand river on some of the most correct maps.

We encamped in the valley on the west bank of the river, having marched but
14.75 miles, with an average descent of over seventeen feet per mile. This fine little
valley is terminated a short distance below our camp, by the close proximity of the
hills on either side, and a deep cañon presents its giant mount to receive the river.

September 7

We recrossed the river at our camp, and proceeded down its southern bank
1,80 mile to the head of the cañon, where a small creek enters, which we crossed, and
immediately began the ascent of the hills to pass around the deep ravines which
enter the cañon in deep chasms. The hills were very rocky, but we found little difficulty in ascending and passing them with our wagons, except from the everlasting
sage, which was large and rank, and the only vegetation on them, although we approached quite close to the base of the tables or mesas, which are elevated from 300
to 400 feet above our path, and are separated by deep ravines from a few hundred
feet to a quarter of a mile in width. The perpendicular rocks at the head of the cañon
are some eighty feet in height, the cañon itself increasing to twice that altitude where
a creek enters it from the northwest half a mile below its head. The course of the
river (At this point the trail is covered by Blue Mesa Reservoir.) in the cañon, for the
first mile, is south-southwest *(magnetic)* and south. It then turns abruptly west, and

continues on broken courses towards the southwestern point of Elk mountain. The rocks are granitic, containing large masses of crystallized quartz, glistening brightly in the sun. After making 3.25 miles over the hills, passing the heads of ravines, we came upon a precipitous descent, the first cañon having terminated, and an open grassy valley succeeding to the hills for two miles. We had ascended, in this short distance, 735 feet above the head of the cañon, or 715 feet above our morning camp. We had, therefore, to make, in a few hundred yards. a descent nearly equal to this ascent, on a natural grade of about one foot in five, full of igneous rocks of all sizes, from fragments and projecting masses, to mighty ledges. The loose surface stones removed, we attached ropes to the first wagon, which, to prevent accidents, was held by a number of men. It arrived safely at the bottom of the hill, 547 feet below, and half a mile distant; and we dispensed with ropes, and descended with the remainder of the wagons, separated a few yards, and soon reached and again crossed the river. This valley was succeeded by another cañon; and we ascended the opposite bank of the river for a similar purpose for which we had labored in the early part of the day. For five miles the ascent was easy, but here we were obliged to cross a deep ravine, and for this purpose were forced close to the base of the mountain to find a practicable descent, which, at best, was very precipitous, as was also the ascent, although not exceeding a hundred yards in length. A mile further on, we again descended to the river, where a narrow strip of grass afforded a night's pasture for our jaded animals, which had been eleven hours in making fourteen miles. One of our wagons had broken an axletree in the passage of the first hill in the morning, and did not arrive at camp until late in the evening. On each side of the river to-day, and as we can see, for some days ahead, the banks rise rapidly towards the precipitous sides of the mesas, which extend back from fifteen to thirty miles to the mountains. These elevated tables are in classes, each class preserving the same level, through on opposite sides of the river, and consisting of the same formations—all of them terminated at the top by a capping of greater or less thickness of igneous rocks, overlaid by a few feet of soil, on which, occasionally, small groves of trees may be seen. They were formed, doubtless, by the upheavel of large plains st the same time; and the immense cracks and crevices of those convulsions have been enlarged, in time, by the elements, and now form the cañones, gorges, ravines, gullies, and passes, which in every direction surround us. While the current of the river is rapid, and the descent very considerable, these tables seem to preserve the same absolute level, and consequently become more elevated above the river as it descends. They are judged to be, to-day, 1,200 feet above it, and not less than 1,500 twenty miles west of us. Sage alone flourished along our path.

Captain Gunnison rode into the cañones several times during the day. He says of the first, "that it would require blasting one-third of the distance for the construction of a road, and solid masonry, with many arches for culverts on the whole line—a stupendous work for an engineer. The second is less formidable, the rocks being more friable, and the curves of larger radius, while the cliffs are but 100 feet in height." The river, at high water, he judged to cover the bottoms in places to the depth of six and eight feet; and from a neighboring hill, he esteemed the country " the roughest, most hilly, and most 'cut up,' he had ever seen. Hills with flat tops, hills with rounded tops, and hills with knife edges and points, and deep chasms, are on every side." Gray and brown headed ducks are numerous on the river; the cock of the plains and blue grouse are common, also deer, antelope, and elk. The average descent of the river from camp to camp to-day, was less than ten feet per mile.

September 8

Last night was clear and cold, ice of some thickness forming in our water-vessels; and the thermometer half an hour before sunrise this morning indicated 23° of Fahrenheit, but the sensation of cold is much less than at a much higher tempera-ture in a moist climate. We were obliged to cross the river twice at this camp to pass around a bluff from a spur of Elk mountain, and to avoid ravines on the south, which enter the river at a gorge a short distance below us. Leroux had gone in advance, leaving a man who had been over the road with him the previous day to point it out to us, but he wandered off in search of mountain sheep, and our pilots, after crossing a spur, descended to the river again, where we lost much time in searching for a ford, the river being narrow and too deep for our wagons; and we were eventually obliged to return to the hills, and follow them for a short distance, when we again crossed to the southern bank of the river, and proceeded immediately from it towards the base of the high tables on that side. We ascended rapidly, having, however, but one sharp ravine to cross, the opposite bank of which we ascended only by dint of hard labor, and descending into another ravine, where we found a small spring of cool water, encamped, with abundant grass on the hills for our animals, having travelled but four miles, our camp being 346 feet above that of the morning, although 200 feet below the crest of the ravine. A large smoke ascending from our last camp, from the grass taking fire after we left it, a larger counter-smoke was seen during the day directly on our route ahead, made doubtless by the Utah Indians, in the heart of whose country we have been travelling for several weeks, and whom we expect daily to meet. as we are approaching their summer hunting-grounds—the elk, which they follow both north and south in the winter, migrating here at this season. Antelope are also abun-dant, and are taken by the Utahs by building a pen, or rather two sides of a triangle, and driving a large district of country, narrowing in until they themselves form the third side, when they seize the game; and a whipping betides the unfortunate *women*, says our guide, if one happens to escape where they are stationed.

As the train left the river, Captain Gunnison ascended a spur on the north side, whence "a small part of the Arkansas mountains could be seen through the gorge of the river, N. 80° E.; the river itself passing him between square-capped hills, which characterize the spurs on either side, S. 75° W., for perhaps twenty miles. From this position, the reason was apparent why the guides pronounced the further progress of the wagons along the river impracticable." "The stream is imbedded in narrow and sinuous cañones, the dark top outline of which resembles a huge snake in motion, as the wavy atmosphere conveys the light to the eye. And the little spurs appear merged into one great connecting ridge, from the mountains at the head of the Rio del Norte to the great Elk mountains on the north. These spurs have their lowest depressions at the bed of Grand (Gunnison) river, a chasm in the porphyritic and crystalline rocks opened for its passage. The red sandstone that has at one time overlaid it, has been washed away. The side creeks from the mountains have cut deep valleys, with perpendicular sides, in the softer rocks; and there are left standing many hills of sandstone, which are protected from decay by what appears to have been lava, cooled under water after spreading over the sediment, which is hardened into argillaceous sandstone in some places, and sand cemented with a ferruginous cement in others. In some parts the capping is removed over great areas, and the stone is found in the bottoms of the streams rounded into pebbles. To look down over the tangent plane in the cañon below, it seems easy to construct a railroad; but immense mounds of cutting, filling, and masonry would be required. There is a number to speak of nearer than the mountains, and that difficult of process for such a work. Cottonwood in clumps on the river, and dwarf cedar and pine scattered on the cliffs and hills, will furnish fuel for wagoners."

September 9

For the second time our guide returned to camp last night ill at ease, and it was evident that his two morning's examination of the route ahead had not only proved less successful than he desired, but had quite surprised his memory. But we were too close upon his trail to admit of longer delay in informing us that we had a serious obstacle before us in the passage of the Rio de la Lagune, (The description given here by Gunnison fits the Lake Fork of the Gunnison River, but the author believes that for some unknown reason Gunnison reverses the location of the Lake Fork and Cebolla Creek.) or Lake Fork, coming into Grand (Gunnison) river from the south, through almost one continuous cañon from the mountain to the river, and that he had failed to find an easy crossing. This morning, therefore, large working parties of soldiers and employes started forward, under their respective commanders, to prepare the crossing of the creek; and at 2 o'clock p.m. we received orders to move on with the train. Ascending from the ravine on which we had encamped, we were forced high up on the mesas, to avoid numerous deep ravines, which we succeeded in turning successfully, when a short, steep ascent around the rocky wall of the table to our left, brought us, four miles from our morning camp, to the top of the difficult passage—a rapid descent of 4,055 feet in length, and 935 in perpendicular height above the stream, covered with stones of all sizes, from pebbles to tons in weight, with small ledges of rocks cropping out at various points. Some of the stones had been removed in the proposed road; but the wagons, with locked wheels, thumped, jarred, and grated over the greater portion, especially those to large and deeply imbedded in the soil to be removed, until their noise quite equalled that of the foaming torrent creek below. At one point, as they passed obliquely over a ridge, it was necessary to attach ropes to the wagons, and employ a number of men to prevent their overturning. Two hours were thus employed in descending with our eighteen wagons, and in twice crossing the creek, in the bed of which we had to descend for a quarter of a mile, before we could gain a permanent footing on the west side. The creek is sixty feet wide by from one to two deep, with an impetuous current falling with a loud noise over a bed of rocks and large stones. Just above its mouth two fine streams, half a mile apart, enter Grand (Gunnison) river from Elk mountain. Day's march five miles, through a heavy growth of sage.

September 10

After considerable labor in removing surface stones and digging down a few yards of the opposite hill, to sideling for our wagons, we doubled our teams, and with ten mules, but not without severe labor—detaining us, however, but six hours—pulled up the load of six to the crest of the western bank of Lake Fork, ascending 480 feet in forty-one hundredths of a mile. By the line followed by our wagons, it is 1.50 mile from crest to crest of the banks of this creek, but in a right line it is only 2,639 feet, or about half a mile, while the perpendicular descent from the east, as already given, is 935 feet. The most practicable means by which this immense ravine can be passed by a road, will be by ascending one of its banks by a heavy grade into the mountains, crossing it by a bridge, and descending the opposite bank—a stupendous labor, for it will be necessary to cut through miles of rocks and to cross large side-ravines. But it becomes narrower below the crossing, and proportionally steeper; and Captain Gunnison, after examining it, though it, perhaps, not impossible, but very difficult to bridge it. (Today there is a bridge crossing the Lake Fork of the Gunnison which was created as the road was rebuilt for the reservoir.)

Leaving Lake Fork we continued along under high bluffs, over very rocky hills with deep intervening gullies, which forced us southward into a valley gorge, which we reached by a steep ascent, and encamped, after a march of 4.69 miles, under a vertical wall of igneous rocks 100 feet in height, at a beautiful spring of cold water in a fine grassy meadow, through which a creek descends to the river, distant two miles. This little valley is part of a depression some four miles in diameter, like a basin in the high table-land among the mesas, which on all sides enclose it to the eye, although Grand (Gunnison) river passes through it, and small streams enter it through deep, wide gorges in all directions. The agreeable and exhilarating effect of the pure mountain air of these elevated regions, ever a fruitful theme of eloquence among trappers and voyageurs, exhibits itself among our men in almost constant boisterous mirth. But violent physical exertion soon puts them out of breath, and our animals, in climbing the hills, unless often halted to breathe, soon become exhausted, and stop from the weight of their loads, but after a few moments rest move on with renewed vigor and strength.

September 12

Crossing the creek, we followed the ravine valley of our camp southward to the top of the mesa, and turning westward, passed from two miles along its summit, and descended with difficulty to a creek two hundred feet below it, only to ascend again, by an equally abrupt path, to the same level, and again immediately descended, by a similar path, to another creek, difficult to cross only because of the dense thicket of willow bushes which line its banks, and again ascended to nearly the same level as before, and then wound more gradually down a long descent to a larger creek, coming through a deep gorge to the south, from snow-peaks, plainly in sight, of the Sierra de la Plata. We left this creek by a more gentle ascent than we had climbed for a week before, through luxuriant fields of grass, in which, indeed, we had travelled during most of the morning, in rear of the mesa adjacent to Grand (Gunnison) river, and passing one or two small ponds of water on the way, descended for five miles to the first branch of Cebolla or Onion creek, the last two miles through a level artemisia field, in which we encamped, on a small grassy space near the creek, having travelled 13.18 miles. While Captain Morris and myself were out in search of a suitable camp, a few tah-bah-was-chi (This is the Tabeguache band of the Ute nation.) Utahs exhibited themselves on their war steeds, near enough to call out to us. We advanced to meet them, and a crowd of men, women, and children soon gathered at our camp.

September 13

Captain Gunnison, this morning, made presents to the Indians; first providing the chief with the articles which he was to distribute to his people, and then a package for himself. They were very importunate for powder and lead, everything else appearing of little value to them. We were anxious to purchase horses, but they would sell them only for arms and ammunition.

We crossed the creek a short distance above our camp, where a practicable ravine afforded us a descent, the bank being forty feet high and very steep, and passing down it ascended the other bank by a similar ravine, opposite our camp, to the rolling sage plain which we crossed to the main branch of Cebolla creek, which we forded, and encamped, after a ride of only 3.75 miles, on a grass field nearby, at the base of a connecting mountain range, which here crossed the valley of Grand (Gunnison) river from Elk towards the Sierra de la Plata—it being necessary to find a path for our wagons before attempting the passage. Captain Morris and myself, therefore, with Leroux as guide, and a party of men, rode forward by one of the two routes followed by Indians and hunters in passing this mountain, and reached the summit in two hours; the scenery becoming more beautiful as we ascended, especially through the gorge of Onion creek to the south, where vertical columns of rocks stood out high and clear against the sky, being part of the Sierra de la Plata—a range of mountains to the west of the Sahwatch and Sierra San Juan—whose sharp summits are broken into a thousand points and angular forms, and its sides streaked with banks of snow. Our route far behind us lay clear and direct at our feet to the mountains about the Coochatopa Pass; and the course of Grand (Gunnison) river, with a level summit for many miles, terminating with a vertical descent of a few hundred feet, and then apparently subsiding into a plain. At our feet to the west lay the Uncompahgra (Uncompahgre) river, rising in the Sierra de la Plata, and flowing northwest through a valley of considerable width, beyond which a range of high land was overlooked by more distant mountains, among which the Salt and Abajo peaks were pointed out to us. The former is directly upon the noted (South Branch of the) Spanish trail leading from California to Abiquiu, New Mexico, and is a favorable resort for the Utah and Navajo Indians for trade; while the latter is near the junction of Grand (Colorado) and Green rivers, considerably below the fords for this trail, or, as Leroux says, below any ford on Grand (Colorado) river known to the New Mexicans, and hence its name. But we had little time to enjoy this majestic scenery, and hastened to examine the descent of the mountain, which we found very difficult, and at various places, as on the ascent, thickly covered with scrubby oak bushes and aspens. The soil is light, but covered with luxuriant grass. We thought it possible to pass this route with wagons; but the other route, followed by the Indians from our camp to the Uncompahgra, lay directly below us while ascending the mountain, and appeared much preferable to the one we had examined; and a small party, sent out to examine it a short distance, reported it passable.

September 14

It was 3.80 miles by this route to the top of the steep ascent of the ridge, and three hours were occupied in its ascent; our barometers giving a difference of level of fourteen hundred feet. The top of the mountain was broad, and near the summit we fortunately found a small basin of water, in our circuitous path to avoid ravines, at which our animals were watered; but it was too stagnant for the men. From the western slope the valley of the Uncompahgra could be seen in the distance; and, striking the dry head of Cedar creek, we commenced our descent to it. This creek was too narrow and ravine-like to allow us to descend its bed, and we accordingly circled round on the hillsides, sometimes in grass fields, at other in dense masses of sage, from which we escaped only to encounter the stiff scrubby branches of oak bushes, and at length, through a mass of them, to make a precipitous descent to the creek, which was itself lined with them. Just before sundown we reached a point where Leroux had, under a rock in a deep thickly-bushed ravine, discovered a little cool and refreshing water, with which our animals were watered from buckets, and ourselves supplied for the night, which now overtook us; and we encamped a mile below on a very little coarse grass, having travelled thirteen miles. Two miles west of this camp our elevation above the sea was 6,962 feet, while it was 8,755 feet at the top of the sharp ascent nine miles east of camp. The average ascent per mile to this point, for the 3.80 miles from our morning camp, is a few inches over 368 feet, and the average descent for the succeeding eleven miles is 163 feet per mile. Some additional distance can be gained by a winding path in the ascent of this ridge, but not sufficient to make it practicable for a railroad, which, if at all, can only be carried on this part of Grand (Gunnison) river immediately along its banks.

September 15

We were still forced to cross Cedar creek several times, each passage requiring considerable labor in cutting down the banks, before it became wide enough for our wagons to pass freely down it, which it did two miles below camp, where we found water in pools. To this point the cacti and sage were troublesome, but were scarcely seen again until we reached the borders of the Uncompahgra; the hills and valley alike, on each side of our route, being a light colored, friable, and clayey soil, almost destitute of vegetation. The valley of the Uncompahgra, efflorescing with salts in many places, is several miles in width, and the stream is lined with cotton-wood trees, willow, and buffalo-berry bushes, and, by crossing it where it was thirty feet wide by one deep, we found an abundance of grass and encamped, having marched 12.30 miles, descending 87.7 feet to the mile for the last ten miles. This river rises, as I have already stated, in the Sierra de la Plata, which appears to set off from the Sierra San Juan, and lie nearly parallel with our path, and from fifty to sixty miles distant. Near us are two or three Indian lodges, the occupants of which were greatly frightened at our sudden appearance. Their young men being absent on the hills hunting, were to timid to return and warn their lodges of our approach, for they had seen us, as we had them, long before reaching these lodges. Those of the women who could, fled to the thickets with their children; but two were too old to run, and were soon assured of their safety. They, however, experienced considerable difficulty in calling the young women from their hiding-places, until their men returned and they no longer feared treachery. The two old women bear unmistakable evidence of having seen the snows of a hundred winters pass away. They are of small stature, and bent forward with years; wearing their coarse hair, still as abundant as in their youth, after the manner of the women of their nation: cut short across the forehead, and passing below the ears, across the nape of the neck, and a little thinned on the edges, it stands off hideously ugly, but gray only in a few locks. Their features are dried and shrunken to a mummy-like appearance, with bleared eyes, and sunken lips covering teeth worn to the gums. The joints of some of their fingers are stiff and distorted, and all are enlarged to ugliness. These poor objects of humanity are clothed in deer-skins, and, on learning that their lives were not in danger, sang and jumped with joy at their escape from what they had supposed inevitable death. The most domestic scene witnessed was that of a mother who visited our camp with her four little children—the five riding the same horse, and all as much at home as mothers and children in a nursery. One sat in front of the mother, and one was swung on her back on a frame covered with skins, and two rode behind her, leaving no place unoccupied from the horse's tail to his neck. Presents were made to these people by Captain Gunnison.

September 16

We travelled 18.25 miles down the Uncompahgra to-day, crossing the stream four miles below our morning camp, and again a few miles before encamping this evening, a short distance above its junction with Grand (Gunnison) river; the descent from camp to camp slightly exceeding forty-one feet to the mile. The country is in all respects like that passed yesterday—cotton-wood, willow, grass in the narrow bottom, and near it heavy sage; but the great mass of the valley land is nearly destitute of vegatation—light, clayey, and arid to such an extent that it is disagreeable to ride over it, as it sends up clouds of dust at every step. We met several small parties of Indians during the day, all of whom followed us to camp; and others continued to arrive until a late hour at night, filling the air as they approached with yells and calls, which were answered by their friends in or near camp—consisting of inquiries and directions as to how and where they were to pass—until we were heartily tired of them. The most of them were sent out of camp, but they built their fires only a few yards from ours, and their noise was little abated by the change, and our safety but little increased. They had, much to his regret, recognized our guide; but he neither showed fear nor want of confidence in them, although he had once shot one of their chiefs, who was attempting to rob him of his horse; and he shared his fire, pipe, and blankets with the chiefs who remained all night with him.

September 17

Si-ree-chi-wap, the principal chief of the band, who is now so old that he exercises but little authority directly—intrusting it to his son, who accompanies him—arrived during the night, and, followed by his sub-chiefs and warriors, this morning repaired to Captain Gunnison's tent to talk and smoke. The Captain informed them that "the President had sent him to look for a good road by which his people, who live towards the rising sun, can visit those who live upon the great water where it sets; that he was their friend, and had authorized him to make them a few presents in his name." The son of Si-ree-chi-wap replied: "This is your land, and you can go over it at any time. There are bad Indians over the mountains, who kill white men, but the Utahs are good, and glad to see the Americans." Presents were then distributed, pipes smoked, and the party moved on, accompanied for several miles by the chiefs. We crossed the point of land lying between the Uncompahgra (Uncompahgre) and Grand (Gunnison) river, reaching the latter at Roubideau's old trading fort, now entirely fallen to ruins. The river is much larger than where we left it a week ago; and its water has here a greenish shade, while there it was colorless. The Uncompahgra, however, is remarkable for this color of its water, and for a pea-green moss, two or three inches long, covering the stones in its bed, even when the stream is shallow and very rapid. A mile below the fort we crossed the river at an excellent ford; (On the 1885 Nell's Topographical and Township Map, this ford is listed as Roubideau's Ford.) the bottom being a mile in width, and covered with abundant grass.

The cañon which we have been so many days passing around, terminates several miles above the junction of the Uncompahgra, where Grand (Gunnison) river receives a large affluent from Elk mountain, known as Smith's fork. The high ridge, varying from 500 to 1,500 feet in height above our path, back of which we passed from Lake Fork in avoiding this cañon, and which is itself cut with deep cañones by the Cebolla and other streams, terminates, towards the valley of the Uncompahgra, in buttes and clay hills, of which there are two ridges; the first and lowest, of gray, and the second of red clay, bordering the river. Alkali is seen in these hills, as it is also in the plain, and is doubtless the chief cause of the barrenness of the soil. From our camp below the mouth of the Coochetopa creek, to the junction of Smith's Fork with Grand (Gunnison) river, there is nothing deserving the name valley. Now and then there is a small open bottom, from a few yards to a mile or two in length, but at the season of high waters the river sweeps over these spaces, and the stream is not followed even by an Indian trail.

The difference of elevation between the head of the cañon and our camp, a few miles below its termination, on the Uncompahgra, separated from Grand

(Gunnison) river by a level bottom only, is 2,077 feet; and as the distance between these points by the river does not exceed seventy miles—of which, perhaps, sixty preserves its cañon character—the average descent will vary but slightly from thirty feet to the mile. But from the continuance, for so great a distance, of vertical rocky walls along the river, upon which the road must be carried, and which can be cut only by blasting, and, from the deep side-chasms to passed, as described by Captain Gunnison on the 7th instant, only by the heaviest masonry, it is evident that a railroad, although possible, can only be constructed in the vicinity of this section of Grand (Gunnison) river, at an enormous expense—for the accurate estimate of which, situated as the work is at so great a distance from civilization, where not only laborers, but their subsistence, must be transported by land carriage nearly 1,000 miles, and where scarcely a stick of timber has been seen for the last 100 miles on the route, nor will be for the succeeding 150 miles, suitable for a string-piece for a small temporary bridge, or even a railroad tie, it is not too much to say, no data exists, nor will until such a labor shall be undertaken.

Ascending from the river bottom, our route passed, parallel with it, over a district of pulverulent clay, the surface occasionally incrusted with salt, with small broken crystals of gypsum scattered freely about. This soil is formed from the wash of the impure clay-slate bluffs on our right, our animals sinking in it to their fetlocks. These bluffs rise one above another until they attain an altitude of 1,000 feet, their summits presenting the appearance, as we descended Grand (Gunnison) river, of an unbroken plain; but as we pass in front of them they are seen to cut into deep ravines by the small streams which descend from them during rains. In a few miles, however, we passed from this soil to a hard one, covered with small fragments of black vesicular volcanic rocks scattered over the surface. The men sent forward to select a camp, failed to find access to the river; and having travelled 20.33 miles at dark, we encamped without water, and on so limited a supply of grass, scattered over the hills, that the most of our animals were tied up to secure their presence in the morning. Our elevation was perhaps 160 feet above the river, and during the afternoon we had repeatedly to cross deep ravines entering the river in cañones, in trap-rock or in sandstone and clay-slate, where they overlie the trap. The land rises from our camp to the river, distant half a mile; and beyond it is soon elevated into a mountain: the stream flowing, consequently, in an immense chasm along the mountain side, made, doubtless, by volcanic action. Much "cutting and filling" would be required in constructing a road near this cañon, which the Utahs call Una-weep, or Red cañon. It extends from a short distance below Roubideau's old fort to near the junction of Grand (Gunnison) river with the (Colorado) Blue or Nah-un-kah-rea of the Indians. The Utahs also give the name of Una-weep to a small stream which enters Grand (Gunnison) river from the south, in this cañon.

231

The wagon tracks at Fool's Hill west of Delta, Colorado can be seen ascending from the middle right of the photo to the right of the cloud at the top.

September 18

At break of day we moved forward for 8.45 miles, over a country like that of yesterday, but less broken, and encamped on a small stream from the west end of Elk mountains, which is on our right, our course being northwest. This little stream the Indians who visit us call Kah-nah (Kannah). The grass, though not abundant, is sufficient for our stock. Descent from the Uncompahgra twenty-nine feet per mile, in round numbers.

September 19

Four miles and a quarter from camp we came to a small creek, running between clay banks twelve feet in depth, which detained us an hour in crossing. The cañon of Grand (Gunnison) river disappears at this point on this bank, and the bottom is covered with a small field of cotton-wood; but we saw no grass either on the creek or river, which is again soon walled in by rocks of sandstone, numerous bluffs of which we passed. The light friable soil of the last two days continued to the

Nah-un-kah-rea (Colorado) river, which we reached in a march of 12.32 miles. The eastern bank of this stream, for miles above and below where we struck it, is perpendicular, and from forty to eighty feet in height—the top of clay and the base of shale. A small gully (at 28-1/4 road in Orchard Mesa south of the Colorado River an arroya leads down to the river.) afforded us the means of cutting a very steep path for our wagons to the river, which we crossed a few hundred yards below, at a point where it was but a little over two feet deep and a hundred yards wide, with a very rapid current—the volume of water being twice that of Grand (Gunnison) river. The opposite bank, although but six feet high, the moment it was cut down and moistened by water thrown up by the leading horses, became so miry that we were occupied three hours in crossing, and encamped near the ford—grass being coarse, and gritty from a recent overflow. This river enters this valley through a cañon or immense gorge, which separates the Elk mountains on its east from the Roan or Book mountains to the west, and, bending from its southern course, unites with Grand (Gunnison) river (The Colorado is the larger of the two rivers. It would be more accurate to state that the Gunnison united with the Colorado. This is the way that it is listed today.) just below us. Roan mountain, which derives its name from the color of its sides of red, gray, white and blue clay, in horizontal strata, destitute of vegetation and washed into many deep gorges and fanciful forms,-sweeps round the west, following a course some miles from the river. The west end of Elk mountain is terminated with a similar formation; and that to the southwest of Grand (Gunnison) river, before its junction with the Blue (Colorado), resembles it, although more rocky, and some of its bluffs are scantily supplied with small cedars and pines. The valley, twenty miles in diameter, enclosed by these mountains, is quite level and very barren, except scattered fields of the greasewood and sage varieties of artemisia—the margins of Grand (Gunnison) and Blue (Colorado) rivers affording but a meagre supply of grass, cotton-wood and willow.

The latter stream at the season of melting snows is greatly swollen, and at every step we see evidences of the great volumes of water which at such times roll forward in its channel or spread out over its bottom, in the deep channels, now dry, and islands now part of the main land, covered with huge trees cast up and left by the angry stream. Average descent during the day, nineteen feet per mile.

September 20

Captain Gunnison, for the first time, succeeded in purchasing horses from the Indians with the public goods which had been brought for that purpose.

The horses were small, but hardy, and we were much in want of them. Our camp was moved down the river but 9.10 miles, as the Indians informed us that we could not reach grass beyond that point before night—an artifice to retain good customers; for there was better grass two hours' march ahead, and our animals fared badly on the gritty blue-grass at our camp. Latitude, 39° 07' 24"; descent, 4 feet 4 inches per mile.

September 21

The clay soil yesterday and this morning was often very smooth and dry, and so hard that our shod horses scarcely left a mark on it. Seven miles below camp the river again enters a cañon, near which we filled our canteens for the night, and continued on for 7.30 miles over the same greasewood plain to Salt creek, which we found a mere rivulet of miserably brackish water, the sands of the bed being covered with incrustations of salt, which also effloresces widely over the plain. Near this creek the plain is washed into little valleys, leaving small knolls and ridges standing, which give it a rolling appearance; and our men find much labor in cutting down the banks of gullies for the passage of our wagons. Bunch-grass is scattered over the hills towards the river, and our animals drink the creek water freely. Many trails lead up this creek, and the Indians inform us that they are used in visiting their neighboring band, the Uintas. Latitude, 39° 13' 12"; average descent per mile during the day, 9 feet 7 inches.

September 22

Captain Gunnison found a bed of coal on a ridge bearing north-northwest from Salt creek cañon, and a mile from it, which he describes as being "100 feet long by 20 broad, and about one foot thick. It is exposed to the weather, but appears to be good and blackened clay banks, are frequent. Latitude by noon observation, 39° 14' 14".

We left Salt creek without a guide—Leroux having gone forward some four days since to examine the route, show those who accompany him the best road to the (South Branch of the) Spanish trail, and not yet returned. We determined, therefore, to keep up the broad, rolling valley between Roan mountain on our right, and the cañon bluffs of the river on the left. The day was very hot and oppressive, and the soil friable, with the usual amount of sage and an increase of cacti; with numerous gullies to cut and fill. We found no point at which we could approach the river until to late an hour in the afternoon to reach it with our train, for it was impossible to travel at night with wagons without a road. We encamped, therefore, without grass, near the dry bed of what proved to be a small intermitting creek of bitter water. Streams of this kind during the day time in the dry season contain no water, but small rivulets break out and flow during the night, but again disappear as the sun becomes hot. So many of our animals gave out, that several of the wagons did not reach camp during the night.

We were here about four miles from the river, which, by following the ravine cut through the cañon wall by the creek, was easily reached on horseback, and only obstructed for wagons by a dry channel cut deep in the clay, at a narrow bottom of fine grass two or three miles in length, with shady groves of cotton-wood on the banks of the stream. The red sandstone cañon walls are nearly vertical, and two hundred feet high; beyond which smaller ledges rise above each other, terrace-like, for some miles towards Salt mountains, which bears south from our camp, some twenty miles beyond the river. The cañon narrows to the width of the river below the groves of cotton-wood. In a ravine by which Captain Gunnison approached the river, four miles below Salt creek, and nearly opposite the mouth of the San Miguel, he says, "sandstone and clayey deposites alternate one above the other, one layer of which is altered by heat, and much of the argillaceous rock is black with the appearance of coal having burnt under it. Coal is found in the cañon near our camp, and can be gathered in place, and there can be no doubt of this being a part of the Green river coal basin formation; at least the formation has the same appearance there as here, and the water from the red sandstone and clay deposits similar crystallizations."

We observe the greatest contrast between the heat of the days and nights in these mountain valleys; the thermometer from noon to 3 o'clock p.m. ranging, for the last several days, from 87° to 92° Fahrenheit, and at night falling below the freezing-point. Yet we find a cactus here which flourishes generally in Texas and warm climates.

The barrenness of these valleys is greatly influenced by the alkaline and saline ingredients of the soil, while their dryness is easily understood by observing the distribution of the aqueous vapors. The moment a cloud begins to form, it rushes towards a mountain chain, is poured in torrents upon its highest peaks, and rushes down its rocky sides into the chasms and gutters in which the beds of streams lie in the valleys, too deep and confined to irrigate the adjacent lands to any distance. The higher mountains are also protected by the clouds to a great extent from the powerful rays of the sun, which scorch the valleys; and hence, in inaccessible places to man, grass and herbage flourish. It is not intended to say that no rain falls upon the valleys and plains, but only a very small proportion is deposited there during the warm season, when the rain comes in showers of sudden formations; but in the colder parts of the year more is diffused over the general surface. We have seen rain falling in showers usually in the afternoon, on the mountain-tops, almost every day since we first came in sight of the Rocky mountains, two months since; whilst in this valley for two weeks we have been scorched at midday by a tropical sun, and in the whole distance scarcely moistened, except once or twice, near the summits of passes, by rain.

The formation of the valleys is against a system of artificial irrigation; their absorbing power being so great that the mountain streams, during the summer, seldom reach far into the plains. It is therefore only at the foot of the mountains which are not too elevated and cold for vegetation to flourish, where the small streams descend, that irrigation can be employed. No part of the route thus far from San Luis valley, therefore, offers a spot of any considerable extent suitable for settlement. Sufficient grass flourishes in the mountain valleys of Grand (Gunnison) river, east of the junction of the Blue (Colorado), for grazing purpose; but it is a significant fact, bearing upon the climate, that elk frequent them only in summer, migrating both to the north and south in autumn, where they remain during the winter and again return in summer.

Leroux, with three companions, left us at this camp to return to New Mexico, having completed his engagement as guide. He expects to travel much at night, and trusts to his knowledge of the country and tact for passing safely through the Indian bands along his route. Day's march, 21.74 miles; ascent, 9 feet 9 inches per mile.

September 26

Having passed three days in camp, keeping our animals at the river to graze, we this morning resumed our march and determined to continue our course back of the river hills. We were not without hope that the fine rain of the previous night *(falling freely for two or three hours)* would furnish a supply of water in pools or in creeks from the mountains. At break of day, therefore, I started, accompanied by one man, armed, as I observed after riding some time, only with a spade and hatchet, to find water, if possible, and grass for a camp; and if successful, a smoke was to guide the party to the point selected. The first two or three creeks passed within a short distance, poured down small muddy streams; but as the sun rose hot and drying, a few hours drained off the surface water, and the beds of creeks soon contained but a few holes of water, and by 10 o'clock even these were fast disappearing. As soon as I had ridden far enough for the day's march, I began my search for grass and water—indispensable items for the camp of a party of exploration, with jaded and weak animals, and months of labor before them. So fruitless was the search, however, that it was not deemed possible to find water; but an extensive view from an elevated position convinced me of the error of deviating from this course, and I therefore made the concerted signal of a camp, trusting to the fortune of a more diligent search—in which threatening showers promised to aid us, and eventually swelled the rain-water creek on which we encamped to the size of a respectable stream, on which and the adjacent hills we found a little bunch-grass. The train arrived, after a march of 16.28 miles, a little before sundown; having passed during the day but one or two small hills and a few gullies. As night closed in, clouds gathered around us; and as I write occasional flashes of lightning and steady-falling rain threaten us with a comfortless night. Average descent during the day, about two feet per mile.

September 27

It continued to rain most of the night, and increased in violence until 10 o'clock in the morning, when it ceased, and we moved slowly forward over a very slippery and miry soil—all the beds of creeks, recently dry, pouring down torrents of water, and water filling every little depression on the surface of the ground; yet the earth was not moistened more than two inches deep, the wagon-wheels turning the dry earth up onto the brick soft clay of the surface. At 12 o'clock a passing shower sent down such a torrent from the mountain, that, although the leading wagons had crossed it without difficulty, the others were unable to follow for some hours; and we therefore encamped just west of this stream, on a hill finely dotted with bunch-grass, after a march of 5.66 miles. Our route here lies but two or three miles from the base of Roan mountain, and is much more direct from Salt creek than by following the river to the (South Branch of the) Spanish trail, (The North Branch of the Old Spanish Trail which Gunnison had been following joins the South Branch about twenty miles east of Green River or near Crescent Junction, Utah.) and thence crossing to the ford on Green river, and is less interrupted by deep gullies; but in wet weather it would be impossible to follow us with heavy loads, and in the dry season no water can be found on this path between Grand (Colorado) and Green rivers.

Captain Gunnison indicates the choice of localities for a railroad track as lying still nearer the base of the mountain, where, however, "much cutting and filling would be required, and many large culverts necessary." The thunder-showers of the morning covered Salt mountain with snow, the effects of which we feel as the wind sweeps round from that quarter; and we can get no wood, and only sage enough to cook our coffee. Ascent, 71 feet per mile.

September 28

We delayed our march until 8 o'clock, to derive as much benefit from the sun and morning drainage as possible, and it was difficult, even at that hour to make any progress—mules miring and wagons stalling even on the descent of the hills, which were destitute of a turf or sward, the whole surface to a considerable depth being of the character of stiff brick-yard clay; but after going two or three miles, the soil became more slaty and gravelly on the ridges, and eventually over the whole surface. We descended a steep bluff in the morning, and passed over two gentle swells during the day, the last of which was the divide between the waters of Grand (Colorado) and Green rivers, and encamped, after a march of 16.71 miles, in which we descended 12 feet 10 inches per mile, just at sundown, on the remnants of a rain-water creek, and a thin supply of grass on the hills. Deep narrow gullies cut in the clay soil, with perpendicular sides, obstructed our progress more than usual to-day, as they were from four to sixteen feet deep, and from one to twelve feet wide.

The mountain on Grand (Colorado) river is very broken, and during the day presented many beautiful rocks standing high above the adjacent ledges and ridges. From one position a majestic shaft stood out clear against the sky; and chimney rocks were almost hourly presented as we rode along, with piles occasionally resembling ruins of immense churches and dwellings, and one or two on eminences, resembling the ruins of mighty cities of adobe buildings.

For a mile, in the morning, we continued our course of yesterday, W.S.W., and then changed to S.W. for seven miles, when we came upon the noted Spanish (South Branch) trail which leads from Salt mountains. We then turned W.N.W., following this trail, and encamped, after a march of 14.07 miles, in which we descended 12 feet 3 inches per mile, at a rain-water pool, a neighboring ravine furnishing a limited supply of grass; but for once, sage was even more scarce than grass, the country being entirely destitute of wood.

From an elevated bluff near camp, Captain Gunnison describes the view as disheartening in the extreme. "Except three or four small cotton-wood trees in the ravine near us, there is not a tree to be seen by the unassisted eye on any part of the horizon. The plain lying between us and the Wahsatch range, a hundred miles to the west, is a series of rocky, parallel chasms, and fantastic sandstone ridges. On the north, Roan mountain, ten miles from us, presents bare masses of sandstone, and on the higher ridges, twenty miles back, a few scattering cedars may be distinguished by the grass; Salt mountain, to the east, is covered half down its sides with snow; and to the south, mass after mass of coarse conglomerate is broken in fragments, or piled in turret-shaped heaps, colored by ferruginous cement from a deep black to a brilliant red, whilst in some rocks there are argillaceous layers, varying to gray or glittering with white. The surface around us is whitened with fields of alkali, precisely resembling fields of snow. The soft clayey earth in many places glistens with selenite, and gypsum appears in masses along the sharp sides of the bluffs, while fragments of obsidian are scattered over the ground."

September 30

Our course for six miles this morning was the same as that of last evening, following the direction of the hills and dry beds of creeks. We then passed through the range of hills on our right, and again resumed our course along the base of Roan mountain; these hills presenting precisely the appearance of immense beds and fields of ashes, being more saline and friable even than those of previous days, and even more destitute of vegetation, the undulating descent being relieved near the Akanaquint or Green river by scattered tuffs of grass. Groves of cotton-wood lined the stream, and a narrow bottom afford grass for our animals for the night, after a march of 14 miles. The distance from Grand (Colorado) river to this ford by a very direct course is 70 miles and from Bitter creek 67 miles by our route, which, except during rains, is entirely without water. By following Grand (Colorado) river, however, some miles below Bitter creek, until the Spanish (South Branch) trail is reached, and, following it, crossing a more broken and gullied country, a spring is said to be passed; but its locality is not known to me.

The greatest difficulty to be overcome in the construction of a railroad on this part of the route would be in obtaining a firm bed for the superstructure in wet weather; and for this purpose it would be necessary to macadamize the road very extensively. Average descent, $12\frac{1}{2}$ feet per mile.

Many Aranaquint or Green river Utahs were on the opposite bank as we encamped, and soon crossed it to beg tobacco, and, if possible, to trade; dressed deer skins being the only article they offer for this purpose.

Our latitude at this camp was 38° 57' 26", and our elevation above the sea 3,873 feet; average descent from camp to camp, $42\frac{1}{2}$ feet per mile.

October 1

We crossed the river by an excellent ford, (The crossing of the Green River is about three miles north of the present day town of Green River, Utah.) which we had observed the Indians crossing, from a few yards below our camp *(on the Spanish trail)* to an island opposite, and from its upper end to the shore. The river is 300 yards wide, with a pebbly bottom, as we forded it, but with quicksands on either side of our path. The water, rising just above the axletrees of our common wagons, flows with a strong current, and is colored by the red sandstone of the country through which it passes, having here the same red muddy character which the Colorado has far below, where it enters the Gulf of California. A fine field of blue-grass in a grove of cotton-wood just above the ford, and the lateness of the hour, determined us to encamp for the benefit of our animals; but a recent overflow had left a fine deposit of sand on the grass, which made it unpalatable to them.

10

1853/JACOB HEINRICH SCHIEL

Jacob Heinrich Schiel was born in 1813 in Stromberg, Germany. This was a wine-making town in the western part of Germany, which was then the Rhenish province of Prussia. Schiel studied at the University of Heidelberg where he received a doctor's degree in philosophy. In 1845 he was a teacher at the University of Heidelberg, lecturing in chemistry and geology. Schiel was the author of four books including the account of his journey through the Rocky Mountains and the Humboldt Range to the Pacific which he published in 1859. This was his story of his experiences as official geologist and surgeon for the Gunnison expedition.

In chapter nine which is a part of the diary that was kept by John W. Gunnison, Jacob H. Schiel is listed incorrectly as a doctor (surgeon), his name is also written as James Schiel, instead of Jacob. Upon Gunnison's death on the 26th day of October 1853, the diary was completed by his assistant, First Lieutenant E. G. Beckwith, then sent to Jefferson Davis, Secretary of War. Jacob Schiels' account of the journey is very interesting as he describes in more detail the flora and fauna and the type of rock and soil that are encountered. But he often lost track of the days and was confused as to the date.

Schiel was well acquainted with a number of the scientific pieces of equipment that were used on the expedition. It would appear that he had some knowledge of medicine though he had never practiced medicine nor did he have a degree in medicine. He enjoyed the buffalo hunts in which he took part, but was quick to recognize the fact that the methods that the American Indian used to hunt the buffalo would be the downfall of both the Indian as well as the buffalo. He was wrong in his calling the prairie dog a marmot, as the marmot and prairie dog are two distinctly different animals.

Schiel's description of the country through which they traveled from Fort Massachusetts to the Green River, is the trail that is known as the East Fork of the North Branch of the Old Spanish Trail in the San Luis Valley. After reaching the area of the present day town of Saguache the trail becomes the North Branch.

August 1

From the camp which we made August 1 on the right bank of the Arkansas, we saw for the first time that evening the Rocky Mountains standing beautiful and distinct before us. The Spanish Peaks and their northern neighbors, the Greenhorn Mountains, (Greenhorn Peak is named after the Jupe Comanche Chief, Cuerno Verde, who was killed east of present day Rye, Colorado by Juan Bautista de Anza in 1779.)[1] lay directly in front of us over the horizon and from a nearby hill James' Peak (James Peak? Pike's Peak was first known as James Peak, but there seems to be some confusion at this point! Edwin James was the first to climb Pike's Peak)[2] could be seen, its summit covered with snow. It was a joyful sight for the entire expedition, for the monotony of the prairie had become very wearisome to all of us. A sojourn on the prairie of only a few weeks has many pleasures. The carefree, untroubled life on one's own; the nomadic camp life of which a certain beneficial ruggedness is a part; the daily change of residence, which at the beginning brings much that is new and interesting; and the beneficial influence of the climate of the high prairie upon health all make it easy to do without beauty of landscape and the little comforts of life. But when the stay is prolonged, when habit has taken the charm from the novel, and even interest in natural history must go almost completely unsatisfied, then the monotony of the prairie becomes palpable indeed. One grows tired of the eternal grass and celebrates the day when he sees the gigantic summits of the Rocky Mountains for the first time almost like a holiday.

August 6

On the sixth of August we had our camp on the Cuchara(s), quite an important mountain stream about forty feet wide and several feet deep. It rises in a mountain in the vicinity of the northern (West) Spanish Peaks and flows into the Huerfano, which carries its waters to the Arkansas. From the adjoining hills we saw before us Pike's Peak (After traveling a little distance from the last point Schiel can now see Pike's Peak to the northwest.) to the north, while only a few miles away to the south and west, respectively, lay the Spanish Peaks and the Sierra (Wet Mountains) Mojada in imposing masses. The terrain, which had become more and more hilly after we left the Arkansas, flattens out toward the mountains into a broad, barren plateau. The soil is at times argillaceous, but the dominant rock is sandstone of a gray or red color, which is supported by a rather soft shale. Numerous rivers and creeks have dug beds through this rock, most of them enclosed by steep, perpendicular walls. These rivers are often so hidden from view that one is astounded to encounter strong rivers in a region where not one trace of water had been suspected. The Mexicans, as is well known, call such narrow canals enclosed by steep cliffs *cañons*, while they designate those with soft, earthy, or slate like walls as *arroyos*.

The vegetation of this entire region presents a very miserable appearance. Here and there a wretched pine or a cottonwood tree are to be seen. Short, entwined cedars with wide-arching branches, on the other hand, are quite frequent and, during the heat of the day, provide welcome shade, for it is not uncommon for the temperature to reach 104 degrees F. in the shade despite the altitude. The only example of a somewhat more luxuriant growth are shrub-like cactus which sometimes reach a height of more than five feet here. Their angular branches covered with small needles are whirled around the trunk and branch out in the same pattern. Unfortunately, they had already bloomed, and the calyxes of the blooms hung from the juicy plant like tiny drinking-cups. Between the hills we always found grass enough for our animals, and the numerous herds of deer, antelope, and occasionally small herds of wild horses we met on our way prove that there can be no lack of grazing places in the entire region. Even the prairie dogs seem to be very happy here, for innumerable packs of these animals are encountered on the plateau, although his prairie companions, the snake and the owl, have become a rarity. These are in general the characteristics of that stretch of land called the Great American Desert, which extend far to the south from the Black Hills along the Rocky Mountains in an average width of 100 to 120 miles and crosses over to the *Llano Estacado*. But the typical nature of this country resembles a real desert as little as the bear, the king of this desert, resembles the king of the African desert.

On the eighth of August we removed our camp to the vicinity of the Huerfano Butte, close to the foot of the mountains. The Huerfano Butte (Huerfano Butte can be seen just east of Interstate Highway 25 between Pueblo and Walsenburg, Colorado.) is an isolated cone of about 150 feet in height and visible from a great distance. It is made of black granite *(quartz and mica)* and a siliceous slate found some miles to the east, where it is interspersed with a porphyritic rock. From this butte the Huerfano or Orphan River, which flows by no farther than a gunshot away, gets its name. The Huerfano is a rather swift-flowing mountain stream eighteen feet wide and one foot deep. It emerges from a narrow valley formed by the Sierra (Wet Mountains) Mojada in the north and a spur of the Sierra Blanca in the south probably to flow into the Arkansas not more than twenty miles west of the Apish(a)pa, which is incorrectly designated as Huerfano on the maps. Its banks are thickly overgrown with cottonwoods, wild plum, cherry, willow, and thorn-bushes, and everything takes on a fresher appearance in the immediate vicinity of the mountains. The soil in the neighborhood is quite light and could be made fertile with little effort through irrigation.

As we came close to the mountains we saw some grizzly bears that were walking around on the steep slope of the mountain and seemed to be watching us suspiciously. They were wonderful examples of bears, but they seemed to want no closer contact with us, and they were soon lost in the mountains. Since in the country through which we had recently come the bear was a rarity, these were the first specimens of these animals which we had a chance to see.

At the foot of the Greenhorns is a little settlement of six families from New Mexico. They have several acres of land in cultivation on which they are planting corn, wheat, beans, and watermelon, and they also have a little herd of cows, horses, and mules. They make an excellent living meanwhile by hunting which is unusually rewarding here. One of our officers had gone with an escort of five men in search of the settlement to get information about the region and perhaps acquire a guide. He returned to camp yesterday with one of the settlers, Massalino (Marcelino Baca), who will guide us into the San Luis Valley. According to the description, the houses of the settlement are built out of air-dried bricks or adobe and are without any windows or other openings except for a low door. In front of and behind each house is an open space twenty yards wide protected by a row of poles driven into the ground and lashed together with rawhide thongs. These yards are supposed to serve as protection against the Utah Indians who the year before killed a part of their cows, destroyed their crops, and stole their horses. The houses, which with the exception of one are joined, are so low that a tall man can reach comfortably to the flat roof. This roof is the general assembly point when strangers approach the settlement and it is not known whether they are friend or foe. Massalino is by birth a New Mexican and about forty-five years old. He belongs to the dying race of Leatherstockings and has spent his entire life in the wilderness. He was by turns a hunter, trapper, voyageur, fighter, and guide and is familiar with the country as far as the Pacific Ocean. Because of the losses at the hands of the Utah Indians, he and his Pawnee wife recently removed to Pueblo on the Arkansas where he and his family are the sole occupants. Here, too, he suffered misfortune. High water destroyed this year's little crop, and he and his family are now entirely dependent upon hunting for subsistence. "I once lived on meat alone for nine years," he said, "and can live well enough now from coffee and the game I shoot." He is reputed a fine hunter. "I never see a grizzly without trying a shot. I try to hit him in the right spot, but if I miss, I have to run. We will have some fun," he declared, pointing to the mountains. There are not many hunters bold enough to shoot at a grizzly bear unless accompanied by a well-armed companion. This formidable animal, able to haul away a buffalo between its front paws, is so tough that it is still dangerous to the hunter even when mortally wounded. The only way to kill him instantaneously, according to the testimony of the hunters, is to hit him in the nape of the neck so as to break his neck with the bullet.

The Marcelino Baca sign marks the location of the farm of Baca on the Arkansas River.

August 6.

We entered the mountains today. We crossed the Huerfano, went through a narrow ravine, and then followed a beautiful valley south which was a half-mile to a mile wide. It was formed from two spurs of the main chain of mountains. Countless heliantus, campanula, papilio flowers, and other plants are blooming in the luxuriant grass, and we moved literally on a beautiful, bright carpet of flowers. Swarms of magnificent magpies encircled us from all sides but avoided our snares with great care. For the first time today I hunted a large grizzly discovered by one of the soldiers in a wooded part of the stream about fifty paces away. But before one of the hunters could get a shot, the bruin had run away and thereby spared the hunters the running, for it is a strict rule on these dangerous hunts that one of the participants, hunter or hunted, must run. After a distance of seven miles we had to put up our tent as it began to rain hard.

As we followed our southern direction the next morning, we came into a ravine through which a little (South Oak Creek) brook flows north toward the Huerfano. The slope of the mountains was so steep that the wagons had to be held with ropes to prevent their overturning. The grass was so high here that it reached to the belly of the horses. We followed the brook for a little distance, opening a path through a forest of quaking asp with our axes. We tried to reach the summit of the Sangre de Cristo pass by turning left but had to put up our tents in a heavy rainstorm, this time on the slope of the mountain in a luxuriant field of grass and flowers. The mountains around us are covered with aspen and small pines although a fire swept over these mountains two years ago and destroyed much of the timber. This fire has left its traces on many trees in the blackened and burned bark.

A large part of our party was busy for two days clearing the forest to the peak of the mountain to make a passage by wagon possible. The trip over the pass was attended by many hardships. The wagons had to be dragged up one by one to be let down on ropes with no less effort on the other side of the pass. Because of the greatly rarefied atmosphere stops had to be made every minute so that man as well as beast could rest and recover. Even though the number of mules per wagon was doubled to twelve on the summit of the pass, they could not accomplish what six mules could do under ordinary circumstances. Likewise, the achievements of our strongest men were reduced to less than half their normal performance.

While the wagon train was busy effecting a painful crossing of the Sangre de Cristo Pass, we had time to acquaint ourselves with the mountains in all directions and investigate more thoroughly those depressions which might be suitable for the transit of a railroad. The novelty and adventurousness of the locality, the long-missed freshness of the vegetation, the grandeur and beauty of the scenery all made this investigation as pleasant as it was interesting. The tasty meal in the evening and relaxation by a blazing campfire made the day's work seem even less strenuous. We do not need to be so sparing of wood here as on the prairie for the sides of the mountains are overgrown with ashes and small pines, and they enclose many small, narrow valleys in whose soil a luxuriant grass grows. Game is at hand in unheard-of abundance. Grouse and pheasant abound, deer and bear are found in every valley and ravine, and the pretty mountain streams are filled with the finest trout.

Captain Gunnison and I rode northwest into the mountains early in the morning led by Massalino and escorted by eight soldiers to investigate a (La Veta) pass, (The first La Veta Pass was used by the D & R G W Railroad to cross the Sangre de Cristo Mountains.)[3] until then known only to hunters, which has a rise less steep than that of the Sangre de Cristo Pass, according to our guide's assurances. We found the guide's account confirmed, for this pass leads down gradually to the Huerfano Valley at a steady decline from the mountain ridge which joins it with the Sangre de Cristo Pass. As we were about to cross a stream on this excursion, Massalino (Marcelino) directed our attention by means of signs to an object on the other side of the water. It was a magnificent white stag grazing peacefully. He did not run until we had gotten within about twenty paces of him. Massalino (Marcelino) did not attempt to shoot and seemed to regard him as a charmed beast. It seems as if the animals in general in this part of the mountains are not familiar with the danger from human beings. On the branch of a tree which stretched out over a little grassy spot near this stream there sat two plump pheasants thirty or forty paces away from us as if waiting for a hunter who might like to shoot them. Gunnison and I had already tried several shots with our revolvers without hitting either of them when Massalino (Marcelino) dismounted, aimed his long rifle, and shot off the head of one of them. While I was tying the fallen bird to my saddle with thongs, Massalino (Marcelino) raised his rifle again and shot his comrade, who seemed not in the least aware of the danger in the proceedings before him. The meat of these birds is unusually tender and tasty, even if the appetite has not been sharpened by a tiring excursion.

August 13

The thirteenth of August was bright and clear, and the day's barometric observations could be used in determining the elevation of the pass. It was computed at 9,396 feet above sea level, while the neighboring mountain peaks are close to ten thousand feet high. A little stream, El Sangre de Cristo, rises in the vicinity of the pass and flows in a southwesterly direction toward the San Luis Valley. The valley (At the head of Sangre de Cristo Creek lies a little valley described by Ruxton as El Vallecito. See chapter six. From El Vallecito to the southwest one enters Sangre de Cristo Cañon.) of the Sangre de Cristo is narrow and has many turns. The banks of the stream are thickly covered with willow bushes and for four days over a distance of five to six miles the entire force was busy making paths and crossings over the stream. During this time I again made an excursion with Captain Gunnison under Massalino's guidance, this time to investigate the mountains south of the Spanish Peaks. We rode up the valley of a stream which coalesced with El Sangre de Cristo Creek bearing the name "Gold Branch." This very winding valley gradually climbs at first in a northeasterly direction, then turns east and after a mile, southeast. After a long, hard ride we climbed a high peak and from there enjoyed a magnificent view of the country which we had recently investigated. The Huerfano, Cuchara(s), and Apish(a)pa flowed at our feet; to the north and south great mountain masses stretched toward heaven; to the west we had the San Luis Valley and beyond the colossal peaks of the Sierra San Juan towered on the horizon. The atmosphere was pure and transparent and allowed objects to be recognized clearly at a great distance. According to the barometer we were almost eleven thousand feet above sea level. Later we climbed still another mountain from which we could look down almost vertically upon the Cuchara(s). In climbing down, we came upon a very fresh trail made by a number of hunters who had come up from Taos. These people travel with horses and packmules on their hunts lasting about fourteen days and the return trip taking four days.

The game is skinned and cut up, and in this condition it remains fresh during the entire time, although no trace of salt is used and rainstorms pour down almost daily around the highest mountain peaks. The only protection which the game requires is against flies, dogs, and wolves. The hunters, therefore, cover it with cloths during the day. At night they spread it out on the ground, lay their saddles on and between it, and sleep in their wool blankets among their treasures.

The main mountain mass, as far as we have come to know it until now, consists of a trachytic porphyry of bluish-gray, rough base in which a great number of feldspar and mica crystals are imbedded. The latter consist of regular, blackish, hexagonal leaflets which lie one upon the other in such profusion that the crystals form what one would be tempted to take for tourmaline crystals were it not for the easily identifiable cleavage of mica in the direction parallel to the end surfaces. This rock, which forms the mountain ridge from Sangre de Cristo Pass to the new pass mentioned above has a very changeable character. Beyond the cañon through which we entered the mountains, it is more gray, and the enclosed feldspar crystals are not glassy but ordinary white feldspar; west of the pass it is bluish-gray, the feldspar crystals diminish, and it is interspersed with a great number of small, black columns of tourmaline or hornblende. Significant quantities of a zeolitic substance called stilbite are not uncommon in this rock.

Of the stratified rocks I found only sandstone, which has been lifted only occasionally to the highest peaks of the mountains, and a red slate supporting it. At the entrance of the mountains the sandstone is white, fine-grained, hard, eroded and worn down, and almost vertically elevated by plutonic rocks. On only one occasion did I find it with a fifteen degree decline to the northeast. The steep slopes of the mountains are covered with fragments of a white silicate which often reach a considerable size and take the form of boulders twenty feet or more in diameter. The little hills at the base of the higher mountains are covered with boulders of all kinds, quartz, porphyry, sandstone, hypersthene, and others. Most or at least many of the summits have sharp, angular, bare ridges from which other ledges branch out laterally, giving the mountains a very strange appearance.

Granite crops out for the first time southwest of the pass in the Sangre de Cristo (Cañon) Valley and forms rugged groups on either side of the valley. The granite is very changeable in its appearance but it has one thing in common, that the mica it contains, whether yellow or white, possesses such a gold or silver luster that the belief arose among the men that we had found a new land of gold. On the right bank of the stream the granite passes successively into gneiss and hornblende rock—hornblende with a few grains of feldspar. On the gneiss lie shale, sandstone, and a blue-gray limestone which has fissured and disintegrated where it is exposed to the air. On the eastern side of the mountains a similar limestone appears. It is very probable that it belongs to the Lower Silurian system whose presence on the North American continent is definitely authenticated.

According to the testimony of our guide several streams in the mountains are supposed to contain gold. The name "Gold Branch Creek," which the mountaineers have given the stream mentioned above, shows that the belief is widespread in this region. We had already met a host of goldseekers on the prairie who were coming with a wagon train from Pike's Peak, where they had been vainly searching half the summer for gold, and were now returning to the States with their disappointed hopes and meager possessions. The possibility of the presence of gold in those regions cannot be discounted, of course, even though none of us succeeded in finding a trace of it. Yet I cannot overcome to this minute a strong doubt as to the presence of great quantities of gold in the vicinity of the peak.

The Sangre de Cristo (Cañon) Valley is not more than twelve to fifteen miles long and leads into the broad San Luis Valley. The latter is enclosed by two mighty mountain chains branching out from the three parks and extending in divided fashion to the south. Although these mountains have received a great many local names, they belong probably to not more than three different geological systems. The San Luis Valley is for the most part sandy and infertile. Artemisia bushes and several varieties of cactus, especially *Cactus opuntia*, make up the vegetation of this valley, which is watered by the Rio Grande del Norte with its numerous tributaries. (The main tributaries of the Rio Grande del Norte from the west side are, Rock Creek, Alamosa River and Conejos, and from the east Trinchera Creek.) Only in the narrow adjoining (Wet Mountain) valley situated higher where frequent rainstorms occur *(which, curiously, rarely happens in wide valleys)* is the vegetation fresh and luxuriant. In these adjoining valleys lie most of the ranches and villages of the New Mexicans. In leaving the Sangre de Cristo (Cañon) Valley, we crossed over a low ridge and came to a broad plain joining the San Luis Valley and reaching to the base of the Sierra Blanca. A march of less than eleven miles brought us to Fort Massachusetts (Fort Massachusetts was located on Ute Creek, southwest of Buck Mountain at the mouth of the cañon of Ute Creek.) which lies concealed at the foot of one of the snow-covered peaks of the Sierra so that one does not see it before he is upon it. The fort has a garrison of several hundred men whose assignment it is to hold in check the dangerous Taos Utahs, as the Utah Indians (The Southern (Mouache, Capote & Weeminuche) Ute and Jicarilla Apache occupied the south end of the San Luis Valley and the Tabeguache or Uncompahgre Ute the north end.)[4] inhabiting the surrounding mountains are called. We stayed several days in camp in order to take on fresh provisions, shoe the horses, and have repairs made on the wagons and harnesses. Antoine Leroux, (Antoine Leroux was the fourth and youngest child of Marie Rose and Jean Sale dit Lajoie. He grew up in St Louis, Missouri and first came west as a trapper with Ashley, arriving in Taos in 1824.)[5] one of the best known mountaineers alive, came up from Taos with some companions to guide us through the Sierra San Juan into the Green River region as far as the so-called "Spanish (South Branch) Trail." After taking leave of the hospitable officers at the fort, we started out to execute one of our chief tasks, the exploration of the Coochetopa Pass. For four days we moved up the San Luis Valley along the base of the Sierra Blanca (The road which they were traveling is the East Fork of the North Branch of the Old Spanish Trail. It followed the west side of the Sangre de Cristo Mountains from Taos north to Rito Alto Creek.) in a northwesterly direction through fields thick with Artemisia, the only thing which grows well in the deep sandy soil. Sometimes we could see fields of beautiful prairie grass toward the river and the river banks covered with trees, but our experienced guide warned us of the marshes, and we had to be satisfied with only the view. According to his statement, the valley is very fertile at the point where the Rio del Norte emerges from a cañon of the Sierra San Juan into the plain. It has wonderful pastures and is rich in game and wild horses.

The slopes of the Sierra Blanca are covered with cedars and pines, but they are of pigmy size and suitable only for firewood. Seen from this side the three-to four-thousand-foot mountains of the Sierra display sharp ledges, although frequently they are more needle-shaped. At the foot of the mountains lie numerous boulders, frequently of considerable size, of quartz, granite, and a kind of basaltic rock. In the mountains, as I discovered on an excursion in Roubideaux (Mosca) Pass, these rocks have shattered and erupted through a rough, bluish-violet mica slate so that all of the rocks together form a real chaos.

Although no large animal population is to be expected in this part of the valley, we still chased some grouse and sandhill cranes out of their hiding places and our hunters supplied us richly with game. Competition for the game sometimes appeared which proved as unpleasant as it was unexpected as in the following incident. One of the hunters, who had come up from Taos with Leroux, shot a fat buck one day and was about to cross a little stream on his horse to retrieve it when a giant bear arose in front of him and gave him to understand that he had no further business there. The hunter had no other course according to the rule mentioned earlier than to turn his horse around and ride off, leaving the bear in undisputed possession of the buck.

August 29

Our camp on August 29th was almost at the northern end of the San Luis Valley on a (San Luis) (The Arkansas River at one time descended south in what is now San Luis Creek.) creek containing many beaver dams, which held back the water and forced it to overflow, thus causing broad swamps to develop to the south. The ground over which we came was frequently covered by effloresced salts and only on the creek did pasturage and brushwood appear once more. The latter consisted primarily of two kinds of currant bushes, one with red and the other with blackberries which had a pleasant bittersweet taste.

Fifteen miles farther north the valley is closed off by a low row of hills to form a beautiful (Homan's) (The area north of Villa Grove is known as Homan's Park named after Sheppard Homan, astronomer for the Gunnison's expedition.) park eight to nine miles wide and fifteen miles long. A number of streams, having their origin here and coalescing into a single creek, water the park, which is rich in luxuriant grazing areas. From here a convenient (Poncha) pass leads over an elevation of 8,600 feet, forming the watershed between the Arkansas and the Rio del Norte to the nearby South Park and the Sierra (Wet Mountains) Mojada. The well-worn paths show that the Indians of the Rio Grande and the Coochetopa (Cochetopa) region make frequent use of this pass. The Sierra Mojada (Sangre de Cristo) or wet mountains, which get their name from the constant rainstorms there, extend from the northern part of the Sierra Blanca to which they are partially joined to the Arkansas. It is in no way to be regarded as a separate mountain system. (The Wet and Sangre de Cristo Mountains are separated by the Wet Mountain Valley.) A march of ten miles in a westward direction brought us to the entrance of Coochetopa Pass. This entrance is marked by an isolated mound of bluish-gray porphyry (Rattlesnake Hill) which is situated like a guard at the gate. The way to the pass leads through the Sawatch (Saguache) Valley, (The east end of the Saguache Valley is where the West and East Forks of the North Branch of the Old Spanish Trail joined before crossing Cochetopa Pass.) one of the most beautiful valleys we saw on the entire journey. It is six or seven miles wide at the San Luis end but becomes narrow five miles farther west. The animals at first sink hoof-deep into the ground, which is light and powdery but becomes firmer and very fertile. Willows and cottonwoods thickly cover the bank of the Sawatch (Saguache) Creek which waters the valley. The game in the underbrush is so thick that startled deer often leap across between our wagons. Grouse, too, are in abundant supply, and we catch beautiful trout, many weighing over two pounds, in the clear, pretty creek. The shape of the mountains, especially on the left bank of the creek, is unusually picturesque, mostly steep and eroded. These mountains offer the purest and most beautiful trap formations. A reddish porphyry with lustrous feldspar and mica provides the material from which these picturesque shapes are formed. The opposite side of the mountains representing the north side of the valley is less steep and covered with little firs down to the valley. Numerous herds of mountain sheep appeared frequently on the peaks of these mountains, protecting themselves from attack by a never-tiring alertness.

It is not more than about thirty English miles from the Sawatch Butte to the top of the Coochetopa (Cochetopa) Pass, but it took four days of the most intense labor to reach the top. Soon trees had to be felled to open a path for the wagons, and the mountain is covered with aspen right to the top; then a stream had to be bridged; and in addition the path led over sandstone and wound around huge boulders of plutonic rock, which made it extremely tiring for the pack animals. About noon of the second of September, we reached the top of the pass as a light storm passed away as if to celebrate the event. Although we were 10,032 feet above sea level, according to the barometric level, the clouds still did not seem any closer than on the plain, and the little rain we received was unusually warm for this altitude. The astronomical observations showed 38° 12' 34" north latitude for the top of the pass, which lies on the great divide of the North American continent. The waters on the east side flow toward the Atlantic, those on the west side toward the Pacific Ocean.

From the top of the Coochetopa (Cochetopa) Pass we climbed down a gradual slope into the valley of Coochetopa (Cochetopa) Creek, which soon empties into the valley of the Grand (Gunnison) River. The latter valley has a width here of a mile and a quarter, but it is compressed into a narrow gorge about eight miles farther west. The valley floor is even, covered with boulders, and apparently subject to annual floods. Grass grows abundantly here, and the banks of the river are clothed in willow bushes and cottonwoods. The mountains forming the upper part of the valley, which consist mostly of high, eroded layers of a white, fine-grained sandstone, have more or less the character of *mesas*, as the New Mexicans call level stretches of land ending on one or more sides in steep precipices. Grand (Gunnison) River is a pretty, clear, cold mountain (Tomichi) stream whose stony bed is a hundred feet wide and three feet deep. It is formed by the confluence of several branches, one rising in the northwest toward Leroux in the Elk Mountains, whose high masses lay before us in the West, the other rising to the north in the mountains lying west of the sources of the Arkansas. After following the east slope of the Elk Mountains, the Grand (Gunnison) River turns south and west and joins the Nahunkahrea or Blue (Colorado) River, which rises in the Middle Park and is incorrectly called the Grand River on all maps.

We followed the valley of the Grand (Gunnison) River almost two weeks, but we had to keep close to the slopes of the mountains for the most part, often at a considerable elevation, since the valley route was only rarely usable. (The North Branch was used by Robidoux and many others.) This was a kind of travel in which great difficulties had to be overcome, of course. In effect, it was as though we had been engaged in a continuous crossing of the Alps since the middle of August but with the difference that some of the resources and comforts which a traveler in inhabited countries does not lack were more than a thousand miles away from us. The wagons had to be dragged up steep mountains and be let down the steeper slopes with ropes; rocky roads had to be cut through, ravines gone around, and strong mountain streams crossed; at times we had to follow a deep stream a quarter mile through the water before we found room to set foot on the bank and from there start to climb a steep mountain. (Blue Mesa Reservoir today.) During the whole time an unusual cheerfulness engendered by the pure mountain air reigned among the men and was expressed in loud, vigorous laughing. Even among the animals this air seems to have a similar invigorating effect. When the teams had to stop after heavy exertion in climbing the mountains to rest and catch their breath, they pulled afterwards with new strength without having to be driven. This pleasant, stimulating quality of pure mountain air is well known to hunters and trappers, and their conversation revolves about it as about a favorite subject.

The difference in temperature during twenty-four hours in these mountains is considerable but less uncomfortable than it would be in the flat land. While the thermometer frequently climbed to 25° C. in the afternoon hours, it had usually fallen to 2 to 4° before sunrise, and on repeated occasions in the morning we found a thick crust of ice on the water in the barrels. The weather was continuously favorable with the exception of a few days. The sky was usually clear with a light, pleasant southwest breeze or at worst only slightly cloudy. We had showers on only three occasions, during which the highest peaks of the mountains became covered with snow.

The farther one comes down into the valley of the Grand (Gunnison) River from Coochetopa (Cochetopa) Creek, the more the sandstone found on the banks of the river recedes into the upper regions of the mountains. In the lower regions of the valley granite, gneiss, a rough siliceous shale, and a fine mica slate are the dominant rocks. At the top of the mountains on the white sandstone and on those peculiar plateaus which form the *mesas* lies a violet-brown porphyry in horizonal layers fifty to a hundred feet thick. It consists of a base of compact feldspar with small crystals of glassy feldspar and mica. Although it resembles in appearance the porphyry found in the Sawatch Valley, it is more difficult to melt as seen in the reaction of thin splinters to the blowpipe. The unusual extension of this rock and the peculiar circumstances of stratification make this porphyry an important and interesting object of investigation at a time when the question of the origin and formation of rocks has received new interest through chemistry. In its composition and entire lithological character, this rock, whose origin was believed to have been established with certainty as plutonic, apparently possesses the characteristic stratification of a sedimentary rock. For days it is encountered over great distances, and its horizontal stratification with layers sometimes pushed up vertically, but always of equal thickness, is seen on the highest mountain peaks without its ever going underground. Since it is more than probable, however, that this rock is of igneous origin, the discovery of the perhaps narrow canal through which the huge mass of rock flowed out of its oven to extraordinary distances must be of interest. A rock very similar to this porphyry appears in the Gray River Valley above the mouth of Cebolla Creek but it has become brown and blackish gray through contact with the granite and very crumbled in the immediate vicinity of the granite. Colossal boulders of this rock, which goes underground here, lie upon the ground in the valley as if they had just climbed out of the ground. Their even surfaces, often worn mirror-smooth from sliding, show that this rock was at one time involved in a slow, sliding movement. If the identity of this rock with the porphyry could be shown with certainty, the solution of the problem of the origin of the latter would be very close. One often sees tower like formations resembling ancient castles hanging over the steep slopes of the mountains, which give shape to the wild romantic valleys and cañons of the Elk Mountains and the southern Sierra de la Plata. They are the remains of a conglomerate lying under the sandstone and consisting of remnants of all sorts of plutonic rocks compressed into an extremely hard mass by a cement of carbonate of lime.

Although we knew that we were in the heart of the land of the Utahs, we had only once any sign of the presence of Indians. When we left our camp on September 8, the grass caught fire a short time afterward, and a thick smoke began to rise. Immediately a second smoke rose up some distance in front of us one of the fires used by the Indians to telegraph the presence of strangers. This is actually the chief hunting ground of the Utahs (Utes) during the summer, as many elk herds move here followed by packs of hunters. There is also abundant deer and antelope in these regions, the latter being hunted by the Utah (Ute) Indians in a strange way, according to Leroux. They build the two sides of a triangle with boulders and shrubbery, and as they drive their game into the corner, the pack of hunters comes closer and closer together until they form the third side of the triangle from which there is no further escape. The wives have to assist in the hunt, and woe to the squaw who permits one bit of game to get through while the men are engaged in the slaughter. Inevitably she will be whipped.

There is no more beautiful sight to a hunter than an elk herd seen up close. Many a hunter would have envied me the sight I saw frequently when I left the wagon train with my assistants to make side-trips into the mountains. One day, instead of following the wagon train, which was forced to hold to the left bank of the Grand (Gunnison) River along the top of the mountains, we went along the right bank of the river to undertake a geological reconnaissance, planning to meet our party about ten miles farther down the river. We were about to cross the river below a creek flowing into it whose ravine broadened into a beautiful pasture-ground near its mouth. Suddenly, through a wide opening in the bushes, our glance fell upon a herd of elk, forty or fifty in number, grazing quietly on the other bank. Surprised, we held still for a while to feast our eyes on the sight of these splendid animals and then tried to cross the river unnoticed. But the hoof beat of our horses and the splashing of the water scared them off, and with their horns laid back they started up the steep walls of the nearby mountain with such agility that a few seconds sufficed to put them out of our sight.

The same day we came so unexpectedly upon the giant elk, we were surprised by a sight which promised us some real excitement. As serious as the situation might have been in this place and circumstance, it had a humorous outcome. We had ridden for several hours down the river on the slope of the mountain, picking up here and there a beautiful cornelian, a chalcedony of unusual shape, or a heliotrope, of which a great number lay strewn about on the ground, or else hammering a hyolite out of a rock cavity in the porphyry. Suddenly C(reutzfeldt) halted his mule with the cry "Indians," looking directly at an open spot about one and a half miles away on the bend of the river, undoubtedly the place where we were to join the caravan. If C. had seen correctly our position was extremely critical. Turning back was not to be thought of, for it would have taken a ride of some twenty miles by returning to the other side of the river and following the wagon tracks to catch up with our party. Furthermore, the wagons could have left only faint, uncertain tracks on the rocky, stone-strewn path which we could easily have missed in the approaching darkness. There was, therefore, nothing else to do but go forward with all possible caution. This we did but concealed ourselves as much as possible in ravines and behind elevations of the terrain. When we had come close enough to the spot to distinguish the objects clearly, we saw that what we had taken for Indian huts was a row of boulders which had strangely assumed the shape of wigwams. The supposed inhabitants of these wigwams consisted of some deer which had been grazing here and had run away as we approached. Soon the wagon train came down from the other side of the mountain, and after crossing the Grand (Gunnison) River, camp was pitched. When I told Leroux how we had been deceived in such a humorous way, he recommended very emphatically that I discontinue all further excursions of this kind if I wanted to keep my scalp a while yet. A few days later the warning of this experienced mountaineer was shown to be well founded. We had climbed down from a *mesa* to the bank of Cebolla or Onion Creek and made camp when we were surrounded in just a few minutes by a host of Tabawatschi (Tabeguache) Indians, who seemed to have grown out of the ground in this apparently uninhabited country. There were several hundred men, women, and children. The men rode beautiful Navajo horses for the most part, which they had undoubtedly stolen from the Navajo Indians, who raise a good many horses and sheep. Even some of the squaws were mounted and sat on horseback just like men. They were for the most part well clothed and did not have at all the famished, degenerate appearance of many of the prairie tribes. A certain prosperity seemed to be the general rule among them. Their warriors were powerfully built, of medium height with broad, high chests but their legs had the usual bowlegged shape of all Indians legs. Their faces maintained a very ugly expression because of the great width of the base of their noses. The speech which they addressed to us at first was overbearing, almost threatening, and they made it very clear that if we did not give them presents they would take them. With the intention of overawing us with their strength and skill, some of the warriors raced their horses madly back and forth, giving the riders a most demoniac appearance. Another means calculated to intimidate us was their pointing to the surrounding mountains while continually chattering and shouting "Utah! Utah!" According to Leroux, who fully understands their language, they were informing us that two thousand Utah warriors were waiting in the neighboring mountains. Very recently they had a great fight with the Comanches and chased them over the mountains. The Utahs had never been defeated by any other Indian tribe. They lived in constant warfare with the Mormons and had killed many of them. They told us still more of the edifying details. But after Leroux had made a speech from our side, they changed their conduct. It sounded about as follows: "We have good weapons, much powder, and much lead. If you want to fight, so be it. We will fight with you and kill many of your warriors. The White Father has many brave warriors. He will punish your transgressions. He has sent us to ride through your land and to see what his red children are doing." The chief made a long speech in which he assured us that the Utahs had always been the best friends of the Americans. He commended us urgently to ask the White Father, when we returned to him, to send yearly presents to the Utahs, too, as he did the other tribes through whose lands his white children go. This was promised him, of course. Peace was concluded, the pipe was smoked, and the next morning the chiefs were summoned to receive some presents. These consisted as usual of woolen blankets, ordinary knives, brass bracelets, strings of pearls, small mirrors, red paint, and other trifles which delight the Indian heart.

The camp on Cebolla Creek was at the foot of a mountain ridge which reaches from the Elk Mountains obliquely through the Grand (Gunnison) River Valley to the Sierra de la Plata, thus connecting the two ranges with each other. The astronomical observations gave the position as 38° 23' north latitude and close to 107.5° west longitude. The barometric reading showed an elevation of 7,026 feet above sea level. From here one can reach the top of the mountains in two hours by following an Indian path. There to the south through the ravine of Cebolla Creek is a beautiful view of the snow-covered Sierra de la Plata, whose sharp, pointed or angular peaks jut into the sky like giant columns. At our feet to the west flows the Uncompahgra, which rises in the Sierra de la Plata and flows in a northwestern direction through a rather broad valley to empty into the Grand (Gunnison) River. Above the western upland tower distant mountains, and Leroux named two of the high peaks as Salt Peak and Abajo Peak. The former lies on the so-called Spanish (south branch) Trail leading from California to Albiquiu in New Mexico and is a favorite gathering place for the Utah and Navajo Indians, who come there to trade. The latter lies in the vicinity of the junction of the Green and Grand (Colorado) rivers below the fords for the trail, hence the name Abajo Peak. On the east side are the neighboring mountains about the Coochetopa Pass, and one can almost follow the entire route traversed from the pass. North of the Grand (Gunnison) River, whose course is visible, the Elk Mountains stretch to the north and northwest, and their summits seem to form here a high plain cut off vertically on the western side.

The passage from Cebolla Creek over the fourteen-hundred-foot mountain ridges to the valley of the Uncompahgra was attended with great difficulties and took a full two days. We had to make our path part-way through cactus and thick fields of artemisia, part-way through thick oak bushes, with long detours to avoid the deep, rocky ravines. The valley of the Uncompahgra is several miles wide with light argillaceous soil and completely without vegetation. Here and there effloresced salt are noticeable. Grass can be found only in places along the river banks, which are also covered with willows, cottonwoods, and buffalo-berry bushes. We had to cross the river, thirty feet across and one foot deep, before we found enough pasturage for our exhausted animals. In the vicinity were some Indian huts whose inhabitants had fled with the exception of two old squaws. These two old women were very wrinkled and shriveled, with bleary eyes, and may well have lived through nearly a century. After the fashion of their people they wore their hair, which was still abundant and only slightly gray, cut short across the forehead and all the way around so that the back stood out bushily, giving them a hideous appearance.

After the runaways had convinced themselves that the two old ones had met no harm, they gradually came back and bore witness to their joy at their rescue from what they believed was certain death by jumping, dancing, and singing. One of the squaws who visited our camp brought along a large number of her descendants with her on the horse. One papoose sat in front of her, one she carried on her back in a kind of basket, and two sat behind her so that the horse was fully occupied from neck to tail. The clothing of these Indians consists of dressed animal-skins. Woolen blankets seem to be a rarity among them. On the next day, September 16, we met several small bands of men who all followed us to our camp, which we put up eighteen miles farther down the river, only a few miles from its mouth. They continued to arrive until late in the night, and their yells and calls to their comrades, asking where best to cross the river, were answered just as loudly by their comrades in the camp. There may have been two hundred warriors assembled in and around the camp when suddenly the war whoop was heard from several sides. This was either in sport or with the intention of testing our courage. They had recognized our guide, who had once shot one of their chiefs as the latter was trying to rob him of his horses. Leroux showed not the least fear though he expressed regret that we might suffer some provocations from the red men because of him. He shared his night's lodging with the chiefs, who remained all night with him. The security officer informed the chiefs that if the war cry was heard again from any side, they would be fired upon. Most of the uninvited guests were sent out of the camp, but they made their fires close by and were now quiet neighbors. The watch was tripled that night, and orders were given to hold ourselves in readiness. We laid our weapons at our sides. Everything turned out all right, however, and most of our guests, who had not escaped noticing our alertness, left us at daybreak.

The principal chief of the band, Sireechiwap, had arrived during the night with his son, who actually held command because of the great age of his father. In the morning he repaired to the tent of the white leaders to speak and smoke. When Captain Gunnison through Leroux had explained the purpose of our coming, he answered: "This is your land and you can pass through it at any time. Across the mountains are bad Indians who kill white men, but the Utahs are good and glad to see the Americans." Presents were then distributed, pipes smoked, and some of the chiefs accompanied us for a distance.

The valley of the Uncompahgra just before emptying into the valley of the Grand (Gunnison) River is several miles wide and the color of the river has become green. This color derives from a moss covering the stones in the river bed. It is not found in the upper part of the river, and the water there is clear and colorless. Leaving the valley for good, we crossed the Grand (Gunnison) River some miles below the mouth of the Uncompahgra. We camped on the right bank of the river on a little creek which comes out of the west end of the Elk Mountains and empties after a short course into the river. The Indians call it Kahnah (Kannah) Creek. The next day after a march of twelve miles over loose, infertile ground we reached the banks of the Nahunkahrea or Blue (Colorado) River. This stream enters the valley of the Grand River here from a magnificent ravine dividing the Elk Mountains from the western Roan Mountains. The Blue (Colorado) River is probably three hundred feet wide here, and its bed is for the most part deep. The current is strong, and the crossing with the wagons threatened to be an insurmountable obstacle. However, after some Indians had showed us a place where the water was not much more than two feet deep, the banks were cut down with axes and spades and the wagons were all brought safely to the right side of the river after more than three hours of great exertion.

The appearance of the Roan Mountains, which we had to our right for more than a week as we followed the course of the Grand (Colorado) River, (From Grand Junction west the river today is known as the Colorado.) is very picturesque. The steep slopes of the mountains are covered with a crumbling green sandstone and a red slate giving them an unusually bright coloring whose charm is nevertheless lessened by the desolate barrenness of the entire region and the complete absence of all vegetation. From the day we climbed down into the valley of the Uncompahgra to the hour we pitched our tents at the foot of the Wasatch Mountains about the middle of October, every agreeable characteristic of the landscape had disappeared with the exception of the view toward these mountains. The route led chiefly over argillaceous soil, sand or sandstone, which comprises several of the smaller mountain chains between the Rocky Mountains and the Wasatch Mountains. The western slope of the Elk and the Roan Mountains are made up of sandstone of all shades of color, a sandy, calcareous clay slate, argillaceous limestone of green and red, a sandy shale, and uppermost a soft, foliating, blackish shale which includes a good deal of fibrous and lamellar gypsum. From there washes down the dry, infertile soil of the lowlands along the Grand (Colorado) and Green rivers.

In the whole region there are only intimations of sedimentary rock containing organic remains. It almost seems as if there were as little organic life in the seas in which the layers of this deserted land were deposited as is to be found here at present. Only once did I find fragments of a dark gray limestone with numerous casts of shells, mostly amonites, together with a great many gryphaea strewn over the ground on the top of a sandstone hill. This was in the vicinity of Grand (Colorado) River where it turns southwest almost exactly on the 39th parallel some twenty miles below the mouth of the Blue (Colorado) River. I did not succeed in finding the rock *in situ*. A close comparison showed that these gryphaea belong to a species found by Pitcher in the cretaceous of North America and named *Gryphaea pitcherii* after him. Not far from the Nahunkahrea (Colorado) is a conglomerate of silica baked so hard that it has attained the hardness of granite, also a hard bluish limestone and a siliceous slate containing much agate. But these rocks do not extend very far even though they were the only sedimentary deposits besides limestone which I could find in the lowlands.

It appears doubtful to me that the Jurassic system really existed in this region as claimed by French naturalist, Mr. Marcou, and represented on his geological map of North America in Petermann's Journal. If so, it must be in such a rudimentary condition that it is very difficult to find, or it must have largely disappeared again.

It is a remarkable feature of the character of the whole country between the Rocky Mountains and the Sierra Nevada of California that whole formations disappear, as it were, before our eyes. The washing away of mountains takes place here on an immense scale and is the more easily observed as no vegetation of any account is present to hide the destruction from the eye. Nature seems here only to demolish without developing any compensatory creative activity. Several days before we found that tower-shaped conglomerate on the Grand (Gunnison) River, we saw stones lying on our path which had no similarity to the surrounding rocks and which afterwards could be identified with the rocks contained in that conglomerate. As these rocks could not have been floated there upstream and to places lying a thousand feet higher than those towers, we must conclude that they are remains of a conglomerate that once spread that far and subsequently disappeared. On the slopes of the mountains in the Grand and Green River region as well as in the level valleys, the ground is strewn with a great many pieces of agate, cornelian, chalcedony, and other members of the quartz family, which could not be referred to any rock in the area. In the neighborhood of the Wasatch Mountains these minerals again make their appearance, but here they can be traced to a rock which still constitutes a large part of that range. The destruction may be followed there step by step. A similar and very striking washing-away process has taken place in the Elk Mountains with the black shale containing gypsum and the strata below it. Before reaching the banks of the Green River, we traveled for days over a black, clayish, absolutely barren soil produced by the disintegration of the mountain masses and found remnants of those strata in many places, especially in the vicinity of Green River. Here they form isolated hills of curious shape and often considerable size. Many have almost the shape of great churches or houses with colossal chimneys towering nearby. Where the dirty black shapes stand close together, one thinks he sees the ruins of a city whose inhabitants are buried under their fallen adobe houses or else flown from the awful, desolate region.

From the elevation of the taller hills lying east of the Green River one can look for great distances over the barren, wasted land. As far as the distant Wasatch Range one sees only a series of open, parallel ravines and fantastically shaped sandstone ridges without a trace of vegetation. A light cover of gypsum gives the soil the appearance of fields of snow. Neither the bald peaks of the northern Roan Mountains, nor the snow-covered Salt Mountains in the east, nor the broken and tower like masses in the south are designed to lessen the gloom of this view.

With the nature of the country it was not possible after crossing Green River to hold to a strict western course, and we had to make a great detour to the north in order to avoid the impassable gorges, ravines, and obstacles of all kinds. After eight days we made camp on the San Rafael, which according to astronomical determination lay on the same parallel as the camp at Green River and not more that twenty miles distant from it, During this time we had more than one occasion to lament the absence of our guide. Leroux had left us at Grand (Colorado) River to attend to other engagements, leaving us to our own devices. Leroux and his companions had to make the return trip to New Mexico by night, staying under cover during the day, for if they had fallen into the hands of the Utahs, they would most certainly have lost their scalps. It took the experience, intrepidity, and cold blood of a man who had spent nearly fifty years in the mountains to deceive the sharp eyes of his deadly enemies and bring such a bold undertaking to a happy conclusion.

Before leaving us Leroux had described exactly the place where we came to the Spanish (South Branch) Trail and by following it could cross the Green River. Finding the fording place, which lies at 38° 75.5' north latitude *(sic)*, was made easier by a number of Akanaquint or Green River Utahs who crossed the river with their horses to wait upon us as we reached its bank. The Green River is probably 800 to 900 feet across here and has the same dirty red color which it has as the Colorado farther down. Its current is strong and its depth between two and a half and three feet.

The Little Mountain, sometimes called the Book Mountain because of its regular appearance, is several miles from the camp we erected on the right bank of the river. This mountain seems to be a continuation of the Roan Mountains and unites the latter with the Wasatch Range. Its steep slope shows horizontal strata several hundred feet high above which tower individual high peaks and ridges. Deep gorges and ravines cut into the mountain and give it the appearance of colossal, half-ruined fortifications. Desolate as the country is, this view is not without interest. Considering the fantastic formations on the other side of the river, the churches, temples, houses, and towers, one cannot escape the feeling that some wild, malicious tribes have dwelled here and destroyed each other in a furious war of extermination. In truth the Indian country is a land of wars of extermination.

The Indians who flocked to our camp seemed to be a cheerful people. They laughed and chattered incessantly, and the trinkets given them brought them great happiness. A piece of bread with some bacon made them dance with joy.

Even though the number of Indians encountered between the Blue (Colorado) River and the Wasatch Mountains was small and the population of this region must be thin, it is still difficult to understand how these people can find sustenance in such an absolutely barren land. Subsistence through hunting is not possible here, for one can travel for weeks without seeing more than a pair of lonely crows or more game than a few contented lizards which seem pre-eminently to represent the animal life here. It is a region where, according to the saying of Kit Carson, the well-known mountaineer, "not a wolf could make a living." Even the bulbous plants, which are an important means of prolonging a miserable existence for the tribes on the other side of the Wasatch Mountains, do not appear here. Only the buffalo-berries, found here and there on the bank of the larger rivers, provide a vegetable nourishment suitable for human beings. The soil is so poor and dry that even the artemisia and cactus fields, still a real annoyance to the traveler in the Grand (Colorado) River region, soon disappear, and only an occasional example of these plants reminds us of their existence. Only in the highest regions is the vegetation somewhat better, for here the frequent rainstorms, which reach the lowlands but rarely in the summer months, maintain the necessary degree of moisture. Here there is frequent opportunity to watch a cloud grow and swell very swiftly. But hardly has the mass attained some size before it begins to encircle the higher peaks or ridges, which alone receive the life giving as well as the destructive effects of water.

11

1853/SOLOMON NUNES CARVALHO

Solomon Nunes Carvalho was born on April 27, 1815 to David Nunes and Sarah D'Azevedo Carvalho in Charleston, South Carolina. His father David was one of the volunteers who helped to defend the city against the British in the War of 1812.

The Spanish-Portuguese ancestry of Solomon Nunes Carvalho can be traced back in England for several generations. His uncle, Emanuel Nunes Carvalho, came to America first. It was probably during his residence in Charleston, South Carolina that he brought his younger brother, David, to the United States.

Solomon became interested in art at a very early age although it is not certain where he studied art. His grandfather on his father's side of the family worked with coral, jet and amber but never achieved an outstanding reputation. This is likely where some of Solomon's early learning stemmed.

After his marriage to Sarah M. Solis of Philadelphia on October 15, 1845, Solomon Nunes Carvalho moved his residence from Bridgetown, Barbados. He listed himself in the city directories of both Philadelphia and Charleston as a professional daguerreo-typist and portraitist.

How Solomon Nunes Carvalho and John C. Fremont became acquainted is not known. Perhaps it was their mutual connection to the city of Charleston. We do know that after a short interview on August 22, 1853, with Colonel John C. Fremont, Carvalho accepted the job as the first photographer to accompany an exploring expedition. Carvalho spent about ten days preparing for the trip, purchasing supplies for both the daguerreotype process and painting materials. He left New York on September 5, 1853 with these supplies as well as half a dozen cases of Alden's preserved coffee, eggs, cocoa, cream and milk, which were to be tested for their quality. Carvalho traveled to Missouri where he joined Col. Fremont's expedition.

The Fremont party left Westport on the Missouri frontier on September 21, 1853. Fremont was accompanied by twenty-two men which included ten Delaware Indians, two Mexicans and a passenger named W. H. Palmer. Specialists were: Mr

Egloffstein, topographical engineer; Mr. Max Strobel, assistant; Oliver Fuller, assistant engineer; Solomon Nunes Carvalho, artist and daguerreo-typist (photographer). Each man carried a bed-roll which consisted of an India-rubber blanket, a buffalo robe which they slept on, with several blankets and another India-rubber blanket over the top to turn away the rain and snow. Each person was also issued a rifle and a Colt revolver.

Fremont had a blacksmith in Westport build a branding iron which was the letter F. All of the horses and mules which Fremont had purchased were branded before leaving on his expedition.

Fremont's party left Missouri, crossing Kansas to the Arkansas River, and traveled up the river to Big Timbers where they spent a week at Bent's Trading post before continuing on. They reached the ruins of Fort William or Bent's Fort on November 30th. Leaving Bent's fort, they traveled up the Arkansas River to the Huerfano River. They proceeded up this river to Medano Pass which they crossed on December 3rd, ascending and descending into the San Luis Valley. Once in the San Luis Valley the party crossed the east end of the Great Sand Dunes and camped in the vicinity of present day Crestone, Colorado. From here they traveled the East Fork of the North Branch of the Old Spanish Trail north along the west edge of the Sangre de Cristo Mountains to Rito Alto Creek. From there they went west to Cochetopa Pass which they crossed on December 14th, following the wagon tracks left by Gunnison's party. Fremont and his men traveled down Cochetopa Creek to the Gunnison River. Arriving at the Gunnison River near Parlin, Colorado, they crossed to the north bank of the river. This they followed west to near Sapinero, where they crossed to the south side. The men followed the tracks of the Gunnison Party west to the area of present-day Montrose, Colorado where they crossed the Uncompahgre River at Johnson Ford. They paralleled the Uncompahgre River northwest to the Gunnison which they crossed at Robidoux Ford west of present-day Delta, Colorado. The party then followed the Gunnison River west to its confluence with the Colorado River which they crossed at present-day Grand Junction, Colorado. Continuing in the tracks of the Gunnison Party, they followed the north bank of the Colorado River to the confluence of Westwater Creek where they turned northwest traveling up an arroyo toward Cresent Junction, Utah. They followed the south side of the Book Cliffs, staying two to three miles from them. Near Cresent Junction they joined the South Branch of the Old Spanish Trail which they followed to the Green River. They crossed the Green River about three miles north of present-day Green River, Utah.

After the expedition crossed the Green River the whole party was forced to walk because the animals were needed to carry the baggage and scientific apparatus of the expedition. Within a few more days they cached all but the most necessary baggage in order to mount the men on the baggage animals as a last resort. As the animals gave out, they were butchered and divided into twenty-two portions, which had to be rationed as six meals for each man. Whenever a horse or mule gave out, a man was forced to walk.

Oliver Fuller became ill and continued to grow weaker. He finally died at the camp at Red Creek Cañon.

Fremont's expedition finally arrived at Parowan, Utah. They were rescued by the Mormons. Carvalho, having lost forty-four pounds and suffering from diarrhea and malnutrition, was unable to continue with the expedition. The Fremont party remained in Parowan, Utah from February 8th to the 21st. Carvalho remained in Parowan for two weeks after the rest of the party continued on. He joined a group going to Salt Lake City where he remained for ten weeks. Carvalho's health was so poor that he had to be lifted in and out of the wagon in which he was transported. Carvalho, in his journal, recorded information which he had gained from visiting with Lieutenant E.G. Beckwith.

After recovering his health during his stay in Salt Lake City, Carvalho traveled to Los Angeles on the Mormon Road/Old Spanish Trail. Carvalho stated "having determined to go to California by the southern route from Great Salt Lake City, through the settlements, and over the trail of Col. Fremont of 1843." He left on May 6, 1854. The Mormon missionaries left Salt Lake on the 5th of May with a wagon train. Carvalho had sent his supplies ahead with the wagons in the company of twenty-three Mormon missionaries, but remained in Salt Lake to finish a portrait before joining the wagons at Petetnit, Utah.

Carvalho arrived in Los Angeles, California on June 10, 1854. His was the only detailed account of the expedition, because John C. Fremont did not complete his notes in detail.

Winter 1853

We travelled up the Arkansas, and passing the ruins, of Bent's Fort (No positive record remains as to the date of completion of Bent's Fort, but evidence pieced together from existing records indicates that the fort was completed in 1833. Bent's Old Fort or Fort William, as it appears in some records, was a 142 foot by 122 foot adobe compound containing twenty-six one or two story apartments. It had two round bastions on opposing corners to defend the walls in case of attack. The livestock at night were driven into two corrals, one on the west side and one on the south. Unable to sell the fort to the US Army, Willian Bent burned it in 1849.)[2] on the opposite side of the river, struck the mouth of the Huerfano; we followed that river to the Huerfano Valley—which is by far the most romantic and beautiful country I ever beheld. Nature seems to have, with a bountiful hand, lavished on this delightful valley all the ingredients necessary for the habitation of man; but in vain the eye seeks through the magnificent vales, over the sloping hills, and undulating plains, for a single vestige to prove that even the foot of an Indian has ever preceded us. Herds of antelope and deer roam undisturbed through the primeval forests, and sustain themselves on the various cereals which grow luxuriantly in the valley.

But where are the people?

Were there ever any inhabitants in this extraordinarily fertile country?

Will the progress of civilization ever extend so far in the interior?

At present, not even the smoke from an Indian wigwam taints the pure air which plays around, and imparts healthful vigor to my frame.

After crossing the Huerfano River, we saw the immence pile of granite rock, which rises perpendicularly to the height of four or five hundred feet, from a perfectly level valley. It appeared like a mammoth sugar loaf, *(called the Huerfano Butte)*. Col. Fremont expressed a desire to have several views of it from different distances.

The main party proceeded on the journey, leaving under my charge the mules which carried our apparatus, and also the blankets and buffalo robes of the whole camp; it being necessary in equalizing the weight, to distribute the different boxes on three or four animals. Mr. Egloffstien, Mr. Fuller, and two Delawares, remained with me.

To make a daguerreotype (Daguerre-o-type was an early method of photography using chemically treated metal or glass plates to produce pictures. It was invented by L. J. M. Daguerre, a French inventor who lived from 1789-1851.) view, generally occupied from one to two hours, the principal part of that time, however, was spent in packing, and reloading the animals. When we came up to the Butte, Mr. Fuller made barometrical observations at its base, and also ascended to the top to make observations, in order to ascertain its exact height. The calculations have not yet been worked out.

If a railroad is ever built through this valley, I suggest that an equestrian statue of Col. J.C. Fremont, be placed on the summit of the Huerfano Butte; his right hand pointing to California, the land he conquered.

When we had completed our work, we found that we were four hours behind camp, equal to twelve miles.

We followed the trail of our party, through the immense fields of artemisia, until night overtook us, travelling until we could no longer distinguish the trail.

Our arms were discharged as a signal to the camp; they answered it by firing off their rifles, but the wind being then high, we could not determine their exact distance or position. Then, taking counsel together, we determined to encamp for the night, on the side of a mountain covered with pines, near by.

We soon had a large fire burning, for the weather was intensely cold and disagreeable. Upon unloading our animals we found that we had with us all the baggage and buffalo robes of the camp, but nothing to eat or drink; the night was so dark that although not more than half a mile from a creek, we preferred to suffer from thirst rather than incur fresh danger which might lurk about it.

I had with me three tin boxes, containing preserved eggs and milk, but I preferred to go supperless to bed, rather than touch the small supply which I had, unknown to the rest, carefully hid away in my boxes, to be used on some more pressing occasion.

Our absence was most keenly felt by the camp, for they had to remain up, around their fires all night, not having any thing to sleep on.

We also watched all night, fearful that our animals should stray away, or that we should be attacked by Indians.

At day dawn we reloaded our animals, found our lost trail, and soon met some of our party whom Colonel Fremont had sent to look for us.

When we got to camp, they were all ready for a start, and waiting for us. A delicious breakfast of buffalo and venison had been prepared, and we discussed its merits with an appetite sharpened by a twenty-four hours fast.

At the very base of the Rocky Mountains, while we were approaching the Sand-hill (Medano) Pass, fresh bear tracks were discovered by our Delawares, who determined to follow in search of the animal. Diverging a little from our line among the trees on the side of the mountain, our bruin was first seen. "A bear hunt! a bear hunt!" was quickly re-echoed by the whole company. The baggage animals were left to themselves while Colonel Fremont and the whole party darted off at full speed to the chase.

Two of our Delawares who first spied him, were half a mile in advance, for they gave the reins to their animals the instant they saw the bear. His bearship seeing strangers approaching at full speed, and being unused to their ways, thought it most prudent to make himself scarce; he turned and slowly descended the hill in an opposite direction; our loud huzzas finally alarmed him and off he went in full tilt, the whole party surrounding him; the first shot from the Delaware brought him to his knees. Three shots killed him.

He was an enormous black bear, and very fat; I partook of but small quantities of it, it being too luscious and greasy for my palate. The meat was brought into camp and served several days for food for the whole party.

The next day I accompanied Colonel Fremont into the Roubidoux Pass, (Robidoux Pass, which Fremont crossed on his fourth expedition in 1848, was the name used in the early days for present-day Mosca Pass. Although credited with being the first white man to use this pass, Antoine Robidoux did not use it until about the mid 1820's. Both Zebulon Montgomery Pike in 1807 and Jacob Fowler in 1822 mentioned seeing evidence of a wagon road crossing the Sangre de Cristo Mountains. In 1787, Manuel Segura led thirty laborers to the confluence of the Saint Charles and Arkansas Rivers where they built a farming community for the Jupe Comanche. They used carretas to transport the goods needed for farming.)[3] from the summit of which I had the first view into the San (Luis) Louis Valley, the head waters of the "Rio Grande del Norte." On the opposite side forty miles across are the " San Juan Mountains," the scene of Col. Fremont's terrible disaster on a former expedition. He pointed out to me the direction of the spot and with a voice tremulous with emotion, related some of the distressing incidents of that awful night. I made a daguerreotype of the pass with the San (Luis) Louis Valley and mountains in the distance.

While exploring in the pass we accidentally came upon a Mexican, almost naked, who had deserted or been left behind by some hunters. Colonel Fremont, whose great heart beats in sympathy for the suffering of his fellow men, made him follow to camp, and although he knew that this man would be an incubus upon the party from his inability to walk, allowed him to accompany the expedition, and supplied him with a part of his own wardrobe. The man subsequently proved perfectly worthless.

On our way down from the pass, Col. Fremont took out his revolver, and at a distance of about twenty paces killed a small, white, delicately formed animal very like an ermine. This was an excellent shot with a sightless pistol.

We entered the San (Luis) Louis Valley through the Sand-hill (Medano) Pass, (Sand Hill or Medano Pass, which is the first pass north of Mosca Pass, was used by Fremont's party in 1853.) and camped at the mouth. Travelling up the valley about twenty miles, we ascended one of the verdant and gentle slopes of the mountains, along which meandered a stream of living water, fringed on its banks with cotton-wood and elms. We selected a camp-ground in an immense natural deer-park, (To-day, Crestone, Colorado can still be described as a natural "deer-park". If you visit the town of Crestone you will find deer eating on the lawns near almost any house, particularly in winter.) and raised our tents under the shelter of wide-spreading cedars.

Scarcely were we comfortably fixed, when a herd of black-tail deer (Black Tail Deer! The species of deer found in the San Luis Valley are mule deer. It is strange that the expedition would call them Black Tailed Deer.) came down the mountain to water within sight of our camp. Cautiously our Indian hunters sallied out, and ere many minutes, the sound of one, two, three—a dozen rifles were heard in quick succession. Every shot brought down a fine fat buck, and our supper that night, consisted of as fine roast venison as ever graced the table of an epicure.

Col. Fremont determined to remain here for several days in order to have a quantity of the meat cured for our use in the mountains. I exercised my skill in rifle shooting for the last time at this camp. Game of all kinds which had hitherto been plentiful, disappeared almost entirely after we left it.

We travelled up the San (Luis) Louis Valley, crossing the Rio Grande del Norte, (It is Saguache Creek that Fremont crossed, not the Rio Grande del Norte, but the Anza campaign map and the Humboldt map both show this to be the Rio Grande. Saguache Creek comes down from Cochetopa Pass where it enters the Saguache (Sarawatch) Valley before continuing on into the San Luis Valley. The Saguache Creek is joined by San Luis Creek before entering the San Luis Lakes.) and entered the Sarawatch (Saguache) Valley through a perfectly level pass. Our journey continued along the valley until we came to the Cochotope, where we camped.

That night it snowed on us for the first time. The snow obliterated the wagon tracks of Capt. Gunnison's expedition, but Colonel Fremont's unerring judgment conducted us in the precise direction by a general ascent through trackless, though sparsely timbered forests, until we approached the summit, on which grew an immense numbers of trees, still in leaf, with only about four inches of snow on the ground.

As we approached this dense forest, we soon perceived that the axe of the white man had forced a passage through for a wagon-road. Many of the larger trees on both sides of the track were deeply cut with a cross, as an emblem of civilization, which satisfied us that Captain Gunnison and Lieutenant Beale had penetrated through to the other side. In this forest, we were surrounded by immense granite mountains, whose summits were covered probably with everlasting snow. The streams from them which had previously been running towards us, now took the opposite direction, supplying us with the gratifying proof that we had completed our travel to the summit, and were now descending the mountains towards the Pacific. After issuing from these woods we camped on the edge of a rivulet.

At this camp Colonel Fremont exhibited such unmistakable marks of consideration for me, that it induced my unwavering perseverance in the exercise of my professional duties subsequently, when any other man would have hesitated, and probably given up, and shrunk dismayed from the encounter.

Near by our camp, a rugged mountain, (The mountain that Carvalho and Fremont climbed is probably Dome Mountain just to the west of Cochetopa Pass. They saw where a wagon road had been cut by the axes of white men, indicated by crosses cut in many of the larger trees on both sides of the road. From Cochetopa Pass Fremont traveled north on the east side of Cochetopa Creek, on the high plateau, to the area of present-day Parlin, Colorado where they crossed the Gunnison River. Then they followed along the north side of Gunnison River to Sapinero, and paralleled the Gunnison River before crossing to the south side of it.) barren of trees, and thickly covered with snow, reared its lofty head high in the blue vault above us. The approach to it was inaccessible by even our surefooted mules. From its summit, the surrounding country could be seen for hundreds of miles. Col. Fremont regretted that such important views as might be made from that point, should be lost, and gave up the idea as impracticable from its dangerous character. I told him that if he would allow two men to assist me in carrying my apparatus up the mountain, I would attempt the ascent on foot, and make the pictures; he pointed out the difficulties, I insisted. He then told me if I was determined to go he would accompany me; this was an unusual thing for him and it proved to me, that he considered the ascent difficult and dangerous, and that his superior judgment might be required to pick the way, for a misstep would have precipitated us on to the rugged rocks at its base; and it also proved that he would not allow his men or officers to encounter perils or dangers in which he did not participate.

After three hours' hard toil we reached the summit and beheld a panorama of unspeakable sublimity spread out before us; continuous chains of mountains reared their snowy peaks far away in the distance, while the Grand (Gunnison) River plunging along in awful sublimity through its rocky bed, was seen for the first time. Above us the cerulean heaven, without a single cloud to mar its beauty, was sublime in its calmness.

Standing as it were in this vestibule of God's holy Temple, I forgot I was of this mundane sphere; the divine part of man elevated itself, undisturbed by the influences of the world. I looked from nature, up to nature's God, more chastened and purified than I ever felt before.

Plunged up to my middle in snow, I made a panorama of the continuous ranges of mountains around us. Colonel Fremont made barometrical and thermometrical observations, and occupied a part of his time in geological examinations. We descended safely, and with a keen appetite, discussed the merits of our dried buffalo and deer meat.

Eating, sleeping, and travelling, continually in the open air, with the thermometer descending, as we gradually ascended the immense slopes of country between the frontiers of Missouri and the Rocky Mountain, until I have found myself in a temperture of 30° below zero, perpared my system for the intence cold, which we endured during our journey through that elevated country. Twice only did our party find it too cold to travel longer than half an hour, without stopping and making a large fire to keep ourselves from freezing. We were all mounted at the time, but we found it necessary to walk a greater part of the way, to keep up a circulation of the blood.

If the human body at temperature heat, say 80° was suddenly exposed to a temperature of 30° below zero, in which we travelled without any extra clothing, no ill effect resulting, we should not have been able to exist for an hour.

Let us then humbly acknowledge that to the great Omnipotent, we owe our being and all the benefits we receive.

My First Journey on foot.

It was a very cold day in December; the snow covered the immense mountain, over which we had to travel, and right merrily we all followed each other's footsteps in the deep snow.

When we arrived at the foot of the rugged mountain, it was found necessary to dismount, and lead our animals along the intricate and tortuous path. As usual I was at the rear of the cavalcade; I threw the bridle over my pony's head, and followed slowly behind him. I plunged frequently up to my neck in chasms of snow. My efforts to extricate myself cost me some time, and when I regained my footing, I discovered my pony about fifty yards ahead, trying to regain the party. I redoubled my exertions to reach him—I halloed all to no purpose—I sank down exhausted on a rock, with the dreadful reality that I was alone, and on foot on the mountains of eternal snow, with a long day's journey before me.

Gathering fresh strength and courage from the serious position I found myself in, I scrambled up that mountain with a heart palpitating so loudly, that I could count its pulsations. In this manner, alternately resting, I reached the top. On looking on the other side, the only indication of the party, was their deep trail in the frozen snow.

I commenced descending, and at considerable distance below me, I fancied I saw a moving object under a tree; continuing in the track, slipping at times a distance of ten or fifteen feet, until some disguised rock brought me up, I reached the bottom, where I found my pony tied to a tree, immediately on the trail.

No shipwrecked mariner on beholding the approach of a friendly vessel to deliver him from certain death, ever felt greater joy than I did, when I realized that it was my horse which I saw.

This incident was most injurious to me, and I felt its effects for several days, both in body and mind. I mounted my pony, and arrived in camp at dark, some four or five hours after the rest of the party.

Captain Wolff saw my pony riderless, and suspecting that he had escaped from me, caught and tied him up in the place where he was sure to be found; thus repaying me a hundred fold for my medical advice and attendance on Salt Creek.

*   *   *   *   *   *

Horse Steaks Fried in Tallow Candles, and Blanc Mange for Dessert.

At Bent's Fort, Colonel Fremont had several pounds of candles made out of buffalo tallow; the want of convenient boxes to convey them, resulted in many of them being broken to pieces, so as to render them useless as candles. On the first of January, 1854, our men were regaled by unexpected, though not unwelcome luxuries.

I had reserved with religious care, two boxes containing one pound each, of Alden's preserved eggs and milk.—*(The yolks of the eggs were beaten to a thick paste with a pound of loaf sugar, the milk was also prepared with powdered sugar, and hermetically sealed in tin cases.)*—These two tins I had stowed away in my boxes, being the remains of the six dozen which had been wantonly destroyed at our six weeks camp on Salt Creek.

Nobody knew I had them. A paper of arrow root, which my wife had placed in my trunk, for diet, in case I was sick, I had also reserved. These three comestibles, boiled in six gallons of water, made as fine a blanc mange as ever was *mangé* on Mount Blanc. This "dessert" I prepared without the knowledge of Colonel Fremont.

Our dinner, in honor of "New Year's Day," consisted, besides our usual "horse soup," of a delicious dish of horse steaks, fried in the remnants of our "tallow candles." But the satisfaction and astonishment of the whole party cannot be portrayed, when I introduced, as dessert, my incomparable blanc mange. "Six gallons of *bona fide*," nourishing food, sweetened and flavored! It is hardly necessary to say that it disappeared in double quick time. The whole camp had a share of it; and we were all sorry that there was "no more left of the same sort."

*   *   *   *   *   *

Several days after we came down from the Cochotope Pass, it became necessary to ascend a very high and excessively steep mountain of snow. When we were half way up, one of the foremost baggage mules lost his balance, from his hind feet sinking deep in the snow. Down he tumbled, heels-over-head, carrying with him nearly the whole cavalcade, fifty odd in number, several hundred feet to the bottom.

It was a serious, yet a most ludicrous spectacle, to witness fifty animals rolling headlong down a snow mountain, gaining fresh impetus as they descended, unable to stop themselves. The bales of buffalo robes, half buried in the snow, lodged against an old pine tree, the blankets scattered everywhere; my boxes of daguerreotype materials uninjured, although buried in the snow. Considerable time was occupied in searching after them.

I found myself standing up to my eyes in snow, high up the mountain, witnessing this curiously interesting, although disastrous accident; for, when we collected ourselves and animals together, we found that one mule and one horse were killed. This scene made a deep impression upon me. Night came upon us before we were ready to leave the spot. We camped on the same place of the night before.

A snow storm commenced raging, which detained us in this situation for another day; when, determined to cross the mountain, we all recommenced the ascent, and successfully arrived, though much exhausted, without further accident, at the top, and encamped on its summit in snow four feet deep.

That night the thermometer sank very low, and the men stood to their waist in snow, guarding the animals to prevent their running away in search of grass, or something to eat.

We descended the mountain the next day. Our tent poles, belonging to the large lodge, were broken by their contact with the trees in the winding path. The lodge, afterwards, became useless, and the men, myself among them, had to sleep out upon the open snow, with no covering but our blankets, etc.

After descending a very steep mountain, on the snows of which we passed the coldest night I experienced during the journey, the thermometer, at daylight, being 30 degrees below zero, we camped on a creek fringed with willows and interspersed with cotton-wood. The country indicating that there might be game about, our Delaware sallied out in quest of some.

We at this time were on rations of meat-biscuit, and had killed our first horse for food. Towards night, our hunters returned, and brought with them the choice parts of a fine fat, young horse that they killed. He was one of three or four wild ones which they discovered grazing some four miles from camp.

Our men, in consequence, received a considerable addition to their stock of provisions, which, when cooked, proved much more palatable than our broken down horses.

The Delawares also discovered recent footprints of Utah Indians. (The Uncompahgre Valley was the home of the Tabeguache or Uncompahgre band of the Ute Indians. They had lived there for many years. In 1765 Juan Luis Maria de Rivera had traveled northwest of Santa Fe, New Mexico on the South Branch of the Old Spanish Trail. He turned north near the Dolores River and traveled to the confluence of the Gunnison and Uncompahgre Rivers where he left evidence of his passing in the form of a cross and the date 1765 on a cottonwood tree. The Spanish continued to travel to this area to trade with the Ute people. In 1868, in an attempt to remove the Tabeguache Ute from the area, the Los Pinos Ute Agency was established on Cochetopa Pass. The Ute Indians refused to stay at the agency during the winter and returned to the Uncompahgre Valley. In 1875 the Tabeguache Ute were moved to the Uncompahgre Ute Agency, which was located south of present-day Montrose, Colorado.)[4] This information caused Colonel Fremont to double the guard and examine the arms of the whole party, who hitherto had been warned by him of the necessity there was for keeping them in perfect order.

Suddenly it occurred to me that my double-barrel gun might be out of order: I had used it as a *walking-stick*, in descending the mountain that day; the snow was so deep that I was obliged to resort to that course to extricate myself from the drifts.

I quietly went to the place where I had laid it down, and attempted to fire it off; both caps exploded, but the gun did not go off, the barrels being filled with frozen snow. The quick ear of Col. Fremont heard the caps explode. He approached me very solemnly and gave me a lecture, setting forth the consequences which might have ensued from a sudden attack of the Indians on our camp. "Under present circumstances, Mr. Carvalho," said he, "I should have to fight for you." His rebuke was merited, and had its effect throughout the camp, for all the men were most particular afterwards in keeping their arms in perfect order.

We traveled that day nearly twenty miles, and encamped outside of a Utah Indian village, containing a large number of lodges and probably several hundred persons.

The men were mostly armed with rifles, powderhorns, and also with their Indian implements of warfare. On our mules was packed the balance of our "fat horse" of the night before.

These Indians received us very kindly, and during the evening we exposed our wares, viz.: blankets, knives, red cloth, vermilion, etc., etc., which we brought along to conciliate the Indians, and also to trade with them for horses and venison.

We made several purchases, and traded for several small lots of fat venison.

About nine o'clock, after placing double guard around our animals and while we were regaling on fat deer meat in Colonel Fremont's lodge, we heard loud noises approaching the camp; voices of women were heard in bitter bewailment. I thought it was a religious ceremony of Indian burial, or something of the kind. Col. Fremont requested me to see from what it proceeded. I found the whole Indian camp in procession assembled around our lodge. The warriors were all armed, headed by a half-breed, who had been some time in Mexico, and had acquired a smattering of the Spanish language; this man acted as interpreter. Understanding the Spanish language, I gleaned from him that the horse our Delawares had killed the evening before, some twenty miles away, belonged to one of the squaws then present, who valued it very highly, and demanded payment.

On informing Colonel Fremont, who denied himself to the Indians, he remarked that "we had no right to kill their horse without remunerating them for it." The man in charge of the baggage was deputed to give them what was a fair compensation for it.

The Indians having seen our assortment, wanted a part of everything we had, including a keg of gunpowder.

To this demand Colonel Fremont gave an absolute refusal, and at the same time emphatically expressed his desire that the men should not sell, barter, or give away a single grain of gunpowder, on pain of his severest displeasure.

The Indians then threatened to attack us. Colonel Fremont defied them. After considerable parleying, we succeeded in pacifying them.

As it was the intention of Colonel Fremont to leave camp at an early hour, I unpacked my daguerreotype apparatus, at daylight, and made several views.

While engaged in this way, one of the Utah Indians brought into camp a beautiful three-year-old colt, and offered to trade him with me; he was a model pony—dark bay color, in splendid order, sound in wind and limb, and full of life and fire. My poor buffalo hunter Pungo had, three days before, been shot down for food, and in consequence I was literally on foot, although I was using one of the baggage animals for the time.

With permission of Colonel Fremont I traded for him; I gave him in exchange one pair of blankets, an old dress coat, a spoiled daguerreotype plate, a knife, half an ounce of vermilion and an old exhausted pony, which we would have been obliged to leave behind; previous to the trade, I had never mounted him, but I saw the Indian ride him, and his movements were easy and graceful. The Indian saddled him for me, as I was otherwise engaged and did not notice him during the operation. By this time the rest of the party were all mounted, and I never jumped on him until the last moment; he winced a little under the bit, the first one he ever had in his mouth, but cantered off at a round pace, I would not at that moment have taken $500 for him. I considered myself safely mounted for the rest of the journey.

After we had proceeded about two miles, my pony prancing and caracoling to the admiration of the whole party, I discovered that I had left my Colt navy revolver in camp. I told Colnel Fremont of my carelessness, and he smilingly sent one of the men back with me to look for it. I must confess I had not the slightest hopes of finding it, nor had he.

At the time we started, there must have been two hundred Utah men, women, and children at our camp, and if one of them had picked it up, it was most unlikely I should ever receive it again. They had shown some hostility, and although I was not afraid to go back, I thought some danger attended it—Frank Dixon accompanied me.

My pony finding his head turned homeward, commenced champing at his bit, and working his head and body endeavoring to get away. I prided myself on being a good horseman, but this fellow was too much for me.

He got the bit between his teeth and off he started at a killing pace for camp. In less than five minutes I found myself in a wild sage bush on the road; the saddle had slipped round his body, which was as smooth as a cylinder, while I, losing my balance, slipped off.

My pony was quietly grazing in the Indian camp, when I, riding double with Frank, arrived there. The most important thing, was my pistol; I proceeded immediately to the spot, and, hidden in the long grass, where I laid it down, I found it.

With the assistance of the Utahs, my pony was captured, and doubling the saddle-blanket, I attempted to draw the girth tightly—he resisted, and gave considerable trouble; but I was finally mounted, and away we cantered after our party, which we overtook after a couple of hour's ride.

This animal continued to trouble me every morning afterwards. On one occasion, I was saddling him, to perform which operation, I had to tie him to a tree, if one was at hand; at the time I now describe, he was tied to a tree, and in vain I endeavored to place the saddle on him, finally, he reared, and planted both feet on my breast, and I barely escaped with my life, yet my pride never suffered me to complain about it. Sometimes one of my comrades would assist me, but on this occasion, Colonel Fremont saw my predicament; in a few minutes, his servant, "Lee," came to me, and said, "he was more accustomed to break horses than I was," and offered to exchange with me, until mine was more managable.

This man rode a cream colored pacer, which Colonel Fremont wanted to take through to California, if possible, as a riding horse for his daughter. I need not say how gladly I accepted this offer. I rode out of camp that morning much lighter in spirits, although suffering somewhat from the bruises I received. The horse I exchanged for, was a pacer, he had no other gait; and unaccustomed to it, I did not notice until one of the Delawares pointed out to me, that there was any defect in him.

Captain Wolff was riding by my side during the day, and expressed in his Indian manner, how surprised he was that I had exchanged my fresh pony for a lame pacer, "one day more, that horse no travel, Carvalho go foot again!"

His prognostications proved, alas, too true, for on the second day, he was so lame that I could not ride him, and I remained on foot, while my beautiful pony was gallantly bearing the cook.

The horse, he said was not lame when he gave him to me, and I could not prove that he was, so I was constrained to submit, but I never saw this man galloping past me, while I was on foot, that I did not regret I was not brought up as an "ostler and professional horsebreaker."

When we left the Utah village, we travelled a long day's journey, and camped on the Grand (Gunnison) River, thirty miles from the last camp; my pony behaved admirably well on the road, and I would not have parted with him on any account.

While at supper, the guard on the look-out gave the alarm that mounted Indians were approaching, the word was given to arm and prepare to receive them.

About fifty or sixty mounted Utah Indians, all armed with rifles, and bows and arrows, displaying their powder horns and cartouch boxes most conspicuously, their horses full of mettle, and gaily caparisoned, came galloping and tearing into camp.

They had also come to be compensated for the horse we had paid for the night before; they insisted that the horse did not belong to the woman, but to one of the men then present, and threatened, if we did not pay them a great deal of red cloth, blankets, vermilion, knives, and gunpowder, they would fall upon us and massacre the whole party.

On these occasions, Colonel Fremont never showed himself, which caused the Indians to have considerable more respect for the "Great Captain," as they usually called him; nor did he ever communicate directly with them, which gave him time to deliberate, and lent a mysterious importance to his messages. Very much alarmed, I entered Colonel Fremont's lodge, and told him their errand and their threats. He at once expressed his determination not to submit to such imposition, and at the same time, laughed at their threats; I could not comprehend his calmness. I deemed our position most alarming, surrounded as we were by armed savages, and I evidently betrayed my alarm in my countenance. Colonel Fremont without apparently noticing my nervous state, remarked that he knew the Indian character perfectly, and he did not hesitate to state, that there was not sufficient powder to load a single rifle in the possession of the whole tribe of Utahs. "If," continued he, "they had any ammunition, they would have surrounded and massacred us, and stolen what they now demand, and are parleying for."

I at once saw that it was a most sensible deduction, and gathered fresh courage. The general aspect of the enemy was at once changed, and I listened to his directions with a different frame of mind than when I first entered.

He tore a leaf from his journal, and handing it to me, said: here take this, and place it against a tree, and at a distance near enough to hit it every time, discharge your Colt's Navy (The Navy Colt revolver, patented in 1851 by Samuel Colt, was new on the gun market. It was a six shot percussion cap revolver. It had probably not been seen by many white men and was certainly a new concept to the Ute Indians. They had become used to seeing the single shot percussion pistols. This new pistol had a revolving cylinder which contained six holes in which to place powder charges and bullets. It could be fired six times before the need to reload the cylinder. The 44 caliber revolver was more powerful than the older 54 caliber pistols. In tests conducted by Colt, the new revolver would penetrate two more one inch boards than the older pistols.)[5] six shooters, fire at intervals of from ten to fifteen seconds—and call the attention of the Indians to the fact, that it is not necessary for white men to load their arms. I did so; after the first shot, they pointed to their own rifles, as much as to say they could do the same, *(if they had happened to have the powder),* I, without lowering my arm, fired a second shot, this startled them.

I discharged it a third time—their curiosity and amazement were increased: the fourth time, I placed the pistol in the hands of the chief and told him to discharge it, which he did, hitting the paper and making another impression of the bullet.

The fifth and sixth times two other Indians discharged it, and the whole six barrels being now fired it was time to replace it in my belt.

I had another one already loaded, which I dexterously substituted, and scared them into an acknowledgment that they were all at our mercy, and we could kill them as fast as we liked, if we were so disposed.

After this exhibition, they forgot their first demand, and proposed to exchange some of their horses for blankets, etc.

We effected a trade for three or four apparently sound, strong animals; Moses," one of the Delaware chiefs, also traded for one, but in a few days they all proved lame and utterly useless as roadsters, and we had to kill them for food.

The Indians with the consent of Colonel Fremont, remained in camp all night; they had ridden thirty miles that day, and were tired. On this occasion, eleven men, fully armed, were on guard at one time.

The Indians who no doubt waited in camp to run our horses off during the night, were much disappointed in not having an opportunity. They quietly departed the next morning, while our whole camp listened to the energetic exclamation of Col. Fremont, that the "price of safety is eternal vigilance."

The crossing of the Grand (Colorado) River, the eastern fork of the Colorado, (South of Grand Junction, Colorado is a two track road which follows the old wagon tracks left by Gunnison and later settlers. This road parallels the Gunnison River and leads to the crossing on the Colorado River. This crossing was at about 28-1/4 Road and can be seen where it came down a natural arroya to the crossing on the Colorado River.) was attended with much difficulty and more danger. The weather was excessively cold, the ice on the margin of either side of the river was over eighteen inches thick; the force of the stream always kept the passage in the center open; the distance between the ice, was at our crossing, about two hundred yards. I supposed the current in the river to run at the rate of six miles an hour. The animals could scarcely keep their footing on the ice, although the men had been engaged for half an hour in strewing it with sand. The river was about six feet deep, making it necessary to swim our animals across; the greatest difficulty was in persuading them to make the abrupt leap from the ice to the roaring gulph, and there was much danger from drowning in attempting to get on the sharp ice on the other side, the water being beyond the depth of the animals, nothing but their heads were above water, consequently the greater portion of their riders' bodies were also immersed in the freezing current.

To arrive at a given point, affording the most facilities for getting upon the ice, it was necessary to swim your horse in a different direction to allow for the powerful current. I think I must have been in the water, at least a quarter of an hour. The awful plunge from the ice into the water, I never shall have the ambition to try again; the weight of my body on the horse, naturally made him go under head and all; I held on as fast as a cabin boy to a main-stay in a gale of wind. If I had lost my balance it is most probable I should have been drowned. I was nearly drowned as it was, and my clothes froze stiff upon me when I came out of it. Some of the Delawares crossed first and built a large fire on the other side, at which we all dried our clothes standing in them.

It is most singular, that with all the exposure that I was subjected to on this journey, I never took the slightest cold, either in my head or on my chest; I do not recollect ever sneezing. While at home, I ever was most susceptible to cold.

The whole party crossed without any accident; Colonel Fremont was the first of our party to leap his horse into the angry flood, inspiring his men, by his fearless example to follow.

On a former expedition, Colonel Fremont crossed the Grand River with a handful of men; but no desolation followed in his path. With the flag of his country in one hand and the genius of Liberty resting on his brow, he penetrated through an enemy's country, converting all hearts as he journeyed, conquering a country of greater extent than Caesar's whole empire, until he arrived at San Francisco, where he became military commandant and governor in chief of California, by the simple will of the people. Fremont's name and deeds, will become as imperishable as Caesar's.

At last we are drawn to the necessity of killing our brave horses for food. The sacrifice of my own pony that had carried me so bravely in my first buffalo hunt, was made; he had been running loose for a week unable to bear even a bundle of blankets. It was a solemn event with me, and rendered more so by the impressive scene which followed.

Colonel Fremont came out to us, and after referring to the dreadful necessities to which we were reduced, said "a detachment of men whom he had sent for succor on a former expedition, had been guilty of eating one of their own number." He expressed his abhorrence of the act, and proposed that we should not under any circumstances whatever, kill our companions to prey upon them. "If we are to die, let us die together like men." He then threatened to shoot the first man that made or hinted at such a proposition.

It was a solemn and impressive sight to see a body of white men, Indians, and Mexicans, on a snowy mountain, at night, some with bare head and clasped hands entering into this solemn compact. I never until that moment realized the awful

278

situation in which I, one of the actors in this scene, was placed.

It was a clear, cold night, on the Eagle Tail River, after a long fast, and a dreary walk, our men had returned supperless to sleep on their snowy bed, and with no prospect of anything to eat in the morning, to refresh them for another day's tramp. It was a standing rule in camp that a rifle discharged between the set of watch at night until daylight, was a signal that Indians were approaching, and this rule had been strictly observed, as a safeguard to the party. I have seen our camp on Salt Creek surrounded with wolves—they even came within its precincts and stole our buffalo meat, but our Delawares would never allow an arm to be discharged. On this occasion, Mr. Fuller was on guard, and it was a few days before he gave out. We had been twenty-four hours without a meal, and as may be supposed, he was as hungry as the rest of us; while patrolling up and down the river on the banks of which we were encamped, his keen eye discovered a beaver swimming across the stream; he watched it with rifle to his shoulder, and as it landed, he fired and killed it.

The sudden discharge of a rifle during this still night, under overhanging mountains, and in the valley of the river where we expected to find Indians, made a tremendous explosion. The sound reverberated along the rocks, and was re-echoed by the valley. Instantly the whole camp was on duty. Colonel Fremont who had been making astronomical observations, had but a few moments previously retired to rest. He rushed out of his lodge, completely armed, the party assembled around it and all were filled with the utmost anxiety and alarm. We did not know the number or character of the enemy, but we were all prepared to do battle to the death. In a few moments, one of the Delawares approached camp dragging after him an immense beaver, which he said Mr. Fuller had killed for breakfast. The sight of something to eat, instead of something to fight, created quite a revolution of feeling; and taking into consideration the extremity, which caused Mr. Fuller to break through the rule, Colonel Fremont passed it off quietly enough. Poor Fuller did not realize the excited condition of the camp, until he was relieved from duty. Our beaver was dressed for breakfast, when Fuller told Colonel Fremont that he was so anxious and delighted at seeing the beaver, that he entirely forgot the rule of the camp.

The divide between Grand (Colorado) River and the Green River, *(the eastern and western forks of the Colorado)* is barren and sterile to a degree. At the season that we crossed, there was no water between the two rivers, a distance of about forty miles. Capt. Gunnison's wagon trail was still plainly visible at the crossing of a gully, now however without water.

That party must have had great difficulty in transporting their wagons across it. From its appearance, a tremendous body of water must have forced a passage through the gully, at that time. Dwarf artemisia grows sparsely on this sandstone formation.

At the roots of the artemisia still remained small quantities of dry powdered snow. To allay my thirst, I have put my head under the bush, and lapped the snow with my tongue. The descent into the valley of the Green River. (The Fremont Expedition had followed the North Branch of the Old Spanish Trail since entering the San Luis Valley through Medano Pass. The North and South Branches of the Old Spanish Trail crossed Colorado into Utah where the two branches joined about twenty miles east of the Green River, near present-day Crescent Junction. The Old Spanish Trail then proceeded to the Green River where the trail crossed about two-and-a-half miles north of the present-day town of Green River, Utah.) was over most dangerous projections of different strata of rock, thrown into its present state by some convulsion of nature.

When we arrived at the river, we saw on the high sand bluffs, on the opposite side, several Indians, whose numbers soon increased. As our party was much exhausted for want of wholesome food, we were buoyed up with hopes that we could obtain supplies from them.

We crossed the river, and were conducted by Indians to a fertile spot on the western bank of it, where their village was. We found that they lived on nothing else but grass-seed, which they collected in the fall. Their women parch it, and grind it

The crossing on the Green River is located about three miles north of the town of Green River, Utah. The island used in crossing can be seen in the middle of the river.

between stones. In this manner it is very palatable, and tastes very much like roasted peanuts.

This, their only article of food, was very scarce, and we could procure only a small supply. I parted with everything out of my daguerreotype boxes that I did not require, and several articles of necessary clothing, for about a quart of it. It is very nourishing, and very easy of digestion. The quantity I had, lasted me for three days. I made a hearty meal of it the night we camped among them.

To the sustaining properties of this cereal, I firmly believe, I owe the strength which enabled me to undergo the physical exertion that was required to reach the settlements.

12

1858/RANDOLPH BARNES MARCY

Captain Randolph Barnes Marcy of the 5th U.S. Infantry arrived at Fort Bridger from Fort Leavenworth as part of General Albert Sidney Johnston's command. They were sent to Utah to settle the unrest created by rumors that Mormons were threatening emigrants and traders who were passing through Utah. The Mormons also reputedly threatened to keep all U.S Troops from entering or crossing Utah. Upon the armies arrival in Utah, the Mormons drove off their cattle and burned their supply wagons. Not being able to purchase supplies in Utah, the army was forced to travel to New Mexico to resupply the troops.[1]

The Charles Fancher emigrant company had attempted to purchase supplies upon entering Utah, but the Mormons refused to sell any to them. An argument ensued, causing bitter feelings on both sides. This resulted in the emigrants being massacred, all but eighteen small children, at Mountain Meadows in 1857.[2]

Captain Marcy left Fort Bridger on November 24, 1857 accompanied by sixty-five men, forty soldiers and twenty-five mountain men. Tim Goodale served as guide and Jim Baker interpreter. From Fort Bridger they descended Henry's Fork to its confluence with the Green River. They continued on to the Colorado River where they joined the North Branch of the Old Spanish Trail. On the 8th of December Marcy and his men reached the Gunnison River which they crossed to the ruins of the fur-trading post of Antoine Robidoux. Here they tried to hire an Indian guide, but the Indians were afraid to cross the mountains in the winter. The expedition crossed the mountains from the Uncompahgre Valley to the Gunnison River then continued up the Gunnison River and became lost north of Cochetopa Pass. Supplies ran out forcing them to eat their animals, including a pet colt belonging to Tim Goodale's Indian wife. Finally Miguel Alona convinced Captain Marcy to allow him to lead the expedition. The young but eager Mexican Miguel Alona led the expedition across Cochetopa Pass to the San Luis Valley. Then he and Mariano Medano hurried along the East Fork of the North Branch of the Old Spanish Trail to Fort Massachusetts for help.

November 24, 1857

Left Fort Bridger with a command of forty enlisted men, and twenty-five mountain men, besides packers and guides. The course lay through an almost trackless wilderness, over lofty and rugged mountains, without a pathway or human habitation to guide or direct, in the very depth of winter, through snows, for many miles together, reaching to the depth of five feet. The beasts of burden very rapidly perished until very few were left; the supplies gave out; the luggage was abandoned; we were driven to subsist upon the carcasses of the dead horses and mules; all the men became greatly emaciated; some were frostbitten, yet not one murmur of discontent escaped the lips of a single man. The mission was one of extreme importance to the movements of the army, and great disaster might befall the command if these devoted men failed to bring succor to the camp. They had one and all volunteered for this service, and, although they might freeze or die, yet they would not complain.

When we left Fort Bridger there was only six inches of snow on the ground, and my guides, as well as other mountain men, were of opinion that we should not, at that early season, find over two feet of snow upon the summit of the mountains. They also believed that we could make the trip to Fort Massachusetts, New Mexico, in twenty-five days; but, to make sure of having enough provisions, I deemed it wise to take thirty day's supply, which, with our luggage, was packed upon sixty-six mules.

After bidding adieu to our friends at Fort Bridger, we proceeded down Henry's Fork to its confluence with Green River, where we forded the latter stream, and followed a trail that led us to the foot of the mountain dividing Green from Grand River. Here we found three lodges of Digger Utes, and engaged one of them to act as guide over the mountain. Our first day's march from here up a very circuitous cañon brought us to the top of this mountain, where we found the snow nearly two feet in depth. We encamped at the head of the cañon, and, after supper, our Indian guide came to me and expressed some doubt as to whether we were in possession of the articles he had been promised for his services, and Jim Baker, the interpreter, advised that they should be shown to him. Accordingly, the knife, powder, lead, and paint were spread out before him; and, although I rather disapproved the proceeding, Baker allowed him to take possession of them.

Before I lay down for the night I posted sentinels around the camp, and directed the guard to keep careful watch upon the Indian. About midnight I was awakened by the sergeant of the guard, who reported that he believed our Indian guide intended deserting, as he had placed his rifle and all his other effects in such a position that he could seize them instantly, and he appeared to be watching for an opportunity to break away. I repeated to the sergeant the order to guard him closely, and directed him, if he made any attempt at deserting us, to seize and tie him.

In the course of an hour the sergeant returned with the intelligence that, in spite of all his vigilance, the fellow had broken away from the guard and escaped. I regretted this, because we wanted his services to pilot us across the summit of the mountain on the following day. We were obliged, however, to set out without him, and, shortly after emerging from the cañon, found ourselves upon a level plateau about ten miles wide. Our track led us across this elevated table-land, which we found terminating in a towering and almost perpendicular cliff of bluff, bordering the valley of Grand River, and some two thousand feet above it. On reaching this lofty escarpment, it did not seem possible that our mules could descend it, and, indeed, I had been previously told that there was but one place for fifty miles along this cliff where the declivity was practicable for animals, and this was at a point where the Indians had cut out a narrow path along the face of the bluff, winding around over rocks and along the brinks of deep chasms. (Jack Nelson, President of the Mesa County Chapter of the Old Spanish Trail Association has studied the Spanish Trail documents for some time. He believes that they descended Mount Garfield to Palisade.)

We bivouacked in the snow directly upon the verge of this precipice, where we had a magnificent view of the valley of Grand River and the Rocky Mountains beyond. Immediately after we halted I sent out Baker to search for the trail leading into the valley, and it was not until late at night that he discovered it. In the morning we entered the tortuous defile and commenced the descent, which we found exceedingly precipitous and slippery. Our pack mules had great difficulty in keeping their footing. Occasionally one of them would fall, and, with his pack, roll over and over for thirty or forty feet down the rocks, until he was brought up by a tree or projecting crag. At length, however, after numerous tumbles and somersaults, we reached the valley at the base, and, to our surprise, found the grass green, and not a particle of snow upon the ground, while, as I said before, directly over our heads, upon the summit of the plateau, it lay two feet deep. We discovered at this place a naturally inclosed pasture, containing about two hundred acres, surrounded by an almost perpendicular trap wall some two hundred feet in height, and with but one opening of not more than a hundred yards wide. Our animals were all turned into this natural *corral*, and a herdsman stationed at the opening secured them as perfectly as if they had been shut up in a stable.

We picked up a horse here that had become very fat upon the rich *bunch* grass. He had probably been lost or abandoned by the Indians. We appropriated the animal, and subsequently used him for food in the mountains.

December 8

We struck Grand (Gunnison) River near the confluence of its two principal branches, the *Uncompadre* and the *Bunkara*.(The Uncompahgre River dumps into the Gunnison River at Delta, Colorado.) We forded them, but with much difficulty, as the water was deep and rapid, and filled with floating ice, and encamped at the base of the "Elk Mountain," near the remains of an old Indian trading establishment, which had formerly been occupied by a man named Robedeau (Robidoux), of St. Louis, who wandered out into this remote wilderness many years ago, but was subsequently driven away and his building burned by the Indians. (Fort Uncompahgre, Robidoux Trading Post, was built about 1828 by Antoine and Louis Robidoux and flourished until 1844.[3] A recreation of this trading post can be seen at Delta, Colorado.)

We were at this point within a few miles from the western base of the Rocky Mountains, which rose in formidable proportions in front of us, and appeared covered with a heavy coating of snow. Thus far our journey had been pleasant, and we had encountered no serious obstacles. Our animals had found abundance of grass, and were in fair condition.

But, as the guide informed me that we were to enter the mountains at this point, their appearance gave me serious apprehensions for the future. We here fell in with a large band of Digger Ute Indians, (The Tabeguache or Uncompahgre Ute occupied the Uncompahgre Valley until the fall of 1881 when they were moved to the Uintah Reservation in Utah.) who were subsisting upon rabbits, bugs, crickets, etc. They came flocking around us as soon as we arrived, examining every thing, and begging for such articles as happened to take their fancy. They were a ragged, villainous-looking set, and we had our hands full in keeping the women from stealing every thing that came in their way.

They had a good many ponies; but, although we offered large prices for some of them, we could not induce them to part with a single one. Their curiosity appeared a good deal exercised to ascertain our business in their country; and when we informed them that we were bound for New Mexico, they expressed great astonishment,and would point to the mountains and shiver as if with cold.

I endeavored to persuade the chief to accompany us as guide to the summit of the mountains, and offered him the value of three horses in goods, but he peremptorily refused, saying that he was not yet ready to die, and that, unless we turned back, or stopped and passed the winter with them, we would all inevitably perish. My interpreter asked him if he took us for a set of old women, who would be intimidated by a little snow; and added, that he had always before taken him for a warrior and a man, but now he had discovered his mistake, and he would advise him to go back to his lodge, cover up warm, and assist his squaw in tending the babies; that we were of the masculine gender; we had started to cross the mountains into New Mexico, and were going to accomplish it at all hazards, and if he did not feel disposed to go, we could dispense with his services. This taunt had no effect upon him, however. He persisted in refusing to go with us, saying that all we had would not be sufficient to induce him to attempt the journey. I then asked him how much snow he supposed we would find in the mountains? He replied that he was not positive as to the exact depth, but that he crossed over the same route we proposed to travel in autumn, when the leaves were commencing to fall, and that he then found about one foot upon the summit; that there had been a great deal of rain in the valley since that time, which he presumed had its equivalent in snow upon the mountains, and he was of opinion that we might encounter from four to five feet, and perhaps even more than that. He concluded by saying, "You may think I do not tell the truth, but if you will only cast your eyes toward the mountains you can see for yourselves that the snow is there."

December 11

Despite the gloomy and discouraging prospects held out to us by the Digger chief, we packed up our mules and commenced the ascent of the western slope of the Rocky Mountains. (From the Uncompahgre River the Old Spanish Trail ascended Cedar Creek to Cerro Summit.) We had proceeded but a few miles when the snow began very seriously to impede our progress. On the second day it became still deeper, with a crust upon the surface, which cut the legs of our animals seriously, and caused some of them to refuse their work. We, however, pushed on, until at length we found the snow so deep that they could no longer force their way through it, and I was now obliged to resort to a new order of march. Up to this time we had, for the security of our animals, adopted the plan of marching with an advanced guard, immediately followed by pack mules, with the main party in rear.

I now placed the greater part of the command in front, in single rank, so as to break a track for the animals.

This was, of course, very hard work upon a few of the leading men; and, in order to equalize the labor as much as possible, I directed that every man, as he came in front, should retain that position a certain length of time, after which he was permitted to turn out of the track and allow all the others to pass him, taking his place in rear. By these alternations the work was very much lightened, and after all the party had passed, a good track was left for the animals. And they really required all our care, as, from the time we entered the mountains, they received no other sustenance than what they derived from the bitter pine-leaves. The effects of this novel and unwholesome forage soon began to manifest itself upon them. They became weak and exhausted, and at length began to give out and die. I was then obliged to *cache*, or hide, all our surplus luggage, which reduced the weight of the packs very considerably. Notwithstanding this, they continued to perish. One day we lost five, and another day as many as eight died out of our little stock. This gave me very serious uneasiness, as our supply of provisions was becoming very small, and I knew, after these were gone, our only dependence for subsistence must be upon our famished animals. Our beef cattle had nearly all been consumed, and our stock of bread was very limited. I felt the necessity of husbanding the strength of my men and animals as much as possible. I therefore ordered the command to throw away every article of baggage they had remaining except one blanket each and their arms and ammunition. They cheerfully complied with the order, and we thus made another very material reduction in the weight of our packs, which enabled our enfeebled animals to proceed with more ease.

The snow increased day after day as we ascended, until it was four feet deep, and was so dry and light that the men, walking in an upright position, would sink to their waists, and could not move. One of the guides made a pair of snow shoes, and attempted to walk upon them, but they sank so deep in the soft snow that it was impossible to use them.

Our only alternative now, in the deepest snow, was for the three or four leading men of the party to lie down and crawl upon their hands and feet, each man following in the tracks of the leader, and all placing their hands and feet in the same holes. This method packed the snow so that, after a few men had passed, it bore up the others, and was sufficiently firm to sustain the mules after all the men had traversed it.

The leading man was generally able to go about fifty yards before he became exhausted; but I had one soldier, named McLead, of the 10th Infantry, whose powers of endurance exceeded those of any other man I have ever known. He would generally, when his turn came to lead the party, make about four times the distance of any other man. He was always in good spirits, and never became weary or discouraged, and his example had a most cheering effect upon his comrades. One bitter cold day, after having labored very hard, we halted for a few moments, and made fires to warm our feet. While standing over the fire, I took out my pipe, and, cutting a little tobacco from a small piece I had remaining, indulged myself in a smoke, the men having used their last tobacco some ten days before. McLead was standing near me at the time, and, being desirous of doing something to show my appreciation of his valuable service, I handed him the precious morsel of tobacco, and asked him if he would not like to smoke." I suggested that he was very fortunate in not being addicted to the habit at a time when tobacco was so very scarce. After a moments hesitation, he said, "*I sometimes take a chew*," when I told him to help himself, which he did, and immediately exclaimed, "I never tasted any thing so good in my life; I would have given ten dollars for that, captain."

Notwithstanding I reduced the rations one half, our provisions were all consumed long before we reached the top of the mountains, and we were then entirely dependent upon our famished animals for food.

Our first repast upon the novel regimen was from a colt belonging to Tim Goodale's Indian wife, who accompanied us, and underwent the hardships of the trip with astonishing patience and fortitude.

She cried very bitterly when the colt was killed, as it had always been her pet; but she realized the necessity of the sacrifice, and was consoled upon my promising her another on our arrival in New Mexico.

We found the meat well-flavored, tender, and palatable. Our next meal was from a very old, lean, and tough mare which had given out and could perform no farther service. This we found any thing but a "*bonne bouche*." We were, however, very hungry, and ate it.

After this our only diet for twelve days consisted of starved mules as they became exhausted and could go no farther. Twelve of my men had frozen their feet so badly as to be unable to walk, and we were obliged to appropriate all our serviceable animals to carry them. I had given up my own horse to one of these men, and took his place in the snow with the others. We had not a single morsel of any thing left to eat except these animals. If we had some salt we would have done better, but that was all gone. I was in the habit of sprinkling a little gunpowder upon my mule-steaks, and it did not then require a very extensive stretch of the imagination to fancy the presence of both pepper and salt.

This lean meat did not, however, by any means satisfy the cravings of the appetite, and we were continually longing for fat meat. Although we consumed large quantities of the mule meat, yet within half an hour from the time we had finished our meals we would feel as hungry as before we had eaten.

One day, as we were making our weary way through the deepest snow near the summit of the mountains, and when we were suffering severely from the intense cold, and the piercing winds which sweep over those high altitudes, my guide, Tim Goodale, called out to me from the front, and pointing toward a snow-bank, said there were some birds he had never but once before seen.

I cast my eyes in the direction indicated, but could discern nothing until the birds rose up and flew away. We subsequently killed two of them, and, upon examination, found them about the size of the partridge of the North, or the pheasant of the South. They were as white as the snow itself, without a single colored feather, and their method of flying, and their appearance in other respects, was very similar to that of the grouse. I was quite confident we had discovered a new variety of that species of bird, until two specimens which were sent to Professor Baird, of the

Smithsonian Institute, showed them to be the "*Sagopus leucurus*," or white-tailed ptarmigan, a species of which but two or three specimens are said to be found in any ornithological collections, and those are in Europe. This beautiful bird, which, in its winter plumage, is as white as the snow upon which we invariably found them, was before supposed to be confined to that part of the Rocky Mountain chain north of latitude 54° north. The specimens sent to Professor Baird are said by him to be the first indications of their occurrence within the limits of our possessions, and it extends their supposed range about a thousand miles to the south.

These birds were the only glimpses of animal life that we had met with, outside of our own party, during thirty days that we were struggling through the deep snow.

January 1, 1858

"This morning dawned upon us with gloomy auspices, far from promising to us a happy New Year. We have been engaged since daylight this morning in wallowing along through snow at least five feet deep, and have only succeeded, by the severest toil, in making about two miles during the entire day. From our bivouac to-night we can see the fires of last night, and in the darkness they do not appear over a rifle-shot distant. The leading men have been obliged to crawl upon their hands and knees to prevent sinking to their necks, and could only go a few yards at a time before they were compelled, in a state of complete exhaustion, to throw themselves down and let others take their places.

"Gallant fellows! Many of them are almost barefooted, and several whose feet have been frozen have suffered intensely from pain and cold. Yet every soldier, without a single exception, has performed every thing I required of him cheerfully and manfully; they have never faltered, or uttered a murmur of complaint. I feel for them from the bottom of my heart, and I should be recreant to my duty as their commander if I neglected to give expression to my profound gratitude for the almost superhuman efforts put forth by them to extricate the party from our perilous position."

At one period of this toilsome journey, while we were ascending the Eagle-tail (Tomichi) River, a branch of the Grand (Gunnison) River, my guide made a mistake, and took the wrong direction for the "Cochetope Pass," the point at which we were aiming, and which was, as I was well aware, the only place where it was possible for us to cross the summit of the chain, (It is easy to see why the party missed the cañon which leads to Cochetopa Pass. If one is not careful in driving east on US Highway 50 from Gunnison, SH 114, which takes you to the pass can easily be missed. Snow covered hills would make it much worse.) as on the north and south of this passway the mountains were much more elevated, and the snow so deep at that season that it would have been utterly impossible for us, in our enfeebled and famished condition, to have forced our way through it. It was only fifty miles south of the Cochetope Pass that General Fremont attempted to penetrate these mountains from New Mexico, (Fremont was trying to find this same pass but from the east side.)[4] and encountered so much snow that all his animals perished, and he was forced to turn back, with the loss of several of his men, before the party was extricated from their perilous position. We traveled the greatest part of the day in the wrong direction; and after we had bivouacked for the night, one of my employés, a Mexican by the name of Miguel Alona, came to me and told me that we had left the right direction in the morning, and, pointing toward a depression in the mountains at a right angle to the course we had taken, some thirty miles distant, said that was the Cochetope Pass. I asked him how it happened that he knew any thing about the country. He replied that he had been there before, and that he knew it well. Whereupon I called up the guide, and upon questioning him in regard to it, he admitted that the face of the country, buried as it was in deep snows, presented so different an appearance from what it did in the summer season, when he had traversed it before, that it was possible he might have been mistaken; but still he believed he was right. I did not blame him, as this might have occurred with any one; but this first exhibition of doubt on his part caused me great uneasiness, and I now regard our situation as involving us in imminent peril. We had advanced too far to retrace our steps, and the only alternative left us was to go forward; and I asked the Mexican if he was willing to act as guide, telling him I would, in addition to his regular pay, make him a handsome present for his services, provided he conducted us in safety to New Mexico; but I also informed him that if at any time I discovered he was leading us in a wrong direction, I should hang him to the first tree.

He was quite displeased at this, saying that he was sorry I should think he would attempt to deceive me. I told him all I required was for him to be sure he was right, and to think over the matter deliberately, and come back and let me know if he was willing to enter into the agreement upon the terms proposed by me. He returned in a short time and said, "I'll risk my neck on it, captain." "Very well," I replied, "you are guide."

From this time the uncertainty of our position, and the knowledge of the fact that if we failed to strike the Cochetope Pass we must all inevitably perish, gave me great anxiety, and prevented me from sleeping for several nights. There was not the slightest sign of a road, trail, or footmark to guide us; all was one vast, illimitable expanse of snow as far as the eye could penetrate; and the mountains rose before us, peak upon peak, until they were lost in the clouds. Not a living animal outside of our own party was seen for many, many long days; all was dreary, desolate solitude; but my noble soldiers struggled manfully ahead, and not a single murmur or complaint ever was heard to come from them; on the contrary, they endeavored to give me encouragement, and requested the senior sergeant to inform me that they had observed for a few days past that I looked melancholy, and they desired him to say to me that they were willing to eat mule meat, or to undergo any other privations that I might think necessary, and that they would work for me as long as they could stand upon their legs. As before stated, I had already required them to throw away all their personal baggage except one blanket each, and the poor fellows were extremely destitute of every thing. They had worn out their shoes, and had patched them with mule hides as long as they would hang together, when some of them were obliged to wrap their feet in pieces of blankets or of their coat-tails to keep them from freezing. Many of them had worn out their pants, and their legs were greatly exposed.

The dazzling reflection of the sun's rays from the snow was very painful, and made several of the men snow blind; but we found a remedy for this by blacking our faces with powder or charcoal.

The greatest deprivation we experienced, however, and the one which caused more suffering among the men than any other, was the want of tobacco. All our tobacco was consumed long before we reached the summit of the mountains, and no one who has not been accustomed to the use of the weed can imagine the intense longing produced by being suddenly deprived of it.

An incident occurred while we were in the mountains which struck me at the time as being one of the most remarkable and touching evidences of devotion that I have ever known evinced among the brute creation.

On leaving Fort Leavenworth with the army for Utah in the previous summer, one of the officers rode a small mule, whose kind and gentle disposition soon caused him to become a favorite among the soldiers, and they named him "Billy." As this officer and myself were often thrown together upon the march, the mule, in the course of a few days, evinced a growing attachment for a mare that I rode. The sentiment was not, however, reciprocated on her part, and she intimated as much by the reversed position of her ears, and free exercise of her feet and teeth whenever Billy came within her reach. But these signal marks of displeasure, instead of discouraging, rather seemed to increase his devotion, and whenever at liberty he invariably sought to get near her, and appeared much distressed when not permitted to follow her.

On leaving Camp Scott for New Mexico Billy was among the number of mules selected for the expedition. During the march I was in the habit, when starting out from camp in the morning, of leading off the party, and directing the packmen to hold the mule until I should get so far in advance with the mare that he could not see us; but the moment he was released he would, in spite of all the efforts of the packers, start off at a most furious pace, and never stop or cease braying until he reached the mare's side. We soon found it impossible to keep him with the other mules, and he was finally permitted to have his own way.

In the course of time we encountered the deep snows in the Rocky Mountains, where the animals could get no forage, and Billy, in common with the others, at length became so weak and jaded that he was unable any longer to leave his place in the caravan and break a track through the snow around to the front. He made frequent attempts to turn out and force his way ahead, but after numerous unsuccessful efforts he would fall down exhausted, and set up a most mournful braying.

The other mules soon began to fail, and to be left, worn out and famished, to die by the wayside. It was not, however, for some time that Billy showed symptoms of becoming one of the victims, until one evening after our arrival at camp I was informed that he had dropped down and been left upon the road during the day. The men all deplored his loss exceedingly, as his devotion to the mare had touched their kind hearts, and many expressions of sympathy were uttered around their bivouac fires on that evening. Much to our surprise, however, about ten o'clock, just as we were about going to sleep, we heard a mule braying about half a mile to the rear upon our trail. Sure enough it proved to be Billy, who, after having rested, had followed upon our tracks and overtaken us. As soon as he reached the side of the mare he lay down and seemed perfectly contented.

The next day I relieved him from his pack, and allowed him to run loose; but during the march he gave out, and was again abandoned to his fate, and this time we certainly never expected to see him more. To our great astonishment, however, about twelve o'clock that night the sonorous but not very musical notes of Billy in the distance aroused us from our slumbers, and again announced his approach. In an instant the men were upon their feet, gave three hearty cheers, and rushed out in a body to meet and escort him into camp.

But this well-meant ovation elicited no response from him. He came reeling and floundering along through the deep snow, perfectly regardless of these honors, pushing aside all those who occupied the trail or interrupted his progress in the least, wandering about until he found the mare, dropped down by her side, and remained until morning.

When we resumed our march on the following day he made another desperate effort to proceed, but soon fell down exhausted, when we reluctantly abandoned him, and saw him no more.

Alas! poor Billy! your constancy deserved a better fate; you may, indeed, be said to have been a victim to unrequited affection.

The method of constructing our bivouac was for each set of two or three men to dig a hole about seven or eight feet square down through the snow to the ground, where a bed was made of soft pine twigs, over which a blanket was spread. Two forked sticks were then set upright in the snow to the windward of the centre, and across them a horizontal pole was laid, and extending from this to the snow a thick covering of pine bushes was placed, forming a sort of roof that shielded us perfectly from the wind. This arrangement, with good fires at the bottom of the pits, enabled us to keep tolerably warm during the coldest nights. We suffered more from the cold during the daytime, and it was while marching that the men froze their feet.

From some cause or other which was incomprehensible to me, the men were often attacked with violent cramps in the stomach, even before they commenced eating mule meat, and the symptoms in all cases were nearly the same. I invariably administered for it a dose of about twenty grains of blue mass, which afforded temporary relief, but on the second or third day following the complaint generally returned in a more aggravated form than at first, I then gave another dose of about thirty grains of the same medicine, which never failed to effect a permanent cure.

After I had placed Miguel in the position of guide, we struggled along up the western slope of the mountains as rapidly as the snow and our exhausted condition would permit, and, at the expiration of ten days, found ourselves upon the summit of a mountain, which the guide pronounced the long-looked-for Cochetope Pass— that Mecca of our most ardent aspirations.

Although I was by no means certain he was right, yet I was much rejoiced, and I now felt in a great measure relieved from the burden of responsibility which had given me such anxiety and distress of mind during the last twenty days and nights.

From the crest of the great continental vertebral column of the Rocky Mountain chain, with one foot standing upon the earth drained by the waters of the Pacific, and the other upon that from which flowed a tributary to the Atlantic, (Several paths cross the Cochetopa Pass area and it is hard to determine which was used by the Marcy expedition. They would have been aware of the creek flowing in a different direction.) we could see in the east, stretching off from the foot of the mountains, a vast plain, extending to the south as far as the eye could reach. This, the guide informed me, was the valley of the Rio del Norte; (The valley of the Rio del Norte referred to here is the San Luis Valley. The Rio Grande del Norte is the main body of water crossing the valley.) and a mountain, (Mount Blanca is the most prominent mountain along the east side of the valley.) which we could discern on the opposite side of this valley, apparently a hundred miles distant, he said was near Fort Massachusetts.

As we still had three good mules remaining, I determined to send forward Mariano and Miguel to Fort Massachusetts, to bring us back supplies, as we were now reduced to a state bordering on starvation. Accordingly, I wrote a letter to the commanding officer, telling him our situation, and requesting him to forward us succor as soon as possible.

FORT MASSACHUSETTS, NEW MEXICO, IN 1852.

Fort Massachussets was built in 1852 on Ute Creek, east of Mount Blanca, to protect the settlers in the San Luis Valley from the Indians. The photo is from Dewitt C. Peters book *Kit Carson's Life and Adventures.*

These men took the good mules and started, and we followed on their tracks, expecting they would return to us with the supplies in about six or seven days; but we continued on the trail, (The snow would have hidden any evidence of a trail, but the North Branch of the Old Spanish Trail descended Saguache Creek and crossed at the north end of the San Luis Valley. The East Fork of the North Branch followed the west side of the Sangre de Cristo Mountains south to Fort Massachusetts.) until finally the snow had covered it up, so that we could no longer see it, and at length, after ten days, as the men did not return, we concluded they must have perished or been lost. On the eleventh day we reached the extended valley (Saguache Valley enters the San Luis Valley from the northwest as one descends from Cochetopa Pass along Saguache Creek.) at the base of the mountains, and, for the first time in thirty days, found a little dry grass appearing above the snow. As our few remaining mules were greatly famished, I concluded to make a halt for a day at this place and let them graze. We had not yet seen a human being outside of our own party since we left Grand (Gunnison) River, thirty-one days before, and we were all anxiously looking out for the return of our messengers from Fort Massachusetts. Nothing appeared, however, until near sunset, when one of the soldiers, upon an elevation near camp, cried out, "There comes two men on horseback;" and, sure enough, in a few moments, up galloped our long-absent companions upon fresh horses, firing their revolvers, and making other demonstrations of joy.

We knew from their fresh horses that they had reached the fort and that we were now saved, and the exhibition of joy manifest among the command exceeded any thing of the kind ever beheld. Some of the men laughed, danced, and screamed with delight, while others *(and I must confess I was not one among the former)* cried like children. I had not slept half an hour at a time for twenty days and nights, and was reduced from 170 to 131 pounds in weight, and, of course, my nervous system was not at that juncture under very good control. My joy was too great, under the circumstances, to find utterance in noise or levity; on the contrary, I mentally offered up sincere thanks to the Almighty for delivering us from the horrible death of starvation.

The mere accident of Miguel's happening to be with us, without any doubt, saved our lives, as without him we could never have found the pass, and must have perished in the mountain.

As soon as Mariano arrived he was surrounded by the men, eagerly entreating him for tobacco, when he produced a large plug of Cavendish, and threw it among them. It was in an instant torn to pieces and distributed, but one man had been omitted in the division, and I heard him offer ten dollars, or a month's pay, for a quid.

Mariano informed me that he had delivered my letter to Captain Bowman, the commanding officer at Fort Massachusetts, who at once dispatched three wagons with supplies for us; that these wagons left the fort with him, and were then probably about fifty miles back, as he had come very rapidly. I at once turned him back, with an order for the man in charge to drive night and day until he met us; and early on the following morning we resumed our march, and had not gone over ten miles, when, much to our delight, we met the wagons, and immediately went into camp. I was obliged to guard them very closely, to prevent the men from getting at the provisions, as I was fully aware of the danger of overeating after long abstinence.

Among other things which Captain Bowman had kindly sent me was a jug of brandy, and, as I thought this a proper occasion to indulge my men in the good cheer that they had been so long deprived of, I issued to each of them a moderate drink of the liquor, but, much to my astonishment, in a short time many of them were very much under the influence of it, and some even crazy drunk. It had acted upon their empty stomachs much more potently than I had anticipated, but I felt no inclination to censure them for this; on the contrary, I entertained a feeling somewhat similar to that of General Jackson when a charge of drunkenness was made to him against an officer who had rendered conspicuous services in the war of 1812, and he replied that Colonel C.'s gallant conduct in battle authorized him to continue drunk during the remainder of his life, if he thought proper. I conceived that my men had a perfect right to get drunk after what they had endured.

We had a most luxurious supper, and all enjoyed it hugely; but during the night, several of the men, not feeling satisfied with the soup I had thought it wise to confine them to, had gone to the wagons and prevailed upon the sentinels to allow them to take enough to gorge themselves so much that the next morning found them suffering most excruciating torture, and one of the poor fellows died the next day.

On the fourth day after this we marched into Fort Massachusetts, and were most hospitably received by the officers and soldiers of the garrison, who supplied us with clothing, provisions, and every thing else we needed.

As we approached the fort, one of the officers complimented us by saying that he took us for a band of prairie Indians. Not more than one half of the men had any caps, and but few had any remains of trousers below the knees. Their feet were tied up with mule hides, pieces of blankets, coat-tails, etc., and they certainly were rough and ragged-looking specimens of United States soldiers. As for myself, I am confident my own wife would not have recognized me. I had set out from Fort Bridger with a wardrobe of stout material suited to the rough work which I expected to encounter, but I had divided this among my destitute men until I was myself reduced to a scanty allowance. Among other garments I had remaining was a soldier's overcoat, from the skirts of which I was in the habit of cutting off pieces to patch my pants and stockings; and as rents in these were of every-day occurrence, by the time I reached the fort there was but very little left of my original coat-tails.

Mariano and Miguel, whom I had sent forward with the message to the commanding officer, had experienced great suffering from hunger upon their trip, and had been obligated to kill one of their mules for food before they arrived at the fort.

Mariano took lodging with a Mexican living in the fort, and immediately ordered a bountiful supper, which he said he devoured with exceeding gusto, and called for more. After this had been disposed of, he says he smoked his pipe and related incidents of his journey to the family until about nine o'clock, when he began to feel hungry again, and offered the hostess two dollars if she would cook him another supper, which she willingly did, and he again did ample justice to its merits.

This he thought would suffice him until morning. Accordingly, he laid dawn and went to sleep; but during the night he awoke, and to his surprise, found himself again very hungry. The family were all abed, and asleep at this time; the fire was out, and he was loth to disturb them, and he endured the cravings of his appetite for some time; but at length, not being able to stand it any longer, he called out to the woman of the house, telling her if she would be so kind as to get up and cook him one more supper he would give her five dollars. This tempting offer had the effect he desired, and he ate the fourth repast, which he smilingly informed me enabled him to worry through the remainder of the night.

Some of my readers may be incredulous regarding the powers of Mariano for accomplishing such gastronomic feats; but when it is considered that he was a half-breed Indian, and had been trained to their habits from infancy, it will not appear at all surprising to those who are familiar with Indian life.

From Fort Massachusetts we marched to Taos, New Mexico, (Just north of San Luis, Colorado the Old Spanish Trail and Taos Trail/Trappers Road become one and the same. This was the main trail to and from the settlements in northern New Mexico.) where I paid off the citizens of my party, and of these Mariano received some five hundred dollars for his arduous and valuable services, which I thought would prove sufficient to supply all his wants for a long period; but my credulity was greatly taxed on the following morning when he told me his money was all gone, and asked me for a loan of five dollars. I said to him, "Is it possible you have been robbed?" He replied, No, but me lose him all at monté, messieur." I gave him the modest loan he solicited, accompanied with a injunction against visiting the monté bank again.

He thanked me for the advice, but at the same time observed, raising his eyes and shrugging his shoulders, "Maybe some time me win, messier."

A few days after this I dispatched him back to Fort Bridger, via the South Pass, with a letter to General Johnston reporting our arrival in New Mexico. The return journey by the general for his services.

As it may be a subject of some interest to those who should ever have occasion to travel through deep snow to know the relative qualities of different animals, and their powers of endurance in this description of work, I will remark that I set out upon this journey with horses, mules, and oxen, the latter to be used as food.

I found, as soon as we struck snow three feet deep, that the mules directly became disheartened, laid down, and would not exert themselves. The horses seemed more ambitious, and would push their way through the snow as long as possible; but they soon became weary, and gave out from exhaustion; while the oxen slowly and deliberately plowed their way through the deep snow for a long time without becoming jaded. Moreover, they seemed to derive much better sustenance from the pine leaves, and from browsing upon other trees, than the horses and mules. I am so well satisfied upon this subject that, if I was ever obligated to make another journey over the mountains in winter *(which God forbid)*, I would take no other animals but oxen. They could be packed with luggage, and used as beef when required. There is also less danger of their stampeding or being stolen by Indians than with horses or mules.

13

1858/WILLIAM WING LORING

W illiam Wing Loring was born December 4, 1818 at Wilmington, Delaware to Reuben and Hannah *Henan* Loring. Little is known of the early years of William. His family moved to Saint Augustine, Florida in 1823. In 1832, William, fourteen years of age, volunteered for service in the Florida Militia. By the end of the Seminole War he had been promoted to Second Lieutenant.[1]

After his service in the Seminole War, William Loring attended the Alexandria Boarding Academy in Alexandria, Virginia where he completed his preparatory schooling before studying law at Georgetown College. Returning to Florida, he practiced law in Saint Augustine in the law office of Senator David Yulee. It seemed that Loring was headed for a career in politics when he served three years in the Florida Legislature, but in 1845 when he ran for the Florida Senate, he was defeated.[2]

In 1846, Congress authorized the formation of a regiment of Mounted Riflemen to protect the new Oregon Territory. Before the troops could take the field, Congress declared war on Mexico. Loring was commissioned Captain on May 27, 1846 and on February 16, 1847 promoted to Major. In the fighting in Mexico, Major Loring was promoted Lieutenant Colonel for gallant and meritorious service in the battles of Contreras and Churubusco, Mexico. During the battle of Chapultepec, Mexico he was wounded in the left arm and it was amputated. After this battle he was promoted to Colonel.[3]

After the Mexican War, Loring took his Mounted Rifles to Oregon. Loring led five companies of Mounted Riflemen and one hundred seventy one wagons along the Oregon Trail. Loring was in command of the Eleventh Military District in Oregon for several years before he was transferred to Fort Union, New Mexico.[4]

While stationed at Fort Union, New Mexico, Loring received orders to accompany Randolph Barnes Marcy and his troops to Utah Territory. After the Mormon War was settled, Colonel William Loring returned to New Mexico along the North Branch of the Spanish Trail. Loring's command which made this trip consisted of three-hundred men and fifty wagons.[5]

The following officers left Fort Union in the spring and returned to New Mexico with Colonel William Loring in the fall: Captains A. W. Bowman and John Trewitt, Lt. A. N. Shipley, Lt. C. D. Hendrea, 3rd Infantry, Lts, Alex. McRae, I. G. Tilford, C. H. McNally, and I. Y. D. Dubois, Rifle Regiment, Sergeant Charles Meinhold, Co. K Rifle Regiment, Dr. I. H. Kellogg, acct'g asst. Surgeon and Mr. Antonine Leroux guide.

From Camp Floyd to Fort Union, Lieut. Shipley acted as Adjutant, Lieut. McNally as A.A. Q. M., I. G. Tilford A.A. C. S., and Lieut. DuBois as Topographical Officer.

Loring left Camp Floyd, located at the present-day town of Fairfield, Utah, on July 19, 1858. The expedition traveled south through Cedar Valley and as far south as Castle Dale where they joined the Spanish Trail. After crossing the Green River, the expedition continued east along the North Branch of the Spanish Trail. They crossed the Colorado River in present-day Grand Junction on August 17, 1858 and followed the Gunnison River to the east. After crossing the Uncompahgre River and traveling up Cedar Creek, somewhere near present-day Cimarron, Colorado, they met a party of pioneers traveling west. They crossed Cochetopa Pass into the San Luis Valley. At the present-day town of Saguache, Colorado they turned south along the West Fork of the North Branch. Loring traveled south along the West Fork and soon after crossing La Garita Creek turned to the southeast. Reaching the Rio Grande del Norte, Loring stayed of the north side and continued east. When the Rio Grande turned south, Loring turned to the southeast, crossing Costilla Creek west of the town of Costilla, New Mexico. Just north of Red River (Questa), New Mexico Loring reached the East Fork of the North Branch of the Old Spanish Trail which he followed south as far as Taos, New Mexico. At Taos, Loring left the Spanish Trail and turned east crossing the Sangre de Cristo Mountains to Fort Union.[6]

At the outbreak of the Civil War, William Wing Loring resigned from the United States Army and became a General in the Confederate Army. General Loring crossed Texas by stagecoach to Richmond, Virginia where he joined his old friend, General Robert E. Lee. General Loring received orders assigning him the command of the Army of the Northwest where he was to keep the Union Army from crossing the Allegheny Ridge.[7]

After commanding troops fighting through the Civil War, Loring surrendered to General Sherman in April, 1865. Loring took up residence in New York until 1869 when he left the United States and joined the Egyptian Army. He assumed command of all of the Egyptian Coastal defenses in 1870. After serving several years as an officer in the Egyptian Army, Loring returned to the United States.[8]

Returning to Florida, Loring became involved in politics as a campaigner for the Democratic Party. He also helped in the promotion of railroads. Loring published a book on Egypt and then began lecturing on his travels in Egypt. He also began gathering information for a book on his Fifty Years a Soldier. However, on December 30, 1886 Loring died in New York City after a short illness.[9]

Camp at a Spring, Aug. 4th.

Left camp without water 9 a.m. In two miles came to water in a rocky tank formed in the bed of an arroya. With little difficulty a tank can be made to hold water in abundance, it is not now permanent. Grass and wood in abundance. A good ridge road for about six miles, heavy sand 3 miles. Road still sandy 1¾ miles to camp. The spring is large and water good, plenty of wood but scarcity of grass, by following down the bed of the creek it is more abundant. There is a trail 3 miles nearer for horsemen from Rocky Bank to this spring. Saw the course of White River yesterday and today, about ten miles distant. It empties into Green River about 3 miles above and St. Raphael 8 miles below the crossing. The mountain forming the great cañon through which Green River runs has been in view several days, also Salt (La Sal) Mountain distant in the southeast. Leroux pointed the direction of Captain Gunnison in '53 up White (Price) River, no remains of the road. From observation we are confirmed in the opinion that a road can be made up White (Price) River to Salt Lake Valley, by the way of Provo Fork or Hubble Creek, possibly the Spanish Fork. General course about east, a few points south and very winding. Distance, 12¾.

Green River, Aug. 5th.

Left spring 5 a.m. In places for five miles the sand is heavy. With some labor a ridge road can be made to avoid it. Five miles from this over a good ridge road there is water in springs in the bed of an arroya, that to the right of the road is the best for animals, and here you find grass, the one to the left was used by the men, it is salty and not good and is only drank when thirsty. Rested here 3 hours. The road is good 7½ miles to Green River, the best grass not abundant, is below, some in an arroya a little way back. Grass is also reported still farther below. The course of Green River is about southeast and 4 or 5 miles from where it comes out of the cañon. The bottom of the river is extensive and thickly covered with cottonwood. General course east by south. Distance, 18.

Aug. 6th.

Remained in camp to rest animals and repair train. A number of Sivareeche

Utahs came into camp, they are very destitute. Say they are not friendly with the Mormons. Cut the bank of Green River and prepared the ford for tomorrow.

Aug. 7th.

Crossed Green River today, the best ford is 1¾ miles above. (The crossing on the Green River is three miles above (north) the present-day town of Green River, Utah. The island used in crossing is still very obvious in the middle of the river.) Upon striking the river you go to the lower end of a small pebbly island near the center of the river, slightly against the current, then with the current diagonally for the opposite side, where there is a good shore to come out, the crossing is little over the ¼ of a mile, camped on elevated ground. Opposite to camp, about 1 mile from the river, grass though scanty may be found. Finding Green River fordable and satisfied that the rivers in advance are so too, we have determined to leave the flat here, which was brought with us from Camp Ford. Cottonwood trees on both sides of the river are large and can be used for flats, bringing plank with you to complete it. We had with us on our wagons, 500 feet. With the aid of cottonwood made a flat 23 feet long and 12 feet wide, crossing the south fork of the Platte River. Eight hundred or 1000 feet on these expeditions ought to be carried. Salt Mountain bears southeast from this camp. Distance, 2½.

13 Mile Spring, Aug. 8th.

Left camp on the eastern bank of Green River at daylight. For a few miles the road is winding and several arroyas to cross, then a straight and very good road to camp. The water is slightly salt, the best is at a spring in a deep arroya, two and ½ miles above there is another spring. Good grass one mile in advance of us, sage bushes for fuel. Country today barren. Salt Mountain bears south of east. Elk Mountain (Elk Mountain today is what we call Grand Mesa, obviously a land mark used by travelers going from west to east.) now in view, north of east, Santaria Mountain west of north. Rocky mount west side of Green River near our encampment while there, a little north of west. Course today southeast. Distance, 13.

An Arroya, Aug. 9th.

Left camp at daylight. Passed between two rocky buttes, the left hand one is in the direct line to camp, struck the Mormon trail (The North and South Branches of the Spanish Trail joined near present-day Crescent Junction, Utah.) which left Green River where we did, but takes a long circuit to a spring 15 or 18 miles south of our road and more distant. At this camp the water is not permanent, good bunch grass within ¾ of a mile of camp, greasebush for wood. Country barren. Course south of east. Distance, 12.

The Water Holes, or Cottonwood Creek, Aug. 10th.

Left camp at daylight, over a broken country to a water hole 9½ miles, grass abundant, water does not look permanent. From here the road in places sandy and heavy. Crossed several arroyas, one with cottonwood trees growing in it one mile from present camp. This camp is situated between two mountain ridges, water is said to be permanent, grass is abundant. Course east by north. Distance, 20¼.

Grand River, Aug. 11th.

Left camp at 6 a.m. Two and ½ miles to Grande (Colorado) River. Camp is contracted, numerous cottonwood trees, the best grass is one mile above, when the river is low, good grass may be found on the opposite side. Several Tabareachee (Tabeguache) Utahs were in camp today. (Loring's expedition camped near the Horse Shoe Bend of the Colorado River near Cisco, Utah. This is also where the Salt Lake Wagon Road reached the Colorado.) Course northeast. Distance, 12.

Grand River, Aug. 12th.

Left camp at daylight. By taking it over the ridge at leaving camp you avoid ¼ of a mile of sandy road and intersect the one made by us. The first part of the road is rolling and sandy with considerable ascent, it is then more level, now then a hill. When you get within 3 miles of the river there is succession of hills, sandy and heavy pulling, making it laborious for animals. The bottom here is extensive with numerous large cottonwood trees, grass abundant and trout found in the river. The road from Green River taken by us is south of that taken by Gunnison, (While Gunnison traveled about two miles from the base of the Book Cliffs, which would have been north of present-day Interstate Highway Seventy. Loring's expedition probably traveled nearly the same route as I-70.) our guide thinking water scarce on the other and very sandy. There is another trail of the Mormons nearer the mountain. From observation and what guides and Indians say it is likely that a good road, escaping sand, with water and grass can be found by following Gray Mountain (Gray Mountain is we what call the Roan Mountains or Book Cliffs.) some distance north of our trail. The Indians say they have a farm near the mountain, at the head of one of the arroyas which we crossed since leaving Green River. When the country is examined a better road may be found with permanent water and plenty of grass. (As automobiles came into use, the need for permanent water and plenty of grass were no longer a concern and Loring's route approximates that of the modern highway.) With the information we now have we would, before leaving Green River, examine the country along the base of the mountain, even if permanent water could not be reached nearer than a mile or two, with a good road and plenty of grass it matters little. Course today north northeast. Distance, 13.

Aug. 13 and 14.

Remained in camp to cut a road on the side of a mountain ridge 4½ miles distant, the cutting is on a precipitous side and immediately above a deep gorge. Engaged more than two days with several hundred men, we succeeded in making a solid and permanent road, and with the exception of two or three slight ascents a very good one. The valley we are in is some six miles in length and two or three in width, surrounded on all sides by high mural precipices. Soil good and covered with large cottonwood trees and sage bush, grass abundant and numerous fish in the river. Since striking it, there have been similar valleys to the one described. Passing through this valley there are numerous Indian trails, leading to Salt (La Sal) mountain and to San Miguel and Dolores rivers. Grand River so far winds through deep cañons, its general course has been north. The mountains are mostly of sandstone with now and then flint.

1½ Miles Off Grand River, Aug. 15.

Left camp at 5 a.m. First 3 miles level road, two short ascents in a distance of 1½ miles to the mural precipice. From here to the top of the ridge it is two miles, ½ mile from the top of the ridge there is a steep descent and then one mile of gentle descent to the valley. Halted to give the animals the benefit of good bunch grass. The river is in too deep a cañon to give them water. In advance one mile the road passes through two rocky buttes resembling huge pillars of agate, back of them a short distance water is in an arroya, where men can get it and animals may be led to it. In the distance of five miles you first pass through a short cañon, and then over a soft road, in places sandy 1½ miles of level road with gentle ascent to a ridge, 2¾ miles of gentle descent and good road to camp, it is 1½ miles from the river. Owing to its steepness wagons cannot approach nearer. With abundance of bunch grass, sage for fuel, we prefer this camp to one on Salt river which is near, the water there be salt. However slightly tinctured injures animals while travelling. Gray mountain which has been in view since leaving the spring on the others side of Green River, is still on our left. We see about where Marcy crossed it last winter (I believe that Loring is mistaken at this point. See chapter twelve.) to Salt creek and where the Mormons left it to come this way. We are still more satisfied that a road with water can be found along the base of this mountain to Green River. Leroux says the Dolores empties into Grand River 10 or 12 miles below where we first struck it, and that San Miguel is the north fork and much the smallest. He thinks the best winter pack trail, with little or no snow, is south of Salt (La Sal) mountain crossing Grand (Colorado) River and following up the Dolores to its head, then around Salt (La Sal) Mountain and across spurs of the San Juan to the head of Rio Mancos, which empties into the San Juan, across the river to the Abiquiu trail, (Loring's Guide Antoine Leroux apparently felt that the North Branch was the better of the two for wagon traffic!) thence to that place. A command with pack animals can go through from Santa Fe to Camp Floyd in 25 or 30 days. General course first 14 miles north, the remainder east. Distance, 16¾.

Grand River, Aug. 16th.

Left camp at 7 a.m. Upon leaving made a considerable descent in 2½ miles, crossing a short plain to, Salt creek. The Mormon trail here passes up a dry creek north of east in the direction of Gray Mountain. Our road immediately after crossing Salt creek ascends a ridge and skirts the mountain buttes along Grand (Colorado) River. Near Salt creek bunch grass is abundant and fresh water is 1½ miles to Grand (Colorado) River where there are cottonwood trees, animals to be driven to it. The road to within 3½ miles of camp continues rough, crossing three or four narrow ridges, thence level and good. Near our encampment the river passes into a cañon "Caxagano" or Little Mountain south of it, Gray mountain continues to follow the course of the river, making a valley of 15 or 16 miles wide, barren with little but sage and grease bush on it, except near the river where the bottom, covered with cottonwood trees, is good soil ¼ to ½ mile wide. Course of the river is west. Eighteen or 20 miles distant is the canon of Gray and Elk Mountain, through which Blue (Colorado) River runs in a southwesterly course and empties into Grand (Gunnison) River. Just before getting to camp on the hills to the right of the road, bunch grass is abundant. Three miles further in advance, opposite to the lone cottonwood tree, blue grass covers the bottom. Course south of east. Distance, 9½.

Blue River, Aug. 17th.

Left camp at daylight. Level road and clay soil, good now but bad in wet weather. Good camps everywhere on the river, soil good and easily irrigated. Crossed the Mormon and numerous Indian trails. Blue (Colorado) River enters into Grand (Gunnison) River 3 miles below. (With no regard to size, most travelers considered the river that they were traveling near as being the Grand (Gunnison) River. Today (1997) we refer to the larger body of water as being the Colorado River.) Little Mountain bears southwest and Elk Mountain north of east. Rested from 11 to 4 when the command forded the river. (There were not many places where travelers could cross the Colorado (Blue) River. One of the best crossings is at 281/4 RD in Orchard Mesa. An arroya descends from the top of the 100 foot mesa or bank to the south edge of the river. The author met two people in Grand Junction who as children walked across the river at this ford during low water.) The ford commences on a pebbly bank which leaves the northern side and runs towards the center of the river. It is soon covered with water and is what the mountain people call a "riffle."

You continue in this direction until you get within fifty yards of a rolled stone island where you strike diagonally for the island on the opposite side, covered with cottonwood trees and grass. A stone having been placed near it to guide you, from here it is easy with a steep ascent to camp. The distance across is about ¼ of a mile. Our wood we get from the island on the north side *(opposite)*, where there are large cottonwood trees, there being none near on this side. One mile in advance bunch grass is very good. A bed of coal is near this camp. Course east southeast. Distance, 16¾.

On an Arroya, Aug. 18th.

Left camp at 7 a.m. Over a level road 1 mile to Grand (Gunnison) River where it bends in the form of a horse shoe, (By looking on a topographical map of the area you can locate this camp.) the bunch grass on the surrounding hills being abundant. We had our animals here last night. The banks are too steep to water them. Ascending from here a dividing ridge, gentle and hard, but precipitous and sandy in its descent, we came into a narrow valley about 2½ miles where there is a good camp upon the river, with wood and grass in abundance. The road then passes over a country cut up with several arroyas, requiring work. To one 4½ miles which comes from Elk Mountain with water and cottonwood trees, it is likely water can be had here almost any season in holes, it being muddy, bridged it. (This is probably White Water Creek which is crossed by Highway 50 today.) Found here one of Marcy's last winter camps. The road is then level and good to Leroux's (Kannah) creek, 4¼ miles. This is a fine little stream coming also from Elk Mountain with abundance of cottonwood trees, hill and bottom grass. Remained here from 11 to 4 p.m. Immediately ascending a ridge and soon after descending into a level and narrow valley, with a good clay road, to an arroya, 6¼ miles, in our front and on our right grass is good and abundant, the water is not thought permanent though the guide thinks it may be found in holes. One mile from us in a northerly direction towards Elk Mountain, there is a creek at its base in which there is always water. Between us and it he thinks Gunnison crossed the ridge. Grand (Gunnison) River is not far from us on our right, but its canon is so rocky and deep that it is difficult getting down to it. About 6 miles after leaving camp this morning passed the mouth of a small creek emptying into Grand (Gunnison) River, which the guide says is the _____ put down on the maps further below Blue (Colorado) River. On the ridge soon after leaving Blue (Colorado) River, San Juan Mountain is in view. The valley here has grown very narrow, high ridge on both sides. General course south. Distance, 18½.

Grand River, Aug. 19th.

Left camp 5 a.m. Country rolling, several high ridges, both steep, in the ascent and descent to water in a ravine 6¼ miles. Diverged to the left taking a ridge to avoid miry and low ground in the valley, in a short distance came to a temporary water hole where we rested, thence into the plain again to Double Creek, 7¼ miles. Abundance of grass, some cottonwood and likely permanent water in holes. Between here and the river you cross a ridge, gentle in the ascent but steep going down 1¾ miles to camp. The valley here is broad and rich, covered with every variety of grass and has numerous cottonwood trees, the mountains well covered with timber 10 or 12 miles distant. On-com-pa-gre (Uncompahgre) creek empties into this river about 3 miles above. (Robidoux Ford crossed the Gunnison River at approximately this location. See Nell's Topographical and Township Map of the State of Colorado produced in 1885.) Heavy rain with thunder and lightning this afternoon. General course E.S.E. Distance, 15¼.

On-com-pa-gre Creek, Aug. 20th.

Left camp at 8 a.m. Ford good, not more than waist deep and 100 yards wide—banks good. In 6 miles crossed a dry creek which empties into the Oncompagre with water in holes and at right angles with what we think must have been the Mormon trail. In 3 miles over a high, level and hard ridge road, came to a well beaten trail that is usually travelled by Indians and possibly the Mormons who were here last spring. Soon after by a gentle descent came into the extensive bottom of the Oncompagre. This bottom extends along the creek for 30 miles, & is in places 1 mile wide, covered with grass in abundance and of every variety. Numerous cottonwood trees along the stream, in the mountains cedar and piñon. The soil is rich, easy of irrigation and rains are frequent. This is in the center of the Utah Indian country and in the immediate vicinity of numerous streams with well timbered and fertile bottoms. Fifteen or twenty miles above there is an extensive valley, great abundance of timber and grass and is the favorite residence of the Utah Indians in the winter. The Mormons have for some time contemplated a settlement in this country. By taking a more direct course from our last camp to this, the distance can be shortened several miles. Saw the peak on the southern side of San Juan mountain, where Las Animas (a stream emptying into San Juan river) takes its rise. On the same side in the same chain of mountains the Rio del Norte also takes its rise; on this side the Dolores and other streams. Portions of the mountains are now covered with snow. Sent an express today to the Headquarters of Dept. of New Mexico with information of our march. General course about east. Distance, 12.

Oncompagre Creek, Aug. 21st.

Left camp 10½ a.m. Remained to let the roads dry, along the creek to a dry creek 8 miles. Here an abundance of berries. Left the bottom of the Oncompagre (The Nell's Map shows the road following the west side of the Uncompahgre River and crossing at Johnsons Ford near present-day Montrose, Colorado.) in consequence of a bluff coming down to the creek, and followed the dry creek ¾ of a mile, turned to the left and followed it up with gentle ascent a ravine ½ of a mile, then a pine ridge road 3 miles. Descended again to the bottom of the creek, 2¼ miles along it with good road to camp. At any time in today's march camps can be made. The bottom here is wider than below and like it covered with cottonwood and the finest description of bunch and blue grass, mixed with rushes. Wood and water convenient. One & ⅓ miles above there is an extensive senigilla covered with grass. At this camp is the best ford of the creek, a prominent butte of white colored sandstone marking it. The creek here runs about south. Little Mountain, Elk and San Juan Mountains and Grand River in view. This is a great resort for the Utah Indians, none have been seen by us. The gap we enter in our ascent of the mountains again bears about east. Out of it Cedar Creek comes. General course southwest by east. Distance, 14½.

Cedar Creek, Aug. 22nd.

Left camp at 10½ a.m. Delayed in consequence of rain last night, to let tents and roads dry. Sent a party ahead to cut out cottonwood and thick brush on the opposite side of the creek. Hard bottom on both sides, from where our camp to the opposite side one mile. In a very gentle ascent and level road entered the gap in 6 miles, and followed Cedar Creek 3½ miles to its first crossing. Found water in holes not enough for the command. Cedar along it and grass on the hills. In the next 2½ miles the cañon narrows, making considerable labor necessary to get the train through. Recrossed the creek and encamped on limited ground. The water here runs in a small rivulet for fifty yards and sinks, ¾ of a mile in advance to ravine on the right there is some grass and water, there we placed our animals, that on the left hand is our road. In 2½ miles, a short distance to the right, near the top of the ridge is a pond with abundance of water and fine bunch grass for a good camp. The mountain we are now ascending is called on some of the maps "On Compagre." Near our camp is where Marcy camped and *cached* a good deal of the property he was compelled to abandon last winter. General course east. Distance, 13.

Devil Rock, Aug. 23rd.

Left camp at 7 a.m. A party of pioneers in advance. (It is sad that more information is not recorded at this point! It would appear that Loring met a party of Emigrants traveling with a destination further west.) Cut the sides of Cedar Creek and the defile to the left, crossing it several times, and finally ascended the dividing ridge by a gentle ascent about 4 miles. Descent more difficult to a ravine where we found water in holes in great abundance one mile from the dividing ridge. Another ascent & then a sideling ridge to a permanent water hole, where we rested from 12 to

3 p.m., good grass and sage for fuel, with a few scattering cottonwood trees and a great abundance of wild ripe currants. From here crossed the ravine, digging down its sides. One mile before reaching Devils creek quite a steep ascent and corresponding descent. When you first strike the creek it runs west, high mountains in the north and east of it. The creek suddenly changing its course and running north between two mountains, forming what is called "Devil's Cañon." In the angle the bottom of the creek is covered with cottonwood. Our camp is in a bottom 50 yards wide surrounded by high mountains covered with fine timber, bunch grass near. General course east. Distance, 8¾.

Northern Fork of Devil's Creek, Aug. 24th.

Left camp at 7 a.m. Considerable labor in cutting out cottonwood, excavating and filling up ravines. Crossed it seven times in 3 miles, beds of rolled stone. As far as we could ascertain Captain Gunnison's trail led from here direct without difficulty across the mountains to Cedar Creek, near our encampment there. Our camp is near the Twin Forks, they rise in the San Juan, called by some Oncompagre Mountains, the one we are on runs west, the other north, both filled with speckled trout. The bottoms large and rich and covered with good grass and cottonwood. Abundance of ripe wild currants, buffalo berry, and black hawes. Rain today. Camped early to rest the animals and enable guides to go ahead and hunt out the best road. An Indian was seen today but he could not be approached. General course east. Distance, 3.

Cebolla Creek, Aug. 25th.

Left camp at 7 a.m. In 1½ miles ascended a mesa, crossed an arroya, passing through thick sage brush. Commenced in two miles the ascent of the mountain, gentle and winding near its top to a pond of permanent water 2 miles, good bunch grass. Another gentle rise and gradual descent to camp on Cebolla Creek 2½ miles. The mountains on either side very high and peaked, covered with pine and piñon, very fine bunch, blue, white and other grasses, with oats and flax. Rich black soil in the valley and on the mountain sides. The Cebolla here comes out of a narrow cañon south of us, its sides so covered with pine and piñon as to hide the view of its course, and runs north 3 miles, entering another rocky, narrow and precipitous cañon. This county seen from a height is broken and tumbled. Since entering the mountains grouse have been abundant, cold last night with white frost. Course varied from southeast to northeast. General direction east. Distance, 7¾.

Ruidas Creek, Aug. 26th.

Left camp 7 a.m. Commenced a somewhat gradual ascent to a mountain ridge ¾ of a mile to its crest. In the descent a distance of ½ a mile to Indian Creek there are two pitches 15 or 20 feet each, where our wagons were let down with ropes, double locking with the mules hitched. We subsequently found a better descent by going a little to the right. Immediately after descending commenced another ascent of ¾ of a mile to the crest of the ridge, steeper than the previous one, descent better to a mountain rivulet, up it ½ of a mile, in places miry, crossing it to the foot of another hill, somewhat steeper than those back, by double teaming can be ascended it is a ½ mile to its crest. From here you have a gradual descent through a small forest to camp. This creek 5 feet wide is a fine mountain rivulet, its valley though contracted is wide enough for camps, abounding in fine bunch and other grasses, wood on the ridges nearby. *(This applies to the creek we have passed today. We are now crossing the span of the San Juan mountains. The Sawatch mountain is in view today.)* The creek runs a little west of north, much better grass can be found passing over these spurs than those we have taken, our time being limited it has been out of our power to look them up. There is little doubt but that a good road can be made over them to San Luis Valley, bridging, maybe, Sagua (Laguna) Creek, shortening the distance at least 75 miles. (See chapter eight this is the route followed by Heap/Beale Expedition.) It was thought that evidence of Gunnison's trail was seen passing over the ridge, but very indistinct. Cold and white frost tonight. General course west of north. Distance, 5½.

Grand River, Aug. 27th.

Left camp at 6 a.m., following the ravine of the creek, crossing several easy hills and then the creek and a spring branch 1¼ miles. Passed over another easy hill and immediately commenced winding around the mountain on our right making 1½ miles, Grand (Gunnison) River in view in a deep cañon some distance below us on our left. Two cañon streams emptying into it from the north and Laguna (Lake Fork of Gunnison) Creek from this side. Changing our course more to the east, passed over a rocky, rolling & winding road, gradually descending 2½ miles, when the descent for ½ a mile to Laguna Creek becomes more precipitous, the creek which is crossed here is 20 yards wide, in a distance of ½ a mile this creek is crossed three times. Here you have an ascent of one mile, steep in places & a gradual descent of 2½ mile to a short ascent, then two miles of descent to camp, ¾ of a mile above and near the mouth of Tabawatche creek and also in rear of us among the sage there is good grass. Cottonwood on the river, and speckled trout in abundance. Two miles before reaching camp crossed a dog creek where there is good grass, and fifty yards above a fine spring. Rain last night. General course northeast. Distance, 13.

Grand River, Aug. 28th.

Left camp at 8¼ a.m. Crossed the (Gunnison) river 50 yards wide with bed good. Half a mile an ascent of 10 yards and crossed the river a second time today, bottoms wider, grass and cottonwood abundant. In 1¾ miles made a third crossing, here there is a good camp, passed over a ridge, gentle ascent, 1 mile to surprise creek, good camp. A gradual ascent turning to the right around a mountain ridge to a spring 2½ miles. A rolling road for two miles to Pioneer creek, a good camp & a good road of one mile to fourth crossing of the river today. The valley is level, five or six miles in length and 1½ miles in width, good grass, cottonwood trees at each end, trout in abundance. Rested here several hours. In 1½ miles commenced the ascent of a mountain ridge, ¾ of a mile to its crest, steep in four places. A gradual descent of 3½ miles to Grand River *(just before reaching the river crossed Phantom creek, it comes out of a cañon near camp and runs northerly into the river)*. The last part of the road today was in places sandy. The bottom here is large; rich soil and abundance of grass, cottonwood and willow, Antelope, Elk and Bear with great numbers of grouse, ducks, and speckled trout. Numerous trails and signs of Indians, from their movements they are frightened at our approach. The general course of the river here is south of west, saw evidence of Gunnison's trail today, but lost all trace of it at this river. A good road can be made from here to Beaver (Cochetopa) Creek across the ridge south of our camp, cutting off some distance. Very cold and frost. The course has varied. General direction N. of E. Distance, 14½.

Goochatope River, Aug. 29th.

Left camp at 7 a.m. Up the river 1½ miles, the soil deep in wet weather and difficult travelling. Crossed the river, banks and bed good. Continued up the valley, road gravelly and better to crossing again, which is good, three miles. Soon came to the valley formed by Grand River running east, its fork from the north and Goochatope (Tomichi), its tributary from the south, extending over 15 or 20 miles. Good soil, easy irrigation, good grasses and cottonwood trees, pine on the mountain sides, speckled trout in the streams. Antelope, bear and grouse, also recent buffalo signs and numerous Indian trails seen. Crossing the valley 4½ miles over a level road to Goochatope. Here near the Point of Rocks its valley narrows to 40 yards. Upon passing the point it opens again, good road 2½ miles along it, to good camp at cottonwood. Rested here 2 hours. Soon after leaving crossed and recrossed the river, good banks and beds. In 7½ miles, with the exception of two short mountain spurs, level and good road to camp. This camp has excellent wood, water and grass. Valley wide and rich soil. Abundance of antelope, deer, bear, grouse, ducks, geese and sand hill cranes, & also recent buffalo signs. Numerous Indian trails seen. Same description applies to the valleys throughout today's march. It is thought that a road could be made across the ridge south of camp today, to Beaver (Cochetopa) Creek, cutting off several miles. Saw Gunnison's trail today at the second crossing of Grand River but soon lost it. Ice last night and cold. General course east. Distance, 18.

Spring Near Beaver Creek, Aug. 30th.

Left camp at 6 a.m. Over good road 1½ miles to fork coming from the mountain on the left. Crossed it and in ½ mile beyond also the river; continued up it 1¼ miles and recrossed, in two miles crossed the Goochatope (Tomichi) again, following the valley 1¾ miles where we suddenly turn to the right and follow the valley of the Eagle Tail, one of its branches, 1¼ miles the valley opens again, numerous others coming into it. Here the command rested, good camps anywhere today. By leaving Goochatope at its first crossing of today, and following up a ravine near, it leads direct into the Eagle Tail Valley, (The trail left the valley after crossing present-day Tomichi Creek near Parlin, Colorado.) and cuts off 4 or 5 miles of the road. While here a large body of Tabawatche (Tabaguache) Utahs rode into camp, professing friendship and appeared very much alarmed that they would not be kindly received. We learned of them that recent New Mexican traders had been amongst them and told of our return through their country, and that it was our intention to make war upon them and that this was the occasion of their leaving the large extent of their country over which we have just passed. This band is the largest and most warlike of any in the Utah nation & occupy a fine country, rich in soil & game. They are nomadic and own large numbers of horses. A talk was held with them and they expressed themselves, notwithstanding their alarm, as very much pleased to see troops passing through their country. We leave Eagle Tail here and turn to the right, after passing over three ridges, at the base of the third, in 5¾ miles to the spring, by clearing out the holes good and clear water may be had for men, to the right about one mile from camp is the creek. With some difficulty animals can be watered. Saw today the ridge which is immediately opposite to our last camp on Grand River. No doubt but that a road can be made there, in a distance of 12 miles. (The original highway 114 did not follow down Cochetopa Creek as it does today, but followed the higher ground where Loring and Gunnison traveled.) Kachoom-pee-ache, a principal chief of the Tabawatche (Tabaguache) band, came with us into camp and remained during the night. Ice and very cold tonight. Course varied from E.N.E. to Southwest, general course south, southeast. Distance, 20.

Head Waters of Sawatch Creek, Aug. 31.

Left camp at spring 6 a.m. Crossed a rolling country to the valley of Bear creek, good camp 3 miles. Left the creek changing course from south to east and following up its fork, a small mountain rivulet, with a wide valley and gradual descent 8 miles to the cañon, leading to the west of Sawatch mountain. One mile in the cañon halted two hours at the junction of three cascades which come from the mountains, followed up the one to the right through which runs a small rivulet, by a gradual ascent, crossing it three or four times. Two & ⅔ miles to good camp at a Spring near the base of the mountain. With little difficulty in a direction south of west reached its summit (The old highway crossed North Cochetopa Pass much the same as it does today (1997). The author believes that this was the route also followed by Gunnison. See chapter nine) in 1¼ miles, the thick pine, balsam and aspen being cut out to enable us to drive. The descent more rocky, winding and timbered, but gradual, ½ & ⅓ of a mile to good camp, from the dividing ridge which separates the waters of the Atlantic and Pacific. There are two valleys in advance, one, 1½ mile and other 1 mile further, both wider and better camps. This mountain is a succession of buttes, rich soil, well timbered, with pine, balsam and aspen, and covered with good bunch and grama grass. The valleys of Goochatopee, Eagle Tail, Beaver and their tributaries are also rich soil, susceptible of cultivation and easily irrigated. A number of Tabawatchee (Tabaguache) Utes were in camp today, as usual very much impressed with the command passing through their country. Mustered companies K Rifles, A, E & F 3rd Infantry since arriving in Camp. Ice tonight. General course southeast. Distance, 16¾.

Sawatch Creek, Sept. 1st.

Left camp at 6 a.m. with some descent, crossing the rivulet frequently through timber, the road in places rocky to the valley below, 7 miles. The rivulet here empties into one from the north and together with others which flow into it from the valley. The course in the cañon E.S.E. the road then runs south ¼ mile, when it turns to the east and in one mile strikes the Sawatch (Saguache) Creek, crossing it, the bed and bank hard, followed it up over a slightly ascending and good road 4 miles, where we halted 2½ hours. With the same load and course continued one mile and then to the left, crossing several rivulets in a distance of 4¼ miles, to the second crossing of the Sawatch. After crossing turned to the right in an easterly direction ¾ of a mile, crossing several rivulet, then south to an excellent camp 2¼ miles. At all the bends in the valley of today, good soil, grass, wood and water. Pine, piñon, and cottonwood found in places. General course east. Distance, 21½.

Carnero Creek, Sept. 2nd.

Left camp 6 a.m. From here a good level road in a southeast course to the Sawatch buttes (The West and East Forks of the North Branch of the Spanish Trail joined near the location of the town of Saguache, Colorado.) 7 miles, and to the last crossing of the creek 1½ miles. Here there is a good camp. Speckled trout in the creek. The Sawatch runs in a northerly (Southeast) direction to the Lake in San Luis Valley. The same fertile soil and good grass continues. San Luis Valley is here about twenty-five or thirty miles wide. Captain Gunnison on entering this pass skirted the northern limit of San Luis Valley, passing the Mosca and Williams (Medano) passes. The objection to that way is the deep sand near Mosca Pass. It bears from the last crossing of the Sawatch, southeast. Rested several hours, changed direction to the south, passing near the south point of the mountains of the pass, over a gravelly road to a fine (Russell) spring, good grass and water, greasewood for fuel, 8 miles. Near the spring miry, just below good bottom. Continued with good road to Carnero Creek, (Remains of the Old Spanish Trail which Loring was following can still be seen south of Carnero Creek and between the La Garita Store and Church.) 9½ miles, abundant bunch and grama grass, water good and creek hard and pebbly. Willow for fuel. Timber can be had one mile distant at the mountain. From the camp to the Sawatch Pass is west of north. Williams (Medano) Pass north of east, Poncha Pass north, Mosca east, Sangre de Christo south of east. General direction south southeast. Distance, 25½.

Garita Creek, Sept. 3rd.

Left camp at 3 p.m. Good road to Garita Creek (The crossing was about where 38 RD crosses La Garita Creek today, Both above and below this point the creek spreads over a lot of marshy area. The Torrez Trading Post was built just south of La Garita Creek, reportedly in 1858. Why did Loring's party not mention this adobe building?) 3½ miles. Grass and fuel not so abundant as at Carnero Creek. Sent an express to Fort Garland. The crossing of the stream is in places miry, and like Carnero Creek, runs about north of east into the Lake. General course Southeast to South. Distance, 3½.

Rio Grande Del Norte, Sept. 4th.

Left camp 6 a.m. in a direct South Southeast course, (The Spanish Trail after leaving La Garita Creek traveled between two small hills which Loring does not mention. It is likely that they reached the south edge of these hills before taking a southeasterly course.) to a slough of the river 16½ miles—the road is level and good, country covered with greasewood. The bottom here ¾ mile wide, is covered with good grass, cottonwood and wild pea, the soil is fertile and extends some distance from the river. The same character of soil, timber and grass extends about 25 miles to Leroux's Pass, from where the river comes out of San Juan Mountain, and runs in a westerly direction. On our way to camp saw the cañon of the _____ Creek where it runs northerly out of the San Juan Mountain, and like the _____ which runs easterly flows into the south side of Rio Grande. San Luis Valley to Poncha Pass, its extreme northern limit, is about 70 miles, and from Leroux's to the Mosca Pass 75 or 80 miles. General course South Southeast. Distance, 16½.

Rio Grande, Sept. 5th.

Left camp 6 a.m. to river land, good grass and wood. Abundance of speckled trout. The valley still broad. General course North (South) of East. Distance, 6.

Fort Garland Day Camp, Sept. 6th.

Left camp at 7 a.m. Continued down the river for 12 miles and halted to rest and graze the animals. The first 6 miles the broad belt of cottonwood continued, since then there has been none on this river. (From the location, Alamosa, where the Rio Grande turns to the south, it is no longer lined with cottonwoods.) Here there is an excellent camp of grass, driftwood and willow for fuel—5½ miles over a road, in wet seasons miry, but now very good, to the meadow about 17 miles from Fort Garland, where the post gets an abundance of hay. Near this camp are successions of springs, willow and sage for fuel, grass excellent. The river valley still broad and soil fertile. Hail and rain today. Snow on the White Mountains east and San Juan Mountains west of us. General course Southeast. Distance, 17½.

Culebra Creek, Sept. 8th.

Left camp at 6 a.m. Ordered Captain Bowman and company, in accordance with orders, to Fort Garland. The road to the Trinchera 4¾ miles is over a sandy mesa, improved by the rain last night. Good wood, water, grass and soil. Crossed the creek, hard bottom, and passed over a similar mesa somewhat sandy and more rolling to Culebra Creek 10¾ miles. Crossed it and then an island ½ mile wide, recrossing the creek to camp, hard bed on both sides, good camping anywhere near the creek. Cottonwood in abundance, valley broad and soil fertile. There are settlements on this creek about 8 miles above. The road to Conejos passes near creek on the other side. Received an express from General Garland, Commanding Department of New Mexico, approving of our suggestion for the disposition of the Command, and congratulating us upon making so successful an expedition. Rain during the night. White and San Juan Mountains still covered with snow. General course S.S.E. Distance, 16.

Latos Creek, Sept. 8th.

Left Camp Culebra 7½ a.m. Passed over a high rolling valley, road tolerably good in any weather to Costilla Creek 10¾ miles. The valley broad with Cottonwood and not much bottom grass and tolerable grama on the hills. Crossed the Conejos trail for the settlements four or five miles above on this creek. Remained to rest and graze animals three hours. While here a band of over 100 Utah Indian warriors came into camp, dressed and painted for war. They said they were in pursuit of a band of Arrapahoes who they had heard were in the valley. From this, both good road to the Conejos trail 8 miles, which leads to Red River, and six miles to this creek, it is small with hard bed, grass tolerable above and below us, good water, and sage for fuel. Instead of going to Fort Garland from the head of the Del Norte and following the old road we have taken a direct course here, making a new road, finding good camps, escaping the Mexican towns *(always miserable)*, cutting off from 30 to 35 miles, and with equally as good a road. We intersect the Fort Garland road ½ mile in advance of the camp. Passed today the cañon of Costilla Creek, a road can be cut through it to Black Lake, intersecting the Taos and Fort Union road, and cutting off nearly 50 miles of the road now travelled between Fort Union and Fort Garland, leaving Taos a long distance to the west. A road can also be made from the Rio Grande where it comes out of the San Juan Mountains by skirting the mountains, passing the Aqua (Ojo) Caliente and so on to the Abiquiu trail 30 or 40 miles from Santa Fe, shortening the distance considerably. General course_____. Distance, 24¾.

Ascequia Near Lama Creek, Sept. 9th.

Left camp Latos 8 a.m. Crossed within 1½ mile two other creeks of the same name as that of our camp. In ½ mile from camp the Fort Garland road, (At this point, Loring reached the East Fork of the North Branch of the Old Spanish Trail. The Loring Expedition followed the East Fork south as far as Taos, New Mexico before leaving it and turning east to Fort Union.) and 9½ miles over a good road to Red River, passing through a Settlement near it under cultivation. Immediately after crossing the river ascended a steep hill over a broken country covered with pine to Lama Creek, 2½ miles. Another ascent more gentle 1½ miles over a similar country to camp. Grass good, but not abundance, pine thick, and water good. General course, south. Distance, 14.

Meadow Near Indian Pueblo, Sept. 10th.

Left camp 6 a.m. In 6 miles crossed San Christobal, descent somewhat steep, ascent better. This valley is well cultivated. Over another ridge and descended into the fine valley of the Rio Hondo, 4½ miles. It is highly cultivated in wheat and corn. From here over a hard and bad road 9½ miles to camp, 2½ miles from Taos. The valley of Taos is one of the largest, richest, and most highly cultivated in New Mexico. Wheat and corn are the principal productions, stock abundant. Course varied very much over the mountain ridges today. General course about west of south. Distance, 19¾.

Taos Creek Cañon, Sept. 11th.

Left camp 7½ a.m. Road passing through the city of Taos. Ordered Capt.

Trevitt and Lieut. Shipley, Commanding Compy F & S, 3rd Infantry, to be relieved from duty with the expedition and to proceed via Bargain (Burgwin?), to Albuquerque in accordance with orders. Passed through the settlements to the entrance of the Cañon of Taos Mountain 3 miles, crossing frequently the Cañon creek to camp 10 miles. The bed of the creek is hard, grass along the road coarse and not abundant, but better at this camp. With the aid of grain our animals have fared very well. General course east. Distance, 13.

Guadaloupita, Sept. 12th.

Left camp 6 a.m. Followed Taos Creek cañon 5 miles about north. Crossed the creek and ascended the dividing ridge of Taos mountain, ascent easy but steep in the ascent, road tolerable. In 4 miles crossed the mountain ridge to a fine little stream, good wood, water and grass. The road then turns a little south of east crossing several short ridges to Black Lake, 9 miles. The Lake is a succession of ponds and has for several miles in its vicinity good camps. The command today is encamped on a little stream running into the Lake, good wood, water and grass. Leaving the command, crossed several mountain spurs over a rough road and crossing Coyote Creek 6 or 7 times and following its course to the Guadaloupita settlement 11 miles. Good camps along it, fine timber, and grama grass in abundance. General course South. Distance, 29.

Fort Union, Sept. 13th.

Left Guadaloupita 8 a.m. Followed Coyote Cañon 3 miles East of South and then 1 mile to a Mexican Settlement. Here the road turns south and passes through in a short distance a narrow gap in a rocky ridge, it then turns south of east and passes over a fine prairie 9 miles to cañon and through it 1¼ mile over prairie to Fort Union. General course_____. Distance, 20¼.

Respectfully, I have the honor to be, your obdt. Svt.

(Signed) —W. W. Loring
Col. Rifle Regiment
Commanding.

14

1859/JUAN BAUTISTA SILVA

Juan Bautista Silva was born about 1809, probably in Santa Fe, Province of New Mexico. He was married in his early twenties to Doloritas *Martinez*. Juan Bautista and Doloritas *Martinez* Silva had six children, Juan Bautista, 1832; Jose Alcario, 1834; Manuel Nieto; Susano, 1839; Jose Juan; and Jose Leone.[1]

In 1859 Silva brought fourteen families into the San Luis Valley on the West Fork of the North Branch of the Old Spanish Trail. They settled at La Loma de San Jose.[2]

In the early part of the 1850s the area around Santa Fe was experiencing a devastating drought. The farmers were having trouble raising their crops to maturity. In 1851 Juan Bautista Silva and a party of men left Santa Fe and traveled along the route that in later years was to be called the West Fork of the North Branch of the Old Spanish Trail. They traveled northwest to the Rio Grande which they crossed just north of San Juan Pueblo. Then they followed the east bank of the Rio Ojo Caliente north to the settlement of Ojo Caliente the northern most of the frontier settlements. From here they headed north to investigate a route which would lead them to the Conejos Land Grant. They followed the route which had long been an Indian Trail along the east side of the San Juan Mountains (known as the Sierra de Las Grullas by the early-day Spanish. See chapters two and three.) They continued north from Ojo Caliente through Comanche Canyon, this route follows the west boundary of Taos County, to the spring west of present-day Tres Piedras. (See chapters one and two as this was a well-known camp site.) Just north of the spring they entered heavy timber in which they marked a trail to prevent having trouble finding it on their return. From here they skirted west of the No Agua country to the west side of Cerro San Antonio, where they camped on the Rio San Antonio. They followed the east bank of the Rio San Antonio north to a point where it turns sharply to the east. Here they crossed the river and continued north to the Rio Conejos.

Several attempts had been made to settle the Conejos Land Grant in the area of the Conejos River. In 1832 and again in 1842 Spanish settlers had moved north, only to be driven out by the Indians.[3] Silva and his party crossed the Rio Conejos and continued north along the foothills. Just south of the La Jara Arroyo they came to a spring which became known as Diamond Spring. Here they turned northwest to La Jara Creek, which they crossed and then continued northwest across the lush pastures created by the two rivers in this low land. After a short distance they crossed what became known as the Alamosa River and continued northwest across the sage-brush-covered hills. They traveled to the east of Greenie Mountain, where they came to another spring, which became known as Spring Creek. They went around the west end of this spring, as it creates a very marshy area to the east. Following the contour of the hills, they traveled northwest to Rock Creek and through a series of small hills where they crossed Raton Creek. From Raton Creek they followed a nearly level plain through more of these small hills. Just south of the Rio Grande they turned west, where they followed an arroyo through a gap in the hills to a site over-looking the bottomland of the Rio Grande and San Francisco Creek. On this small plateau they decided to make their homes. The party returned to Santa Fe along this same route. Probably somewhere in the area of the Rio Conejos, the Silva party was stopped by Indians and they were treated very badly although their records do not indicate exactly what happened. Often times when the Indians captured a party like this one they would take all of their personal belongings, horses, guns and clothing, leaving them to return to the settlements the best they could.

Guadalupe, the first permanent settlement on the Conejos Land Grant, was established in August of 1854. This brought to an end the long period where the farmers and stockmen stayed on the grant only during the summer months. These settlers from Abiquiu were under the leadership of Lafayette Head. They built their plaza on the north side of the Conejos River and called it Plaza de Guadalupe. The settlers fulfilled the requirements just in time. The Conejos Land Grant of 1842 re-quired that a permanent settlement be established within twelve years after the decree.

On May 6, 1859 Juan Bautista Silva and fourteen carretas pulled by oxen and mules left Santa Fe. Each of these fourteen carretas represented a family that was hoping to journey to an area where the pastures and game were plentiful. The carretas were loaded with corn, peas, farm implements and only the most necessary items. A small herd of sheep and goats were also driven along with the expedition. The party planned to kill game along the trail so as to conserve these animals. The caravan followed the trail which they had scouted eight years earlier. They were successful in killing rabbits which were used to make stew. They also killed a buffalo which was dried to make jerky. Near Guadalupe the Nestor Vigil family gave up and remained, hoping to travel to La Loma de San Jose later. The Silva party continued on to the north arriving at the site which had been chosen eight years earlier. They dropped to their knees and gave thanks to the La Conguistadora for a safe journey. They named their new home La Loma de San Jose.

May 6- June 6 1859

Diary and summary of a trek to a very distant country and dangerous one for those who would attempt to settle in a place of clear waters and meadows and pastures stocked with wild deer and elk.

With the faith of all placed in the pure St. Joseph, the most pure husband of the all conquering Virgin who is our light, with the grace of God we will arrive safely.

On the sixth day of May, 1859, after so much disorder, we set forth to where we hope the future of the fourteen families disposed to suffer the hardship of this long trip awaits us.

Those so disposed are: Juan Bautista Silva, and my brother Alcadio, and my nephew Professor Luis Alarid, Maria Refugio Alarid, and Jesus Maria Alarid, Antonio Jose and Soledad Ortega, Juan Francisco Chavez, Agapito Lucero and family, Hilario Atencio and family, Jose Manuel and Jose Pablo Martinez and families, Nestor Vigil who comes from El Rito, Francisco Ignacio Espinosa and family and Guadalupe Torrez and family.

Carretas of this type were the first wheeled vehicles used in the San Luis Valley.

This trip is very difficult, even with the ox-carts and oxen (Carretas, pronounced car-ray'-tah, are two wheeled carts made entirely of wood. They were the first wheeled vehicles to travel the North Branch of the Old Spanish Trail into the San Luis Valley. Manuel Segura brought carretas north on the East Fork of the Old Spanish Trail in 1787 and Juan Bautista Silva the West Fork in 1859.) and the teams of mules that with the fourteen carts carry the families. We carry the bare necessities, seed corn and peas, and we hope for meat wherever it can be found. We travel alert to the Indians and their treachery that in our first advance was so cruel.("Treachery and cruel on our first advance". What did the Indians do? It is a shame that Juan did not provide more detail!)

We leave Santa Fe because of the drought.

We have traveled for a week in that which is a deserted, difficult and rough territory and have not yet encountered bands of Indians, but there is no lack of alertness on the part of those who carry rifles. We camp circled for the night with only cooking fires.

We awaken every morning to see if we can find the end of the high mountainous route we are following.

With the help of the Virgin of Conquest our arrival will be one of happiness and a great future for all.

Still, we find ourselves in good health and eat well.

It has been twenty days since we left Santa Fe. We have seen bands of Indians in the distance, but they are not aware of us. (The Southern Ute and Jicarilla Apache occupied the area of the present day New Mexico/Colorado state line until about 1868.)

We have seen several buffalo, and a surplus of rabbits, so there is no lack of meat to cook. At the end of the day our backs were tired, but we prayed for another, and our sleep beneath the stars was profound, always giving thanks to the Virgin of the Conquest that she guides us well.

Just a noise is cause for alarm, but we have able and knowledgeable men, and all is put in order.(Ruida which means noise is the word used by Silva so I would assume that one of the carreta wheels became dry and began to squeal. The men probably removed the wheel and greased the wooden axle with fat from an animal that they had killed.) Our road worsens, and if we had not marked pines on our first trip it would be doubly difficult to follow the main route. (This same route had been followed by Vargas, Pike and some of it by Anza and Fowler, but Silva was the first to travel it with wheeled vehicles. Lafayette Head had brought eighty families of settlers to Guadalupe from Abiquiu, New Mexico over La Manga Pass to the southwest.) We determine that St. Joseph will be our patron Saint when we arrive and complete this act of our Savior.

The land is so beautiful and so bountiful that there will be happiness and plenty for everyone.

At the most, it would take us another two weeks, some thought, for us to arrive at our destination.

The first thing we do is give thanks to blessed St. Joseph.

Today we used the rifle to kill a buffalo, (The buffalo was probably killed near the Rio San Antonio south of present day Antonito, Colorado. Vargas in 1694 killed some on the same river east of Antonito.) and we expect to dry the meat in the sun.

The thoughts of everyone are in Santa Fe, and we hope that our relatives are praying for us.

The goats have given birth, and so they give us milk in exchange for the pasturage we find for them.

Today Nestor Vigil and family drop out, unable to go on, perhaps they will follow later. (Nestor Vigil stayed at Guadalupe which was then still part of New Mexico. Guadalupe was settled in 1854 on the north side of the Rio Conejos.)

The 1858 Año Rock was a marker on the West Fork of the North Branch of the Old Spanish Trail at the point where it crossed Raton Creek. This marker can be seen at the Rio Grande County Museum and Cultural Center in Del Norte, CO.

Little Lucy was confirmed and we are anxious to arrive at our destination, so rough is our journey. Perhaps we will arrive in one more day.

There are more impenetrable mountains, but our mules and oxen are strong.

Today, the sixth of June, we arrived at our destination, tired and dirty. (On June 6, 1859 the fourteen families arrived at La Loma de San Jose. The ruins of the settlement are located east and south of present day Del Norte, Colorado up on the higher ground just out of the bottom land of the old creek bed of San Francisco Creek. The creek was diverted and the old creek bed is now a ranch meadow.)

In the name of St. Joseph we made camp on the hill of St. Joseph and have knelt to give thanks to the great Virgin of the Conquest for having arrived safely.

Our first day everyone awakened and every family commenced the great task of fixing up their places. There is much work ahead, but it is a beautiful camp, with plenty of room. We have laid out the plan for our community on the Plaza de Alta, (La Loma de San Jose) as it will be called, and we will buy our sites, and as soon as possible we will build homes, and for the rest of our days we will give thanks to our Lord.

The Silva Ditch was built to carry water diverted from San Francisco Creek to Dry Pole Creek then on to the crops at La Loma de San José.

323

To begin planting the seed we have brought, we will have to dig the irrigation ditches in order to water the crops, and I and my brother Alcadio will be the ones put to this work, and we will call it the Silva Ditch. It will take years, but it will be accomplished.

The housewives busy themselves with the cooking and the children. My nephew, Jesus Maria Alarid is in charge of teaching them the catechism and of the school, the parents to pay him in grain, meat and young goats and in any way they can.

On arising, the entire day is one of work. Some cut firewood and pine for building houses and the jacal, (Church) which are of great importance.

The first houses built at this site were jacals which are made of poles placed vertically in a trench. Adobe was then used to fill in the cracks between the poles. Additional poles were used to cover the top which was covered with perhaps six to eight inches of adobe.

Days have passed of great labor, but we fulfill our wish to have a place to live without encampment and to have the proposed jacal where we will be able to say our prayers of supplication to our good Creator.

We find ourselves very happy in our situation, We have plans for fourteen houses, and they will be of adobe. (Today the foundations of eighteen adobe homes can be seen at this site.)[4]

Having so much work to do, I have not written much. Our days are what we hoped they would be, and so much to do that our days are of faith and enjoyment of a happy life, all pleased with what we have accomplished and with what is yet to be done, because now it is turning cold. The sheds and fences will keep the animals well.

Today is the day to celebrate what we have accomplished, Professor J.M. Alarid has given a children's program, and we have enjoyed, and we give thanks to the Virgin of Conquest who brought us with her guidance to this success. Our days are filled with happiness and we shall continue going forward until our plan for the Silva Ditch and good homes for each family are accomplished by the will of St. Joseph and our Virgin of Conquest.

—By *Juan Bautista Silva,*
July 20, 1859
Thanks be to God.

15

1859/ALBERT D. RICHERDSON

Albert Richerdson traveled throughout the west for a period of ten years from 1857-1867 keeping notes on what he saw in his travels. On his return to the east in 1867 he published his notes in a book titled *Beyond the Mississippi*.

In 1859 he traveled north from Santa Fe, New Mexico on the East Fork of the North Branch of the Old Spanish Trail. Richerdson had hoped to return east along the Santa Fe Trail to Kansas City, but the Kiowa Indians were raiding along the trail. The Kiowa had captured the last two east-bound stage coaches and killed the passengers. As the Santa Fe Trail was blocked and seemed that it might be for months, Richerdson planned to travel north on the Old Spanish Trail/Trappers Road. Richerdson, hoping to find someone to guide him to Taos, became lucky and met Kit Carson in the dining room of the hotel where he was staying and traveled from Santa Fe to Taos with Carson.

Miners were arriving in Taos, everyday, leaving the colder climate near Denver to spend the winter months in New Mexico. Richerdson, after inquiring from the travelers about the trail north, finally consulted Kit Carson as to its safety. Richerdson left Taos, on October 25, 1859. Kit Carson rode with him for an hour to show him Mount Blanca to be used as a landmark in his route north. He traveled north on the Old Spanish Trail/Trappers Road spending the first night at Charles Beaubean trading post at Rio Colorado (the present-day Red River at Questa, New Mexico). He continued north through the small ranches and farms, impressed by the yields of the corn and wheat in the irrigated fields. He spent the second night at the trading-house of a German emigrant, Mr. Posthoff at Costilla, New Mexico.[1] This place was part of the Sangre de Cristo Land Grant owned at this time by Charles Beaubien. Stephen Luis Lee and Narciso Beaubien were the original owners. Both residents of Taos, they petitioned Governor Manuel Armijo of Santa Fe, New Mexico on December 27, 1843 for land that later became Costilla County in Southern Colorado. The Grant was authorized on January 12, 1844 by Governor Armijo. The boundaries were paced and the grantees were placed in possession of the property.

Although groups of settlers tried to build homes and plant crops along both the Culebra and Costilla Rivers in 1845, they were driven out by the continual harassment of the Indians.

Both Lee and young Beaubien were killed in the Taos Rebellion of 1847 when the Mexican and Indian people revolted against the new United States Government. Charles Beaubien inherited his son's half of the grant. He then purchased from Lee's widow the other half for one hundred dollars.[2]

Carlos (Charles) Beaubien, owner of the Sangre de Cristo Land Grant, encouraged settlers to establish a settlement along Costilla Creek by 1849.

The Jacals road north of Costilla crossed the south end of San Pedro Mesa for travel between the mesa and the Sangre de Cristo Mountains. Richerdson stopped to rest and allow his horse to graze on Culebra Creek before continuing on to Fort Garland.

Fort Garland was named after Brevet General John Garland, commander of the 8th Infantry and the Military Department of New Mexico. It was established by the War Department on June 24, 1858. The site was leased to the United States Army from Charles Beaubien since this land was a part of his Sangre de Cristo Land Grant. At the time the fort was built, this location in present-day Costilla County, Colorado was in the Territory of New Mexico.

The fort was built by Company E, U.S. Mounted Riflemen and Company A, 3rd Infantry under the command of Captain Thomas Duncan of the Mounted Riflemen.

Twenty-five years later, on November 30, 1883, Fort Garland was closed. The last troops stationed there were Company A, 222nd U.S. Infantry under Captain Javan B. Irvine. After lowering the flag for the last time, the troops boarded the Denver & Rio Grande Railroad bound for Fort Lewis, near Durango, Colorado.[3]

Richerdson spent the night with the sutler at Fort Garland John M. Francisco. At Fort Garland he left the Trail and continued up Ute creek to the area of Fort Massachusetts before crossing the upper plateau east to Sangre de Cristo Creek. He followed Sangre de Cristo Creek/Trappers Road across Sangre de Cristo Pass to Pueblo, then continued north to Denver.[4]

October 1859

Leaving Santa Fe at ten our road was nearly all hills; led over barren plains and among snow-streaked mountains; but passed some rich valley-farms, with speckled ripening corn and plump wheat.

Turning our horses out to graze, we lunched upon bread and dried buffalo meat, and smoked our mid-day cigars upon the grassy bank of a clear stream, in the Cañada a battle-ground of the Mexican war. Starting again we struck the Rio Grande, (The Old Spanish Trail divided at San Juan Pueblo. The East Fork of the North Branch angled to the northeast toward Taos.) here an insignificant stream in a narrow valley. At four, P.M., the sun had disappeared; so we halted at a spacious adobe whose swarthy owner received us in great dirt and dignity. We performed our ablutions in the little acequia or irrigating canal; supped on mutton, *frijoles* and eggs and slept on floor-mattresses with yellow-haired saints and a pink-faced virgin staring down from the walls.

Breakfasting at daylight before our host was up, we left a quarter-eagle upon his table and started on. We galloped through El Ambudo (Embudo), (Embudo was also visited by Anza. See chapter three.) *(the funnel)*. We entered a dark cold canyon, its frowning walls crowned with odorous pine and hemlock. At two, P.M., sore in every joint, from the ride of eighty miles, equal to one hundred and twenty upon level roads, I reached Taos, and was soon housed under Carson's roof.

From Taos to Denver, three hundred miles due north, a lonely mountain trail led through the range of the murderous Utes. I lingered, hoping to find companions for the journey, but as winter was at hand no one was starting northward. Miners were daily arriving *from* Denver to pass the cold months in (New) Mexico. Some declared the trail as safe as Broadway. Others pronounced the journey madness, and its inevitable price a lost scalp. As the Fort Smith fever had left my crown bare, taking this would be no easy matter. But I felt like the Scotchman about his head, that while 'nae much of a' scalp it would be 'a sair loss' to me. A third class of immigrants had no apprehensions about the savages, but laid great stress upon the danger of perishing among mountain snows.

Despairingly I appealed to Kit Carson as final authority. He replied with a smile that the road, (From Taos, New Mexico to San Luis, Colorado the Taos Trail/ Trappers Road and the Old Spanish Trail are one and the same.) always perilous to a stranger unfamiliar with Indian warfare, was more so toward winter than during the warm months. Just now too there was some possible danger from the Utes. Still if I deemed the trip necessary he had little doubt that I could make it successfully.

I bought a thin, iron-gray pony, two years and a half old, so Liliputian that satirical friends advised me to start upon a rocking horse instead. Even Carson was skeptical of the little brute's capacity. My own confidence was serene, based upon long experience with the hardy creatures, during which I had never known one to die from overwork or any other cause. The entire cost of pony, saddle, bridle, spurs and lariat was thirty-six dollars.

October 25, 1859

On the twenty-fifth of October, with Liliput almost buried under rider, heavy blankets and plethoric saddle-bags, I bade adieu to kind friends in Taos, and galloped away toward the latest El Dorado. Carson obligingly accompanied me for an hour. Pointing at an isolated mountain, (Mount Blanca.) a dozen miles away he said;

'Your general course is directly toward that butte.'

'Shall I reach it to night ?'

'Hardly! I see you have not learned to estimate distances in this clear atmosphere. Next time we meet, remember to tell me how long you were in getting to it.'

Soon he turned homeward and I was sorry to lose sight of his kind, trust-inspiring face.

After a solitary mountain ride of twenty-eight miles I dismounted at Beaubean's trading-post, beside a rushing transparent little stream bearing the name Colorado, so frequent in Spanish nomenclature. Beaubean (Beaubien) (Carlos Beaubien was owner of the Sangre de Cristo Land Grant. The grant covered most of the land from Mount Blanca south to the Rio Colorado or Red River and from the Rio Grande to the tops of the mountain peaks to the east.) was a Frenchman whom long intercourse with this mixed population had converted into a bewildered polyglot. With profuse bows and in a medly of French, German, Spanish, English, and Indian, he begged me to pardon his poor lodgings and his fare so unfit to set before a gentleman. As a sequel to this preamble he gave me a supper of mutton and eggs, the best meal I had eaten in New Mexico, served upon snowy linen, in a pleasant room. Then through the long evening I lounged in a luxurious arm-chair, reading before my cheerful fire with many glances through the skeleton window at tall snow-crowned mountains, with yawning black canyons between.

The dirt floor was smooth and hard. The mud walls, dressed with a trowel and whitewashed, could hardly be distinguished from the finest plastering. They were hung with pictures of saints, and crucifixes, curiously intermingled with views of horse races and cock fights. The mattress upon the floor, covered with fine blankets of whitest wool, was quite luxurious. That afternoon in a wretched hovel across the narrow street, a little child had fallen into the fire and been burned to death. Now shrieks and moans rending the air, showed that in one dusky bosom under all its rags and wretchedness the mother-heart was beating.

October 26, 1859

Soon after sunrise I rode on among scattered ranches with valley-fields of corn and wheat. Irrigation makes the parched, sandy soil wonderfully productive. In most wheat-growing States a yield of fifteen fold from the seed is an excellent crop. But this seeming desert often produces fifty fold and sometimes a hundred fold. It is not adapted to Indian corn on account of the cold nights. In winter farmers do not feed stock; the cattle subsist upon a wild sage so tall that it is seldom hidden by the snow.

Crossing the Costilla (Costilla, rib, was settled in 1849. In ten years it had grown. See chapter six.) river I dined at the trading-house of Mr. Posthoff, a German resident of gentlemanly manners and liberal culture, with whom I spent an agreeable afternoon and night.

Nearby was a Mexican grist-mill—not the human variety already depicted but yet almost as primitive. It is simply a horizontal water-wheel connected by an up-right shaft with the millstone one story above. The stone, revolving no faster than the wheel, grinds but slowly, and having no bolting apparatus turns out very coarse flour. There are a few improved steam mills in the Territory. Day's travel twenty-one miles.

My morning route over the desert abounded in wild sage, cactus, and great herds of antelopes. At noon as usual I broiled a bit of pork upon a long stick by my

Fort Garland was built in 1858 and was used as a military post until 1883.

little camp-fire, and made tea in my drinking cup. Liliput found excellent grazing on the banks of the Culebra (snake) creek. (Culebra Creek is mentioned in most of the previous chapters, the name has been in use a long time) The afternoon ride was delightful—among grand old mountains with ever shifting colors, water worn sides and whitened crests-a.

At last from a hill-top, I had a dim shadow-like view of Fort Garland far below, its adobe walls dotting the fair valley of a creek fringed with cottonwoods, and the Stars and Stripes floating over it. Late in the cold evening I reached it, after a day's journey of thirty-three miles.

The post-sutler Mr. Francisco (John M. Francisco later founded Fort Francisco, the forerunner of La Veta, Colorado.) was far-famed for his hospitality. Around his cheerful fire I found several gentlemen who brought the latest word of old comrades and new mines in the gold region. One told me that of seven intimate friends who resided in Santa Fe fourteen years before, he was now the only survivor. All the rest had been killed by Indians or in drunken affrays.

October 27, 1859

This morning I reached the mountain (Blanca) which Carson had pointed out

Travelers who proceed north along the East Fork of the North Branch of the Old Spanish Trail have this view of Mount Blanca but not from near Taos.

to me from Taos, the distance having proved three day's journey, or more than a hundred miles. Here my course turned eastward through the Sangre de Christo *(blood of Christ)* canyon, leading from the waters of the Rio Grande to those of the Arkansas. Its tall upright walls are worn by streams pouring down their sides, and streaked with elk paths.

The trail crossed the little (Sangre de Cristo) creek a dozen times in a single mile, and soon left it to follow another stream. Liliput climbed the steady ascent but slowly, for at that great altitude the atmosphere is thin, makes breathing difficult, and compels both bipeds and quadrupeds to pause frequently.

As night approached the air grew nipping and eager. I had trusted to luck for a camping place, and was nearly a day's travel from human habitation. But just before sundown I overtook two young adventurers with an ox team and a load of wheat. (This statement indicates that wagons were continuing to use Gunnison's Road which was built six years earlier.) Despite their rough attire and sun-browned faces, the moment they spoke, they betrayed Yankee origin and they proved to be natives of Medfield, Massachusetts. Gladly I accepted their hearty invitation to lodge with them.

We climbed wearily a long sharp hill and stood upon the summit (Sangre de Cristo Pass) of a high divide. Behind us, within pistol shot, were streams running into the Rio Grande del Norte, which rises among the eternal snows of the Rocky Mountains and continues its sinuous course to the tropical waters of the gulf. Before us were springs which feed the Arkansas; and far to the east over hill and dale, forest and desert, we could discern its wooded valley sixty miles away.

The scenery was inspiring, but the cold and approaching darkness were not. Descending a long terraced hill, we halted for the night. The wayworn animals were turned loose to graze; supper was cooked and eaten by a log fire; after a long chat, our couch was extemporized in the open air by spreading a blanket upon the frozen ground, and we huddled close under a buffalo robe, without even a tree overhead.

As the guest, my new companions had placed me in the middle where the temperature was endurable; though whether sleeping or waking I had a dim consciousness of cold. They found it intolerable, and often arose to warm themselves by the fire.

October 28, 1859

Soon after sunrise I bade them adieu and was again on the road. The first creek I crossed, though running water, was frozen so hard that it bore pony and rider, and gave me new appreciation of the intense cold of the night.

Thus far I had not forgotten the alleged danger of this solitary journey, and had plumed myself a little upon facing it. But now I met a miner from Pike's Peak coming *on foot* over the same route and bearing upon his shoulders his blankets, provisions, frying pan, ax and rifle. Our brief exchange of greetings showed that he regarded the journey as a mere pleasure excursion and it made me a little ashamed of myself.

Through the day, the mountain scenery was varied and pictuesque. After nightfall I reached Maxwell's ranch on the Greenhorn river. Ever since starting, I had anticipated here an agreeable and luxurious resting place. Maxwell had thousands of sheep and cattle, and his dwelling *(the only one within sixty miles)* was eagerly looked forward to by every traveler. To my sore disappointment I found that only the day previous he had removed his cattle and men to a distant ranch, leaving no soul here save one villainous-looking Mexican. This unprepossessing host wore a tattered hat, woolen shirt, buckskin breeches and moccasins; and his black matted hair shaded a face which would have hanged him before any intelligent jury. But he was the very pink of courtesy offering hospitality in bastard Spanish with unceasing genuflections of welcome clearly the *only* soap and water with which his person was familiar.

I tied Liliput in a ruinous out-building and gladdened his faithful heart with corn. The dwelling had a rough dirt-floor and was pierced with holes in lieu of doors and windows. Through great gaps in the roof I saw the deep blue sky and the twinkling stars. But a cheerful blaze glowed in the spacious fire-place, and mine host of the rueful countenance prepared a capital supper of broiled venison, biscuit, and coffee. Obsequiously declining my invitation to join me at the meal, and vowing that he would ne'er consent, he not only consented but did ample justice to his own cooking.

Spreading my blanket in one corner and directing him to make his bed in another, I lay down with one hand ostentatiously resting upon the revolver under my pillow. My clothing had become ludicrously ragged. I had carefully concealed my watch; and marvelous indeed must have been the cupidity which that wardrobe, steed, or equipment could excite. But I had been told again and again that an ignorant Mexican would kill a man any day for ten dollars; and if this peon was not a cutthroat his face would have justified a suit against Nature for libel. Studying it drowsily by the flickering light of the log fire I fell asleep.

October 29, 1859

Waking at three o'clock I instinctively imitated his example. But the jugular veins still continued perfect and the Mexican slept soundly under his sheep skin, until aroused to cook breakfast and feed Liliput for a hard day's journey.

Overwhelming me with thanks for a pecuniary acknowledgment of his hospitality, he uttered a vehement 'Adios Senor;' and I was on the road while the stars were yet shining.

Upon a mountainous desert I crossed the imaginary line which then bound New Mexico on the north. Later, when Colorado Territory was organized it took a slice from the northern border, and also included portions of Kansas, Nebraska, and Utah.

Before noon I descended into the broad rich valley of the Arkansas. (near present-day Pueblo, Colorado) Here the stream is a hundred yards wide, shaded with a narrow belt of tall cottonwoods, and its banks covered with waving grass. The river was like an old friend. I had journeyed sixteen hundred miles since leaving it at Fort Smith, eight hundred miles nearer the Mississippi, many weeks before.

Turning out Liliput for a grassy feast, I dined with the conductor of a Mexican flour train for Denver, a Maine Yankee who for twenty years had been roaming over the world by sea and land. Soon after, I struck the Fontaine qui Bouille (present-day Fountain Creek which dumps into the Arkansas River.) creek, and followed up its bank during the whole afternoon.

Spent the night at a pleasant ranch kept by an intelligent American family. It was homelike once more to be under a civilized roof and to encounter, for the first time during a journey of a thousand miles, women who spoke English. One of the ladies had been my neighbor in Kansas; but long roving had disguised me so effectually that for the first half hour she failed to recognize me. Day's travel forty-four miles.

October 30, 1859

Journeyed up the Fontaine qui Bouille directly toward Pike's Peak, which, with its dark wooded sides, and irregular turreted summit, towers far above all adjacent mountains.

Plump antelopes abounded, so tame that when I stopped my pony a long herd of one hundred and twenty-seven in single file crossed the path before me, within a stone's throw. Some were beautifully spotted and all exquisitely graceful.

Just before dark in the gigantic shadow of Pike's Peak, I reached a little sign-board labeled in bold capitals 'Colorado Avenue.' I had not seen a human being since morning, and the idea of a city in these solitudes savored of the Ludicrous; but there it stood, unmistakable evidence of civilization and speculation.

A mile beyond, passing around an intervening hill, I reached Colorado City, (Colorado Springs) founded a few weeks before, and containing fifteen or twenty log-cabins. In front of one stood an old Kansas friend, who came inquiringly forward and at last penetrating my panoply of dirt and rags gave me heartiest greeting. Day's travel thirty-five miles.

October 31, 1859

A morning visit to the curious Fontaine qui Bouille, *(fountains which boil,)* two miles from Colorado City, at the head of the creek I had followed up since leaving the Arkansas. The three fountains, bubbling up from the ground and not boiling with heat, are very strongly impregnated with soda. One, whose basin is three feet in diameter, seems to rise from the midst of a great rock which it has incrusted with soda to the thickness of several inches. A column of water nearly as large as the body of a man gushes up with great force. The supplying channel must be far under ground; for between this and one of the other fountains runs a fresh water creek twenty feet below their level.

The Indians regard these springs with awe and reverence. They believe that an angel or rather a spirit troubles the waters and cause the bubbling by breathing in them. Before going on war expeditions the Arapahoes formerly threw beads and knives into the fountain, and hung the adjacent trees with deer-skins and quivers as propitiatory offerings to the invisible deity. The Coloradoans mixed their flour in this water without adding soda or saleratus, and it made the lightest and best of bread. Mingled with tartaric acid and lemon-juice, the water foams like champagne, and is more palatable than that from any artificial soda fountain.

It is said to possess rare medicinal qualities. The railroad will make the spring a popular summer resort. The vicinity combines more objects of interest and grandeur than any other spot on the continent: Pike's Peak, the great South Park, the Garden of the Gods and the Fontaine qui Bouille.

Pressing onward toward Denver, I found still another old Kansas friend lunching upon the prairie under the shade of his wagon. After he identified me, we broke bread together and then fought our battles o'er again.

In the afternoon I crossed the high divide between the shining waters of the Arkansas and those of the Platte—an ascent so gentle that with the exception of two or three short hills, it is hardly perceptible. At night I came to a road-side fire beside an ample tent whose solitary sleeper rubbing his eyes, cordially offered me lodging; for hospitality is preeminently a frontier virtue, and every stranger is tendered food and shelter. My host was of a hunting party, and his two companions were seeking their stray horses. I turned Liliput—now foot-sore from his long journey—out to graze; and, thanks to the kindness of Colorado friends, who had stuffed my pockets with venison, was able to prepare an ample supper by the roaring fire. Then stretching upon the ground with saddle for a pillow, slept soundly after a day's journey of fifty miles.

November 1, 1859

At sunrise I was again upon the road. Soon after, from the summit of a hill I could see Denver distinctly, though it was more than twenty miles distant. A lady upon a spirited horse overtook me and accompanied me into the city. From visiting a sister at a saw-mill in the deep pineries she was returning home, a morning ride of twenty-five miles. Ruddy cheeks and a symmetrical form had rewarded her fondness for this health-inspiring exercise.

Descending easy hills over a sand soil we reached the Platte valley, for miles trenched and gullied by miners, some still hard at work and realizing five dollars per day to the man.

Passing many rude shanties for the sale of whisky and tobacco, along the well-trodden road, soon after noon we galloped into Denver. Here ended my mountain journey, the most enjoyable trip I had ever made. It removed the last vestiges of my Fort Smith illness. The whole desert and mountain region from the British Possessions to New Mexico, and westward to the Pacific, is one of the healthiest in the world. Rains fall only from July to September; the air is so dry that fresh meat cut in strips in summer, and quarters in winter, and hung up, will cure without smoking or salting, so that it may be carried to any part of the globe. In such an air lung and throat complaints have no chance. I have known persons supposed to be hopelessly consumptive, and only able to travel lying upon feather beds in ox wagons, who after crossing the plains and sleeping in the open air, enjoyed for years a comfortable degree of health.

Denver had developed wonderfully during the four months of my absence. Frame and brick edifices were displacing mud-roofed log-cabins. Two theaters were in full blast; and at first glance I could recognize only two buildings. When I left there was no uncoined gold in circulation; now it was the only currency—incontestable evidence that the mines were a fact. Upon every counter stood little scales, and whenever one made a purchase, whether to the amount of ten cents or a thousand dollars, he produced a buck-skin pouch of gold dust and poured out the amount for weighing.

'Praise the bridge which carries you safely over.' In spite of Kit Carson's incredulity, Liliput had brought me three hundred miles in seven and-a-half days' travel. He reached Denver with tender feet, galled back and a spot on each flank as large as my hand, made raw by the spur; for his many virtues were tempered by the vice of laziness. Still I disposed of steed and equipments at a sum which reduced the cost of the trip to precisely thirteen dollars. Liliput, placed in a ranch soon grew fat, and the next spring sold for a hundred and twenty-five dollars.

16

1867/JOHN LAWRENCE

John Lawrence was born November 15, 1835 in St. Louis, Missouri. Orphaned when he was six years old, he received what education came his way in an orphanage. At age fourteen Lawrence ran away and worked on farms in Iowa and Minnesota, breaking prairie sod using six yoke of oxen.

In return for his passage, Lawrence came to Denver, Colorado driving a freight wagon pulled by six yoke of oxen. He was then twenty three years of age. He tried his hand at mining, but soon decided that there was more money to be made by freighting from Omaha to Denver. In 1860 John Lawrence crossed Sangre de Cristo Pass into the San Luis Valley, arriving at Fort Garland with freight wagons. He traveled another thirty five miles southwest to the settlement of Guadalupe on the Conejos River.[1] In 1854 Major Lafayette Head brought eighty four families to found Guadalupe on the north bank of the Conejos River on the site of an ancient Indian village.[2] By the time John Lawrence arrived, the town was reduced to twelve families. Guadalupe was plagued by the high water of the Conejos River in the spring, the settlement was moved to the south side of the river, and the name was changed to Conejos.

Lawrence left Conejos on February 28, 1867 and traveled north on the West Fork of the North Branch of the Old Spanish Trail to Saguache, Colorado. After arriving at Saguache Lawrence and the people traveling with him measured off homesteads. The land which John Lawrence filed on is three miles west of the present-day town of Saguache and the house that he built is still standing today (1997). Lawrence farmed, raised livestock and accumulated nearly one thousand two hundred acres of land. At the height of his operation he claimed ownership to nineteen thousand head of sheep.

The "founder of Saguache county" accomplished much during his lifetime. During the Civil War, John Lawrence served with the New Mexico Volunteers at Fort Garland. Being an avid reader and having a good memory, he educated himself better than most of the men of the time. He learned to talk Spanish as well as the Ute language, which he would find useful many times. John Lawrence frequently served as an interpreter for the Mexican people in Denver. On one of these trips he drew up the bill organizing Saguache County. He was part owner in a hardware business. Lawrence served several terms in the Colorado State Legislature, several terms as Saguache County Assessor, County Judge, Mayor of Saguache, and Saguache County Commissioner. Lawrence also helped organize and build the first school in Saguache, serving on the school board twenty five years.

John Lawrence kept a diary for forty years. The excerpts from the Lawrence Diary that follow are just a few of those that mention travel on the early-day roads. These roads were part of the Old Spanish Trail which led to California.[3] The route that he used in traveling from Conejos to Saguache in 1867 was the same, route mentioned in chapter three, which Juan Bautista de Anza used eighty-eight years before (the West Fork of the North Branch of the Old Spanish Trail).[4] In Lawrence's frequent travels to the village of San Luis (La Culebra), they traveled to the east of Saguache, then along the west side of the Sangre de Cristo Mountains. This is the East Fork of the North Branch of the Old Spanish Trail.[5] The East Fork ran along the west side of the Sangre de Cristo Mountains although the term "North Branch" was not used until the 1950s when it was introduced by Leroy Hafen. This part of the North Branch was probably used by both Clovis and Folsum Man as evidence of both are found along the trail. That would make part of this trail at least twelve thousand years old.[6]

Also mentioned is the use of the West Fork of the Trail to the Rio Grande. It followed the north bank of the river to the southward bend and then went east to Fort Garland. This is the same route mentioned in chapter eight by the Beale-Heap Expedition.[7] The route to the west of Saguache to the Indian Agency is marked on an old survey plat map as the Old California Road. This was often used by the Saguache people to take supplies to the Ute Agencies at Los Pinos and the Uncompaghre.

February, 1867

In accordance with a command of God, which says, "In the sweat of thy brow shalt thou eat bread all the days of thy life," I, John Lawrence, having passed thirty-one years of my life, eating bread, and rather poor bread, in this way was anxious to change it for better, and as to make such change it was necessary to change from my old to a new home. I therefore changed from Conejos to Saguache, and that I may better appreciate such change, I was prompted to keep this memorandum, dating from the 28th of February A.D. 1867, being the day on which I started from Conejos.

February 28, 1867

Started from Conejos for Saguache with two ox teams and one horse team, loaded with wheat, oats, provisions, and impliments for farming, was accompanied by Sylvester Larus who had his *(wooden wheeled)* cart (Carreta) loaded with work bench and lumber, was also accompanied by Langino Verte, who came with me to farm on shears, also had along with me Andres Woodson who is a Navajo Indian boy belonging to J.B. Woodson. (Andres and Gabriel Woodson were Navajo slaves that had been purchased by J. B. Woodson. Their names show up on a list in Conejos County Records compiled by Indian Agent Lafayette Head for the U.S. Government at the end of the Civil War.)[8] We arrived safe at Rio de la Jara (La Jara Creek) said night without any axident with the exception that one of the wheals of Beral's cart break down and we had to leave it with all its load on the road. The road this day was very heavey, snowy and muddy. James B. Woodson and Santiago came to our camp this night. (John Lawrence was following the West Fork of the North Branch of the Old Spanish Trail along the east edge of the San Juan Mountains. This trail was probably first used as a game trail. As animals were hunted by man, man also began to use the trail. It has been known by many names throughout history, including the Spanish Trail, Juaquin's Road, the Trail of the Sheep, Del Norte/Conejos Road and the West Fork of the North Branch. The latter is a term first used by Leroy Hafen in the 1950s to distinguish between the East and West Forks of the North Branch of what the trappers called the Old Spanish Trail. This trail was used by Vargas in 1694, Anza in 1779, Pike in 1807, Jacob Fowler in 1822, Beale and Heap in 1853, Silva in 1859 and John Lawrence in 1867.

The best way to view this trail is from an airplane. Nearly eighty percent of the West Fork is visible today.)

March 1, 1867

This day we stayed in camp as we had to get the herd of cattle together.

March 2, 1867

Started with the herd of cattle belonging to J.B. Woodson and Santiago Manchego accompained by Longino Verte, Juan de Jesus Manchezo and José Ant. Moran as renters, also Andres and Gabriel Woodson, the two Navajo boys of Woodson's, also José Andres Chavez as herder boy for Santiago Manchego. We had a fine day and arrived at night and camped at the Piefra (Piedra) Pintada. Woodson and Manchego turned back to Conejos at el Rio de la Jara (La Jara Creek). (Lawrence's camp on the 2nd of March would be used again many times in the next forty years as he traveled to and from Conejos. This camp was near the location of the original town of La Jara which was established around 1870 by Mancil Garrett. The town served as a pony express stop, way station, post office and a stage stop in later years.)

March 3, 1867

Started with the whole outfit and crossed el Rio Grande del Norte. Camped below La Loma. Everything all right. (On March 3rd Lawrence camped near the town of La Loma Del Norte which was established in 1861. This was one of many Spanish Plazas established in the area that used the name La Loma in conjunction with an additional name.)

March 4, 1867

...snowed all day and very cold. Killed a collote (coyote).

March 5, 1867

In the morning it was snowing but cleared up about ten o'clock. We cut the logs out of the road from where we camped to the crossing of the river...camped on el Rio de la Garita. (This route follows along the seven west road which is seven miles west of the present-day North Gunbarrel/Highway 285. It proceeded to the old town of La Garita, located on the south bank of La Garita Creek. This was the site of the Torrez Trading Post. The post was built in about 1858 for trade with the Ute Indians who inhabited the San Luis Valley.)

March 6, 1867

Passed a disagreeable night, but got up early and hitched up cattle and started...at el Rio del Carnero I delivered a bull of Woodson's to Ant. Masceno, and got one bull from him. I also delivered a bull for Juan to one of the Chacons, said bulls all yearlings. I then started on and passed the teams and came to the mouth of the *(Saguache)* valley, where I pitched camp for the night, unhitched the horses, tied two calfs, that I had been hauling, to the wheals and went over to Russells. I come back early and met the wagons. Went with them to camp...Juan killed a libre *(deer)*. (The town of Carnero was located where the present-day La Garita Store is located (1997). In Frank White's book "La Garita", he states that Spanish-speaking people first settled in the Carnero Creek area about 1858. The name Carnero in the author's Velázquez Spanish/English dictionary gives the meaning as a burial place. The author believes that the early day Spanish people mistakenly thought that the bones laying on the hill west of the La Garita Church represented a burial site. In Col. Fauntleroy's diary in 1855, he stated that this area was strewn with human remains.

La Garita Church which features a six-armed cross so it may be viewed from any direction.

This was the result of a smallpox epidemic in 1854 in which the Mouache Ute and Jicarilla Apache were given disease-ridden blankets. It is noticable in Gwinn Harris Heap's diary in chapter seven that no mention is made of this burial place although Beale and Heap passed through the same area.)

March 7, 1867

...measured off seven claims, went back to camp, hitched up and moved the whole outfit in and pitched our permanent camp... (The home of John Lawrence can be seen about 3.5 miles west of Saguache, on the north side of Z Road. There has been some talk that this building is to be torn down. Something needs to be done to preserve such an outstanding piece of history!

John Lawrence left Conejos on February 28, 1867 with seed, farm implements and tools to take up farming in the Saguache area. At La Jara Creek where they camped the first night, they gathered cattle belonging to his partner, James B. Woodson. On March 2, 1867 they started traveling again, arriving at Piedra Pintada (Rock Creek) where they camped for the night. Then on March 3, they traveled as far as the Rio Grande which they crossed before setting up camp for the night at La

341

Loma Del Norte which was established in 1861. It snowed on March 4th so they apparently stayed in camp. On March 5, 1867 they cut the logs out of the road from where they camped to the crossing of the river. They traveled as far as the Rio de La Garita where they camped for the night. March 6, after delivering a yearling bull to Antonio Masceno, who was living on Carnero Creek they traveled to the mouth of the Saguache Valley where they camped. On March 7, 1867 Lawrence measured off seven claims and moved their outfit to their permanent camp.

The original house at this site was started on March 12, 1867. It was three rooms built of logs with stone chimneys. The roofs of the cabins were made of pole rafters covered with dirt, per Lawrence's description.

John Lawrence had Beral, the local carpenter who had come from Conejos with him in February of 1867, build him an adobe brick mold. Then on June 21, 1867, Gabriel picked up a load of straw and Guadalupe started to make adobes for the Lawrence house. Lumber was hauled from the Ute Agency. Adobes were made when there was time between the farming chores. The materials were continually stockpiled. Then on February 28, 1870, Beral and Woodson began work on the Lawrence house. All of the farm hands worked on the house. The house was completed on March 24, 1870 in time for the spring planting season. Wooden floors were added in November while Lawrence was busy at the Ute Agency.

The John Lawrence house which is located three and a half miles west of Saguache, Colorado.

The distance from Conejos to Saguache is about seventy-five miles and usually under good conditions required five days to make the trip. The stopping points were Old La Jara, Piedra, La Loma Del Norte which was East Del Norte, Old La Garita or Carnero with arrival in Saguache on the fifth night.)

June 9, 1867

I went down below accompanied by Gabriel and Moran. I there learned that Isaah Young was going to the river with teams to bring Mearses stuff. I thought it would be the best chance for me to get over the river (the Rio Grande), as I had to go to Conejos...when I got there to the river I found I could not cross without risk. While there Mears hurt his leg. I then went and tuck him to Fort Garland. I was gone the 10th, 11, 12, 13, 14, 15, 16, and got home the 17th about noon. The water was high and I had to brake a new road from La Lome to Fort Garland.

June 22, 1867

...Russell came up with me and brought up 17 head of Head's cattle to be kept here until the Rio Grande went down as his man that went with them could not get across and had to bring them back.

June 27, 1867

I started to Conejos, we all got to the river & ferried & swam the horses & got all across by night. In the morning we had to cross from the bank of the river to the high land. It was very muddy & we had to pull the wagons across by hand, the horses being barely able to pull themselves across alone. I was gone the 28th...to the 7th, eleven days in all...

April 23, 1868

...Woodson and Dulany started to Fort Garland with potatoes...

These wagon ruts worn in the stone up to a foot deep are located between Monte Vista and Del Norte, Colorado.

May 8, 1868

I started by way of Conejos to the Moreno mines, having one load of potatoes and one of flour. I was gone 42 days, getting back with the wagon on the 18th of June...when I got back I found Woodson and family with Fullerton & family at Godfreys expecting to have an indian war, but it was all settled on the evening of my arrival, but in the meantime they sent to Fort Garland for soldiers. They arrived on the morning of the 20th and as things were all settled we have made a pleasure time up to the following date.

July 22, 1868

We all started for La Culebra...got back August 1st about two o'clock. (La Culebra that Lawrence referred to was the settlement of San Luis de Culebra, was the original name for the Spanish settlement of San Luis, Colorado. In 1851 Jesus Jacques and Carlos (Charles) Beaubien led fifty families from Taos, New Mexico to settle on Culebra Creek. This was part of the Sangre de Cristo Land Grant owned by Carlos Beaubien. Their arrival on April 5th created a great change in lifestyle for the farmers and stockmen who previously stayed on the grant only during the summer months. The settlement was located three-fourths of a mile below the present day town of San Luis, Colorado in Costilla County and it was called San Luis de Culebra.

Taos residents Stephen Luis Lee and Narciso Beaubien were the original owners of the Sangre de Cristo Land Grant. On December 27, 1843 these men petitioned Governor Manuel Armijo of Santa Fe, New Mexico for land that later became Costilla County in Southern Colorado. The grant was authorized on January 12, 1844 by Governor Armijo. Its boundaries were paced and the grantees were placed in possession of the property. Groups of settlers attempted to build homes and plant crops along the Culebra and Costilla Rivers in 1845, but were driven out by the continual harassment by the Indians.

Both Lee and young Beaubien were killed in the Taos Rebellion of 1847, in which the Mexican and Indian people revolted against the new United States Government. Charles Beaubien inherited his son's half of the grant and purchased from Lee's widow the other half for one hundred dollars.) On our arrival the crops looked as well as heart could wish. The wheat and oats all headed out beautiful and the corn commencing to silk out, but in less than an hour after our arrival a hail storm wide enough to take in our whole crop passed over when hail fell to the depth of an inch and a half and from the size of a hazelnut entirely distroying the crop...

September 25, 1869

We started over to the Agency... and got home the 4th, being absent 10 days. The Indian goods got in & near two thirds of them were distributed while we were there... (The Los Pinos Ute Indian Agency near Cochetopa Pass was built as part of the treaty of 1868. The agency was to be built on the Los Pinos River in La Plata County for the Tabeguache band and the three (Mouache, Capote and Weeminuche) Southern Ute bands. When the Tabeguache reached the Cochetopa Creek area about fifty-five miles west of Saguache, they were still about sixty miles from the Los Pinos River but they refused to go any farther. This tributary of Cochetopa Creek which they had reached was named Los Pinos Creek to conform to the name specified in the treaty. The Southern Ute continued to receive their rations from the old agency at Abiquiu, New Mexico until 1877 when the Southern Ute Agency was established at Ignacio.

The first agent at the Los Pinos Agency in Saguache County, Colorado was Second Lieutenant Calvin T. Speer of the 11th United States Infantry. He arrived on Los Pinos Creek on July 31, 1869 and construction began on the agency buildings. The road from Saguache was in poor condition and it took eleven days for goods to be transported the fifty-five miles.

The cattle that were taken to the agency were placed in a corral until all the other items were given to the Ute. The cattle were then driven from the corral and frightened into running across the meadows nearby and killed as if they were buffalo. This often resulted in someone falling with their horse and being injured. People from Saguache often attended the agency during allotment day to see this excitement.

The Los Pinos Agency was short-lived. After the area was surveyed, the agency was found not to be on the reservation as originally believed. Another problem was that it was located at a high enough elevation that the growing season was too short for most crops and due to the long cold winters the Utes refused to stay there except during the summer months. In 1875 the Utes were moved to the Uncompaghre Agency near Montrose, Colorado.)

November 23, 1870

I started to the mill at La Culebra (San Luis). Woodson & Fullerton started with their families & horse teams on the 24th and at noon overtook & camped out with me the 25th. They then went on ahead of me to Culebra. Jim had his ox team along with me & Moran had a team going to the mill. We got in to the mill on the night of the 27th. A few days after I got there Woodson & his father-in-law went over to Cucharas, Huerfano County, where Woodson settled up with J.M. Francisco *(Co. John Francisco)*...I started home with the ox teams on Dec. 14th and Woodson & family started the 15th. The first night I camped at the Trenchera...The next day I came to the point of the bosque on the Rio Grande *(the grove at Alamosa)*. there Woodson overtook me. it snowed 3 inches during the night. We all came up to the point where the road turned off to the Garita and camped for the night in an old house of Royals...very cold...on the 18th we all started for home. Woodson got in about 2 hours before sundown & I and Andres got in about 10 o'clock at night. From the Carnero the snow was very deep being about one foot at the Russell ranch.

November 1, 1871

We all hands started to Culebra to the mill. Woodson also went in the carriage with his wife & family...we were gone 12 days...the first part of the road was good, but the last half was heavy with snow. Ricardo Martin & wife stayed here while we were gone.

November 19, 1871

We started to Culebra with 2 ox wagons with wheat and one horse wagon with cabbage. Woodson & I went by Ft. Garland and traded off our cabage & vegitables. We got our grinding done & I got 1000 feet of lumber at the mill above Culebra for which I payed $25...

July 26, 1872

Woodson & family & I started to Culebra in the carriage. We drove the boy colts, Prince & Sam. We overtook the ox wagons the second day. we traveled with them 2 days and went in to Culebra on the 4th, the ox wagons getting in the 6th. We had to wait 6 days for the grinding. The ox wagon got home in 16 days & we in the same time...we lost the bull dog on the trip. at Conejos Mrs. Woodson got one of her Primos (cousins) to come home with her. The weather was very wet while we were gone & the ox wagons mired down a great many times and it rained continually on us the last two days and the road was one flood of water.

August 17, 1872

Bob Morrison started to the Agency with the ox teams with 22 sacks of flour. I also went on horseback...

October 2, 1872

Uray (Uray, or Ouray, is the name of the Chief of the Tabeguache or Uncompahgre band of the Ute Indian nation from 1855-1880. His name is spelled many ways in various documents, but the most common spelling is Ouray. Ouray was born in 1833 in northern New Mexico to a Tabeguache Ute mother and a Jicarilla Apache father.

When Ouray's mother died, his father remarried. Ouray and his brother Quenche were left with a Spanish couple while his father and step-mother returned to the western slope. Ouray was raised near Taos and spent much of his early years working at a hacienda near there. Ouray spent a great deal of time tending sheep, gathering firewood and doing other chores. He learned Spanish, English, Ute and Apache as well as sign language. Ouray, having learned these languages, also knew much about each culture.

Ouray had grown to be an adult by 1850 and left Taos to join his mother's people. He was in the Taos area during the American invasion of New Mexico on August 18, 1846 so he witnessed the power of the United States Army. Ouray knew that it was futile for his people to fight the Americans, as they would be easily overpowered. He always counseled his people to remain peaceful with the whites.

Ouray was probably suffering from Brights Disease at this point and went to Ojo Caliente hoping that the hot water would make him feel better. Ojo Caliente is a natural hot spring, which contains a combination of five geothermal waters iron, arsenic, lithia, soda and sodium. Though named by the early Spanish settlers, these springs were used by the Indians long before the white man set foot on the North American continent.) went past on his way from Ojo Caliente to the Agency. he got a carnero from me.

October 23, 1872

I fixed up the School Superintendent Register...a lot of wagons with freight for the Agency got in to Mearses (Otto Mears) while I was down. I also got 1/2 gal. of oil from Russell. I was also sworn in as road overseer and gave my bond. I started two wagons to the agency this morning with oats & vegitables.

October 24, 1872

I started to the (Ute) Agency on horseback. I overtook the wagons near the top of the range. We camped together on the other side of the mountain and got in to the Agency the next day at noon. We got the wagons unloaded by dark. on the 26th we loaded them up with 2500 feet of lumber and started home. I stayed at the Agency and about noon Mears got in and on the 27th we started home. we then...took the lumber down to Pumphreys.

November 7, 1875

The four ox teams started to the new Agency (The road to the Agency was a continuation of the North Branch of the Old Spanish Trail which crossed Cochetopa Pass.) loaded with potatoes, oats, & vegetables. I started with 4 yoke of cattle to each wagon though some of them were unbroke steers. The wagons got home on Jan. 3, 1876. That is, two of them, with the hands and 5 yoke of cattle, and one yoke that the agent at the Un-com-pa-ga-ra (Uncompahgre) loaned me to come out with. They being gone 58 days. we had to leave 2 of the wagons at Cimaron and also 13 head of oxen. The Cimaron (Cimarron) is about 35 miles this side of the new Agency. The oxen we left there was so entirely worn out by being footsore that we could not move them, and the ones we started out with (7 *yoke*) were unfit for travel and of them one was left on the hill this side of the old Agency, and one up at Fullertons.

I had Pedro Manchego, Francisco Manchego, Francisco Gallegos, and Anto-nio Moreno as drivers and they all worked very faithful. It was the hardest & worst trip I ever went on in my life, having snow and wind from the time I started until I got back. and in all the home trip having to travel in snow from one to five feet deep and at times having to pass over drifts from 10 to 15 feet deep. In comimg home I left the boys with the wagons at Cibolla (Cebolla) and came on ahead on horseback, as I had General along, and got home on Jan. 1st, 1876...

July 14, 1878

At noon William & Bob took me to town and from there I started to Pueblo to attend the Democratic State Convention. I went from here to Del Norte on the buck board that carries the U.S. mail and from there I went to Alamosa with Walter Conley, and from Alamosa I went to Pueblo on the cars...

April 10, 1880

    All hands farmed. I wrote some at a report I was writing to print in the Saguache Chronicle about the toll roads & Cochetopa Pass. a very large travel goes by here every day.

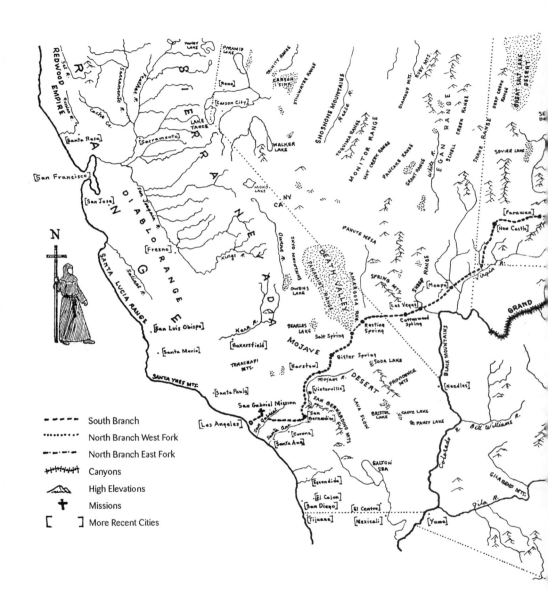

Legend:
- – – – – South Branch
- ········· North Branch West Fork
- –·–·–· North Branch East Fork
- ┼┼┼┼┼┼┼ Canyons
- ⛰ High Elevations
- ✝ Missions
- [   ] More Recent Cities

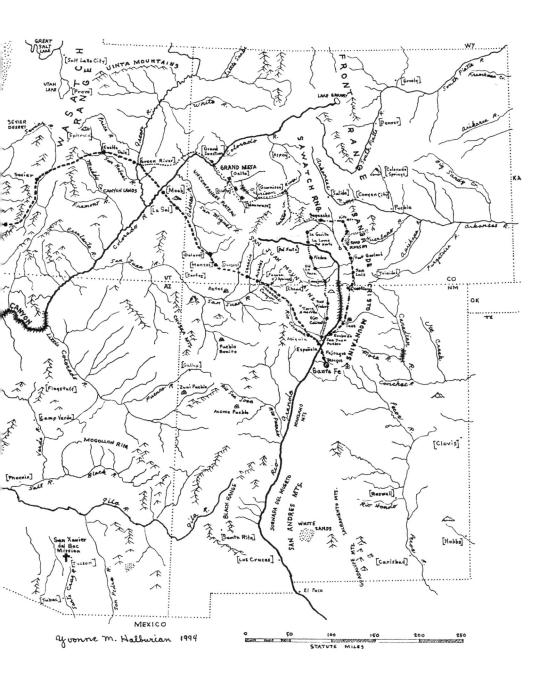

Yvonne M. Halburian 1994

STATUTE MILES

351

APPENDIX

The following seven people used the North Branch of the Old Spanish Trail. Although they did not leave enough of a diary to be included as a separate chapter, they are nonetheless important. It is the desire of this author that this book prompt and encourage other accounts of the Old Spanish Trail to come forward.

OñATE

Juan de Oñate arrived at San Juan Pueblo on July 11, 1598 and continued north to Picurís Pueblo which is located in a little valley west of the Sangre de Cristo Mountains. After looking over the Pueblo, the expedition crossed the Picurís Mountains to Taos Pueblo. Oñate was back in San Juan Pueblo by the 19th of July.[1]

MENDINUETA

Pedro Fermin de Mendinueta's soldiers traveled north, probably on the West Fork of the North Branch. By 1768 this trail had become well known. The soldiers built a fort on top of the hill of San Antonio, where fifty soldiers were stationed to watch the ford of the Rio Grande for the approach of Comanche.[2]

SEGURA

Manuel Segura left Taos soon after August 10, 1787 and traveled along the East Fork of the North Branch of the Old Spanish Trail. Segura was accompanied by thirty Spanish laborers who carted tools, implements and seeds. Their journeey took them along the west side of the Sangre de Cristo Mountains, north on the Old Spanish Trail as far as the Great Sand Dunes before turning east through Mosca Pass.[3]

ROBIDOUX

On February 20, 1824, Antoine Robidoux was granted a passport to travel from Saint Louis, Missouri west across the Indian Territory to the Mexican border. He crossed Mosca Pass into the San Luis Valley and traveled south along the west side of the Sangre de Cristo Mountains on the East Fork of the North Branch of the Old Spanish Trail.

The following is from Gwinn Harris Heap's diary:

"We were now traveling on an Indian trail; for the wagon trail, which I believe was made by Roubideau's (Robidoux) wagons, deviated to the right, and went through the pass named after him.

June 15, 1853 Bidding adieu to our kind friends at the fort, we resumed our journey at noon, and traveled down Utah Creek south-southwest, until it debouched in the valley of San Luis, when we altered our course to west by north. In six miles from Fort Massachusetts, we crossed the trail of Roubideau's wagons from the upper Arkansas settlements; they entered through Roubideau's Pass in the Sierra Mojada (Sangre de Cristo).[4]

In 1828 Antoine Robidoux built Fort Uncompahgre on the Gunnison River and Fort Uintah on the Uintah River in Utah about 1832. From 1828-1844 Antoine used the North Branch of the Old Spanish Trail to transport supplies to his trading posts."[5]

WHITMAN

Marcus Whitman and Asa L. Lovejoy left the mission at Waiilatpu near present-day Walla, Washington on October 3, 1842. They traveled the 528 miles to Fort Hall in fourteen days. Hearing that the Sioux and Pawnee were at war, the men set out for the Spanish Trail. After resting for two days the two men hired a new guide and then proceeded on to Fort Uintah.

Whitman and Lovejoy arrived at Fort Uintah about November 1st. At Fort Uintah they hired a different guide to take them to the Fort Uncompahgre on the Gunnison River. They reached the Colorado River which they forded near present-day Grand Junction, Colorado. Lovejoy describes the crossing of the Colorado River as follows:

"This stream was some one hundred and fifty, or two hundred yards wide, and looked upon by our guide as very dangerous to cross in the present condition. But the Doctor, nothing daunted, was the first to take the water. He mounted his horse, and the guide and myself pushed them off into the boiling, foaming stream.

Away they went completely under water—horse and all; but directly came up, and after buffeting the waves and foaming current, he made to the ice on the opposite side. The guide and myself forced in the pack, animals; followed the doctor's example, and were soon drying our frozen clothes by a comfortable fire."

At Fort Uncompahgre the two men hired a third guide. After traveling about a week with the party, he became lost. Marcus Whitman and the guide returned to Fort Uncompahgre where Whitman hired the fourth guide. After returning to where he had left Asa Lovejoy, the party continued across the mountains to the area of present-day Gunnison, Colorado. They ran out of food and were forced to eat Whitman's dog and one of the pack animals. After crossing Cochetopa Pass into the San Luis Valley the party met a group of travelers from Taos. These travelers were able to supply them with enough food to last until they reached Taos. Whitman, Lovejoy and their guide reached Taos about the middle of December.[6]

WHOOTEN

In 1852 Dick Whooten purchased sheep at about a dollar each in Taos Valley. He was accompanied by several hunters and herders who drove the flock of sheep north along the west side of the Sangre de Cristo Mountains to Rito Alto (Leroux) Creek before turning west. Proceeding west, they crossed Cochetopa Pass to the Gunnison River. Near present-day Montrose, Whooten quarreled with the Utes and pulled one chief from his horse and gave the Utes to understand that he would not be bullied. Whooten continued west along the North Branch of the Old Spanish Trail to the Green River. After crossing the Green River, Whooten continued north to the Oregon-California Trail which he followed to Sacramento, California. The miners in California were hungry for meat of any kind and the sheep were sold at a tremendous profit.[7]

WORTHINGTON

Worthington, who came to the San Luis Valley in the early 1880's, tells of having been called upon to perform a funeral service for a child of a young couple. The child had died as they reached the San Luis Valley. After the service was performed the couple continued on to California along the California Road/North Branch of the Old Spanish Trail.[8]

NOTES & REFERENCES

CHAPTER 1. 1694/DON DIEGO de VARGAS

1.Kessell, *REMOTE BEYOND COMPARE The Journals of Don Diego de Vargas* University of New Mexico Press, Albuquerque, NM 1989.
2.Simmons, *THE LAST CONQUISTADOR Juan de Oñate and the Settling of the Far Southwest* University of Oklahoma Press, Norman, OK 1991.
3.Vargas, *JOURNAL OF THE VARGAS EXPEDITION INTO COLORADO, 1694* Archivo General de la Nación, Mexico City, copy from Adams State College, Alamosa, CO.
4.Kessell, *REMOTE BEYOND COMPARE The Journals of Don Diego de Vargas* University of New Mexico Press, Albuquerque, NM 1989.

CHAPTER 2. 1705/ROQUE MADRID

1.Hendricks & Wilson, *THE NAVAJOS IN 1705 Roque Madrid's Campaign Journal* University of New Mexico, Albuquerque, NM 1996.
2.Chávez, *ORIGINS OF NEW MEXICO FAMILIES A Genealogy of the Spanish Colonial Period* Museum of New Mexico Press, Santa Fe, NM 1992.
3.Hendricks & Wilson, *THE NAVAJOS IN 1705 Roque Madrid's Campaign Journal* University of New Mexico, Albuquerque, NM 1996.
4.ibid.
5.Chávez, *ORIGINS OF NEW MEXICO FAMILIES A Genealogy of the Spanish Colonial Period* Museum of New Mexico Press, Santa Fe, NM 1992.
6.Hendricks & Wilson, *THE NAVAJOS IN 1705 Roque Madrid's Campaign Journal* University of New Mexico, Albuquerque, NM 1996.
7.Simmons, *THE LAST CONQUISTADOR Juan de Oñate and the Settling of the Far Southwest* University of Oklahoma Press, Norman, OK 1991.
8.Cassells, *THE ARCHAEOLOGY OF COLORADO* Johnson Books, Boulder, CO 1983 & 1997.
9.Harrington, *ETHNOGEOGRAPHY OF THE TEWA INDIANS 29th ANNUAL REPORT 1907-08* Bureau of American Ethnology, Washington, D. C. 1916 pg. 182.
10.ibid pg. 174.
11.Camp, *THE NEW HUNTER'S ENCYCLOPEDIA* The Stackpole Company, Harrisburg, PA 1966.

CHAPTER 3. 1779/JUAN BAUTISTA de ANZA

1.Garate, *ANZA A Basque Legacy on New Spain's Northern Frontier* unpublished 1997.
2.Bowman, *ANZA and the Northwest Frontier of New Spain* Southwest Museum Papers, Los Angeles, CA 1967.
3.Simmons, *THE LAST CONQUISTADOR Juan de Oñate and the Settling of the Far Southwest* University of Oklahoma Press, Norman, OK 1991.
4.Thomas, Alfred B. *FORGOTTEN FRONTIERS A Study of the Spanish Indian Policy of Don Juan Bautista de Anza, Governor of New Mexico, 1777-87.* University of Oklahoma Press, Norman, OK 1932.

CHAPTER 4. 1807/ZEBULON MONTGOMERY PIKE

1.Coues, *THE EXPEDITIONS OF ZEBULON MONTGOMERY PIKE, To Headwaters of the Mississippi River, Through Lousiana Territory, and in New Spain, During the Years 1805-6-7.* Ross & Haines, Inc. Minneapolis, MN, 1965. reprinted by Dover Publications, Inc. New York, NY 1987.
2.Hollon, *THE LOST PATHFINDER: Zebulon Montgomery Pike* University of Oklahoma Press, Nornon, OK 1949.
3.ibid.
4.ibid.
5.ibid.
6.ibid.
7.Coues, *THE EXPEDITIONS OF ZEBULON MONTGOMERY PIKE, To Headwaters of the Mississippi River, Through Lousiana Territory, and in New Spain, During the Years 1805-6-7.* Ross & Haines, Inc. Minneapolis, MN, 1965. reprinted by Dover Publications, Inc. New York, NY 1987.
8.Simmons, *THE LAST CONQUISTADOR Juan de Oñate and the Settling of the Far Southwest* University of Oklahoma Press, Norman, OK 1991.

CHAPTER 5. 1822/JACOB FOWLER

1.Kessler, *COLORADO'S OLDEST WAGON ROAD* Taos, New Mexico to San Carlos de los Jupes, Colorado. SLV Magazine August/September 1997.
2.Griswold, *RIO GRANDE Along the Rio Grande* Griswold, Denver, CO 1986.

CHAPTER 6. 1846/GEORGE FREDERICK RUXTON

1.Haley, *APACHES A History and Culture Portrait,* Doubleday & Company, Inc., Garden City, NY 1981.
2.Kessler, *RE-TRACING THE OLD SPANISH TRAIL NORTH BRANCH* Adobe Village Press, Monte Vista, CO 1995.
3.Parkhill, *THE BLAZED TRAIL OF ANTOINE LEROUX* Westernlore Press, Los Angeles, CA 1965.

4.Kessler, *COLORADO'S OLDEST WAGON ROAD* Taos, New Mexico to San Carlos de los Jupes, Colorado. SLV Magazine August/September 1997.

CHAPTER 7. 1848/GEORGE DOUGLAS BREWERTON
1.Hafen & Hafen, *OLD SPANISH TRAIL Santa Fe to Los Angeles* Arthur H. Clark Co., 1954. Reprinted by University of Nebraska Press, Lincoln, NE 1993, pg. 180.
2.Quaife, *KIT CARSON'S AUTOBIOGRAPHY* University of Nebraska Press, Lincoln, NE 1966, pg.123.
3.ibid.
4.ibid.
5.ibid.
6.Hafen & Hafen, *OLD SPANISH TRAIL Santa Fe to Los Angeles* Arthur H. Clark Co., 1954. Reprinted by University of Nebraska Press, Lincoln, NE 1993, pg.336.
7.Brewerton, *OVERLAND WITH KIT CARSON a narrative of the Old Spanish Trail in 1848* University of Nebraska Press, Lincoln, NE 1993, pg. 129-136.

CHAPTER 8. 1853/GWINN HARRIS HEAP
1.Lavender, *BENT'S FORT* Doubleday & Company, Inc 1954, reprinted by Univesity of Nebrasks Press, 1972.
2.Kessler, *COLORADO'S OLDEST WAGON ROAD* Taos, New   Mexico to San Carlos de los Jupes, Colorado. SLV Magazine August/September 1997.
3.Teeuwen, *LA CULTURA CONSTANTE de SAN LUIS* San Luis Museum and Cultural Center. San Luis, CO 1985.
4.White, *LA GARITA* published by Author 1971.
5.Wallace, *ANTOINE ROBIDOUX 1794-1860* A Biography of a Western Venturer Glen Dawson, Los Angeles, CA 1953.

CHAPTER 9. 1853/JOHN WILLIAMS GUNNISON
1.Walker, *THE WAGONMASTERS High Plains Freighting from the Earliest Days of the Santa Fe Trail to 1880,* University of Oklahoma Press, Norman, OK, 1966.

CHAPTER 10. 1853/JACOB HEINRICH SCHIEL
1.Kessler, *ANZA'S 1779 COMANCHE CAMPAIGN* Monte Vista, CO 1994.
2.Carson, *AMONG THE ETERNAL SNOWS* First Ascent Press, Colorado Springs, CO 1995.
3.Griswold, *RIO GRANDE Along the Rio Grande* Griswold, Denver, CO 1986.
4.Smith, *OURAY Chief of the Utes* Wayfinder Press, Ridgeway, CO 1986.
5.Parkhill, *THE BLAZED TRAIL OF ANTOINE LEROUX* Westernlore Press, Los Angeles, CA 1965.

CHAPTER 11. 1853/SOLOMON NUNES CARVALHO

1.Carvalho, *INCIDENTS OF TRAVEL AND ADVENTURE in the Far West*, Derby & Jackson, 119 Nassau St. Cincinnati:H.W. Derby & Co. 1857, reprinted by: The Jewish Publication Society of America, Philadelphia, PA 1954.

2.Thompson, *BENT'S OLD FORT: LIFE IN AN ADOBE CASTLE, 1833-1849* The Colorado Historical Society, Denver, CO 1979.

3.Johns, *STORMS BREWED IN OTHER MEN'S WORLDS* Texas A. & M. University Press, College Station, TX 1995.

4.Smith, *OURAY Chief of the Utes* Wayfinder Press, Ridgeway, CO 1986.

5.Peterson & Elman, *THE GREAT GUNS* Ridge Press, Grosset & Dunlap, Inc. New York, NY 1971.

CHAPTER 12. 1858/RANDOLPH BARNES MARCY

1.Marcy, *THIRTY YEARS OF ARMY LIFE ON THE BORDER* Harper Brothers, NY 1866.

2.Brooks, *THE MOUNTAIN MEADOWS MASSACRE* University of Oklahoma, Norman, OK 1950.

3.Wallace, *ANTOINE ROBIDOUX 1794-1860* A Biography of a Western Venturer Glen Dawson, Los Angeles, CA 1953.

4.Richmond, *TRAIL TO DISASTER* Colorado Historical Society, Denver, CO 1990.

CHAPTER 13. 1858/WILLIAM WING LORING

1.Hafen, *COLONEL LORING'S EXPEDITION ACROSS COLORADO IN 1858* Colorado Magazine Vol. XXIII-No. 2, March, 1946.

2.Wessels, *BORN TO BE A SOLDIER* Texas Christian University Press, Fort Worth, TX 1971.

3.Heitman, *HISTORICAL REGISTER AND DICTIONARY OF THE UNITED STATES ARMY, I 642;*

4.Hafen, *COLONEL LORING'S EXPEDITION ACROSS COLORADO IN 1858* Colorado Magazine Vol. XXIII-No. 2, March, 1946.

5.Wessels, *BORN TO BE A SOLDIER* Texas Christian University Press, Fort Worth, TX 1971.

6.Hafen, *COLONEL LORING'S EXPEDITION ACROSS COLORADO IN 1858* Colorado Magazine Vol. XXIII-No. 2, March, 1946.

7.Wessels, *BORN TO BE A SOLDIER* Texas Christian University Press, Fort Worth, TX 1971.

8.Hafen, *COLONEL LORING'S EXPEDITION ACROSS COLORADO IN 1858* Colorado Magazine Vol. XXIII-No. 2, March, 1946.

9.Wessels, *BORN TO BE A SOLDIER* Texas Christian University Press, Fort Worth, TX 1971.

CHAPTER 14. 1959/JUAN BAUTISTA SILVA

1.Palmer, *A GENEALOGICAL RECORD OF THE DESCENDENTS OF MANUEL de JESUS MARTINEZ*, Colorado Springs, CO 1996.
2.Richmond, *SAN JOSE* San Luis Valley Historian VI/1=1-87; VI/2=89-148.
3.Mead, *CONEJOS COUNTRY* Century One Press, Colorado Springs, CO 1984.
4.Richmond, *SAN JOSE* San Luis Valley Historian VI/1=1-87; VI/2=89-148.

CHAPTER 15. 1859/ALBERT D. RICHERDSON

1.Richerdson, *BEYOND THE MISSISSIPPI: FROM THE GREAT RIVER TO THE GREAT OCEAN life and adventure on the prairies, mountains and Pacific Coast, 1857-1867.* American Publishing Company, Hartford, CT 1867.
2.Teeuwen, *LA CULTURA CONSTANTE de SAN LUIS* San Luis Museum and Cultural Center. San Luis, CO 1985.
3.Hodge, *FORT GARLAND: A Window onto Southwest History* SLV Historian Vol. XXIV #2, Alamosa, CO 1992.
4.Richerdson, *BEYOND THE MISSISSIPPI: FROM THE GREAT RIVER TO THE GREAT OCEAN life and adventure on the prairies, mountains and Pacific Coast, 1857-1867.* American Publishing Company, Hartford, CT 1867.

CHAPTER 16. 1867/JOHN LAWRENCE

1.Martin, *FRONTIER EYEWITNESS Diary of John Lawrence, 1867-1908.*
2.Mead, *CONEJOS COUNTRY* Century One Press, Colorado Springs, CO 1984.
3.Kessler, *RE-TRACING THE OLD SPANISH TRAIL NORTH BRANCH* Adobe Village Press, Monte Vista, CO 1995.
4.Kessler, *ANZA'S 1779 COMANCHE CAMPAIGN* Monte Vista, CO 1994.
5.Hafen & Hafen, *OLD SPANISH TRAIL Santa Fe to Los Angeles* Arthur H. Clark Co., 1954. Reprinted by University of Nebraska Press, Lincoln, NE 1993.
6.Cassells, *THE ARCHAEOLOGY OF COLORADO* Johnson Books, Boulder, CO 1983 & 1997.
7.Heap, *CENTRAL ROUTE TO THE PACIFIC, from The Valley of the Mississippi to California: Journal of the Expedition* Arno Press, New York Times Co. NY 1981.
8.San Luis Valley Historian Vol. V No.1. pg. 22-28.

APPENDIX

1.Simmons, *THE LAST CONQUISTADOR Juan de Oñate and the Settling of the Far Southwest* University of Oklahoma Press, Norman, OK 1991.
2.Thomas, *THE PLAINS INDIANS AND NEW MEXICO* University of Oklahoma Press, Norman, OK 1932.

3.Kessler, *COLORADO'S OLDEST WAGON ROAD* Taos, New Mexico to San Carlos de los Jupes, Colorado. SLV Magazine August/September 1997.

4.Heap, *CENTRAL ROUTE TO THE PACIFIC, from The Valley of the Mississippi to California: Journal of the Expedition* Arno Press, New York Times Co. NY 1981.

5.Wallace, *ANTOINE ROBIDOUX 1794-1860* A Biography of a Western Venturer Glen Dawson, Los Angeles, CA 1953.

6.Jones, *THE GREAT COMMAND: THE STORY OF MARCUS AND NARCISSA WHITMAN AND THE OREGON COUNTRY PIONEERS* Little Brown Press, 1959.

7.Baxter, *LAS CARNERADAS: SHEEP TRADE IN NEW MEXICO 1700-1860* University of New Mexico Press, Albuquerque, NM 1987.

8.Worthington, *THE SUNNY SAN LUIS VALLEY* 1883 Dorothy W. Sabin reprinted in 1965.

BIBLIOGRAPHY &
SUGGESTED READING

Anza, Juan Bautista de. *SPANISH DIARY OF 1779* Archivo General de la Nación, Mexico City, Mexico, copy from the University of New Mexico, Albuquerque, NM. (Obtained for the author by Marc Simmons)

Baxter, John O. *LAS CARNERADAS: SHEEP TRADE IN NEW MEXICO 1700-1860* University of New Mexico Press, Albuquerque, NM 1987.

Beckwith, Lt. E. C. *REPORT OF EXPLORATION OF A ROUTE FOR THE PACIFIC RAILROAD* Capt. Gunnison, Topography Engineers Near the 38th & 39 Parallels of Lattitude, 1854.

Bowman, J. N. & R. F. Heizer. *ANZA and the Northwest Frontier of New Spain* Southwest Museum Papers, Los Angeles, CA 1967.

Brewerton, George Douglas. *OVERLAND WITH KIT CARSON a narrative of the Old Spanish Trail in 1848* University of Nebraska Press, Lincoln, NE 1993.

Brooks, Juanita. *THE MOUNTAIN MEADOWS MASSACRE* University of Oklahoma, Norman, OK 1950.

Camp, Raymond R. Editor, *THE NEW HUNTER'S ENCYCLOPEDIA* The Stackpole Company, Harrisburg, PA 1966.

Carson, Phil. *AMONG THE ETERNAL SNOWS* First Ascent Press, Colorado Springs, CO 1995.

Carter, Carrol Joe. *PIKE IN COLORADO* The Old Army Press, Fort Collins, CO 1978.

Carvalho, Solomon Nunes. *INCIDENTS OF TRAVEL AND ADVENTURE in the Far West,* Derby & Jackson, 119 Nassau St. Cincinnati: H.W. Derby & Co. 1857, reprinted by: The Jewish Publication Society of America, Philadelphia, PA 1954.

Cassells, E. Steve. *THE ARCHAEOLOGY OF COLORADO* Johnson Books, Boulder, CO 1983 & 1997.

Chávez, Fray Angélico. *ORIGINS OF NEW MEXICO FAMILIES A Genealogy of the Spanish Colonial Period* Museum of New Mexico Press, Santa Fe, NM 1992.

Colville, Ruth Marie. *LA VEREDA, A Trail Through Time* San Luis Valley Historical Society, Alamosa, CO 1995.

Coues, Elliott, Edited by. *THE JOURNAL OF JACOB FOWLER Narrating an Adventure from Arkansas through The Indian Territory, Oklahoma, Kansas, Colorado, and New Mexico, to the Sources of Rio Grande Del Norte, 1821-22,* Ross & Haines, Inc. Minneapolis, MN 1965.

Coues, Elliott. *THE EXPEDITIONS OF ZEBULON MONTGOMERY PIKE, To Headwaters of the Mississippi River, Through Lousiana Territory, and in New Spain, During the Years 1805-6-7.* Ross & Haines, Inc. Minneapolis, MN, 1965. reprinted by Dover Publications, Inc. New York, NY 1987.

Espinosa, J. Manuel. "*Journal of the Vargas Expedition into Colorado, 1694,*" The Colorado Magazine. Vol. XVI, No. 3 (May 1939).

Garate, Donald T. *ANZA A Basque Legacy on New Spain's Northern Frontier* unpublished 1997.

Gates, Zethyl. *MARIANO MEDINA, COLORADO MOUNTAIN MAN* Johnson Publishing Co. Boulder, CO 1981.

Griswold, Phelps R. *RIO GRANDE Along the Rio Grande* Griswold, Denver, CO 1986.

Hafen, Leroy R. & Ann W. *OLD SPANISH TRAIL Santa Fe to Los Angeles* Arthur H. Clark Co., 1954. Reprinted by University of Nebraska Press, Lincoln, NE 1993.

A WINTER RESCUE MARCH ACROSS THE ROCKIES Colorado Magazine Vol. IV 1927.

Hafen, Ann. *COLONEL LORING'S EXPEDITION ACROSS COLORADO IN 1858* Colorado Magazine Vol. XXIII-No. 2, March, 1946.

Haley, James L. *APACHES A History and Culture Portrait,* Doubleday & Company, Inc., Garden City, NY 1981.

Hammond, George P. & Agapito Rey. *DON JUAN DE OñATE, COLONIZER OF NEW MEXICO, 1595-1628* University of New Mexico Press, Albuquerque, NM 1953.

Harlan, George. *POSTMARKS AND PLACES* published by the author Crestone, CO 1976.

Harrington, John P. *ETHNOGEOGRAPHY OF THE TEWA INDIANS 29th ANNUAL REPORT 1907-08* Bureau of American Ethnology, Washington, D. C. 1916.

Heap, Gwinn Harris. *CENTRAL ROUTE TO THE PACIFIC, from The Valley of the Mississippi to California: Journal of the Expedition* Arno Press, New York Times Co. NY 1981.

Heitman, Francis. B. *HISTORICAL REGISTER AND DICTIONARY OF THE UNITED STATES ARMY, I 642;*

Hendricks, Rick & John P. Wilson. *THE NAVAJOS IN 1705 Roque Madrid's Campaign Journal* University of New Mexico, Albuquerque, NM 1996.

Hodge, Betty. *FORT GARLAND: A Window onto Southwest History* SLV Historian Vol. XXIV #2, Alamosa, CO 1992.

Hollon, W. Eugene. *THE LOST PATHFINDER: Zebulon Montgomery Pike* University of Oklahoma Press, Nornon, OK 1949.

Johns, Elizabeth A. H. *STORMS BREWED IN OTHER MEN'S WORLDS* Texas A. & M. University Press, College Station, TX 1995.

Jones, Nard. *THE GREAT COMMAND: THE STORY OF MARCUS AND NARCISSA WHITMAN AND THE OREGON COUNTRY PIONEERS* Little Brown Press, 1959.

Kessell, John L. ed. *REMOTE BEYOND COMPARE The Journals of Don Diego de Vargas* University of New Mexico Press, Albuquerque, NM 1989.

Kessler, Ron. *ANZA'S 1779 COMANCHE CAMPAIGN* Monte Vista, CO 1994.

RE-TRACING THE OLD SPANISH TRAIL NORTH BRANCH Adobe Village Press, Monte Vista, CO 1995.

COLORADO'S OLDEST WAGON ROAD Taos, New Mexico to San Carlos de los Jupes, Colorado. SLV Magazine August/September 1997.

Lavender, David. *BENT'S FORT* Doubleday & Company, Inc 1954, reprinted by Univesity of Nebrasks Press, 1972.

Madrid, Roque. *ROQUE MADRID'S NAVAJO CAMPAIGN JOURNAL OF 1705* New Mexico State Records and Archives Center, Santa FE, NM.

Marcy, Randolph Barnes. *THIRTY YEARS OF ARMY LIFE ON THE BORDER* Harper Brothers, NY 1866.

Martin, Bernice. *FRONTIER EYEWITNESS Diary of John Lawrence, 1867-1908.*

Mead, Frances Harvey. *CONEJOS COUNTRY* Century One Press, Colorado Springs, CO 1984.

Nevins, Allan. *FREMONT Pathmaker of the West* University of   Nebraska Press, Lincoln, NE 1992.

Nixon, Oliver W. *HOW MARCUS WHITMAN SAVED OREGON* Star Publishing Co., Chicago, IL 1896.

Palmer, John C. *A GENEALOGICAL RECORD OF THE DESCENDENTS OF MANUEL de JESUS MARTINEZ*, Colorado Springs, CO 1996.

Parkhill, Forbes. *THE BLAZED TRAIL OF ANTOINE LEROUX* Westernlore Press, Los Angeles, CA 1965.

Peterson, Harold L. & Robert Elman. *THE GREAT GUNS* Ridge Press, Grosset & Dunlap, Inc. New York, NY 1971.

Quaife, Milo Milton. *KIT CARSON'S AUTOBIOGRAPHY* University of Nebraska Press, Lincoln, NE 1966.

Richerdson, Albert D. *BEYOND THE MISSISSIPPI: FROM THE GREAT RIVER TO THE GREAT OCEAN life and adventure on the prairies, mountains and Pacific Coast, 1857-1867.* American Publishing Company, Hartford, CT 1867.

Richmond, Patricia Joy. *SAN JOSE* San Luis Valley Historian VI/1=1-87; VI/2=89-148.
       TRAIL TO DISASTER Colorado Historical Society, Denver, CO 1990.

Rockwell, Wilson. *THE UTES A Forgotten People* Sage Books, Denver, CO 1956.

Rounds, Glen *MOUNTAIN MEN* Edited and Illustrated by Glen Rounds Holiday House, Inc. 1966.

Ruxton, George Frederick. *ADVENTURES IN MEXICO AND THE ROCKY MOUNTAINS* University of Oklahoma Press, Norman, OK 1950.

Ruxton, George Frederick. *ADVENTURES IN MEXICO AND THE ROCKY MOUNTAINS* The Rio Grande Press, Inc., Glorieta, NM 1973.

Ruxton, George Frederick. *LIFE IN THE FAR WEST* University of Oklahoma Press, Norman, OK 1951.

Sage, Rufus B. *His Letters and Papers 1836-1847 with an annotated reprint of his "SCENES IN THE ROCKY MOUNTAINS AND IN OREGON, CALIFORNIA, NEW MEXICO, TEXAS AND THE GRAND PRAIRIES."*, The Arthur H. Clark Company, Glendale, CA 1956.

Sage, Rufus B. *ROCKY MOUNTAIN LIFE OR, STARTLING SCENES AND PERILOUS ADVENTURES IN THE FAR WEST, DURING AN EXPEDITION OF THREE YEARS* University of Nebraska Press, Lincoln, NE 1982.

Schiel, Jacob H. *JOURNEY THROUGH THE ROCKY MOUNTAINS AND THE HUMBOLDT MOUNTAINS TO THE PACIFIC OCEAN* Translated from German and Edited by Thomas N. Bonner University of Oklahoma Press, Norman, OK 1959. (pages 29 through 61)

Simmons, Marc. *THE LAST CONQUISTADOR Juan de Oñate and the Settling of the Far Southwest* University of Oklahoma Press, Norman, OK 1991.

Smith, P. David. *OURAY Chief of the Utes* Wayfinder Press, Ridgeway, CO 1986.

Teeuwen, Randall. *LA CULTURA CONSTANTE de SAN LUIS* San Luis Museum and Cultural Center. San Luis, CO 1985.

Thomas, Alfred B. *FORGOTTEN FRONTIERS A Study of the Spanish Indian Policy of Don Juan Bautista de Anza, Governor of New Mexico, 1777-87.* University of Oklahoma Press, Norman, OK 1932.

THE PLAINS INDIANS AND NEW MEXICO University of Oklahoma Press, Norman, OK 1932.

Thompson, Enid. *BENT'S OLD FORT: LIFE IN AN ADOBE CASTLE, 1833-1849* The Colorado Historical Society, Denver, CO 1979.

Vargas, don Diego de. *JOURNAL OF THE VARGAS EXPEDITION INTO COLORADO, 1694* Archivo General de la Nación, Mexico City, Mexico copy from Adams State College, Alamosa, CO.

Wallace, William Swilling. *ANTOINE ROBIDOUX 1794-1860* A Biography of a Western Venturer Glen Dawson, Los Angeles, CA 1953.

Walker, Henry Pickering. *THE WAGONMASTERS High Plains Freighting from the Earliest Days of the Santa Fe Trail to 1880,* University of Oklahoma Press, Norman, OK, 1966.

White, Frank. *LA GARITA* published by Author 1971.

Wessels, William L. *BORN TO BE A SOLDIER* Texas Christian University Press, Fort Worth, TX 1971.

Worthington, Rev William. *THE SUNNY SAN LUIS VALLEY* 1883 Dorothy W. Sabin reprinted in 1965.

INDEX

Pecos 26,55
Peno, Baptiste 85,86
Pentacigo 177
Phantom Creek 311
Plaza de Armas 19,45
Picurís 20,21,23,27,31,35,40,43,44,46,353
Piedra 13
Piedra Creek 57
Piedra del Carnero 43,45   **also see Tres Piedras**
Piedra Pintada 339,341
Pike, George Washington 64
Pike, Isabelle Brown 64
Pike, James Brown 64
Pikes Peak 129,132,135,136,162,163,164,241,248,333,334,335
Pike, Zebulon M. 55,64,65,66,67,68,71,80,84,89,98,128,212,267,321,339
Pilar 43,44,45   **also see Ciéneguilla**
Pinole 180
Pojoaque Pueblo 12,53,62,84
Poncha Pass 52
Pope, William 139
Posthoff 326,330
Pryor, Nathaniel 85
Pueblo 136,243,327,348
Pueblo, Colorado 65,87,86,87,117,136,200,242,334
Puerta 217
Puncha 220
Purgatoire River 160

Questa, New Mexico 147,300,326
Quiros, Diego Arias de 21,25,27,29,31,32,34,37,41

Raton Creek 9,319
Rattlesnake Hill 58,198,214,250
Red Cañon 231
Red River 26,31,32,65,67,68,73,75,76,78,80,124,126,135,149,209,300,316,326,329
Richerdson, Albert D. 61,90,128,326,327
Rio Colorado 57,61,124,125,129,147,149,209,214,326,329
Rio Conejos 48,69,71,80,98,108,318,319,322
Rio Culebra 18,61,92,129
Rio Grande 12,18,20,39,43,44,58,65,69,73,106,117,118,140,159,160,170,171,209,210,214,217,250,
314,315,316,318,319,328,329,332,338,341,343,346,353
Rio Grande del Norte 20,44,57,68,71,75,95,103,118,208,209,214,216,248,267,268,293,300,332,340
Rio Grande Gorge 43,45,95
Rio Hondo 177,316
Rio Mancos 304
Rio Napestle 62,132
Rio Salado 194
Rio San Antonio 18,55,318,322
Rio San Carlos 87,135
Rio Tusas 55   **also see Rio de las Nutrias**

Rio Ojo Caliente 39,318
Rio Uncompagre 178
Rio de La Culebra 32,58,61
Rio de La Garita 171,340,342
Rio de La Laguna 176,177,224
Rio de La Lara 339
Rio de las Nutrias 48,55   **also see Rio Tusas**
Rio de las Timbres 57   **also see Alamosa Riverr**
Rio de los Conejos 56
Rio de los Pinos 43,47,48,56
Rio de San Antonio 34,55,322
Rio de San Lorenzo 57
Rio del Carnero 340
Rio del Datil 61
Rio del Norte 20,32,34,39,40,43,44,45,55,57,60,71,75,78,80,81,84,170,211,224,
249,250,293,307
Rio del Ojo del Agua Caliente 38
Rio del Pino 56
Rito Alto Creek 140,147,198,213,249,263,355   **also see Leroux Creek**
River of the Cranes 48   **also see Rio de Los Grullas**
Rivera, Juan Luis Maria 272
Roan Mountains 233,234,237,238,257,258,259,260,303
Robidoux, Antoine 182,251,267,282,285,354
Robidoux Ford 190,263,307
Robidoux, Louis 182,285
Robidoux Pass 166,198,211,266
Robidoux Road 166
Robidoux Trading Post 285
Rock Creek 57,248,319,341
Rocky Mountains 84,118,119,126,132,135,145,153,154,155,161,235,240,241,242,258,266,269,
284,285,286,289,292,293,332
Robidoux 166,182   **also see Robideau**
Robinson, Dr.John Hamilton 65,66,73,75,82
Roubideau 182
Roubideau's 166
Roubideau's Ford 230
Roubideau's Fort 181,182,230,231
Roubideau's Pass 159,166,169,198,205,211,212,249,266,354
Roubideau's Wagons 159,169,354
Roy, Alexander 65
Roy, Baptiste 85
Roxas, Carlos de 49
Russell Spring 160,171,314
Ruxton, George Augustus Frederick 60,61,92,116,117,147,149,205,246
Rye, Colorado 52,135,241

Saguache 12,13,58,140,147,168,171,172,173,198,215,240,300,313,337,338,339,341,343,345,349
Saguache Butte 214
Saguache County 337,338,345
Saguache Creek 58,140,172,250,268,294,295,313

Ute 29,30,32,35,36,37,38,48,52,56,57,59,61,62,143,174,185,186,188,191,226,248,253,272,283, 285,313,321,328,337,347,348,355
Ute Agency 338,342
Ute Creek 207,248

Van Biber, Jesse 85,101,103,111
Vargas, Don Diego de 17,18,20,21,25,27,28,29,31,32,33,34,35,37,38,39,40,41,93,119,128,321,322,339
Vargas, Eusébio de 30,35,37
Vasquez, A.F. Baronet 65
Vegas de Santa Clara 183,192,193
Velarde 20
Verte, Longino 339
Vigil, Nestor 319,320,322

Wagner 187,188
Wahsatch Range 238,258,259,260
Walters, Dick 90,91,104
Walters, Richard 85
Walters, Taylor 85,86,95,99,100,101,102,104,107
Ward, Eli 85,102
Weeminuche 248,345
Westport 12,159,161,162,165,168,170,194,197,198,263
Westwater Creek 198,263
Wet Mountains 162,163,165,167,171,199,200,211,241,242,248,250
Wet Mountains Valley 67
Wheeler 140,190
Whitewater Creek 306
Whitman, Marcus 354,355
Whooten, Dick 355
William's Pass 198,205,212,215,314
Wilkinson, Lieutenant James B. 65
Wilson John 65
Wolfskill, William 11
Woodson, Andres 339
Woodson, Gabriel 339,342
Woodson, J.B. 339,341,342,344,346
Worthington 355

Yé, Don Juan de 23,24,25,26,31
Yount 11
Young, Henry 192,193
Yuta 125,126